Health, Poverty and Human Development

Perspectives and Issues

Editors:

Ulimiri V. Somayajulu
C.P. Prakasam
N. Audinarayana
K.E. Vaidyanathan

Indian Association for Social Sciences and Health (IASSH)

GRP

GLOBAL RESEARCH PUBLICATIONS
NEW DELHI (INDIA)

First Published – 2011

ISBN. 978-81-89630-24-9

Published by

GLOBAL RESEARCH PUBLICATIONS
4830/24, 1st Floor, Ansari Road
Darya Ganj, New Delhi-110002 (India)
Phone : 23245225. Fax : 91-11-23272135
E-mail: globalresearchpublications@gmail.com, grpindia@vsnl.net

Contents

SECTION - 2
Health and Nutrition Inequalities, Policies and Programmes

SECTION - 3
Reproductive and Sexual Health, Poverty and Human Development

Preface

Indian Association for Social Sciences and Health (IASSH) is an Indian chapter of Asia Pacific Network (APNET) of the International Forum for Social Sciences and Health (IFSSH). The major objectives of IASSH include : bringing together scientists, researchers, and policy makers to one forum to explore and work in the areas of social and cultural dimensions of illness, health and health care in the country; strengthening networking with similar organisations in India and abroad; linking social scientists, health activists, and policy makers; and initiating steps to evolve an equitable health care system in the country through appropriate and affordabale health sector reforms.

IASSH's first conference was at Tirupati in 2003, followed by Mumbai in 2005, Delhi in 2006, Surat in 2007, Bhubaneswar in 2008, and Puducherry in 2009. The 7th conference of IASSH was held at Centre for Study of Social Exclusion and Inclusive Policy, Faculty of Social Sciences, Banaras Hindu University, during March 5-7, 2010 on the theme "Health, Poverty and Human Development"-.

Though the twenty first century has resulted in health advancement which seemed impossible in the past centuries, the challenges are daunting. The Statistics indicate that the developing nations account for ninety per cent of the disease burden, but have access to only ten per cent of the resources used for health. This striking imbalance can be attributed to the higher levels of poverty in spite of efforts towards development and advancement of technology. The relation between health and poverty is double edged with ill health leading to poverty and poverty breeding ill health. There is an urgent need to understand the linkages between poor health, poverty and development so as to make any dent in this vicious cycle which not only impinges on the health but has major bearing on socio-economic and political well being of nations. The need of the hour is to identify the inequalities in development and involve all the development sectors in the efforts towards eradication of poverty and health development. The 7th conference was an attempt to bring intellectuals from all walks of life to make fruitful deliberations on these issues. This book is an edited volume of selected papers presented at the conference and has 21 chapters under 4 sections. We sincerely hope that the book would be of immense use to the researchers, health activists, planners, programme mangers and policy makers.

IASSH acknowledges the financial support extended by UNFPA, UNICEF, RBI, ICMR and BARC. We are also thankful to Dr. Panjab Singh, VC, and Dr. A.K. Pandey, of BHU, Varanasi for their active support in oragisning the conference. We are grateful to all the authors of the papers.

Ulimiri V. Somayajulu
C.P. Prakasam
N. Audinarayana
K.E. Vaidyanathan

List of Contributors

M.H. Suryanarayana, Indira Gandhi Institute of Development Research, Mumbai 400 065.

N. Audinarayana, Professor and Head., Dept. of Sociology and Population Studies, Director, School of Social Sciences, Bharathiar University, Coimbatore-641 046.

C.P. Prakasam, Rtd. Prof. International Institute for Population Sciences, Mumbai.

Talwar Sabanna, Associate Professor, Department of Economics, Karnatak University, P.G.Centre, Belgaum-591156, Karnataka.

K.E. Vaidyanathan, 3028, 13th Main Road, Anna Nagar, Chennai-600040.

Ulimiri V. Somayajulu, CEO, Sigma Research and Consulting, New Delhi- 110 049.

Tilak Mukherji, Chief Mentor, Sigma Research and Consulting, New Delhi-110 049.

M.V. Vaithilingam, Department of Fertility Studies, International Institute for Population Sciences, Mumbai.

Samar Kumar Biswas, Senior Lecturer, Department of Anthropology, University of North Bengal, Darjeeling-734013, West Bengal.

Somenath Bhattacharjee, Assistant Professor, Department of Anthropology, Assam University, Diphu Campus, Diphu, Karbi Anglong. ASSAM-782460.

M.S.R. Murthy, Retd. Professor, Department of Population Studies, Sri Venkateswara University, Tirupati.

Venkata Putcha, Consultant, Accostats Solutions Ltd & Sarma Memorial Research Fund, Visakhapatnam.

Hemant Meitei, Department of Economics, Manipur University, Imphal, 795003.

Manishankar K., National AIDS Control Organisation, Ministry of Health & Family Welfare, 6th Floor, Chandralok Building, 36, Janpath New Delhi,110001.

Masayuki Kakehashi, Hiroshima University, Hiroshima, 734-8551, Japan.

Arni S.R. Srinivasa Rao, Indian Statistical Institute, 203 B.T. Road, Kolkata, 700108.

P.B. Shankar Narayan, Asst. Professor, Department of Social Work, Pondicherry University, Puducherry- 605 014.

Sunitha Kuppuswamy, Lecturer, Department of Media Sciences, Anna University, Chennai-600 025.

Pradosh Debnath, Sr. ITES Manager, Tathya Dot Com Pvt. Ltd. Kazi Nazrul Islam Avenue, Kolkata.

Reeti Debnath, Lecturer, NSHM College of Management and Technology, NSHM Knowledge Campus, Kolkata.

Anindita Chowdhury, Department of Applied Psychology, Calcutta University, 92, A.P.C. Road, Kolkata-700 009.

S. Radhakrishnan, Deputy Director-M & E, Pathfinder, Pune.

Biranchi Jena, Senior Partner, Emergency & Health Systems Research, GVK-Emergency Management and Research Institute, Devar Yamzal, Medchal Road, Secunderabad-500014.

Debasis Bhardwaj, Partner, Analytics & OR, GVK-Emergency Management and Research Institute, Devar Yamzal, Medchal Road, Secunderabad-500014.

G.V. Ramana Rao, Executive Partner, Emergency Medicine Learning & Care and Research, GVK-Emergency Management and Research Institute, Devar Yamzal, Medchal Road, Secunderabad- 500014.

Balaiah Donta, National Institute for Research in Reproductive Health Jehangir Merwangi Street, Parel, Mumbai-400 012.

D.D. Naik, National Institute for Research in Reproductive Health Jehangir Merwangi Street, Parel, Mumbai-400 012.

Umesh Iddya, National Institute for Research in Reproductive Health Jehangir Merwangi Street, Parel, Mumbai-400 012.

Anil Bandivedekar, Municipal Corporation of Greater Mumbai, Mumbai-400 012.

Pallavi Banjare, Research Scholar, Department of Humanities & Social Sciences, National Institute Of Technology (NIT), Rourkela, Orissa.

Jalandar Pradhan, Assistant Professor, Department of Humanities & Social Sciences, National Institute Of Technology (NIT), Rourkela, Orissa.

M. Ganesan, Senior Project Officer, IITM's Rural Technology and Business Incubator, Department of Electrical Engineering, Indian Institute of Technology Madras, Chennai-600 036.

Suma Prashant, Project Manager, IITM's Rural Technology and Business Incubator, Department of Electrical Engineering, Indian Institute of Technology Madras, Chennai-600 036.

N. Janakiraman, Project Associate, IITM's Rural Technology and Business Incubator, Department of Electrical Engineering, Indian Institute of Technology Madras, Chennai-600 036.

Nuwan Waidyanatha, Senior Researcher, LIRNEasia, 12 Balcombe Place, Colombo, Sri Lanka 08, Sri Lanka.

Ranjeeta, Research Scholar, Centre for the Study of Regional Development, Jawaharlal Nehru University, New Delhi.

G.M. Subba Rao, Scientist 'C' (Communication & Journalism), Extension and Training Division, National Institute of Nutrition (NIN), Jamai-Osmania PO, Hyderabad-500007.

T. Vijayapushapm, Scientist 'D' (Sociology), Extension and Training Division, National Institute of Nutrition (NIN), Jamai-Osmania PO, Hyderabad-500007.

Vinod Pavarala, Dean & Professor of Communication, SN School of Arts & Communication, University of Hyderabad, Gachibowli, Hyderabad.

Balaiah Donta, National Institute for Research in Reproductive Health Jehangir Merwangi Street, Parel, Mumbai-400 012.

D.D. Naik, National Institute for Research in Reproductive Health Jehangir Merwangi Street, Parel, Mumbai-400 012.

Umesh Iddya, National Institute for Research in Reproductive Health Jehangir Merwangi Street, Parel, Mumbai-400 012.

Anil Bandivedekar, Municipal Corporation of Greater Mumbai, Mumbai-400 012.

Pallavi Banjare, Research Scholar, Department of Humanities & Social Sciences, National Institute Of Technology (NIT), Rourkela, Orissa.

Jalandar Pradhan, Assistant Professor, Department of Humanities & Social Sciences, National Institute Of Technology (NIT), Rourkela, Orissa.

M. Ganesan, Senior Project Officer, IITM's Rural Technology and Business Incubator, Department of Electrical Engineering, Indian Institute of Technology Madras, Chennai-600 036.

Suma Prashant, Project Manager, IITM's Rural Technology and Business Incubator, Department of Electrical Engineering, Indian Institute of Technology Madras, Chennai-600 036.

N. Janakiraman, Project Associate, IITM's Rural Technology and Business Incubator, Department of Electrical Engineering, Indian Institute of Technology Madras, Chennai-600 036.

Nuwan Waidyanatha, Senior Researcher, LIRNEasia, 12 Balcombe Place, Colombo, Sri Lanka 08, Sri Lanka.

Ranjeeta, Research Scholar, Centre for the Study of Regional Development, Jawaharlal Nehru University, New Delhi.

G.M. Subba Rao, Scientist 'C' (Communication & Journalism), Extension and Training Division, National Institute of Nutrition (NIN), Jamai-Osmania PO, Hyderabad-500007.

T. Vijayapushapm, Scientist 'D' (Sociology), Extension and Training Division, National Institute of Nutrition (NIN), Jamai-Osmania PO, Hyderabad-500007.

Vinod Pavarala, Dean & Professor of Communication, SN School of Arts & Communication, University of Hyderabad, Gachibowli, Hyderabad.

SECTION - 1

Health, Poverty and Human Development Interrelationships

1

Redefining Poverty Line: Catastrophic Health Expenses, Morbidity and Implications

M.H. Suryanarayana

Introduction

Pursuit of policies for poverty reduction and human development has led to successive revisions in the concept of poverty and hence, the poverty line depending upon information availability, empirical perceptions, methodological innovations, policy imperatives and priorities. This holds good for both academic and official versions in India. A decade prior to India's Independence, the National Planning Committee under Pandit Nehru declared in 1938 that policy objective should to "ensure an adequate standard of living for the masses, in other words, to get rid of the appalling poverty of the people" (Nehru 1946). Towards this end, the Committee defined goals for the total population in terms of nutrition (involving a balanced diet of 2400 to 2800 calories per adult worker), clothing (30 yards per capita per annum) and housing (100 sq. ft per capita). More than a decade after the country got Independence, a working group set up by the Government of India defined a national minimum of Rs 20 per capita per month (Rs 25 for urban areas) at 1960/61 prices (Perspective Planning Division (PPD), 1962). This minimum, considered adequate to ensure minimum energy requirements for an active and healthy life and also minimum clothing and shelter, did not include expenditures on health and education, which are to be provided by the State as per the Indian Constitution. The Planning Commission Task Force on Projection of Minimum Needs and Effective Consumption Demand defined the poor as "those whose per capita consumption expenditure lies below the midpoint of the monthly per capita expenditure class having a daily calorie intake of 2,400 in rural areas and 2,100 in urban areas" (PPD, 1981, p. 81). The poverty lines corresponding to these norms were worked out with reference to the NSS data for the year 1973-74. The poverty line turned out to be Rs 49.09 per capita per month at 1973-74 prices for rural all-India. The Expert Group (PPD, 1993) has also recommended this poverty line.

This question of defining a normative minimum has received considerable attention in the international context too in the wake of 'Stabilization and Structural Adjustment Programmes' pursued at the behest of international institutions like the IMF and the World Bank. It is in this context, that the World Bank proposed its 'A Dollar A Day' poverty line based on a sample of poverty line estimates from 33 countries. The 'Copenhagen Declaration' at the *UN* World Summit on Social Development in 1995 has described poverty as "...a condition characterized by severe deprivation of basic human needs, including *food, safe drinking water,* sanitation facilities, *health,* shelter, *education* and information." The Millennium Development Goals are in fact based on this explicit recognition of the multiple dominions of deprivation and need for reducing them for a sustained reduction in poverty.

In general, the emphasis has been on defining a threshold minimum level of living to measure deprivation and identify policy imperatives with reference to economic profiles of poverty. A major limitation of this approach has been its failure to recognize that poverty reduction is not simply a question of reducing the deprivation of the current poor. To ensure that the reduction in poverty is sustained, it is also important to ensure that the vulnerable non-poor do not slip into poverty. If so, what are the factors that lead to such 'slips" and what are the possible options? This paper provides a perspective on some such issues from the point of view of redefining the poverty line. The paper is organised as follows: Section 2 provides a brief review of panel studies on households profiles of poverty and the possible causes for the changing profiles. Section 3 examines their methodological implications for redefining the poverty line and some empirical evidence in the Indian context. Section 4 examines morbidity profiles across economic status of households and their implications for defining a threshold minimum. The final section concludes the paper.

Causes of Vulnerability and Implications

Studies for developing countries across the world have shown that sustained reduction in poverty would not be feasible unless measures are taken to provide social protection to the vulnerable non-poor. For instance, consider the findings for the state of Andhra Pradesh. About 65% of the households in 36 villages in the districts of Nalgonda, Khammam and East Godavari in Andhra Pradesh were poor 25 years ago. As a result of public policy intervention for poverty reduction, 14% of households could move out of poverty. Ceteris paribus, this would have meant a similar reduction of aggregate poverty in these villages. Instead, poverty scenario continued to be about the same even after a quarter-century of economic development. This has happened because during the same period, about 12% of non-poor households have moved *into* poverty due to financial and health crises. Prompt and appropriate policy support in terms of access to credit and medical facilities would have prevented the deterioration in their economic status (Krishna et al., 2004a).

Another study for Kenya has come out with similar findings. The sample is located in 20 villages in western Kenya. The findings show that 19% of households in these villages crossed the poverty line during the past 25 years. These changes are not reflected in the estimates of poverty for these villages because households of similar magnitude fell into poverty for reasons like ill health, medical care and expenses on funeral rites (Krishna et al., 2004b).[1]

In other words, these studies show that sustained reduction cannot be achieved only by a set of policies and programmes, however much well targeted to the currently poor, for subsistence minimum consumption. Equal weightage should be assigned to a programme on tacking potential causes of vulnerable non-poor's decent into poverty. A strategy based on an appreciation of the asymmetric causes for mobility into and out of poverty would call for an appropriate policy response to the causes of vulnerability.

Under the economic reform programme, the Government has already provided for, *inter alia,* user charges for services in public health facilities to the non-poor in particular since the early 1990s (GoI 2007a). But the health insurance coverage of the population is quite dismal.[2] This would involve catastrophic payments for health. Hence, the current official estimates of poverty line, which does not provide for medical out-of-pocket expenses would involve underestimation of the poor and hence, Type I error from a positive perspective in estimate as well as policy targeting.[3] Therefore, the question of revising the poverty line to accommodate health expenses and choice of cost-effective strategy towards health care and poverty reduction assumes importance. But, the health care requirements of the population are not constant but random, which would imply that it would not be possible to define a unique minimum for health care expenditure. In other words, there would be pronounced variance in health status across households in the same economic profile. This in turn would call for an adequate appreciation of the morbidity profile of the population from an economic perspective. Such an appreciation would facilitate a cost-effective intervention in the health sector. This is because health programmes and interventions based only on aggregate mortality/morbidity estimates have ended up as lopsided cost-ineffective strategies and situations like the one obtaining in Kerala, that is, paradox of low mortality and high morbidity.

In order to provide a perspective on some of the issues involved, the following section discusses some methodological options for accommodating medical expenses while defining and estimating poverty with some illustrations for India.

Methodological Implications

If catastrophic health expenses, however defined, were a major cause of household slippage into poverty and hence failure of conventional poverty reduction strategy, some relevant policy related questions would be as follows:

(i) Would it make sense to redefine the poverty line by taking into account out-of-pocket health expenses, that is adopt the (medical out-of-pocket expenses in the threshold (MIT) approach?

(ii) Would it be a better alternative to subtract medical expenses from household income or what is called the medical out-of-pocket expenses subtracted from income (MSI) approach?

(iii) If neither of the options makes sense for whatever reasons, what would be the policy imperatives?

As regards the choice between adding medical expenses to the poverty line and subtracting them from household income[4], it may be noted that the two alternative poverty estimates would differ from the current estimates with reference to the calorie-based poverty lines, which do not provide for health expenses. Both would indicate Type I error in the current official estimates. We provide one such illustration for the MSI approach based on the National Sample Survey data for 2004-05. Table 3 provides estimates of poverty alternative to the official estimates by adjusting household expenditure for health expenses (Table 3). They indicate that the extent of Type I error (percentage point underestimation) in the official estimates of poverty for 2004-05 would be 3.6 per cent for rural and three percent for urban India. This works out to an absolute difference of 28 and seven million people respectively. In other words, the number of poor in India is currently under-counted by about 35 million. It also would imply that methodological adjustments matter quite perceptibly for rural than for urban India.

The profile across states is as follows. The extent of Type I error (as measured by percentage point difference) varies across states. It varies from 1.12 in Jammu & Kashmir to 5.83 in Uttar Pradesh in the rural sector, and 0.14 in Assam to 4.63 in Rajasthan in the urban sector. Immeserizing impact of medical expenses (as measured by percentage point difference made to the official estimate of poverty by providing for medical expenses) in the rural sector is one of the highest in states like Uttar Pradesh, Madhya Pradesh and Chhattisgarh, where it exceeds five percentage points. As regards the urban sector, incidence of poverty is one of the highest in Rajasthan and Uttar Pradesh where poverty is underestimated by 4.60 percentage points. Rural households are vulnerable to catastrophic implications of health expenses even in economically prosperous states like Gujarat and Maharashtra. The association between extent of deprivation (adjusted or unadjusted) and absolute (percentage point) error is in fact negative and statistically significant (Table 2). If one considers relative (percentage) error in estimation, the association is positive and significant.

The estimates presented above are made with some simplifying assumptions like the following: (i) households have limited resources; and (ii) all medical expenses are essential. Available evidence indicates that in rural India households from lower and middle expenditure brackets depend more on borrowings than own resources to meet expenses on hospitalization (Table 3). In other words, resources are fixed at least for these groups of households. Studies have also shown that one-fourth of those who are hospitalized fall below the poverty line (Peters et al., 2002, p. 5).

It may also be noted that such estimates of Type I error based on observed health OoP expenditures have positive perspective. They would also involve another from of Type I error, that is, from a normative perspective. This is because several households leave their morbidities untreated for fear of catastrophic consequences. Hence, they do not incur any

Table 1
Official and Health Expenditure Adjusted Poverty Estimates: Type I Errors, 2004-05

	Rural				*Urban*			
			Type I Error				*Type I Error*	
State *Percentage point*	*Official*	*Adjusted*	*Percentage Point*	*Percentage*	*Official*	*Adjusted*	*Percentage Point*	*Percentage*
Andhra Pradesh	10.47	11.64	-1.17	-10.05	27.36	30.7	-3.34	-10.88
Assam	22.09	23.37	-1.28	-5.48	3.64	3.77	-0.13	-3.45
Bihar	42.59	45.32	-2.73	-6.02	36.09	37.69	-1.60	-4.25
Chhattisgarh	40.77	46.35	-5.58	-12.04	42.18	45.01	-2.83	-6.29
Dadra and Nagar	39.64	40.06	-3.44	-15.41	19.17	19.17	-1.38	-9.39
Delhi	6.89	6.89	-3.57	-21.22	16.34	16.81	-0.96	-6.22
Goa	5.64	5.64	-2.67	-20.23	19.71	22.9	-0.48	-13.08
Gujarat	18.89	22.33	-1.12	-20.78	13.31	14.69	-0.71	-8.75
Haryana	13.25	16.82	-3.76	-7.53	14.48	15.44	-1.56	-7.15
Himachal Pradesh	10.53	13.2	-3.47	-14.37	3.19	3.67	-2.15	-6.19
Jammu and Kashmir	4.27	5.39	-4.23	-24.27	7.4	8.11	-3.77	-15.87
Jharkhand	46.15	49.91	-5.41	-12.82	20.25	21.81	-3.36	-7.29
Karnataka	20.67	24.14	-4.03	-11.99	32.61	34.76	-2.93	-8.36
Kerala	13.2	17.43	-4	-7.86	19.99	23.76	-1.90	-4.08
Madhya Pradesh	36.79	42.2	-2.63	-22.58	42.72	46.08	-1.78	-22.06
Maharashtra	29.57	33.6	-3.47	-15.92	32.1	35.03	-4.63	-12.53
Orissa	46.9	50.9	-1.99	-7.97	44.72	46.62	-2.70	-10.73
Punjab	9.02	11.65	-5.82	-14.87	6.29	8.07	-4.60	-13.25
Rajasthan	18.32	21.79	-3.83	-8.61	32.31	36.94	-1.17	-3.11

Contd.

State	Rural				Urban			
			Type I Error				Type I Error	
Percentage point	Official	Adjusted	Percentage Point	Percentage	Official	Adjusted	Percentage Point	Percentage
Tamil Nadu	22.99	24.98	-4.55	-13.82	22.46	25.16	-1.90	-12.34
Uttar Pradesh	33.32	39.14	-1.17	-10.05	30.13	34.73	-2.72	-9.44
Uttaranchal	40.65	44.48	-1.28	-5.48	36.5	37.67	-3.34	-10.88
West Bengal	28.37	32.92	-2.73	-6.02	13.5	15.4	-0.13	-3.45
All India	28.2	32.04	(-) 3.84	(-) 11.99	26.09	28.81	-1.60	-4.25

Source: Based on Agrawal, Chandrasekhar, Suryanarayana (2009)

Table 2
Pair wise Correlations (Rural)

	Official	*Adjusted*	*Percentage Point Difference*	*Percentage Difference*
Official	1.0000			
Adjusted	0.9968(0.00)	1.0000		
Percentage point Type I error	(-)0.5640(0.0096)	(-) 0.6278(0.0030)	1.0000	
Percentage Type I Error	0.7081(0.0005)	0.6611(0.0015)	0.0663(0.7811)	1.0000
Official	1.0000			
Adjusted	0.9971(0.0000)	1.0000		
Percentage point Type I Error	(-) 0.5436(0.0132)	(-) 0.6061(0.0046)	1.0000	
Percentage Type I Error	0.4278(0.0599)	0.3727(0.1055)	0.3588(0.1203)	1.0000

Notes: Figures in parentheses are t statistics and Estimates of Spearman's rank correlation too throw up a similar profile.

Table 3

Per 1000 Distribution of Household Total Expenditure on Treatment on Account of Hospitalization During the Last 365 Days by Source of Finance for Each MPCE Class

Rural					Urban				
	Source of Finance					Source of Finance			
MPCE Classes (Rs.)	*Household Income/ Savings*	*Borro-wings*	*Others**	*Total*	*MPCE Classes (Rs.)*	*House-hold Income/ Savings*	*Borro-wings*	*Others**	*Total*
Less than 225	332	435	233	1000	Less than 300	541	308	151	1000
225 - 255	265	556	178	1000	300 - 350	338	401	262	1000
255 - 300	314	488	198	1000	350 - 425	322	334	343	1000
300 - 340	349	462	189	1000	425 - 500	345	486	169	1000
340 - 380	379	461	161	1000	500 - 575	472	359	169	1000
380 - 420	347	402	251	1000	575 - 665	419	407	174	1000
420 - 470	391	451	158	1000	665 - 775	573	295	132	1000
470 - 525	399	435	166	1000	775 - 915	526	283	191	1000
525 - 615	420	411	169	1000	915 - 1120	625	191	184	1000
615 - 775	418	406	176	1000	1120 - 1500	585	203	212	1000
775 - 950	419	411	170	1000	1500 - 1925	707	116	177	1000
950 or more	485	331	184	1000	1925 or more	665	107	229	1000
All	409	411	181	1000	all	578	227	195	1000

*include contribution from friends & relatives and sale of ornaments and other physical assets, draught animals, etc.

Source: GoI (2006), p. 35

medical expenditure and by overlooking such expenses both MIT and MIS approaches commit Type I error from a normative perspective. This will have serious implications for policy choice and evaluation.

In sum, there are a number of questions regarding choice of minimum health expenditure and identifying associated morbidity profiles as follows:

(i) How should one define a critical minimum for health care expenditure? Should one consider all medical expenses irrespective of the morbidity profile of the household? Should one identify a critical minimum bundle of diseases to define this minimum?

(ii) Should they be made conditional on family size and composition, health status and insurance coverage?

(iii) Should they be restricted to a sub-set associated with deprivation only?

(iv) What are the policy imperatives given the different stages of epidemiological transition across states/ regions?

In order to address the questions listed above, the following section provides morbidity profiles of Kerala and all-India as some evidence.

Morbidity Profiles: Some Illustrations

This section addresses the question if morbidity profiles and hence, health care needs were constant across income groups and regions in India. One may examine this issue in terms of two alternative approaches, which would provide different types of insights:

(i) To begin with, one may examine the extent of relative inequalities in morbidity by individual disease or broad groups of diseases across per capita consumer expenditure. For this purpose, one may draw (i) pseudo-Lorenz curve for morbidity by diseases with reference to per capita consumer expenditure; and (ii) Lorenz curves for per capita consumer expenditure distribution. Generally pseudo-Lorenz curves lie below the Line of Equal Distribution for any normal item, which belongs proportionately more to the rich. Within this class, a finer distinction could be made depending upon whether the pseudo-Lorenz curve lies above or below the Lorenz curve for consumer expenditure distribution. However, for items, which are owned disproportionately more by the poor than by the rich, pseudo-Lorenz curves would lie above the Line of Equal Distribution. Such a scenario would generate negative values for pseudo-Lorenz ratios. Accordingly, depending upon the sign and size of the estimated pseudo-Lorenz ratios one could classify them as between those associated with deprivation and otherwise. The three broad categories of diseases would be as follows:

- Diseases | Deprivation: Pseudo-Lorenz ratios would be negative.
- Diseases | Normal state: Pseudo-Lorenz ratios would be positive but less than Lorenz ratio for per capita consumer expenditure distribution.
- Diseases | Affluence: Pseudo-Lorenz ratios would be positive but greater than Lorenz ratio for per capita consumer expenditure distribution.

(ii) A similar distinction as between diseases associated with the poor and those associated with the rich could be made by developing a concept of elasticity similar to Engel elasticity of consumer demand in Economics. Engel elasticity of consumer demand measures the response of consumer demand to income/total expenditure and is given by the ratio of percentage change in demand to percentage change in income/ total expenditure. If it is negative, it is called an inferior good consumed largely by the poor. If it is positive and greater than one, it is called a luxury consumed largely by the rich. In a similar way, we estimate Engel elasticity of number of persons reporting a given illness; if it were negative, it would indicate that the illness is prevalent and reported largely by the poor people.[5]

Some relevant results are as follows:

- Morbidity rate in general is more for the rich than for the poor in both the sectors in Kerala and India as a whole. Between Kerala and all-India, the relative share of the rich is more at the all-India level than in Kerala (Figures 1 & 2).
- The pseudo-Lorenz curves are not smooth and convex; in fact, they are horizontal at several stretches implying zero morbidity for households in some ranges of per capita consumer expenditure at both lower and upper ends of consumer expenditure distribution (Figures 1 & 2). In other words, this would imply morbidity profiles of population classified solely with reference to income poor and non-poor categories would sometimes be misleading.

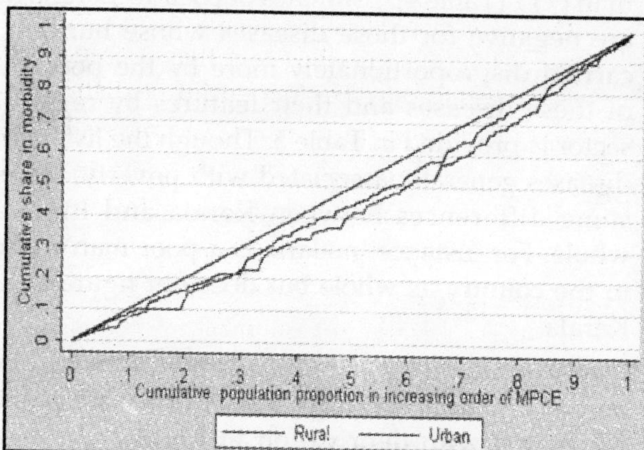

Figure 1: Pseudo-Lorenz Curve for Morbidity: Kerala

- However, this aggregate profile does not hold uniformly the same at the level of individual diseases. This is borne out by pseudo-Lorenz curves and ratios for disease-specific morbidity. Pseudo-Lorenz curves lie above/below the Line of Equal Distribution

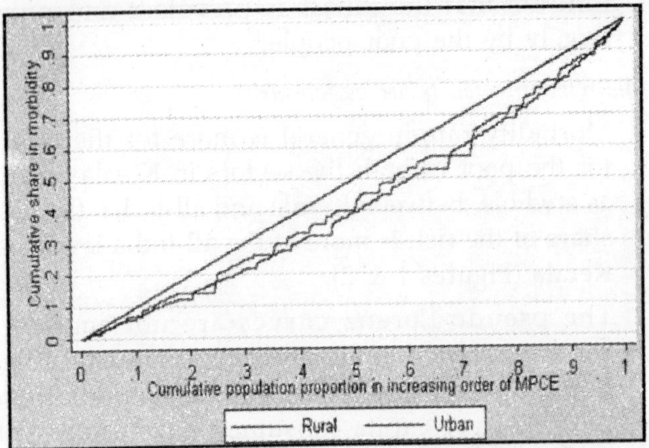

Figure 2: Pseudo-Lorenz Curve for Morbidity: India

depending upon the nature of diseases (not reported). Consistent with such a profile, estimates of pseudo-Lorenz ratios range from less than (-) 1 to greater than (+) 1 (Table 4). Estimates of pseudo-Lorenz ratios are negative for those diseases whose burdens are carried disproportionately more by the poor. A list of these diseases and their features by region and sector is provided in Table 5. Though the list includes diseases generally associated with poverty, there are some differences between Kerala and India as a whole. For instance, malaria is a poor man's disease in the country as whole but does not figure at all in Kerala.

- Engel elasticity estimates confirm the general perception that Tuberculosis and asthma are generally associated with deprivation in Kerala.. As regards India, tuberculosis is an inferior disease in both rural and urban sectors but asthma is only in urban India. The estimates of sector wise shares in total reported morbidity is less than or about one per cent for tuberculosis in both Kerala and India. Bronchial asthma, with a share of more than 3 per cent (5 per cent in rural Kerala) has a significant presence

Table 4
Estimates of Psuedo-Lorenz Ratios of Morbidity by Disease and Sector: Kerala vs. India

Disease	*Code*	*India*		*Kerala*	
		Rural	*Urban*	*Rural*	*Urban*
Diarrhoea/ dysentery	1	-0.1032	-0.1946	0.0624	0.0399
Gastritis/ gastric or peptic ulcer	2	0.0172	-0.0413	0.0403	0.0611
Worm infestation	3	-0.1068	-0.0966	-0.2178	0.1371
Amoebiosis	4	-0.0844	-0.0664	0.2147	.
Hepatitis/Jaundice	5	-0.0878	-0.0950	.	0.4439
Heart disease	6	0.3145	0.2434	0.1944	0.1637
Hypertension	7	0.3676	0.3015	0.1348	0.1896
Respiratory including ear/nose/throat ailments	8	0.1041	0.0272	0.0670	0.0568
Tuberculosis	9	-0.1014	-0.3232	-0.1893	-0.3898
Bronchial asthma	10	0.0556	-0.0376	-0.0603	-0.1865
Disorders of joints and bones	11	0.1117	0.0718	0.0326	0.0418
Diseases of kidney/urinary system	12	0.1207	0.1891	0.0138	-0.1900
Prostatic disorders	13	-0.2105	0.2114	-0.7357	.
Gynaecological disorders	14	0.0132	0.0246	0.3142	0.1978
Neurological disorders	15	0.1419	0.0234	0.1352	-0.0124
Psychiatric disorders	16	0.0657	-0.0308	-0.0092	-0.3041
Conjunctivitis	17	0.0348	-0.0048	-0.2544	0.1288
Glaucoma	18	-0.0883	0.0380	0.3704	-0.2110
Cataract	19	-0.0586	-0.1579	-0.1410	-0.0574
Diseases of skin	20	-0.0155	-0.1893	-0.0056	0.0141
Goitre	21	0.3004	0.2439	0.3835	0.6968

Contd.

Disease	Code	India		Kerala	
		Rural	*Urban*	*Rural*	*Urban*
Diabetes mellitus	22	0.4328	0.3276	0.1911	0.2052
Under-nutrition	23	-0.1397	0.0340	-0.2713	.
Anemia	24	-0.1108	-0.1868	-0.1845	-0.8187
Sexually transmitted diseases	25	0.1315	0.3124	.	.
Malaria	26	-0.1052	-0.1671	.	.
Eruptive	27	-0.0953	-0.1659	0.0346	.
Mumps	28	-0.1932	-0.1084	0.4965	.
Diphtheria	29	-0.4363	-0.0425	.	-0.6790
Whooping cough	30	-0.0873	-0.0543	-0.1635	0.4130
Fever of unknown origin	31	-0.1076	-0.1506	-0.0793	-0.0028
Tetanus	32	0.3098	0.6133	-0.6620	.
Filariasis/Elephantiasis	33	-0.0622	-0.2353	.	-0.6986
Locomotor	34	-0.0401	-0.1247	-0.1555	-0.5324
Visual including blindness (excluding cataract)	35	-0.0693	-0.1439	0.1677	-0.1038
Speech	36	-0.2114	-0.0758	-0.2711	-0.8166
Hearing	37	-0.0594	0.0483	-0.1532	0.1123
Diseases of Mouth/Teeth/Gum	38	0.2290	0.1425	0.1998	0.3446
Accidents/Injuries/Burns/Fractures/Poisoning	39	-0.0151	-0.1075	-0.1520	-0.3589
Cancer and other tumors	40	0.1112	0.0561	-0.1357	-0.2971
Other diagnosed ailments	41	-0.0218	-0.0159	-0.0893	-0.0991
Other undiagnosed ailments	99	-0.0517	-0.0973	0.0700	-0.3451
MPCE Lorenz ratio	-	0.2573	0.3262	0.2830	0.3292

Note: MPCE = Monthly per capita consumer expenditure

Table 5
Diseases Associated with Deprivation: A Disaggregate Profile

Sector	*Common to Kerala & India*	*Only in Kerala*	*Only in India*
Rural	Worm infestation, tuberculosis, bronchial asthma, prostatic disorders, cataract, diseases of skin, under- nutrition, anaemia, whooping cough, fever of unknown origin, locomotor, speech, hearing, accidents et al, other diagnosed diseases	Bronchial asthma, psychiatric disorders, conjunctivitis, tetanus, cancer & other tumors	Diarrhoea/dysentery, amoebiosis, hepatitis/Jaundice, glaucoma, malaria, eruptive, mumps, diphtheria, filariasis/elephantiasis, visual, other undiagnosed diseases
Urban	Tuberculosis, bronchial asthma, diseases of kidney/urinary system, psychiatric disorders, cataract, anaemia, diphtheria, fever of unknown origin, filariasis/elephantiasis, locomotor, visual, speech, accidents et al, other diagnosed diseases, other undiagnosed diseases	Diseases of kidney/urinary system, neurological disorders, glaucoma, cancer & other tumors	Diarrhoea/dysentery, gastritis/gastric or peptic ulcer, worm infestation, amoebiosis, hepatitis/Jaundice, conjunctivitis, diseases of skin, malaria, eruptive, mumps, whooping cough

(Tables 6-7); (b) the sub-set of undiagnosed diseases is associated largely with the poor in both rural and urban India but only in urban Kerala.

- The share of diseases associated with deprivation is less than 50 per cent in both rural and urban Kerala but more than 50 per cent in India as a whole. In rural India, diseases of poverty account for about two-thirds of the reported cases (Table 8).
- Disease profile with reference Engel elasticity rules, differ between Kerala and India: (a) Inferior diseases with elasticites less than (-) 1 are conspicuous by their absence in urban India. Diphtheria is the only such disease found in rural India with a share in total rural reported morbidity cases of just 1.70 per cent; (b) In rural Kerala, prostatic disorders and tetanus are the only two diseases with Engel elasticities less than (-) 1. But their share in total reported morbidity cases is just 0.16 per cent. But the profile is different for urban Kerala. There are about eight such diseases, which, though individually insignificant, collectively account for 6.35 per cent of total urban morbidity cases.
- Having identified the diseases reported proportionately more by the poor, it would be useful to identify those diseases, which afflict the rich proportionately more, to avoid Type II errors in targeting medical facilities. Following consumer economic theory, we may classify all those diseases with Engel elasticities more than one as diseases of affluence. Such profiles based on disaggregate estimates of Engel elasticities are provided in Table 9. Such diseases are virtually insignificant in Kerala. They account for 1.23 and 1.75 per cent of reported morbidity cases in rural and urban Kerala respectively. As regards India, they have significant presence. Their respective shares in total rural and urban morbidity cases are 7.83 and 6.83 per cent.

Table 6
Estimates of Expenditure Elasticities and Morbidity by Disease and Sector: India

		Rural India		*Urban India*	
Disease	*Code*	*Exp. Elasticity*	*Morbidity (%)*	*Exp. Elasticity*	*Morbidity (%)*
Diarrhoea/ dysentery	1	-0.401	5.48	-0.597	3.71
Gastritis/gastric or peptic ulcer	2	0.067	4.04	-0.127	2.70
Worm infestation	3	-0.415	0.45	-0.296	0.37
Amoebiosis	4	-0.328	0.44	-0.204	0.22
Hepatitis/Jaundice	5	-0.341	0.42	-0.291	0.51
Heart disease	6	1.222	1.89	0.746	4.75
Hypertension	7	1.429	3.53	0.924	9.40
Respiratory including ear/nose/throat ailments	8	0.405	7.04	0.083	7.22
Tuberculosis	9	-0.394	1.33	-0.991	0.74
Bronchial asthma	10	0.216	3.81	-0.115	3.15
Disorders of joints and bones	11	0.434	6.46	0.220	6.81
Diseases of kidney/urinary system	12	0.469	0.92	0.580	1.12
Prostatic disorders	13	-0.818	0.14	0.648	0.09
Gynaecological disorders	14	0.051	1.30	0.076	0.95
Neurological disorders	15	0.552	1.91	0.072	2.32
Psychiatric disorders	16	0.255	0.70	-0.094	0.63
Conjunctivitis	17	0.135	0.41	-0.015	0.47
Glaucoma	18	-0.343	0.24	0.117	0.32
Cataract	19	-0.228	1.64	-0.484	1.39
Diseases of skin	20	-0.060	2.44	-0.580	1.75

Contd.

Disease	Code	Rural India		Urban India	
		Exp. Elasticity	Morbidity (%)	Exp. Elasticity	Morbidity (%)
Goitre	21	1.168	0.11	0.748	0.13
Diabetes mellitus	22	1.682	2.26	1.004	6.82
Under-nutrition	23	-0.543	0.11	0.104	0.22
Anaemia	24	-0.431	0.47	-0.573	0.50
Sexually transmitted diseases	25	0.511	0.09	0.958	0.00
Malaria	26	-0.409	2.06	-0.512	0.96
Eruptive	27	-0.371	0.58	-0.509	0.21
Mumps	28	-0.751	0.29	-0.332	0.22
Diphtheria	29	-1.696	0.14	-0.130	0.23
Whooping cough	30	-0.339	2.59	-0.166	2.25
Fever of unknown origin	31	-0.418	20.55	-0.462	15.00
Tetanus	32	1.204	0.04	1.880	0.02
Filariasis/Elephantiasis	33	-0.242	0.12	-0.721	0.13
Locomotor	34	-0.156	1.99	-0.382	1.60
Visual including blindness (excluding cataract)	35	-0.270	1.23	-0.441	0.75
Speech	36	-0.822	0.23	-0.233	0.37
Hearing	37	-0.231	0.97	0.148	0.94
Diseases of Mouth/Teeth/Gum	38	0.890	0.97	0.437	1.10
Accidents/Injuries/Burns/Fractures/Poisoning	39	-0.059	2.73	-0.330	2.60
Cancer and other tumors	40	0.432	0.50	0.172	0.58
Other diagnosed ailments	41	-0.085	14.61	-0.049	14.68
Other undiagnosed ailments	99	-0.201	2.80	-0.298	2.08

Table 7
Estimates of Expenditure Elasticities and Morbidity by Disease and Sector: Kerala

Disease	Code	Rural Kerala		Urban Kerala	
		Exp. Elasticity	Morbidity (%)	Exp. Elasticity	Morbidity (%)
Diarrhoea/ dysentery	1	0.221	0.87	0.121	0.61
Gastritis/gastric or peptic ulcer	2	0.143	2.65	0.186	1.83
Worm infestation	3	-0.770	0.33	0.416	0.62
Amoebiosis	4	0.759	0.30		0.00
Hepatitis/Jaundice	5		0.00	1.348	0.10
Heart disease	6	0.687	3.57	0.497	4.78
Hypertension	7	0.477	7.61	0.576	9.84
Respiratory including ear/nose/throat ailments	8	0.237	12.29	0.172	13.79
Tuberculosis	9	-0.669	0.63	-1.184	0.68
Bronchial asthma	10	-0.213	5.20	-0.567	3.27
Disorders of joints and bones	11	0.115	8.97	0.127	7.44
Diseases of kidney/urinary system	12	0.049	0.72	-0.577	1.27
Prostatic disorders	13	-2.600	0.10		0.00
Gynaecological disorders	14	1.110	0.73	0.601	1.23
Neurological disorders	15	0.478	2.59	-0.038	3.10
Psychiatric disorders	16	-0.033	1.57	-0.924	0.74
Conjunctivitis	17	-0.899	0.21	0.391	0.42
Glaucoma	18	1.309	0.19	-0.641	0.12
Cataract	19	-0.498	1.23	-0.174	0.78
Diseases of skin	20	-0.020	2.01	0.043	0.99

Contd.

Disease	Code	Rural Kerala Exp. Elasticity	Rural Kerala Morbidity (%)	Urban Kerala Exp. Elasticity	Urban Kerala Morbidity (%)
Goitre	21	1.355	0.24	2.117	0.32
Diabetes mellitus	22	0.675	5.92	0.623	8.52
Under-nutrition	23	-0.959	0.03		0.00
Anemia	24	-0.652	0.26	-2.487	0.25
Sexually transmitted diseases	25		0.00		0.00
Malaria	26		0.00		0.00
Eruptive	27	0.122	0.45		0.00
Mumps	28	1.755	0.07		0.00
Diphtheria	29		0.00	-2.063	0.18
Whooping cough	30	-0.578	1.04	1.254	1.10
Fever of unknown origin	31	-0.280	15.40	-0.009	17.47
Tetanus	32	-2.340	0.06		0.00
Filariasis/Elephantiasis	33		0.00	-2.122	0.32
Locomotor	34	-0.550	1.46	-1.617	1.37
Visual including blindness (excluding cataract)	35	0.593	0.79	-0.315	0.19
Speech	36	-0.958	0.28	-2.480	0.26
Hearing	37	-0.541	0.56	0.341	1.14
Diseases of Mouth/Teeth/Gum	38	0.706	0.68	1.047	0.23
Accidents/Injuries/Burns/Fractures/Poisoning	39	-0.537	2.06	-1.090	2.33
Cancer and other tumors	40	-0.480	0.43	-0.903	0.39
Other diagnosed ailments	41	-0.316	16.46	-0.301	13.36
Other undiagnosed ailments	99	0.247	2.04	-1.048	0.96

Table 8
Share (%) of Diseases Associated with Deprivation

Sector	*Kerala*	*India*
Rural	49.30	64.01
Urban	47.01	57.21

- Generally coronary heart diseases, diabetes and hypertension are considered as life style diseases. Among them, only diabetes mellitus has elasticity greater than one for rural and urban India; heart disease and hypertension too have elasticities greater than one only for rural India. As regards Kerala, none of them are luxury diseases. This could also be interpreted to represent a process whereby the diseases of affluence and deprivation converge in Kerala. In other words, this may represent a shift a in the epidemiology of diseases in Kerala.

Table 9
Diseases Associated with Affluence: A Disaggregate Profile

Sector	*Common to Kerala & India*	*Only in Kerala*	*Only in India*
Rural	*Goitre*	Gynaecological disorders, mumps, glaucoma	Heart diseases, hyper tension, diabetes mellitus, tetanus,
Urban		Hepatitis/Jaundice, goiter, whooping cough, diseases of moth teeth and gum	Diabetes mellitus, tetanus

The preceding discussion implies that it would not be possible to identify a unique critical bundle of diseases across states in India for purposes of defining minimum medical out-of-pocket expenses. The bundle would differ across states. Its implication would be to define a state-specific bundle and estimates the expenses associated with it. Alternatively, one might formulate a health insurance programme like the *Yeshasvini* in Karnataka and treat its monthly premium as the critical minimum health expenditure to facilitate the MIT/MIS approach.

Conclusions

The concept of absolute poverty has relevance to a context marked by material deprivation and limited growth in income, which would call for a policy agenda to ensure a subsistence minimum for the population. However, with growth and development involving structural changes, and findings on the asymmetric causes of mobility into and out of poverty, the policy agenda can no longer be cast in terms of ensuring a subsistence minimum but in terms of inclusion in the mainstream growth process and ensuring security for the vulnerable also. This would call for an integrated perspective to provide for growth and inclusion of and security for the poor and vulnerable. Consistent with such changes in emphasis and policy imperatives, norms and measures should be revised for policy formulation, implementation and evaluation.

The economic reform programme, which provides for, *inter alia,* user charges for services in public health facilities to the non-poor in particular would imply irrelevance of the conventional (current) official poverty line, which has been formulated assuming that the State would provide free health and education. Current health insurance coverage of the population is quite small, which would involve catastrophic payments for health. Hence, the current official estimate of poverty line, which does not provide for medical out-of-pocket expenses would involve Type I error in poverty estimates and policy targeting from positive as well as normative perspectives. The estimated errors from a positive perspective are considerable and as a percentage of the true extent of deprivation bear positive association with the latter. Therefore, the question of revising the poverty line to accommodate health expenses and choice of cost-effective strategy towards health care and poverty reduction assumes importance.

But, the health care requirements of the population are not constant but stochastic. Further, morbidity profiles differ across income groups, sectors and states. Hence, it would not be possible to define a unique minimum for health care expenditure across states. Therefore, the Government may explore options to define a state-specific critical bundle of diseases and estimate the expenses associated with it. Alternatively, one might formulate a health insurance programme like the *Yeshasvini* in Karnataka and treat its monthly premium as the critical minimum health expenditure to facilitate the MIT/MIS approach.

References

Agrawal, Ankush, S. Chandrashekhar, and M.H. Suryanarayana (2009): How to Accommodate Health Expenses in Poverty Lines/Estimates? Some Issues" (mimeo).

Government of India (2001): *National Human Development Report 2001*, Planning Commission, New Delhi.

Government of India (2006): *Morbidity, Health Care and the Condition of the Aged: NSS 60th round (January-June 2004)*, Report No. 507 (60.25.0/1), National Sample Survey Organisation, New Delhi.

Government of India (2006a): *Economic Survey 2005-2006*, Ministry of Finance, New Delhi.

Government of India (2006b): *Morbidity, Health Care and The Condition of the Aged, NSS 60th Round (January –June 2004)*, NSS Report No 507, National Sample Survey Organisation, New Delhi.

Government of India (2007a): *Economic Survey 2006-2007*, Ministry of Finance, New Delhi.

Government of India (2007b): *Poverty Estimates for 2004-05*, Press Information Bureau, New Delhi.

Government of India (2007c): *Nutritional Intake in India 2004-2005*: NSS 61st Round (July 2004 – June 2005), NSS Report No 513, National Sample Survey Organisation, New Delhi.

Gumber, A. and Berman, P (1997): "Measurement and Pattern of Morbidity and the Utilization of Health Services: Some Emerging Issues from Recent Health Interviews in India", *Journal of Health & Population in Developing Countries*, Vol. 1, No.1, pp. 16-43.

International Institute for Population Sciences and Macro International (2007): *National Family Health Survey (NFHS-3) 2005-06 India: Volume I*, IIPS, Mumbai.

Krishna, Anirudh, et al., (2004a): "Falling into Poverty in Villages of Andhra Pradesh: Why Poverty Avoidance Policies are needed?" *Economic and Political Weekly*, July 17.

Krishna, Anirudh, et al., (2004b): "Escaping poverty and becoming poor in 20 Kenyan villages", *Journal of Human Development*, July.

Nehru, Jawaharlal (1946): *The Discovery of India*, The John Day Company, New York.

Perspective Planning Division (1962): "Perspective of Development: 1961-1976: Implications of Planning for a Minimum Level of Living. A Decade of Development", reprinted in Srinivasan, T.N and P.K. Bhardhan (eds.) (1974): *Poverty and Income Distribution in India*, Statistical Publishing Society, Calcutta, pp. 9-38.

Perspective Planning Division (1981): *A Technical Note on the Sixth Plan of India (1980-85)*, Planning Commission, New Delhi.

Perspective Planning Division (1993): *Report of the Expert Group on Estimation of Proportion and Number of Poor*, Planning Commission, New Delhi.

Peters, David H., Abdo S. Yazbeck, Rashmi R. Sharma, G.N.V. Ramana, Lant H. Pritchett and Adam Wagstaff (2002): *Better Health Systems for India's Poor: Findings, Analysis, and Options*, The World Bank, Washington, DC.

Rajeshwari, R.,R. Balasubramanian, M. Muniyandi, S. Geetha-ramani, X. Thresa and P. Venkatesan (1999): "Socio-economic impact of tuberculosis on patients and family in India". *The International Journal of Tuberculosis and Ling Diseases*, Vol. 3, pp. 869-877.

Sebm B. (2003): "Drivers of Escape and Descent: Changing Household Fortunes in Rural Bangladesh", *World Development*, Vol. 31, pp 513-534.

Short, Kathleen and Thesia I. Garner (2002): "Experimental poverty measures: accounting for medical expenditures" *Monthly Labor Review*, pp. 312.

Suryanarayana, M.H. (2008): "Exploring Economic Profiles of Morbidity: Measures and Illustrations with Indian Data" *Artha Vijnana*, Golden Jubilee Special Issue, Vol. L, No. 4, pp. 313-331.

Suryanarayana, M.H. (2009): *Nutritional Norms for Poverty: Issues and Implications*,

Concept paper prepared for the Expert Group to Review the Methodology for Estimation of Poverty, http://www.planningcommission.nic.in/eg_poverty.htm.

Van Damme, W. (2004): "Out-of-pocket health expenditure and debt in poor households: evidence from Cambodia", *Tropical Medicine and International Health*, Vol. 9, pp. 273-280.

Footnotes

1. For further corroboration, see Rrajeshwari et al. 1999; Sen 2003, and van Damme 2004.
2. The extent of insurance coverage is not only inadequate but also limited to just 10 per cent of the population (Peters et al., 2002; p.4).
3. Out-of-pocket expenses are those incurred by the patient or the family for health care, including purchase of medicines and transport. These do not include opportunity costs like forgone income or employment.
4. See Short and Garner (2002).
5. For methodological details and estimates, see Suryanarayana (2008).

2

Role of Poverty in Determining Health Status of Urban Elderly: An Analysis of Empirical Data from Coimbatore City

N. Audinarayana

Introduction

With advanced demographic transition caused by persistent reduction in mortality and increased longevity combined with moderate but continued fertility decline, while the young population started to decrease, the size of the old age population has stared to increase to a greater extent. This has lead to population ageing all over the world, more conspicuously in more developed counties and in the recent past, to a moderate extent in less developed countries like India. For instance, while the per cent of population 60 years or more was only 5.6 in 1961, which has increased to a level of 7.5 % in 2001. While this increase of elderly population (60+ years hereafter) on the one side indicates the developments taken place in the fields of science and technology, medicine and health in Indian context; on the other side, continued increase of such population posed many challenges to the Government as well as policy makers.

Of the major challenges to be faced with large share of elderly population, poverty may be ranked as number one. This is because of the major reasons like lack of proper social security measures during old age, in addition to moderate to fewer earnings during their working ages and thereby, no/ less savings/owning of assets as well as less number of children to extend economic support. Further, during old age, majority of them won't work for wages/income, which in turn forbid the headship status of the family and mostly would not be considered for major family decisions. All these in turn cut off them from the monetary resources. Conversely, even majority of the elderly tend to give/spend whatever little money they have to their children and grandchildren because of the traditional bonds. Thus, there is a possibility that majority of the persons during old age become poor and live in poverty conditions. Another crucial aspect that posses challenge for the elderly is the risk of ill-health status. On the one side, as age advances, biologically the functions of the most organs of the body would be deteriorated and thereby, a large majority of them would fell sick. In addition to physical ill-health, they would also tend to be unwell psychologically because of loneliness, lack of companionship, ill-treatment and disrespect by children/sons/daughters-in-law. That is why it is often believed that old age is synonymous to poverty and ill-health. Moreover, at times there are arguments and counter arguments that during old age whether poverty and unhealthy status are complement to each other or poverty is the root cause for the prevalence of disease or sickness, especially in developing countries like India (Ettner, 1996; Ecob and Simth, 1999; Zimmer. 2006; Chandrasekhar and Mukhopadhyay, 2008). Another fact often argued is that the poverty conditions among elderly would be comparatively higher in urban areas than in rural areas, because of maintaining higher standard of living and cost of living in the former setting than the latter (Chandrasekhar and Mukhopadhyay, 2008; Montgomery, 2009). Equally, important is that receiving health services is somewhat costlier in urban areas, especially from private health facilities, because public health facilities would be limited and no separate queue or section/ward is allotted for the elderly persons. Moreover, it is also noticed that majority of the elderly do not avail

Government health facilities due to lack of proper and/or sympathetic care from the doctors (Raju, 2002). In fact the National Policy on Older Persons, which has been designed to address the issues relating to the elderly, does not give specific recommendations on the heath of the elderly (Gupta et al., 2001).

In view of the foregoing discussion, this chapter takes a fresh look into the issues of poverty and physical health of the elderly persons, with the examination of empirical data, primarily focusing on whether there exists a causal association between these two indicators in a well developed urban setting of Tamil Nadu? It also aims to find out other major factors that would affect the health status of elderly. Moreover, these issues are studied with the help of multivariate analyses since such attempts are fewer in Indian context.

Theoretical Perspectives and Empirical Support

Researchers around the world have argued that elderly who are living under poverty conditions suffer more with ill-health and such proposition has also been empirically supported to a large extent (Bucklund et al., 1996; Berkman and Gurland, 1998; Deaton and Paxson, 1998; Zimmer and Amorn-sirisomboon, 2001; Grundy and Sloggett, 2002; Beydoun and Popkin, 2005; Montgomery and Hewett, 2005; Matthews et al., 2006). Such detrimental effect of poverty on elderly' health status could be, on the one side, elderly who live in poor conditions are not able to eat necessary and nutritious food, which is the basic determinant of health, and also not able to keep up personal hygiene. On the other side, poor economic status among elderly deprives them to seek health care because of physical immobility and/or higher expenses needed for transport, consultation fee and medicines if they want to visit private health practitioners/centres because of the crowd/time taken at public health facilities. In Indian context, a few studies have examined the association between various economic measures (personal/household income, per capita consumption expenditure, household standard of living index and/or wealth index) and health status, viz., chronic illness and perceived health status. In addition to poverty, another economic indicator, more number of earning members in the family where elderly reside, also likely to depress their risk of falling ill-health since large economic resources pooled together as well as one or the other of them likely to take care of the elderly in a proper fashion.

As already discussed, deterioration of health with advancing age is well established and among the poor such association would be more pertinent. Likewise, elderly women, that too, widowed are more likely to suffer largely with ill-health than their men and currently married counterparts. While cultural/traditional norms/customs do not allow women and widowed to participate in income-generating activities during their working ages; on the other side in most societies property inheritance to women is absent. Further, if women/widowed fell sick the treatment seeking would be generally delayed and at times even neglected/not sought. Elderly who have some education, by and large, tend to be with fair/good health because of knowledge about keeping up personal and household hygiene, nutritious food intake and health service providers. In Indian context, the role of caste, an indicator of social status, in determining the health status can't be ruled out. Generally, elderly belonging to Scheduled Castes, the lower social strata, suffer more with ill-health because of the abject poverty among them, in addition to large percent of illiteracy and engaging themselves in menial jobs, which are conducive to infection. There is some evidence that elderly who live in nuclear family and with spouse only tend to suffer more with ill-health than their counterparts. Such pattern may be because of poverty conditions among them and no accompanying person for visiting health facility. In Indian context, some of the studies in the recent past have examined one or the other propositions with primary data from different settings adopting multivariate techniques (Yadava et al., 1996; Dreze and Srinivasan, 1997; Gupta and Sankar, 2001; Raju, 2002; Audinarayana, 2005; Kumar et al., 2005; Alam, 2008; Pandey, 2009).

Data and Methodology

Data Source

Data for the present study was collected from 778 elderly persons (60 years or more) from Coimbatore city, Tamil Nadu during 2009 as part of a major research project entitled "*Care of the Elderly across their Living Arrangements in an Urban Setting of Tamil Nadu*". The elderly were selected (on census basis) from 8 clusters (streets or parts of streets), which were selected on the basis of simple random sampling technique, belonging to 4 Wards (out of 72 Wards) in Coimbatore Municipal Corporation – 2 Wards each with lower and higher literacy rates among elderly population according to 2001 census.

Dependent Variable

In the present study, *self-reported current health status* is used as the measure of health status of the elderly. This measure is a comprehensive one and widely used and collected in empirical research in different settings around the world and India (McCallum et al., 1994; Idler and Kasi, 1995; Berkman and Gurland, 1998; Ecob and Smith, 1999; Rahman and Barsky, 2003; Audinarayana; 2005; Zimmer, 2006; Alam, 2008; Pandey, 2009). For this, information has been collected from the elderly persons about their health status with the following ratings, viz., Unhealthy, Fair and Good; however, for the purpose of analysis this information is used as dichotomous, 'Ill-healthy' (score = 1) and 'Fair or Good' (score = 0).

Explanatory Variables

Though a number of background characteristics of the elderly as well as households are collected in the present study, selected variables are only considered for analysis depending upon the theoretical perspectives and levels of strong association with the dependent variable. Among these, since the central focus is on poverty and its causal effect on health status, in the present study '*per capita monthly household income*' (PCMHI hereafter) is used as a measure of poverty. Though this measure has its own limitations, it is presumed that broadly the economic conditions of the elderly would be represented by this measure. For this purpose, the monthly household income has been computed based on the income / wages from different sources, viz., work participation, pension after retirement from service, old age pension, rent earned on houses/shopping places/business establishments, by all those earning members of family. From this, the total household monthly income has been computed and divided by total number of family members living in the same household wherein the elderly live so as to get 'per capita monthly household income'. Finally, based on the frequency distribution, this variable has been categorised into: 'Very Poor', 'Poor', 'Fair', and 'Better' levels of household income.

Among the other variables, '*Current Age*' of the elderly is used as continuous variable, '*Gender*' as 'male' and 'female', '*Marital Status*' as 'currently married' and 'others', and '*Caste*' in terms of 'Scheduled Castes', 'Most Backward Castes', 'Backward Castes' and 'Forward Castes' based on the Government of Tamil Nadu's classification. '*Educational Status*' of the elderly categorised into 'Illiterates (No education)' and 'Some Education'. '*Type of Family*' as 'Nuclear Family (Single Married couple with/without unmarried children and widowed/divorced/separated persons)' and 'Joint Family (Two or more married couples of the same or different generations with/without children and widowed/divorced/separated persons)', '*No. of Earning Members*' classified into 'Nobody/1', '2 – 3', and '4 +', and '*Living Arrangements* of the elderly categorised into 'Alone', 'With Spouse only', 'With Unmarried Children/Others' and 'With Married Children'.

Data Analysis

The analysis has been carried out in the following manner. Firstly, the frequency distribution of the elderly by their background characteristics and a cross-tabular analysis of self-reported health status of the elderly across their PCMHI with chi-square test of significance have been carried out. Later, logistic regression analysis (full model) performed keeping the health status of the elderly (dichotomous) as dependent variable and rest as explanatory variables. Finally, forward step-wise logistic regression analysis is executed with the same variables in order to know the strength of significance of poverty as well as other major variables on their health status of the elderly.

Results

Profile of Elderly

Selected background characteristics of the sample elderly is provided in Table 1. A simple majority of the elderly respondents are in the age group of 60-64 years followed by 75 years and above. About one-fifth is in the age group of 65-69 and rest in 70-74 years. The average age of the sample

Table 1
Background Characteristics and Self-reported Health Status of Elderly

Background Characteristics	*Percentage*	*Frequency*
Current Age (in years)		
60 – 64	28.5	222
65 – 69	24.6	191
70 – 74	20.8	162
75 +	26.1	203
Gender		
Male	46.8	364
Female	53.2	414
Marital Status	45.9	357
Married Widowed/Separated/Divorced	54.1	421
Caste		
Scheduled Castes	21.6	168
Most Backward Castes	8.9	69
Backward Castes	50.6	394
Forward Castes	18.9	147
Educational Status		
No Education (Illiterates)	45.1	351
Some Education	54.9	427

Contd.

Background Characteristics	*Percentage*	*Frequency*
Living Arrangements		
Alone	10.0	78
With Spouse only	47.4	369
With Married Children	23.3	181
Unmarried Children/Others	19.3	150
Type of Family		
Joint Family	19.0	148
Nuclear Family	81.0	630
No. of Earning Members		
1 or Nobody	14.7	114
2 - 3	49.4	384
4 +	36.0	280
Per Capita Monthly Income		
Very Poor	25.2	196
Poor	26.3	205
Fair	25.2	196
Better	23.3	181
Total	100.0	778

elderly is about 69.7 years. In the sample, the share of women and widowed/separated/divorced elderly is more compared to men and currently married. About half of the sample elderly are from backward castes, whereas slightly more than one-fifth is from Scheduled Castes. More than fifty percent of the elderly could be able to have some education, slightly less than half of the elderly live with spouse only and a large per cent belonging to nuclear families. Likewise, in a large number of families where elderly live about 2-3 and 4 & above earning members are available. Based on PCMHI, about one-fourth each of the elderly are said to be 'very poor', 'poor', 'fair' and 'better'.

Elderly' Self-Reported Health Status across their PCMHI

In order to know the gross differentials in self-reported health status across the elderly' PCMHI, data has been analysed and presented in Table 2. From this Table, it is evident that the per cent of elderly who reported as 'unhealthy' is higher among those who are belonging to 'very poor' and 'poor' PCMHI levels as compared to those who are belonging to 'fair' and 'better' PCMHI categories. Obviously, the per cent of elderly who reported that their health status as 'fair/good' has increased with an increase in the levels of PCMHI. These results are also supported by the chi-square test of significance to a higher extent.

Table 2
Self-reported Health Status of Elderly (%) by Per Capita Monthly Household Income

Per Capita Monthly Household Income	*Self-reported Health Status*		*No. of Elderly*
	Good/Fair	*Unhealthy*	
Per Capita Monthly Income			
Very Poor	65.8	34.2	196
Poor	76.6	23.4	205
Fair	81.9	18.4	196
Better	89.5	10.5	181
Total	78.1	21.9	778
Chi-Square; Sig. Level	*32.607;*	*0.001*	

Results Based on Logistic Regression Analysis

Results based on logistic regression analysis (full model) presented in Table 3 (cols. 2-3) highlight that, controlling for all the other variables used in the model, PCMHI has statistically strong association with self-reported health status. For instance, from panel 1 of Table 3, it can be seen that elderly persons who are said to be 'very poor' and 'poor' in terms of PCMHI have a tendency to report 4.1 and 2.4 times ($p<0.001$ and $p<0.01$, respectively) higher as ill-healthy than those who are 'better' in their per capita monthly income. Such odds are 1.8 times higher in the case of 'fair' PCMHI category with somewhat level of significance ($p<0.05$) as compared to those of 'better' PCMHI. As expected, the likelihood of reporting sickness by the elderly significantly ($p<0.01$) increases with an increase in their current age. Another interesting fact noticed here is that the odds of reporting 'ill-health' by elderly

Table 3

Results of Logistic / Step-wise Logistic Regression Analysis on Self Reported Ill-health Status of Elderly

	Full Model		*Step 1*		*Step 2*		*Step 3*	
Explanatory Variables	*Coeff.*	*OR*	*Coeff.*	*OR*	*Coeff.*	*OR*	*Coeff.*	*OR*
Per Capita Monthly								
Income *(Ref.: Better)*		1.000		1.000		1.000		1.000
Fair	0.577	1.780^{+}	0.652	1.918***	0.684	1.983*	0.551	1.735^{+}
Poor	0.881	2.414**	0.958	2.607***	1.037	2.821***	0.831	2.295**
Very Poor	1.420	4.138***	1.488	4.428***	1.560	4.760***	1.373	3.948***
Current Age (in Years)	0.030	1.031**	–	–	0.035	1.036***	0.039	1.040***
Caste								
(Ref.: Forward Castes)		1.000						1.000
Backward Castes	0.213	1.238	–	–	–	–	0.191	1.211
Most Backward Castes	0.450	1.569					0.387	1.472
Scheduled Castes	0.980	2.663**					0.854	2.350**
Gender								
Male *(Ref.)*		1.000	–	–	–	–	–	–
Female	0.180	1.197						
Marital Status								
Wid./ Sep./ Div. *(Ref.)*		1.000	–	–	–	–	–	–
Married	-1.117	0.327***						
Educational Status								
Some Education *(Ref.)*		1.000	–	–	–	–	–	–
No Education	-0.081	0.922						

Contd.

Explanatory Variables	Full Model		Step 1		Step 2		Step 3	
	Coeff.	*OR*	*Coeff.*	*OR*	*Coeff.*	*OR*	*Coeff.*	*OR*
Type of Family								
Joint Family *(Ref.)*		1.000	–	–	–	–	–	–
Nuclear Family	-1.144	0.318***						
No. of Earning Members								
1 or Nobody *(Ref.)*		1.000	–	–	–	–	–	–
2 - 3	-0.608	0.545*						
4 +	-0.773	0.462*						
Living Arrangement								
Married Children (Ref.)		1.000	–	–	–	–	–	–
Alone	-0.530	0.589						
With Spouse only	1.295	3.649***						
With Unmarried Children/Others	0.387	1.471						
Constant	-3.046	0.048**	-2.143	0.117***	-4.696	0.009***	-5.134	0.006***
-2 Log likelihood	733.143		783.436		773.606		762.190	
Chi-square (d. f.)	83.780 (16)		33.496 (3)		43.317 (4) 0.001;		54.742 (7)	
Level of Sig.; N	0.001; 778		0.001; 778		778		0.001; 778	
Nagelkerke $R^2 * 100$	15.7		6.5		8.3		10.5	

Note:

— = Variables not included in the model; Coeff. = Beta Coefficients; OR = Odds Ratio

+, *, **, and *** = Beta Coefficients are significant at 0.10, 0.05, 0.01 and 0.001 levels, respectively.

are 2.7 and 3.6 times ($p<0.01$ and $p<0.001$, respectively) higher among those from Scheduled Castes and those living with spouse only as compared to those who belong to Forward Castes and co-residing with married children. It is also conspicuous to note that elderly living in nuclear families, currently married and households in which 2-3 and 4 or more number of earning members are there have exhibited lesser probability of reporting bad health than their counterparts and also turn out as highly significant ($p<0.001$ in the case of former two variables and $p<0.05$ in each case of latter two categories of variable). Noticeably, female elderly appear to be reporting with illness to a higher extent as against their male elderly, and elderly who have no education felt lower level of poor health as against to those who have some education; but both these patterns did not turn out as statistically significant.

Results Based on Step-wise Logistic Regression Analysis

In order to know the strength of poverty conditions and also the principal factors that determine elderly' self-reported health status, step-wise logistic regression analysis has been carried out and the results are presented in Table 3 (cols. 4-9). Among all the variables, at step one (cols. 4-5), the poverty variable entered as the principal factor that affects the self-reported health status. For instance, it is evident that the elderly who are in 'very poor' and 'poor' conditions tend to health status as 'ill-health' rate as compared to those who are 'better' in their PCMHI; and interestingly, such effect remained highly significant till step three, i.e., in the presence of two more factors. Besides poverty factor, the following variables, viz., current age and belonging to Scheduled Castes, exhibited a highly significant net effect on elderly' sickness status at step two and three, consecutively. Thus, the self-reported ill-health of the elderly is mainly determined by their level of poverty, in addition to their current age and caste background (those belonging to relatively lower socio-economic strata at the society level).

Discussion and Implications

From the foregoing analyses and discussion, it can be inferred that lower/poor income level is an important determinant of ill-health among the elderly. Moreover, the positive relationship between poverty and ill-health is found to be consistent and strong even in the presence of elderly' other selected background factors. Other major factors that influence reporting of bad health among elderly are their current age, and lower social strata (Scheduled Castes). On the other hand, while elderly who reside in nuclear families, currently married and to a certain extent more numbers of earning members in the families wherein elderly who live with less number of members are less likely to report ill-health than their counterparts, elderly reside with spouse only tend to report sickness at a higher extent than those who co-reside with married children.

The findings of this study clearly exhibit that poorer and poor elderly are more vulnerable to ill-health and thereby reported ill-health status to a higher extent. Reasons for such a pattern are discussed at length in the beginning of this chapter and there is ample empirical evidence to this pattern from different settings of the world and India. Current age also appear to play a crucial role in determining the self-reported ill-health status. This is obvious because of biological as well as physiological deterioration in the functions of various parts of the body, in addition to not able to take nutritious food besides not able to purchase such food because of their poor conditions. Another crucial aspect noted here is that the elderly belonged to Scheduled Castes tend to report ill-health status to a higher extent than those from forward castes. In fact the poverty conditions, by and large, are higher among the former group than the latter group, in addition to the possibility of a large extent of the elderly among them as widowed/separated, especially among women, because of early marriage who are more vulnerable to poverty conditions.

The findings of this study demand certain policy interventions.

1. Firstly, in view of the increased demand for health of the elderly, immediate intervention is required in improving/providing of public health infrastructure/facilities in urban areas with special attention to the needs of elderly like geriatric wards, doctors specialised in geriatric medicine and separate sections for out-patients' health care with convenient timings.
2. Attempts also have to be made for the provision of anti-poverty programmes (like the NREGA implemented in rural areas) and strong safety net for the urban elderly. Increasing the amount of 'Old Age Pension' for the elderly also may be looked into depending upon the diversified settings/states of India.
3. Increase of elderly' disposal income may be tried either through subsidised food and services, or by increasing their avenues for earning in the informal sector during post retirement age and/or after age 60 years.
4. Suitable social security measures may be designed and implemented for the middle aged persons who are participating in income generating activities. Additionally, reasonable interest rate and/or suitable savings schemes have to be worked out by the Government so as to encourage the savings among such persons, which would be much helpful for them to live comparatively in a better way after their retirement and/or during old age.
5. Providing health insurance to the elderly would also may be thought of by the Government and insurance companies with reasonably lower premiums so as to protect them from serious illnesses during their fag end of their life. Though some Multi-national Companies provide health insurance to the parents of their employees, its coverage is very limited. Such a provision can be made suitably for all those parents whose children are employees in the organised sector.

6. In India, though there is a law making the sons and daughters (children) responsible for the support of their parents' maintenance and welfare as well as senior citizens (The Maintenance and Welfare of Parents and Senior Citizens Act, 2007), its effectiveness is yet to be assessed. This is because many cases are pending in family courts of the different states. Awareness about it has to be created among the elderly and it is better to educate the children about the need and importance of taking care of their parents when they fell sick.

References

Alam, M (2008): *Ageing, Socio-economic Disparities and Health Outcomes: Some Evidence from Rural India.* Working Series No: E/290/2008, Delhi, Institute of Economic Growth, University of Delhi Enclave, North Campus.

Audinarayana, N (2005): "Self-reported Chronic Morbidity and Perceived Health Status Among the Elderly in Tamil Nadu: Patterns, Differentials and Determinants", in *The Elderly: Emerging Issues,* Bangladesh Association of Gerontology (Ed.), Dhaka, Bangladesh Association of Gerontology, pp. 145-170

Berkman, Cathy S., and Barry J. Gurland (1998): "The Relationship among Income, Other Socioeconomic Indicators, and Functional Level in Older Persons", *Journal of Aging and Health,* 10: 81-98.

Beydoun, May A., and Barry M. Popkin (2005): "The Impact of Socio-economic Factors on Functional Status Decline among Community-dwelling Older Adults in China", *Social Science and Medicine,* 57: S145-S157.

Bucklund, Eric, Paul D. Sorlie, and Norman J. Johnson (1996): "The Relationship among Income, Other Socio-economic Indicators, and Functional Level in Older Adults in China", *Social Science and Medicine,* 60: 2045-2057.

Chandrasekhar, S., and Abhiroop Mukhopadhyay (2008): *Multiple Dimensions of Urban Well-Being: Evidence from India.* Poverty, Gender, and Youth Working Papers No. 2008/11, New York, The Population Council, Inc.

Deaton, A. S., and C. H. Paxson (1998): "Aging and Inequality in Income and Health", *American Economic Review: Papers and Proceedings*, 88: 248-253.

Dreze, J., and P. V. Srinivasan (1997): "Widowhood and Poverty in Rural India: Some Reflections from Household Survey Data", *Journal of Development Economics*, 54: 217-234.

Ecob, Russell and George Davey Smith (1999): "Income and Health: What is the Nature of Relationship?", *Social Science and Medicine*, 48: 693-705.

Ettner, S. L (1996): "New Evidence on the Relationship between Income and Health", *Journal of Health Economics*, 15: 67-85.

Grundy, Emily, and Andy Sloggett (2002): "Health Inequalities in the Older Population: The Role of Personal Capital, Social Resources and Socio-economic Circumstances", *Social Science and Medicine*, 56: 935-947.

Gupta, Indrani, and D. Sankar (2001): *Health of the Elderly in India: A Multivariate Analysis*. Discussion Paper Series No. 46, Delhi, Institute of Economic Growth, University of Delhi Enclave, North Campus.

Gupta, Indrani, P. Dasgupta, and M. Sawhney (2001): "Health of the Elderly in India: Some Aspects of Vulnerability", *BOLD, Quarterly Journal of the International Institute on Ageing*. 11, 3:

Idler, E.L., and S.V. Kasl (1995): "Self-reporting of Health: Do they also Predict Change in Functional Ability?", *Journal of Gerontology*, 50, 6: S344-54.

Kumar, Alok, Haruo Sagaza, K.N.S. Yadava, and Brijesh P. Singh (2005): "Some Health Related Issues of Elderly People in Rural Northern India", in *The Elderly: Emerging Issues*, Bangladesh Association of Gerontology (Ed.), Dhaka, BAG, pp. 171-203.

MaCallum, J., B. Shadbolt, and D. Wang (1994): "Self-rated Health and Survival: A 7-year follow-up Study of Australian Elderly", *American Journal of Public Health*, 847: 1100-1105.

Matthews, Ruth J., Carol Jagger, and Ruth M. Hancock (2006): "Does Socio-economic Advantage lead to a Longer, Healthier Old Age?", *Social Science and Medicine*, 62: 2489-2499.

Montgomery, Mark R., and Paul C. Hewett (2005): "Urban Poverty and Health in Developing Countries: Household and Neighborhood Effects", *Demography*, 42: 397-425.

Montgomery, Mark R. (2009): "Urban Poverty and Health in Developing Countries", *Population Bulletin*, 64, 2.

Pandey, Manoj K. (2009): *Poverty and Disability among Indian Elderly: Evidence from Household Survey*. ASARC Working Paper No: 2009/14, Delhi, Institute of Economic Growth, University of Delhi Enclave, North Campus.

Rahman, M. Omar, and Arthur J. Barsky (2003): "Self-reported Health Among Older Bangladeshis: How Good a Health Indicator is it?", *The Geronotologist*, 43: 856-863.

Raju, Siva S. (2002): *Health Status of the Urban Elderly: A Medico-Social Study*. Delhi: B. R. Publishing Corporation.

Zimmer, Zachary (2006): *Poverty, Wealth Inequality and Health Among Older Adults in Rural Combodia*. Policy Research Division Working Papers No. 217, New York, The Population Council, Inc.

Zimmer, Zachary, and Pattama Amornsirisomboon (2001): "Socioeconomic Status and Health Among Older Adults in Thailand: An Examination using Multiple Indicators", *Social Science and Medicine*, 52: 1297-1311.

Yadava, K. N. S., Surendar, S. Yadava and Ron E. Robers (1996): "Ageing and Health Hazards in Rural Northern India", *Health and Population: Perspectives and Issues* 19, 1: 1-18

3

Influence of Household Poverty on Women Nutrition Status in Two Selected States: NFHS-3 Data Analysis

C.P. Prakasam

Introduction

The health impact of the linkages between women nutritional status and household poverty are most clearly seen in terms of overwork, hazardous work, and poor nutrition. Nutrition is a key area where the combined effects of household poverty and women ill health, leading to ill-health of women and children, more so with girl child, and inter-generational transmission of poverty may occur through the under-nourishment/overwork of pregnant or lactating women.

There are groups of people in all societies who are systematically at disadvantage because they are discriminated against at individual and community level. Discrimination occurs in public institutions, such as the legal system or the education and health services, as well as in the household and in the community.Men, women and children who are discriminated against often end up excluded from society, the economy and political participation. They are more likely to be poor and denied access to income, assets and services. At the household level women and girl child are discriminated with regard to food, clothing and better eduction.These people suffer from certain conditions of ill-health because of social exclusion leading to subsequent poverty (DFID, 2005).Socially excluded people are often denied the opportunities available to others to increase their income and escape from poverty by their own efforts. So, even though the economy may grow and general income levels may rise, excluded people are likely to be left behind, and make up an increasing proportion of those who remain in poverty (DFID, 2005).

Poverty and women's health need special attention as women's health problems and access to health care are affected not only by poverty, but also other household environmental factors. Even women in less poor households may not place priority on meeting their own health needs.There is a debeate that poverty alone can not explain all the health problems of women. According to WHO (2005), the correlation between poverty and poor health for women is not a direct one. Economic growth does not necessarily guarantee better health or higher status for all women because the benefits are not equally distributed. A deteriorating economic situation can create severe health risks for women even when they do not live in extreme poverty (WHO 2005). Hence measurement of household poverty and its influence on women's health is a compex phenomenon and it can be measured through proxy variable than attempting to measure it directly.

Objectives

Keeping in view above points, an attempt is made to understand the influence of Poverty on women, with the following specific objectives:

1. To understand the influence of household poverty on women's health
2. To establish interrelation between household poverty and women's health from two selected states viz: Bihar and Tamil Nadu, representing one developing state and one developed state.

Data and Methodology

Measuring Poverty or status of "Poor" is a multidimentional phenomenon. However researchers identified two main approaches to know "Poverty line" below which population can be classified as "Poor" viz: Absolute or Relative. An absolute approach defines poverty according to a minimum standard of living based on a person's physiological needs for water, clothing and shelter. In contrast, the relative approach defines poverty in relation to a generally accepted standard of living in a specific society at a specific time and goes beyond basic physiological needs (Jane F., Ceema N; 2002). In this paper, poverty according to a minimum standard of Housing condition (living) has been considered. Research studies (Montgomery, M, et.al; 2000, Moser, C and Holland, J; 1997, Phipps, Shelley, and Peter Burton, 1995, Jenkins, Stephen, 1991) define the household production of health (HHPH) as .a dynamic behavioural process through which households combine their (internal) knowledge, resources and behavioural norms and patterns with available (external) technologies, services, information and skills to restore, maintain and promote the health of their members of the household. A set of household amenities, and Household resources (Life-style indicators) have been considered as proxy variables for measuring status of Poverty and the variables are lsited in Table 1.

Data for the present study has been drawn from National Family Health survey (NFHS-3), coordinated by the International Institute for Population Sciences (IIPS, 2007) during 2005-06. Information related to Household amenities, Household Furniture, Type of House, Household family structure, number of members in the house, and relation of household members with the head of the household was collected to understand the level of poverty at household level. The selected variables are given in Table 1. By using the household assests, poverty index has been derived by applying Factor analysis (Guilford, J.P, 1952; Harman, H, 1960; Kaiser, H.F, 1960).

Table 1

List of Variables Considered for Analysis in Measuring Influence of Household Poverty on Health of Currently Married Women in Bihar and Tamil Nadu: NFHS-3 Data Analysis

Variables/Indicators	*Description*
Dependent Variable: (Y)	Anemia: Sever-1, Moderte-2,Mild – 3,Not Anemic-4
Indirect (Back Ground variables)	
B1. Level of Education	Illiterate- 0, Primary-1, Secondary-2, Higher-3
B2. Place of residence	Urban-1, Rural-2
B3. Husband's Education	Illiterate- 0, Primary-1, Secondary-2, Higher-3
B4. Religion	Hindu–1, Muslim-2, Others-3
B5. Work status of Women for Cash	Not paid–0, Working for cash-1
Direct (Household level) Household Factors	
H1. Electricity	No- 0, Yes-1
H2. Source of Drinking Water	Piped-4, Well-3, Surface Water- 2, Other-1
H3. Time to get drinking Water	Within the premises- 4, <15 minutes-2,>15 minutes-1
H4. Main type of fuel used for cooking	Wood-1 Crop Residues/ Dung Cake/Coal/coke/ Lignite/charcoal-2
H5. Food Cooked on Stove, Chullah or Open fire:	Kerosene -3, Electricity/L.P.G/ Bio-gas-4 Stove-4, Chullah-3, Open fire-2, Other-1
H6. Type of Toilet facility	Flush Toilet-4, Pit toilet/latrine-3, Dry toilet-1, No facility (bush, field etc)-0
H7. House Hold Goods:	Radio, TV, Refrigerator, Cycle, Sewing Machine, Motorcycle/Scooter: Yes-1, No-0
H8. Household Furniture	Mattress, Pressure Cooker, Chair, Cot/bed, table, fan Yes-1, No-0
H9. Type of House	Pucca-2, Not Pucca-1
H10. Household family Structure	Nuclear-2, Joint& Extended-1
H11. Ownership of House	Own this house or other houres-2, No-1
H12. Number of Household Members	1-4 Members-4, 5-9 Members-2, 10+ Members-1
H13. Number of Children under 5	No Children-4, 1-3 Children-2, 4 and above children-1

In this study Women's Nutritional status has been identifyed through her "Anemia" status.Anemia is a major health problem in India, especially among women and children. Anemia can result in maternal mortality, weakness, diminished physical and maternal capacity, and increased reproductive morbidity. Anemia among women generally decreases with increasing education and household wealth.Anemia is characterized by a low level of haemoglobin in blood. NFHS-3 (IIPS, 2007) undertook direct measurement of the haemoglobin level of women in the age group 15-49 years .In this study women's anemic condition with mild, moderate and severe levels were derived from NFHS-3 (IIPS, 2007) for the states of Tamil Nadu and Bihar.

To establish the interrelation between household poverty and women health, two states viz: Tamil Nadu and Bihar have been idendified. Based on the wealth index calculated using NFHS-3 data, the state of Bihar is poorer than the nation as a whole and only 9 percent of Bihar's households are in the *highest* wealth quartile,compared with one-fifth of households in India (NFHS-3,Bihar). Where as in Tamil Nadu, only 12 percent of the households are in the *lowest* wealth quintiles. Apart from wealth quintiles, nearly 70 percent women in the age group 20-24 years got married below age 18 years in Bihar and TFR is found to be very high (4.0) whereas only 22 percent in Tamil Nadu got married at less than 18 years and TFR was 1.8. Only 35 percent of currently married women age 15-49 years were employed in Bihar and in Tamil Nadu 48 percent women were employed. Sixty seven percent of women in Bihar and 53 percent in Tamil Nadu found to be anemic and among them 17 percent with moderate and severe anaemia in Bihar and it was only 2 percent in Tamil Nadu (NFHS-3, IIPS2006). Comparing these two states data will reveal the household poverty differentials and its influence on women's health status which has been identified as percentage of women with anemia.

Proxy Measures of Poverty

It has been argued by the researchers (Deaton (1997), Jane Falkingham and Ceema Namazie (2002), that considering household percapita income and consumption as a measure of poverty are prone to measurement errors.Asset indices or household asset have been applied extensively in the recent period. In this study by considering NFHS-3 data, household assets have been identified and given in Table1. Scores have been given with scores ranging from "1" to "4". Higher score indicates better household facilities, indicating not poor or "well" and lower score indicates "poor".Considering Source of Drinking Water (H2), Piped water is given a score "4" explains that household had better economic status (Not Poor) to have piped water at home than the household who depends on surface water as source of water. Simillarly time to get drinking water (H3), "within the premises" is given higher score because household had better facilitiy,gives indirect evidence of better economic situation than time required being "more than15 minutes to get water". It is assumed that housewife will spend more time in getting water which is a proxy indicator of "Poverty", affect her health condition.

In case of Household goods (H7: electronic and Transport), availability of each item is scored as "1" and non availability as "0". Higher score indicates better living and lower score indicates "poor"household. Simillarly Household furniture (H8) has been scored according to its availability as "1" and non availability as "0". The total score has been divided in to poor/not poor.

Other variables viz: Type of House, Household family structure and ownership of house is given score in increasing order indicating higher score reflecting better living (Table 1).

Number of household members (H12) and Number of Children under 5(H13) indicate household density and economic burdern.

To derive a composite index, the scores for each holdhold item viz: H1, H2, etc. (Table 1) are not additive because the unit of measurement and degree of ranks are different and preparing a composit index leads to error. For comparitive purpose, proper weights have to be derived and with the multiplication of weights, these varible scores can be added. Hence Factor Analytic Technique (Factor Analysis) has been used to determine a composite index through which it is possible to clasify the household under different category of "poverty". Factor analysis is often used in data reduction to identify a small number of factors that explain most of the variance observed in a much larger number of manifest variables. Factor Analysis first starts with calculation of Pearson product-moment correlations, computed between all trait variables. Principal component analysis was then carried out using unity in the major diagonal. Following the Kaiser (1960) criterion, all factors with Eigen values greater than 1.0 have been selected. These factors were then rotated according to the varimax criterion. Subsequently factor scores are calculated utilizing the factor loading. The derived scores which are a composit score of household amenities given in Table 1 depicts Poverty status of household. The calculated scores will have inbuilt characteristics of having zero mean and unit variance and thus the households classified in to four quartiles according to Poverty score (-1 to -.5, -.5 to 0, 0 to +0.5, +0.5 to +1.0). According to these quartiles, Poverty at the household level has been further analysed. For further reading on Factor analysis one can see Guilford, J.P (1952), Harman, H, (1960), Kaiser, H.F (1960).

Results

Women's Nutritional Status and Background and Household Variables

Anemia status by haemoglobin level of women was clasified in NFHS-3 as mild anemia 10.0-11.9 g/dl, moderate amemia 7.0-9.9g/dl, and severe anemia as less than 7 g/dl. In the present study considering above clasification status women's health has been derived. The association of anemia status of women with back ground variables in Tamil Nadu and Bihar has been analysed and given in Table 2.

It has been observed from Table 2 that background variables of women including level of Literacy, Religion, Partner Education, and Number of children less than five years living in the house are significantly associated with

Table 2

Percentage of Women with Degree of Anemia by Background Characteristics in Tamil Nadu and Bihar: NFHS-3 Data

	Tamil Nadu					*Bihar*				
	Anemia					*Anemia*				
Background Variables	*Sever*	*Moderate*	*Mild*	*Not Anemic*	*Total Women*	*Sever*	*Moderate*	*Mild*	*Not Anemic*	*Total Women*
Level of Literacy										
Illiterate	517(43.8)	447(37.8)	183(15.5)	34(2.9)	1181(100.0)	694(33.1)	1021(48.7)	354(16.9)	28(1.3)	2097(100.0)
Literate	2389(50.4)	1675(35.4)	591(12.5)	83(1.8)	4738(100.0)	668(38.8)	821(47.47)	222(12.9)	10(0.6)	1721(100.0)
Total	2906(49.1)	2122(35.9)	774(13.1)	117(2.0)	5919(100.0)	1362(35.7)	1842(48.2)	576(15.1)	38(1.0)	3818(100.0)
$\chi^2 = 22.825^{**}$						24.194**				
Religion#										
Hindu	2532(48.5)	1914(36.7)	671(12.8)	105(2.0)	5222(100.0)	1108(35.6)	1504(48.4)	464(14.9)	32(1.0)	3108(100.0)
Muslim	118(46.8)	86(34.1)	43(17.1)	5(2.0)	252(100.0)	246(35.2)	335(47.9)	112(16.0)	6(0.9)	699(100.0)
Others	256(57.5)	122(27.4)	60(13.5)	7(1.6)	445(100.0)	8(72.7)	3(27.3)	0	0	11(100.0)
Total	2906(49.1)	2122(35.9)	774(13.1)	117(2.0)	5919(100.0)	1362(35.7)	1842(48.2)	576(15.1)	38(1.0)	3818(100.0)
$\chi^2 = 20.803^{**}$	#Chi-square is calculated for Hindu and Non Hindu categories.						7.705 NS			
Partner Education										
Illiterate	370(43.2)	324(37.8)	135(15.8)	28(3.3)	857(100.0)	340(30.7)	540(48.7)	212(19.1)	16(1.4)	1108(100.0)
Literate	1860(49.6)	1337(35.6)	488(13.0)	67(1.8)	3752(100.0)	742(36.3)	1005(49.1)	283(13.8)	16(0.8)	2046(100.0)
Total	2230(48.4)	1661(36.0)	623(13.5)	95(2.1)	4609(100.0)	1082(34.3)	1545(49.0)	495(15.7)	32(1.0)	3154(100.0)
$\chi^2 = 18.140^{**}$						22.523**				
Work status respondent women										
Not working	1507(49.6)	1073(35.3)	401(13.2)	56(1.8)	3037(100.0)	1012(37.4)	1282(47.4)	388(14.3)	22(0.8)	2704(100.0)
working	1397(48.5)	1049(36.4)	373(13.0)	61(2.1)	2880(100.0)	350(31.4)	560(50.3)	188(16.9)	16(1.4)	1114(100.0)
Total	2904(49.1)	2122(35.9)	774(13.1)	117(2.0)	5917(100.0)	1362(35.7)	1842(48.2)	576(15.1)	38(1.0)	3818(100.0)
$\chi^2 = 1.500$, NS						15.731*				

Contd.

	Tamil Nadu					Bihar				
	Anemia					Anemia				
Background Variables	*Sever*	*Moderate*	*Mild*	*Not Anemic*	*Total Women*	*Sever*	*Moderate*	*Mild*	*Not Anemic*	*Total Women*
Household structure										
Nuclear	2017(48.7)	1484(35.8)	557(13.4)	87(2.1)	4145(100.0)	685(34.6)	985(49.8)	288(14.6)	20(1.0)	1978(100.0)
Joint&Extend	889(50.1)	638(36.0)	217(12.2)	30(1.7)	1774(100.0)	677(36.8)	857(46.6)	288(15.7)	18(1.0)	1840(100.0)
Total	2906(49.1)	2122(35.9)	774(13.1)	117(2.0)	5919(100.0)	1362(35.7)	1842(48.2)	576(15.1)	38(1.0)	3818(100.0)
χ^2 = 2.969, NS						4.064N.S.				
Children under five										
One	2(20.0)	7(70.0)	1(10.0)	0	10(100.0)	34(30.1)	55(48.7)	21(18.6)	3(2.7)	113(100.0)
Two	782(47.1)	633(38.1)	226(13.6)	21(1.3)	1662(100.0)	696(34.7)	970(48.4)	319(15.9)	20(1.0)	1005(100.0)
3 and more	2122(50.0)	1482(34.9)	547(12.9)	96(2.3)	4247(100.0)	632(37.2)	817(48.1)	236(13.9)	15(0.9)	1700(100.0)
Total	2906(49.1)	2122(35.9)	774(13.1)	117(2.0)	5919(100.0)	1362(35.7)	1842(48.2)	576(15.1)	38(1.0)	3818(100.0)
χ^2 = 17.191*						9.404, NS				
Ownership of house										
Not own	919(49.7)	638(34.5)	255(13.8)	37(2.0)	1849(100.0)	319(36.9)	403(46.6)	134(15.5)	9(1.0)	865(100.0)
own	1987(48.8)	1484(36.5)	519(12.8)	80(2.0)	4070(100.0)	1042(35.3)	1437(48.7)	441(15.0)	29(1.0)	2949(100.0)
Total	2906(49.1)	2122(35.9)	774(13.1)	117(2.0)	5919(100.0)	1361(35.7)	1840(48.2)	575(15.1)	38(1.0)	3814(100.0)
χ^2 = 2.618,NS						1.231, N.S.				

*P<.01, **P<.001, N.S. =Not Significant

Women's anemia status in Tamil Nadu.Around 49 percent of women were sever anemic, 36 percent were moderately and 13 percent mild anemic. Only 2 percent of women were not anemic (Table 2).

The association of Women's health (Anemia) and background varaibles in Bihar revealed that Level of literacy, Partner education, Work status of respondent women are found to have significant association (Table 2). Among the women, nearly 36 percent were sever, 48.2 women were moderate and 15 percent were mild anemic. Only one percent of Bihar women in the reproductive age are not anemic. Analysis revealed that in Tamil Nadu and Bihar states, Anemia is found to be very high and healthy women were only 1 to 2 percent.

Poverty and Women's Nutritional Status

By using Factor Analysis technique with Principal Component Analysis for extraction factors, and Varimax method for rotation of factors with Kaiser Normalization, the component scores have been calculated. The extracted factors with components and communality for Tamil Nadu and Bihar states are given in Table 3. Four factors for Tamil Nadu and three factors for Bihar have been selected by factor analysis method. Among these, factor 2 which in Tamil Nadu and Bihar showed more than 1 eigen value, has been selected. Further the scores calculated for each component were plotted and with zero mean and unit standard deviation. From the Figure 1 and Figure 2, it was evident that factor 2 scores for Tamil Nadu and Bihar are more suitable for classifying household poverty status. Considering factor two scores as Poverty index variables, correlation coefficient has been calculated. Further the score data according to households classified in to four quartiles according to Poverty score (-1 to -.5, -.5 to 0, 0 to +0.5, +0.5 to +1.0).

As the household amenities and economic status of rural population are different from that of urban population, analysis has been done separately for rual and urban data.

Table 3

Factor Structure of Selected Household Variables or Measuring Povery in Tamil Nadu and Bihar: NFHS-3 Data

	Tamil Nadu						*Bihar*				
	Communalities		*Component*				*Communalities*		*Component*		
Household Variables for Poverty Measurement	*Initial*	*Extraction*	*1*	*2*	*3*	*4*	*Initial*	*Extraction*	*1*	*2*	*3*
Source of Drinking water (H2)	1.000	.756	.352	-.103	.256	.021	1.000	.869	.240	-.047	.032
Time to get water (H3)	1.000	.452	-.179	.512	-.109	.053	1.000	.510	.142	.078	-.038
Type of toilet (H6)	1.000	.704	.060	.016	-.481	-.064	1.000	.731	-.138	.442	.020
Electricity (H1)	1.000	.554	.056	.318	.101	.037	1.000	.616	-.041	.375	.072
Type of cooking fuel used(H4)	1.000	.875	.367	-.096	-.009	.020	1.000	.819	.216	.012	.049
Amenities coded grouped(H7,8)	1.000	.489	-.113	.464	.035	-.051	1.000	.465	.061	.198	-.134
Type of house (H9)	1.000	.457	.083	.235	-.041	.012	1.000	.599	.040	.290	.009
Household members (H12)	1.000	.608	.148	-.100	.082	.534	1.000	.662	.073	-.070	.654
Children under five (H13)	1.000	.502	-.180	.323	.016	.447	1.000	.592	-.048	.105	.615
Ownership of house (H11)	1.000	.675	.119	-.039	.521	-.030	1.000	.652	.226	-.137	-.017
Food cooked on stove (H5)	1.000	.803	.314	-.125	-.212	.002	1.000	.898	.246	-.057	.024

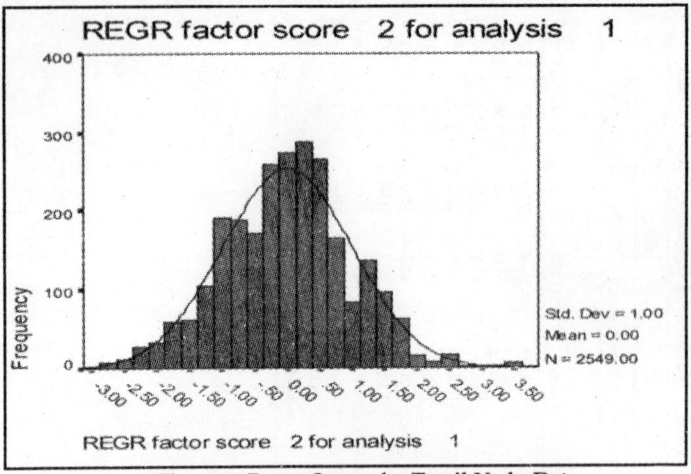

Figure 1: Factor Scores for Tamil Nadu Data

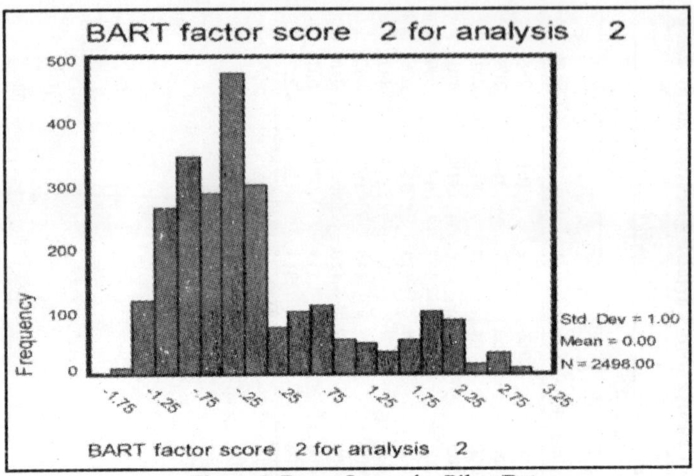

Figure 2: Factor Scores for Bihar Data

Association between Poverty and Background varaiables has been tested. The results reveal that (Table 4) Level of Literacy, Partner education, Respondent education and Anemia (Women Health) are significantly associated with Poverty level in rural areas of Tamil Nadu and Bihar. The background variables including Anemia are not significantly associated with Poverty status in urban Tamil Nadu. In urban Bihar, Poverty and anemia (women's health) are not significantly associated and this reveals that there may be other factors which are influencing anemic status of urban women than household poverty.

Correlation cofficient between the Anemia status of women and Poverty quartiles for rural and urban areas has been calculated for Tamil Nadu and Bihar. Results presented in Table 4 indicate negative significant relation for Tamil Nadu and Bihar. In rural areas of Tamil Nadu and Bihar, Poverty and anemia (women's health) are negatively related (Table 4) but it is different except in urban area of Bihar.

Summary and Conclusions

In this paper an attempt is made to establish interrelationship between Household poverty, which is measured with household assests and facilities with women's health. Over all Poverty affects health of human beings especially women at household level. People in lower socioeconomic groups experience poorer health than those in higher income group. Considering Household assets and amenities and anemia status of women, data for Tamil Nadu and Bihar has been collected from NFHS-3. By applying Factor Analytic Technique household assests have been grouped in to four levels of poverty (Quartiles). Association between Poverty quartiles with anemia status of women has been assessed. From the survey data analysis the results revealed that:

- Women's health status (Anemia) in these two States viz: Tamil Nadu and Bihar is found to be poor and majority of women suffer with sever to moderate anemia. Though Tamil Nadu is a progressive state, in the context of women health condition, it was found to be same with developing state like Bihar.
- Background variabels viz: Women's literacy level, and Partner Education, have significant influence on Women's health in both the states. However religion and children under five (child dependency) show significant influence on women's health in Tamil Nadu while Work status of respondent affects the women's health status in Bihar.

Table 4
Association between Poverty and Background Variables in Tamil Nadu and Bihar

Chi-Square Analysis	*Tamil Nadu*		*Bihar*	
	Urban	*Rural*	*Urban*	*Rural*
Poverty with Anemia	12.929 (NS)	15.060 **	13.744 (NS)	20.563*
Poverty with Level of Literacy	2.913 (NS)	15.496 **	12.857**	105.170**
Poverty with Partner Education	2.711(NS)	33.373**	41.539**	166.864**
Poverty with Respondent Education	8.997(NS)	16.314**	23.504**	270.103**

N.S. =Not Significant ** P<.001 *P<.01

- With proper scoring, household assests and facilities have been grouped and by applying factor analysis technique Poverty status of women has been derived. There exists association between Poverty at household and Woman's health (anemic status) in rural areas of Tamil Nadu and Bihar. In urban areas, Poverty at household could not reveal significant impact on Women's health in both the states. Rural and Urban Poverty is different as the asset owenership in Rural and Urban is different. Hence further analysis has been done. The results are given in Table 5. The results show (Table 5) in Rural Tamil Nadu and Bihar anamic condition is having significant relation with Poverty than urban areas in both states.It can be viewed that household assests and facilities may be better in urban areas than rural areas and hence while measuring urban poverty; different sets of variables should be considered to measure poverty and its influence on women's health.

Table 5
Correlation between Poverty Quartiles and Anemia for Urban, Rural and Total Areas of Tamil Nadu, Bihar: NFHS-3 Data

	Total#		*Urban#*		*Rural#*	
Poverty Quartile	*Poverty Quartile*	*Anemia*	*Poverty Quartile*	*Anemia*	*Poverty Quartile*	*Anemia*
Poverty quartile	1.000	-.054**	1.000	-.038	1.000	-.063
Anemia	-.053**	1.000	.090*	1.000	-.052*	1.000

** Correlation is significant at the 0.01 level (2-tailed).
# Tamil Nadu: Total N=2549, Urban=899, Rural=1650, Bihar : N:Total=2992, Urban=634, Rural= 1857

A common criticism levied at the quantitative measurement of poverty based on household survey data is that household assests and facilities may not some times reveal better economic status. Though these assests are acquired over a period of time by spending their financial resourses, may not addup to quality of life in improving health condition of women. Further these household assests become economic burden and cut their financial resources and influence adversly on health of individual more so women. Therefore these quantitative measures should be considered as "proxy" variables to "Poverty".

While measuring Poverty, different sets of variables should be condidered for Urban and rural areas. Further, currently married women's health is also affected apart from socio economic condition; it is affected with psychological conditions which depends on people living in the household and their relation with her and number of dependent children. However to improve the women's health, poverty at household level should be removed by providing subsidised food grains, and constructing low cost housing. Policies and programs should be implemented in empowering women by providing skill based training programs which will improve her economic status and health, and indirectly remove poverty at household level.

References

DFID (2005): "Reducing Poverty by Tackling Social Exclusion" Department of International Development, A DFID Policy Paper, September, pp: 1-20.

Guilford, J.P. (1952): "When Not to Factor Analyze" Psychological Bulletin, 49, 26-37.

Harmon, H. (1960): Modern Factor Analysis, University of Chicago Press.

International Institute for Population Sciences (IIPS) and Macro International (2007): "National Family Health Survey (NFHS-3), 2005-2006: India", Mumbai.

Jane Falklngham and Ceema Namazie (2002): "Measuring Health and Poverty: A Review of Approaches to Identifying the Poor" Health System Resource Centre, DFID.

Jenkins, Stephen (1991): Poverty Measurement and the Within-Household Distribution: Agenda for Action, Journal of Social Policy, 20, 457.483;

Kaiser, H.F., "The Application of Electronic Computers to Factor Analysis", Educational and Psychological Measurements, 20 (1960), 141-151

Montgomery, M, Gragnolati, M., Burke, K and Paredes, E. (2000): "Measuring living standards with proxy variables", Demography, Vol 37, No.2, pp: 155-74

Moser, C and Holland, J (1997): "Household Responses to Poverty and Vulnerability" Volume 4, Confronting Crisis in Chawana, Lusaka Zambia, Washington DC, World Bank.

Phipps, Shelley, and Peter Burton, 1995, "Sharing Within Families: Implications for the Measurement of Poverty Among Individuals in Canada", The Canadian Journal of Economics, 28:1, 177.204.

WHO (2005):"Human Rights, Health and Poverty Reduction Stratagies", Health and Human Rights Publication Series, Issue No.5, April 2005, WHO/ETH/HDP/05.1

4

Access to Maternal Health Services in Backward Regions: An Intra-Regional Study

Talwar Sabanna

Introduction

In industrialised countries, there are an average nine maternal deaths per 100000 live births, whereas this figure can be as high as 1000 or more per 100000 live births in the most disadvantaged countries. In settings where high fertility is the norm, women face such risks with each pregnancy (Chen M.A., Houser A.N., WHO)

India has a high maternal mortality ratio-approximately 453 deaths per 100,000 births in 1993. This ratio is 57 times the ratio in the United States. The World Health Organization (WHO) and United Nations Children's Fund (UNICEF) estimate that India's maternal mortality ratio is lower than ratios for Bangladesh and Nepal but higher than those for Pakistan and Sri Lanka. The level of maternal mortality varies greatly by state, with Kerala having the lowest ratio (87) and two states (Madhya Pradesh and Orissa) having ratios over 700. This differential maternal mortality is most likely related to differences in the socio-economic status of women and access to health care services among the states.

Poor nutritional status-and its concomitant problems of poor body weight and height, poor weight gain during pregnancy, low hemoglobin levels-is one of the primary underlying cause of maternal mortality in India. The causes that lead to the unnecessary deaths of so many women, most in the prime of their lives, originate long before their pregnancies, and extend far beyond the realm of medical care. They are the result of a complex interaction of factors rooted in the social and economic contexts in which Indian women are placed. Thus, apart from the immediate cause of maternal mortality, the long chain of invisible causes behind those which are most apparent, need to be examined more closely (Acharya I.B and Cleland J., Bhatia J.C., Krishnan T.N., Ramachandran L.).

Generally, malnourishment, poor medical facilities and unfavourable social conditions are the major underlying causes for high maternal mortality. Nutritional anaemia, a serious problem in pregnancy, affects 50 percent of the women of childbearing age in Southeast Asia. A severely malnourished woman is at higher risk on two fronts: she is more susceptible to miscarriages and stillbirths, and to excessive bleeding and infections. This means that she has to go through about eight pregnancies to have five live births (of which only three or four may see adulthood), exposing herself to potentially grave consequences each time (Mukhopadhyay Alok, Navaneethan K. and Dharmalingam A., Govindaswamy P. and Ramesh B.M.).

Poorer and less educated women and those living in rural areas are far less likely to give birth in the presence of a skilled health worker than better-educated women who live in wealthier households or urban areas. The reasons for this include physical inaccessibility and prohibitive costs, but may also be the result of inappropriate socio-cultural practices. It is not enough for services to be available; they must also be of high quality and should be provided in a way that is both culturally appropriate and responsive to women's needs (Navaneethan K. and Dharmalingam A.).

Antenatal care is particularly important because many women have nutritional deficiencies when they begin their pregnancy. Iron deficiency anaemia and defiencies of vitamin A and iodine are commonplace. It is estimated that almost half of all pregnant women and one third of non-pregnant women worldwide have anaemia, a deficiency that significantly increases the risks to health for both mothers and infants. Maternal deficiencies in micronutrients may also affect the infant's birth weight and chance of survival, and poor vitamin A intake increases the mother's risk of night blindness (Pathmanatnan I. et.al., Govender V. and Penn-Kekana L.).

The choice of Hyderabad–Karnataka region from Karnataka state, Telangana region from Andhra Pradesh state and Marathwada region from Maharashtra state for the present study is prompted, because, the regions are most backward areas, maternal mortality is high, access to maternal health services is low due to poverty, illiteracy and lack of awareness among women. Thus, maternal health status of women is a major problem for the over all development of the women in these regions. In this context, the chief purpose with which this study is undertaken is to present about access to maternal health services in backward regions.

Objectives

The following aspects have been the focus of analysis in the present paper:

1. To analyse the access to ante-natal care (ANC) services in three backward regions.
2. To compare reasons for not receiving ante-natal care (ANC) services in three backward regions.
3. To find out the place of delivery and person conducted delivery in three backward regions.

Data Sources

Data relating to maternal health services of women in backward regions was collected from the selected sample villages and urban areas (cities–district headquarters are treated as urban areas) of the study regions through personal interview method. Further, the study covers one district from each region i.e., Gulbarga district from Hyderabad-Karnataka region, Mahaboobnagar district from Telangana region and Osmanabad district from Marathwada region.

To analyse the maternal health services of women in the study regions, 450 women respondents from rural areas and 450 women respondents from urban areas from three study regions (300 women respondents from each district/region: of this 150 women respondents from rural areas and 150 women respondents from urban areas) were interviewed. Thus, the total 900 women respondents were selected and interviewed for the present study.

The study collected data on the access to maternal health care services during pregnancy and the birth of the reference child. They are:

Ante-Natal Check-up: Information on ante-natal care during pregnancy with all children born during the study: whether ante-natal care was obtained, who provided the ante-natal care (For example: health professional or trained/traditional birth attendant), number of ante-natal check-ups, timing of first ante-natal check-up, medical tests conducted during pregnancy and reasons for not receiving ante-natal care.

Place of Delivery: The place of delivery is an important determinant for reducing the risk of infant and maternal death. Women were asked whether their last baby was born at home or at any health institution (public hospitals or other health care institutions).

Assistance during Delivery: Assistance during delivery is an important component in the reproductive health care services: it can reduce the risk of obstructed labour during delivery and is highly associated with place of delivery. Information was collected about who assisted during delivery: health personnel (doctor, Auxiliary Nurse Midwife (ANM), nurse or midwife, trained traditional birth attendant, friends or relatives).

Findings

Maternal health care is defined as "The field of work related to the physical, mental and emotional health of women immediately before, during and after childbirth". Pre-natal care ensures that the health of the expectant mother, more specifically her nutritional status, is periodically supervised, and avoidable complications of pregnancy are prevented or treated. Intra-natal services provide skilled care and attention by trained health personnel during child birth. Post-natal care includes checks on the mother's health after delivery that makes it possible for a gynecologist to diagnose and prevent some of the chronic and disabling conditions common in women (Shivakami M., 2008, p.9). In this context following findings present the access to maternal health services in three backward regions:

Ante-Natal Check-up

Ante-natal care (ANC) or check-up refers to pregnancy-related health care provided by a doctor or a health worker in a medical facility or at home. The safe mother hood initiative proclaims that all pregnant women must receive basic professional ante-natal care. Ideally ante-natal care should monitor a pregnancy for signs of complications, detect and treat pre-existing and concurrent problems of pregnancy, and provide advice and counseling on preventive care, diet during pregnancy, delivery care, post-natal care, and related issues. The Reproductive and Child Health Programme recommends that as part of ante-natal care, women receive two doses of tetanus toxoid vacine, adequate amounts of iron and folic acid tablets or syrup to prevent and treat anemia, and at least three ante-natal check-ups that include blood pressure checks and other procedures to detect pregnancy complications (NFHS II 1998-99, p.280). In this context we have asked women respondents whether they saw anyone for ante-natal care for their most recent birth. Table 1 shows that 73 percent women respondents in rural areas and 86 percent women respondents in urban areas received ante-natal care for their most-recent birth. However, 27 percent women respondents in rural areas and 14 percent women respondents in urban areas reported that they did not receive ante-natal care.

Table 1
Ante-Natal Check-up by Women in Study Regions

Regions	Rural Areas			Urban Areas			Total			
	Yes	No	Total	Yes	No	Total	Yes	No	Total	
Hyderabad-Karnataka	89(64.96)	48(35.04)	137(100.00)	109(84.50)	20(15.50)	129(100.00)	198(74.44)	68(25.56)	266(100.00)	χ^2 =13.32 Significant at 1%
Telangana	105(77.21)	31(22.79)	136(100.00)	121(92.37)	10(7.63)	131(100.00)	226(84.64)	41(15.35)	267(100.00)	χ^2=8.94 Significant at 5%
Marthwada	106(76.81)	32(23.19)	138(100.00)	110(80.88)	26(19.12)	136(100.00)	216(78.83)	58(21.17)	274(100.00)	χ^2 =1.19 NS
All Regions	300(72.99)	111(27.01)	411(100.00)	340(85.86)	56(14.14)	396(100.00)	640(79.31)	167(20.69)	807(100.00)	

Source: Field study.
Note: Figures in brackets denote Percentage.

Similar trend was observed in all regions of study areas. For instance, in rural areas women respondents who went to health centres for ante-natal check-up constitutes 77 percent in Telangana region, 77 percent in Marathwada region and 65percent in Hyderabad-Karnataka region. However, the percent of women respondents who received ante-natal check-up were higher in urban areas than in rural areas. For instance, 92 percent women in Telangana region, 85 percent women respondents in Hyderabad-Karnataka region and 81 percent women respondents in Marathwada region received ante-natal services during their last pregnancy period. This shows that there are wide variations in the use of ante-natal care services among the women in rural and urban areas in these regions. The value of chi-square is significant at 1 percent level in Hyderabad-Karnataka region, 5 percent level in Telangana region and non-significant in Marathwada region.

Place of Ante-Natal Check-ups

Women respondents who received ante-natal care services during their last pregnancy were asked about the place where they have received ante-natal care. Study results shown in Table 2 indicate that 73 percent and 27 percent women respondents in rural areas and 45 percent and 55 percent women respondents in urban areas received ante-natal care services in Government Hospitals/PHCs and Private Hospitals, respectively.

The distribution of data according to the region for rural areas in study regions present that 74 percent women in Telangana region, 74 percent women in Marathwada region and 72 percent women in Hyderabad-Karnataka region received ante-natal care in Government Hospitals /PHCs. As against this, 57 percent women in Hyderabad-Karnataka region, 55 percent women in Telangana region and 53 percent women in Marathwada region received ante-natal care in Private Hospitals. This shows the differentials in rural and urban areas who received ante-natal care primarily in Government Hospitals/PHCs and Private Hospitals, respectively. The chi-square value is significant at 1 percent level in all regions.

Table 2

Place of Ante-Natal Check-up by Women in Study Regions

Source	*Hyderabad-Karnataka*		*Telangana Region*		*Marathwada Region*		*All Regions*	
	Rural	*Urban*	*Rural*	*Urban*	*Rural*	*Urban*	*Rural*	*Urban*
Government Hospital/PHCs	64(71.91)	47(43.12)	78(74.29)	54(44.63)	78(73.58)	52(47.27)	220(73.33)	153(45.00)
Private Hospital	25(28.09)	62(56.88)	27(25.71)	67(55.37)	28(26.42)	58(52.73)	80(26.67)	187(55.00)
Total	89(100.00)	109(100.00)	105(100.00)	121(100.00)	106(100.00)	110(100.00)	300(100.00)	340(100.00)
	χ^2=16.49 Significant at 1%		χ^2=17.01 Significant at 1%		χ^2=15.60 Significant at 1%			

Source: Field study.

Note: Figures in brackets denote Percentage.

Person Attended Ante-Natal Check-up

Further, women respondents were asked to whom they saw for their ante-natal check-up. From Table 3 it is found that 61 percent and 79 percent women received ante-natal care from doctors followed by 30 percent and 20 percent women from ANM/Nurse and 9 percent and about 1 percent women from mid-wife in rural and urban areas, respectively.

Region–wise distribution of data for rural areas reveals that 64 percent in Telangana region, 60 percent in Marathwada region and 58 percent in Hyderabad-Karnataka region received ante-natal care from Doctors. Whereas, in case of urban areas, 83 percent in Hyderabad-Karnataka region, 74 percent in Telangana region and 89 percent in Marathwada region received ante-natal care from doctors. Thus, receiving ante-natal care from doctors is much more common in urban areas than in rural areas. However, other service providers like ANM/nurse and mid-wife are predominant types for ante-natal care service providers in the study area. The chi-square value is significant at 1 percent level in Hyderabad-Karnataka region, 5 percent level in Marathwada region and non-significant in Telangana region.

Number of Ante-Natal Care Visits

The number of ante–natal care visits and the timing of the first visit are important for the health of the mother and the outcome of the pregnancy. The World Health Organization recommends that all pregnant women should have at least four ante-natal care (ANC) assessments by or under the supervision of a skilled attendant. These assessments should be spaced at regular intervals throughout pregnancy, commencing as early as possible in the first trimester (NFHS III 2005-06, p.196). In the light of this, women respondents who received ante-natal care during their last pregnancy were asked about the total number of ante-natal care visits they had. It is found from Table 4 that 56 percent women respondents in rural areas had up to 3 ANC visits, whereas 56 percent women respondents in urban areas had 7 to 9 ANC visits during their last pregnancy. Further, 25 percent women

Table 3
Person Attended Ante-Natal Check-up

Person Attended	Hyderabad-Karnataka		Telangana Region		Marathwada Region		All Regions	
	Rural	*Urban*	*Rural*	*Urban*	*Rural*	*Urban*	*Rural*	*Urban*
Doctor	52(58.43)	91(83.49)	67(63.81)	89(73.55)	64(60.38)	88(88.89)	183(61.00)	268(78.82)
ANM/Nurse	29(32.58)	17(15.60)	30(28.57)	31(25.62)	32(30.19)	21(21.21)	91(30.33)	69(20.30)
Mid-Wife	8(8.99)	1(0.91)	8(7.62)	1(0.83)	10(9.43)	1(1.01)	26(8.67)	3(0.88)
Total	89(100.00)	109(100.00)	105(100.00)	121(100.00)	106(100.00)	110(100.00)	300(100.00)	340(100.00)
	χ^2=17.38 Significant at 1%		χ^2=11.04NS		χ^2=12.67 Significant at 5%			

Source: Field study.
Note: Figures in brackets denote Percentage.

Table 4
Number of Ante-Natal Care visits by Women

Time	*Hyderabad-Karnataka*		*Telangana Region*		*Marathwada Region*		*All Regions*	
	Rural	*Urban*	*Rural*	*Urban*	*Rural*	*Urban*	*Rural*	*Urban*
Up to 3 times	51(57.30)	9(8.26)	65(61.90)	9(7.44)	52(49.06)	8(7.27)	168(56.00)	26(7.65)
4 to 6 times	27(30.34)	39(35.78)	22(20.95)	48(39.67)	27(25.47)	36(32.73)	76(25.33)	123(36.18)
7 to 9 times	11(12.36)	61(55.96)	18(17.15)	64(52.89)	27(25.47)	66(60.00)	56(18.67)	191(56.18)
Total	89(100.00)	109(100.00)	105(100.00)	121(100.00)	106(100.00)	110(100.00)	300(100.00)	340(100.00)
	χ^2=67.05 Significant at 1%		χ^2=77.10 Significant at 1%		χ^2=49.59 Significant at 1%			

Source: Field study.
Note: Figures in brackets denote Percentage.

respondents in rural areas and 36 percent women respondents in urban areas had 4-6 ante-natal care visits. Only 19 percent women respondents in rural areas had 7 to 9 ante-natal care visits.

Examining the region-wise data in rural areas, it is found that 62 percent women in Telangana region, 57 percent women in Hyderabad-Karnataka region and 49 percent women in Marathwada region visited up to 3 times for ante–natal check-up. Further, 30 percent women in Hyderabad-Karnataka region, 25 percent women in Marathwada region and 21 percent women in Telangana region visited 4 to 6 times for ante-natal check-up. As against this, in case of urban areas, 60 percent women in Marathwada region, 56 percent women in Hyderabad-Karnataka region and 53 percent women in Telangana region had 7 to 9 ante-natal care visits. This presents that number of ante-natal care visits is more among urban women and less among rural women. The shorter distance to place of ante-natal care services and the comparative cost of travel in urban areas, as well as the higher educational attainment of mothers in urban areas could be the factors in explaining the higher number of ante-natal care visits in urban areas. The chi-square value is significant at 1 percent in all regions.

Timing of First Ante-Natal Check-up

The first ante-natal check-up should take place at the latest during the second trimester of pregnancy (NFHS III 2005-06, p.196). In this context, women respondents who received ante-natal care for their last pregnancy were asked about the month in which they had their first ANC visit. Table 5 shows that only 35 percent women had their first ante-natal care visit in the first trimester of pregnancy in rural areas. More than half (59 percent) women in urban areas had their first ante-natal care visit in the first trimester of pregnancy. Further, 65 percent women in rural areas and 41 percent women in urban areas had their first ante-natal care visit in the second trimester (4-6 months). Thus, visit for ante-natal care during the first trimester was more common in urban areas than rural areas. The chi-square value is significant at 1 percent level in

Table 5
Timing of First Ante-natal Care by Women

	Hyderabad-Karnataka		*Telangana Region*		*Marathwada Region*		*All Regions*	
Months	*Rural*	*Urban*	*Rural*	*Urban*	*Rural*	*Urban*	*Rural*	*Urban*
Up to 3 months	33(37.08)	61(55.96)	28(26.67)	79(65.29)	44(41.51)	62(56.36)	105(35.00)	202(59.41)
4 to 6 months	56(62.92)	48(44.04)	77(73.33)	42(34.71)	62(58.49)	48(43.64)	195(65.00)	138(40.59)
Total	89(100.00)	109(100.00)	105(100.00)	121(100.00)	106(100.00)	110(100.00)	300(100.00)	340(100.00)
	χ^2 =5.46NS		χ^2 =35.08Significant at 1%		χ^2 =4.44NS			

Source: Field study.
Note: Figures in brackets denote Percentage.

Telangana region and non-significant in Hyderabad-Karnataka and Marathwada regions.

Further, region-wise analysis of the data reveals that in rural areas, 41 percent women in Marathwada region, 37 percent women in Hyderabad-Karnataka region and 27 percent women in Telangana region had their first ante-natal care visit during the first trimester (up to 3 months). In case of urban areas, 65 percent women in Telangana region, 56 percent women in Marathwada region and 56 percent women in Hyderabad-Karnataka region had their first ante-natal visit during their first trimester of pregnancy (i.e., up to 3 months). Further, 73 percent women in Telangana region, 63 percent women in Hyderabad-Karnataka region and 58 percent women in Marathwada region had their first ante-natal care visit during 4 to 6 months pregnancy period. About 44 percent women in Hyderabad-Karnataka region, 43 percent women in Marathwada region and 35 percent women in Telangana region visited hospitals for ant-natal check-up during their second trimester period (4-6 months). The analysis indicates that initiating the ante-natal check-up during first semester is less common in rural areas of the study regions.

Tests Performed

The effectiveness of ante-natal care in ensuring safe motherhood depends on the test and measurement done and the advice given as part of ante-natal care package. The women who received ante-natal care services were asked whether they got tests like weight / blood pressure/blood test during their last pregnancy.

The results presented in Table 6 show that 38 percent women in rural areas and 70 percent women in urban areas had undergone such examination or test during their last pregnancy. The region-wise distribution of data of the women respondents in rural areas reveals that 41 percent women in Marathwada region, 40 percent women in Telangana region and 33 percent women in Hyderabad-Karnataka region, got such test during their last pregnancy. In urban areas, 74

Table 6

Performed Weight /Height/Blood Pressure/Blood Test During Pregnancy

	Rural Areas			*Urban Areas*			*Total*			
Regions	*Yes*	*No*	*Total*	*Yes*	*No*	*Total*	*Yes*	*No*	*Total*	
Hyderabad-Karnataka	29(32.58)	60(67.42)	89(100.00)	73(66.97)	36(33.03)	109(100.00)	102(51.51)	96(48.49)	198(100.00)	χ^2=21.76 Significant at 1%
Telangana	42(40.00)	63(60.00)	105(100.00)	84(69.42)	37(30.58)	121(100.00)	126(55.75)	100(44.25)	226(100.00)	χ^2=20.16 Significant at 1%
Marthwada	44(41.51)	62(58.49)	106(100.00)	82(74.54)	28(25.46)	110(100.00)	126(58.33)	90(41.67)	216(100.00)	χ^2=24.53 Significant at 1%
All Regions	115(38.33)	185(61.67)	300(100.00)	239(70.29)	101(29.71)	340(100.00)	354(55.31)	286(44.69)	640(100.00)	

Source: Field study.

Note: Figures in brackets denote Percentage.

percent in Marathwada region, 69 percent women in Telangana region and 67 percent women in Hyderabad-Karnataka region reported so. Thus, it is clear that women from urban areas got all the tests more than their rural counterparts. The chi-square value is significant at 1 percent level in all regions.

Reasons for Not Receiving Ante-Natal Check-up

Table 7 presents the data about women respondents/ mothers who did not receive ante-natal check-up in a health centre and reasons for not receiving ante-natal care. Of the total respondents in the study regions, 116 women in rural areas and 56 women in urban areas did not receive ante-natal care. In rural areas, 41 percent pregnant women who did not receive any ante-natal check-ups thought 'it was not necessary' with other reasons mentioned being 'cost too much (16 per cent)', 'not customary (14 percent)', 'too far/no transport (13 percent)', 'lack of knowledge (12 percent)' and 'family did not allow (3 percent)'. In urban areas, 45 percent women stated that ante-natal care was 'not necessary' with other reasons being 'cost too much (25 percent), 'lack of knowledge (14 percent)', 'not customary (9 percent)', 'family did not allow (5 percent)' and 'too far/no transport (2 percent)'.

In rural areas, 44 percent women in Hyderabad-Karnataka region, 42 percent women in Telangana region and 38 percent women in Marathwada region felt that ante natal care was 'not necessary'. In urban areas, 55 percent in Hyderabad-Karnataka region, 50 percent in Telangana region and 35 percent in Marathwada region mentioned so. 'Cost too much' was the second major reason for not availing ante natal care services-mentioned by 22 percent and 23 percent in Marathwada region, 15 percent and 20 percent in Hyderabad-Karnataka region and 14 percent and 40 percent in Telangana region in rural and urban areas, respectively. This shows that ante-natal care services are not taken seriously by women during their pregnancy due to traditional society, negligence and poverty in these backward regions. Thus there is a need to educate mothers and families about the availability and

Table 7
Reasons for Not Receiving Ante-Natal Care by Women in Study Regions

	Hyderabad-Karnataka		*Telangana Region*		*Marathwada Region*		*All Regions*	
Months	*Rural*	*Urban*	*Rural*	*Urban*	*Rural*	*Urban*	*Rural*	*Urban*
Not necessary	21(43.75)	11(55.00)	15(41.67)	5(50.00)	12(37.50)	9(34.62)	48(41.38)	25(44.64)
Not customary	6(12.50)	1(5.00)	4(11.11)	0(0.00)	6(18.75)	4(15.38)	16(13.79)	5(8.93)
Cost is too much	7(14.58)	4(20.00)	5(13.89)	4(40.00)	7(21.88)	6(23.08)	19(16.38)	14(25.00)
Too far / no transport facilities	6(12.50)	1(5.00)	7(19.44)	0(0.00)	2(6.25)	0(0.00)	15(12.93)	1(1.79)
Family did not allow	4(8.33)	0(0.00)	0(0.00)	0(0.00)	0(0.00)	3(11.54)	4(3.45)	3(5.36)
Lack of knowledge	4(8.34)	3(15.00)	5(13.89)	1(10.00)	5(15.62)	4(15.38)	14(12.07)	8(14.28)
Total	48(100.00)	20(100.00)	36(100.00)	10(100.00)	32(100.00)	26(100.00)	116(100.00)	56(100.00)
	χ^2 =4.27NS		χ^2 =5.99NS		χ^2 =5.45NS			

Source: Field study.
Note: Figures in brackets denote Percentage.

benefits of ante-natal check-ups to help to overcome traditional attitudes and other hurdles that prevent mothers from seeking ante-natal care.

Person who Assisted Delivery

Obstetric care from a trained provider during delivery is recognized as central for the reduction of maternal and neonatal mortality. Births delivered at home without the assistance of trained health professionals are more risky than those carried out with the assistance of trained health professionals. Table 8 gives the results about the person who assisted the delivery. About 36 percent women in rural areas reported that their last delivery was assisted by mid-wife, 27 percent mentioned about doctor, 20 percent mentioned ANM/Nurse and 17 percent got assistance of relatives/ friends. In urban areas, 67 per cent mentioned about deliveries/births assisted by doctor, followed by mid-wife (16 per cent), ANM/Nurse (14 per cent) and relatives/friends (4 per cent).

The proportion of women whose last delivery or birth was assisted by doctor constitute 33 percent in Telangana region, 31 percent in Marathwada region and 16 percent in Hyderabad-Karnataka region. The percentage of women who got assistance from midwife is 38, 36 and 33 per cent in Hyderabad-Karnataka region, Telangana region and Marathwada region, respectively. In urban areas, proportion of women whose deliveries/ births were assisted by doctor is 70 per cent in Hyderabad-Karnataka region, 69 per cent in Telangana region and 63 per cent in Marathwada region. Thus, getting delivery/birth assistance from Doctors is higher in urban areas than in rural areas.

Place of Delivery

Another important thrust of the Reproductive and Child Health Programme is to encourage deliveries in proper hygienic conditions under the supervision of trained health professionals. For this purpose, women respondents were asked about the place of delivery during their last pregnancy.

Table 8

Person Assisted Delivery in Study Regions

	Hyderabad-Karnataka		*Telangana Region*		*Marathwada Region*		*All Regions*	
Person Assisted	*Rural*	*Urban*	*Rural*	*Urban*	*Rural*	*Urban*	*Rural*	*Urban*
Doctor	14(15.73)	76(69.73)	35(33.33)	83(68.59)	33(31.13)	69(62.73)	82(27.33)	228(67.06)
ANM/Nurse	18(20.22)	12(11.01)	19(18.10)	13(10.74)	24(22.64)	21(19.09)	61(20.33)	46(13.53)
Mid-Wife	34(38.20)	14(12.84)	38(36.19)	24(19.83)	35(33.02)	16(14.54)	107(35.67)	54(15.88)
Relatives/ Friends	23(25.85)	7(6.42)	13(12.38)	1(0.84)	14(13.21)	4(3.64)	50(16.67)	12(3.53)
Total	89(100.00)	109(100.00)	105(100.00)	121(100.00)	106(100.00)	110(100.00)	300(100.00)	340(100.00)
	χ^2=59.36Significant at 1%		χ^2=24.90Significant at 1%		χ^2=26.01Significant at 1%			

Source: Field study.

Note: Figures in brackets denote Percentage.

In rural areas, 50 percent women had the last delivery at home, while 36 per cent had the delivery in Government Hospitals/ PHCs with 15 per cent mentioning about delivery at Private Hospital. In urban areas, 53 percent women delivered at Private Hospital and 25 percent had at Government Hospital. However, still 23 percent women delivered at home. This shows that about half of deliveries in rural areas took place in non- institutional situations like home. However, it is satisfactory to note that institutional delivery are widely common among urban women across the study regions.

Region-wise analysis shows that in rural areas, 55 percent women in Hyderabad-Karnataka region, 49 percent women in Telangana region and 46 percent women in Marathwada region had home delivery. And 56 percent women in Hyderabad-Karnataka region, 53 percent women in Telangana region and 49 percent women in Marathwada region had deliveries in Private Hospitals. Further, study results highlight that 33 percent and 21 percent women in Hyderabad-Karnataka region, 38 percent and 26 percent women in Telangana region and 36 percent and 26 percent women in Marathwada region had delivery at Government Hospitals in rural and urban areas respectively. Thus, institutional deliveries, particularly in Private Hospitals, are more common among urban women than rural women across the study regions. One factor contributing to these patterns may be a heightened awareness of the benefits of professional medical care during both pregnancy and delivery among urban women.

Conclusion and Suggestions

Utilisation of maternal health care services (ante-natal check, tests performed, institutional delivery, assistance of health personnel during delivery) was less in the study regions. Further, utilisation of maternal health care services differs within region, i.e., rural women access less maternal health services than urban women. The rural-urban differential in the use of maternal health care services is likely to be due to differences in the availability of maternal health care facilities

Table 9

Place of Delivery During Last Pregnancy

Person Assisted	*Hyderabad-Karnataka*		*Telangana Region*		*Marathwada Region*		*All Regions*	
	Rural	*Urban*	*Rural*	*Urban*	*Rural*	*Urban*	*Rural*	*Urban*
Government Hospital/PHC's	29(32.58)	23(21.10)	40(38.10)	32(26.45)	38(35.85)	29(26.36)	107(35.67)	84(24.71)
Private Hospital	11(12.36)	61(55.96)	14(13.33)	64(52.89)	19(17.92)	54(49.09)	44(14.67)	179(52.65)
At Home	49(55.06)	25(22.94)	51(48.57)	25(20.66)	49(46.23)	27(24.55)	149(49.66)	77(22.64)
Total	89(100.00)	109(100.00)	105(100.00)	121(100.00)	106(100.00)	110(100.00)	300 (100.00)	340(100.00)
	χ^2=41.60Significant at 1%		χ^2=40.76Significant at 1%		χ^2=24.53Significant at 1%			

Source: Field study.
Note: Figures in brackets denote Percentage

including the distance to the health care centre. However, the magnitude of regional differences is not the same for all the maternal health care indicators among the backward regions. The regional level characteristics such as the availability and accessibility of health care facilities and programme factors could be responsible for less utilisation of maternal health care services among women in the study regions. Moreover, the role of various socio-economic, cultural and programmatic factors in influencing the pattern of utilisation has varied in their effects depending on the state and the type of service.

Further, study also found that women's literacy is an important predictor for the use of maternal health care services in all the three regions. Illiterate women are less likely to use maternal health care services for delivery assistance and place of delivery compared to literate women in the study regions. Further, the literature gives several reasons for higher utilisation of maternal health care services by educated mothers than uneducated mothers. Educated women may have a greater decision making power on health related matters and also attach a higher value to the welfare and their health. Further, educated mothers will have more confidence in handling the officials and have the ability and willingness to travel outside the home to seek services.

The study concludes that determinants of maternal health care services are not same across regions and for different maternal health care indicators. Although illiterate women are less likely to use maternal health care services, there was no difference among the educated. The differential in access to health care facilities between rural-urban areas is an important factor responsible for lower utilisation of maternal health care services, particularly for institutional delivery and delivery assistance by health personnel in the rural areas of the three regions. Also, the health workers in the rural areas are playing a pivotal role in providing ante-natal care in backward regions.

The following suggestions are made to overcome these discriminations in the regions:

- Government should make an effort to improve the health status of women.
- Government should initiate an integrated approach to provide maternal health care through primary health care services in rural areas by taking the needs and preferences into account.
- Government and NGOs should encourage women in study regions to utilize a range of information, education and communication activities to improve their maternal health status.
- Efforts should be made to create awareness among women to use and extend appropriate technologies at all levels so that women have better care at lower cost in backward regions.
- By strengthening community based maternal health care delivery systems, especially in rural areas, the Government should upgrade existing facilities, and create relevant new ones if necessary.
- Government should strengthen referral facilities- hospitals as well as health facilities – and locate them appropriately. They need to be equipped to handle emergency situations effectively and efficiently.

References

Acharya L.B. and Cleland J. (2000): *"Maternal and Child Health Services in Rural Nepal: Does Access or Quality Matter More?"*, Health Policy and Planning, 15(2), 223-229.

Amit S.Ray and Saradindu Bhaduri (2001): *"The Political Economy of Rural Health Care In India"*, Voluntary Health Association of India, New Delhi.

Anita N.H., Dutta G.P. and Kasbekar A.B. (2000): *"Health and Medical Care A People's Movement"*, Foundation for Research in Community Health, Pune.

Bhatia J.C. (1995): *"Levels and Causes of Maternal Mortality in South India"*, Studies in Family Planning, 24(5), 310-318.

Chen M. A. (2000): *" Perpetual Mourning: Widowhood in Rural India"*, Oxford University Press, Oxford.

Govender V. and Penn-Kekana L., (2008): *"Gender Biases and Discrimination: A Review of Health care Interpersonal Interactions"*, Global Public Health, 3 suppl 1; 90-103.

Government of India (1998-99 & 2005-06): *"National Family Health Survey (II & III)"*, International Institute for Population Sciences, Mumbai.

Govindaswamy P. and Ramesh B.M. (1997): *"Maternal Education and Utilisation of Maternal and Child Health Services in India"*, NFHS Survey Subject Reports No.5, International Institute for Population Sciences, Mumbai.

Houser A.N. (2009): *"Women and Long-term Care: Research Report"*, Washington D.C.

Krishnan T.N. (1976): *"Demographic Transition in Kerala: Facts and Factors"*, Economic and Political Weekly, 11, 1203-1224.

Leena Sumaraj (1991): *"Women and Medical Care"*, Ashish Publication House, New Delhi.

Mukhopadhyaya Alok (1992): *"State of India's Health"*, Voluntary Health Association of India, New Delhi

Navaneetham K. and Dharmalingam A. (2000): *"Utilisation of Maternal Health Care Services in South India"*, Centre for Development Studies, Thiruvananthapuram.

Rajani R.Ved and Avtar Singh Dua (2005) *"Burden of Disease in India"* National Commission on Macro Economics and Health, Ministry of Health and Family Welfare, Government of India, New Delhi

Pathmanathan I et.al., (2003): *"Investing in Maternal Health: Learning from Malaysia and Sri Lanka"*, The World Bank, Washington D.C

Ramachandran L. (1989): *" The Effect of Ante-natal and Natal Services on Pregnancy Outcome, and Health of the Mother and Child"*, Journal of Family Welfare, 35(5), 34-46.

Ram Kumar (1990): *"Women Health Development and Administration Principals and Practices"*, Vol.II , Deep and Deep Publications New Delhi.

Sivakami M., (2008): *"Determinants of Maternal Health Care Service Use: A Regional Analysis in Karnataka"*, Institute for Social and Economic Change, Bangalore.

The World Bank (1996): *"Improving Women's Health in India"*, The World Bank Report, Washington D.C.

Veeramatha C.S, Praksh Rao A. and Lingaraju M., (2002): *"Functioning of Health and Family Welfare Training Institutions in Karnataka"*, Population Research Centre, Institute of Social and Economic Change Nagarbhavi, Bangalore.

WHO (2004): *"Global Health Risks: Mortality and Burden of Disease Attributable to Selected Major Risks"*, Geneva.

5

Persons with Disabilities in India: Socio-economic Differentials and their Implications

K.E. Vaidyanathan

Introduction

The aim of this paper is to assess the differentials among persons with disabilities (PWDs) in key socioeconomic variables such as social acceptance, education, nature of work, health care and other factors. The two main sources of data on disability in India are the 2001 census and NSS 58th round of 2002. The 2001 census found 21.91 million PWD (2.13 percent of the population), while the 2002 NSS estimate was 18.5 million or 1.8 percent of the population. The results differ for different disabilities largely due to differences in definitions and measurement procedures. Nevertheless the data reveal important socioeconomic differentials among PWDs and among households having PWDs.

The NSSO undertook the first comprehensive survey of disabled persons in its 36th round during the second half of 1981, the International Year of the Disabled Persons. After a gap of ten years, a second survey on the disabled was carried out in the 47th round during July-December 2002. The objective of these surveys was to provide the data base regarding the incidence and prevalence of disability in the country. The basic framework of these surveys viz., the concepts, definitions and operational procedures was kept the same. While the earlier surveys were restricted to only the physically handicapped persons, in the surveys conducted during NSS 36th and 47th rounds, an extended definition was used to cover all the physically disabled persons. Information was collected from all persons with one or more of the three physical disabilities - visual, communication (i.e. hearing and/ or speech) and locomotor. The particulars of disability of the disabled persons, such as, the type of disability, degree of disability, cause, age at onset of disability, type of aids and appliance used, etc. were collected along with some socio-economic characteristics. After a gap of eleven years, the third survey on the disabled was carried out in the 58th round during July-December 2002. In this round, the coverage was extended to include mental disability also, keeping all other concepts, definitions and procedures for physical disability same as those of the 47th round. The decision to include mental disability in the survey was taken on the basis of a pre-test of the questions on mental disability, both for the listing and detailed schedules. Along with the particulars of physical and mental disabilities, the socio-economic characteristics of the disabled persons such as their age, literacy, vocational training, employment, cause of disability, age at onset of disability, etc. were also collected.

Sources of Data and their Limitations

The field work for the 58th round survey was carried out during the second half of 2002 starting from July and continuing up to December-over a period of six months.

Geographical Coverage: The survey covered whole of India except (i) Leh and Kargil districts of Jammu & Kashmir, (ii) interior villages of Nagaland located beyond 5 kms. from the bus routes and (iii) villages in Andaman and Nicobar Islands which were inaccessible throughout the year.

Survey Work: The survey period was divided into two sub-rounds of three months duration each. Equal number of

Table 1
Estimated* Number (In '00) of Disabled Persons by Type of Disability /Sex for Rural/Urban India

All-India						*(in 00)*
	Rural			*Urban*		
Type of Disability	*Male*	*Female*	*Persons*	*Male*	*Female*	*Persons*
(1)	(2)	(3)	(4)	(5)	(6)	(7)
Any disability**	83102	57748	140850	25811	18249	44060
Mental disability						
Mental retardation	4434	2561	6995	1824	1128	2951
Mental illness	5022	3377	8399	1623	988	2611
Physical disability						
Visual disability						
Blindness	7494	8536	16030	1793	2311	4104
Low vision	2982	3563	6545	711	877	1588
Hearing disability	12516	11171	23687	3617	3313	6930
Speech disability	9495	6532	16027	3416	2102	5518
Locomotor disability	49987	29839	79826	16352	10162	26514
Estimated persons (00)	3923611	3711319	7634930	1545555	1391996	2937551

* *estimates are obtained by using survey proportions on the projected population.*
** *at least one of mental, visual, hearing, speech and locomotor disability.*
Source: NSS, 2002, Statement 2

sample first stage units was allocated to each of these sub-rounds with a view to ensuring uniform spread of the interviews over the entire survey period.

Sample Design: A stratified multi-stage sample design was adopted for the 58th round. The first stage units were in most cases 1991 census villages in rural areas and urban blocks-demarcated by the Urban Frame Survey-in urban areas. The ultimate stage units were households-constituting a group of persons normally living together and taking food from a common kitchen. The survey followed the standard NSS practices of stratification, allocation of samples to various states into stratum, selection of sample, etc.

Sample Size: The number of sample villages and urban blocks surveyed in Central sample was 4637 and 3354, respectively. A total of 45571 and 24731 households were surveyed in rural and urban areas, respectively.

Definition of Disability: A person with restrictions or lack of abilities to perform an activity in the manner or within the range considered normal for a human being was treated as having disability. It excluded illness/injury of recent origin (morbidity) resulting into temporary loss of ability to see, hear, speak or move. The definitions of various disabilities are given in the Annex.

The measurement of disability is subject to many limitations. Omission to report disability in the census is very common due to cultural reasons. The definition of disability has a subjective element. What is normal for one person, may not be considered as normal by another person. Temporary disabilities arising from illness and accidents are excluded from the survey, unless these are considered as permanent. The sample size is small in the case of smaller states and Union territories, besides for the elderly population. These could have a bearing on the final estimates.. The cause of disability was not recorded for one-third of the reported cases of disability.

Findings

The results presented in this report relate to both physical and mental disabilities, namely, (i) mental disability, (ii) visual

Table 2
Number of Disabled Persons Per 1,00,000 Persons for Each Sex and Sector

All-India

	Disabled Persons Per 1,00,000 Persons								
	Rural			*Urban*			*Rural + Urban*		
Type of Disability	*Male*	*Female*	*Persons*	*Male*	*Female*	*Persons*	*Male*	*Female*	*Persons*
(1)	*(2)*	*(3)*	*(4)*	*(5)*	*(6)*	*(7)*	*(8)*	*(9)*	*(10)*
Mental retardation	113	69	92	118	81	100	115	72	94
Mental illness	128	91	110	105	71	89	122	86	105
Blindness	191	230	210	116	166	140	171	214	192
Low vision	76	95	86	46	62	54	68	87	77
Hearing disability	319	301	310	234	238	236	296	285	291
Speech disability	242	176	210	221	151	187	237	169	204
Locomotor disability	1274	804	1046	1058	730	901	1217	785	1008
Any disability	2118	1556	1846	1670	1311	1499	2000	1493	1755

Source: NSS, 2002, Statement 4

disability, (iii) hearing disability, (iv) speech disability and (v) locomotor disability. More specifically, the report gives the incidence and prevalence of different forms of disability and the distribution of the disability by cause of disability (as reported by the informant), marital status, educational level, living arrangements, activity status, etc. The aggregated estimates of the disability in rural and urban India are given in Table 1, separately for each sex and type of disability. These estimates are obtained by applying survey proportions to the projected population.

According to the survey estimates, the number of disabled persons in the country was 18.49 million during July to December, 2002 comprising of 10.9 million males and 7.6 million females. They accounted for about 1.8 per cent of the total estimated population. Among the different types of disabilities, the number of persons having locomotor disability (10.6 million) was the highest followed by the number of persons with hearing disability (3.1 million) and visual disability.(2.8 million). About 10.63 per cent of the disabled persons had more than one type of following disabilities, (i) mental disability in the form of (a) mental retardation or (b) mental illness, (ii) visual disability in the form of (a) blindness or (b) low vision, (iii) hearing disability, (iv) speech disability, and (v) locomotor disability. In the case of locomotor disability, multiple types of locomotor disability were also considered as multiple disabilities

Rural-Urban and Gender Differentials

About 8.4 per cent and 6.1 per cent of the total estimated households in rural and urban India, respectively reported to have at least one disabled person in the household. Since average size of households in rural areas (5.7) is higher than the average household size in urban (5.5), there are more disabled in rural areas than in urban areas.. The prevalence rate is the number of disabled persons found during the survey per 100,000 persons. The prevalence rate observed during the survey is given below:

Table 3
Per 1000 Distribution of Disabled Persons by Marital Status by Type of Disability for Each Sex and Sector

	Male					Female				
Type of Disability	*Never Married Rural*	*Currently Married*	*Wido-wed*	*Divorced/ Separated*	*Total*	*Never Married*	*Currently Married*	*Wido-wed*	*Divorced/ Deparated*	*Total*
Mentally retarded	920	63	3	13	1000	899	47	23	31	1000
Mentally ill	506	398	35	61	1000	338	393	171	97	1000
Blindness	264	538	187	11	1000	132	275	580	13	1000
Low vision	146	662	173	18	1000	92	273	626	5	1000
Speech disabled	348	529	113	10	1000	292	318	365	24	1000
Hearing disabled	728	240	23	8	1000	697	197	74	32	1000
Locomotor disabled	483	456	53	8	1000	437	334	206	23	1000
All disabled	471	448	69	12	1000	376	316	281	26	1000
Urban										
Mentally retarded	963	27	4	6	1000	941	29	10	20	1000
Mentally ill	640	283	32	46	1000	522	220	190	68	1000
Blindness	269	589	136	6	1000	297	198	495	10	1000
Low vision	236	612	146	6	1000	88	305	599	8	1000
Speech disabled	391	488	110	11	1000	298	297	386	18	1000
Hearing disabled	767	207	16	11	1000	721	158	98	22	1000
Locomotor disabled	453	493	48	6	1000	418	319	248	16	1000
All disabled	484	450	57	9	1000	415	284	283	18	1000

Contd.

Type of Disability	Male					Female				
	Never Married Rural	Currently Married	Wido-wed	Divorced/ Separated	Total	Never Married	Currently Married	Wido-wed	Divorced/ Deparated	Total
Rural + urban										
Mentally retarded	931	53	3	11	1000	911	41	19	28	1000
Mentally ill	536	371	35	57	1000	377	356	175	91	1000
Blindness	265	547	178	10	1000	165	259	563	12	1000
Low vision	162	653	169	16	1000	91	278	621	6	1000
Speech disabled	737	232	21	9	1000	293	314	370	23	1000
Hearing disabled	357	521	113	10	1000	703	188	79	30	1000
Locomotor disabled	476	464	52	8	1000	433	330	216	21	1000
All disabled	474	449	66	11	1000	385	309	282	24	1000

Source: NSS, 2002, Statement 9

	Prevalence Rate (%)		
	Male	*Female*	*Persons*
Rural	2.12	1.56	1.85
Urban	1.67	1.31	1.50
Rural + Urban	2.00	1.49	1.76

The prevalence of disability was 1.85 per cent among the rural residents and 1.50 per cent among the urban residents. Between the two sexes, the prevalence of disability was marginally higher among males than among females. The rate for males was 2.12 per cent and 1.67 per cent respectively in rural and urban areas while that for females was 1.56 percent and 1.31 percent. The prevalence of locomotor disability is highest in the country–it was 1046 in the rural and 901 in the urban per 1,00,000 persons and for obvious reasons, it was highest among the aged who experienced the incidence through out their life. The second in the list is the hearing disability. For every 1,00,000 persons living in rural areas 310 persons were having hearing disability. The corresponding figure was 236 in urban area. However, the prevalence rate was lowest among the mentally disabled.

The incidence rate is the number of disabled persons who became disabled during the last 365 days per 100,000 persons.. For any disability the incidence rate for rural and urban by sex are given below:

	The Incidence Rate (%)		
	Male	*Female*	*Persons*
Rural	0.77	0.61	0.69
Urban	0.75	0.58	0.67
Rural plus urban	0.76	0.60	0.69

About 69 persons were born or otherwise became disabled per 100,000 persons in rural India during the reference year. The incidence rates were almost the same in both the rural and urban India. As in the case of prevalence rate, the incidence rate is also observed to be higher among males than that among females. The rates among males were 77 and 75, respectively in rural and urban India as against 61 and 58, respectively among females. About 84 percent of the mentally retarded and 82 per cent of the persons having speech disability were born with disability. For persons with other type of disability the incidence by birth is not as significant as in the case of the mentally retarded or persons with speech disability. Most of them become disabled during the course of life. Incidence for some of the disabilities (e.g visual disability, hearing disability) is largely associated with the process of ageing.

Social Inequalities-Marital Status, Education and Living Arrangements

Marital Status

Statement 9 gives the distribution of disabled persons by marital status for each sex and sector at the all-India level. It is seen that at the all-India level, out of 1000 disabled males residing in the rural areas – 471 were never married, 448 were currently married while in the urban areas, the corresponding numbers were 484 and 450. Out of 1000 disabled females residing in the rural areas – 378 were never married, 316 were currently married while in the urban areas, the corresponding numbers were 415 and 284. The male- female differences in these proportions are quite significant, and disability can be regarded as a greater disadvantage for females to get married. The proportion of either the never married or the currently married among disabled males is found to be much higher than among females in both the sectors. About 30 to 31 per cent of disabled females in India were either widowed, divorced or separated as against 7 to 8 per cent of disabled males (widowed, divorced or separated). Sharp changes are observed in the distributions over the types of disability. Most of the mentally retarded seem to lead an unmarried life. Similar is the situation, although a little better, for persons having hearing disability.

Literacy Among the Disabled: Literates, for the purpose of this survey, were those who could read and write a simple

Table 4

Per 1000 Distribution of Disabled Persons (5 Years And Above) by Level of General Education and Sector

All-India

	Rural				*Urban*				*Rural + Urban*			
		Literate				*Literate*				*Literate*		
Type of Disability	*Not Literate*	*Upto Primary*	*Middle*	*Secondary & Above*	*Not Literate*	*Upto Primary*	*Middle*	*Secondary & Above*	*Not Literate*	*Upto Primary*	*Middle*	*Secondary & Above*
(1)	*(2)*	*(3)*	*(4)*	*(5)*	*(7)*	*(8)*	*(9)*	*(10)*	*(11)*	*(12)*	*(13)*	*(14)*
Mental retardation	887	90	20	3	809	150	36	5	866	106	24	3
Mental illness	620	208	97	71	488	237	121	150	591	215	102	89
With blindness	826	113	37	23	546	257	76	119	773	141	45	41
With low vision	774	157	39	27	576	235	73	114	738	172	45	43
Hearing	695	211	60	32	463	306	110	121	646	231	70	50
Speech	715	210	49	25	527	314	84	74	670	235	57	38
Locomotor	486	290	128	96	318	301	162	216	447	292	136	124
Any disability	590	244	97	69	400	288	137	175	547	254	106	92

Source: NSS, 2002, Statement 10

message with understanding. Those who were unable to do so were considered as illiterates. The different levels of general education of those who were considered as literates were ascertained. The distribution of disabled persons (age 5 years and above) by level of general education (including illiteracy) is given in Statement 10 separately for rural and urban sectors of all-India. About 55 per cent of the disabled in India were illiterate.The proportion of illiterate was about 59 per cent in the rural and 40 per cent in the urban among the disabled. It was highest among the mentally retarded (87 per cent) followed by the visually disabled (74 to 77 per cent). On the other hand, about 9 per cent were of the category "secondary and above". Only about 7 per cent of the disabled in rural India reported educational level "secondary and above" as against 18 per cent in urban India. This urban bias could be due to the availability of infrastructural facilities in the urban areas, particularly for the disabled. Along with the general educational level of the disabled, information relating to whether or not any vocational course had been completed by them was collected. The vocational courses have been broadly divided into two categories–engineering and non-engineering courses. The data have been tabulated for the disabled of age 10 years and above and are presented in Statement 11 for all-India. Out of 1000 disabled persons living in rural India, only 15 completed any vocational course. In urban India, a comparatively higher number of disabled persons (35) have done so. Of them, about 20 to 26 per cent completed courses in engineering streams and the rest 74 to 80 per cent in non-engineering streams.

School Enrolment of Disabled Children

For the disabled persons of age 5-18 years, the particulars of enrolment in general (Ordinary) as well as in the special school was collected. The information on attendance in pre-schools was also collected. The proportion of disabled persons of age 5-18 years who attended the pre-school intervention programme is given in Statement 12 for each sex separately for rural and urban sector of all-India and the proportion of persons enrolled in the ordinary and special school is given in Statement 13. In India, about 13 per cent of the disabled persons of age 5-18 years attended the pre-school intervention programme. The proportion was 20 per cent in the urban and was almost half of urban at 11 per cent in the rural. Surprisingly, proportion of disabled persons of age 5-18 years attending the pre-school intervention programme was highest among urban girls although the proportion was more for boys in the rural.

Table 5
Number of Persons Per 1000 Disabled Persons of Age 5 -18 Years by Enrolment Status and Type of Disability for Each Sex and Sector

All-India

	Number Per 1000 of Disabled Children					
	Currently Enrolled in Ordinary School			*Currently Enrolled in Special School*		
Type of Disability	*Male*	*Female*	*Persons*	*Male*	*Female*	*Persons*
(1)	*(2)*	*(3)*	*(4)*	*(5)*	*(6)*	*(7)*
Rural						
Mental retardation	155	95	134	45	9	32
Mental illness	163	74	128	24	12	19
Blindness	239	154	203	19	17	18
Low vision	472	437	456	11	0	6
Hearing	540	454	503	0	11	5
Speech	412	341	383	12	7	10
Locomotor	601	501	562	4	1	2
Any disability	511	420	475	8	4	6
Urban						
Mental retardation	128	100	117	141	137	139
Mental illness	145	128	138	102	81	94
Blindness	254	110	143	74	716	569
Low vision	628	629	629	0	42	19
Hearing	490	469	480	47	46	47
Speech	338	270	311	240	266	250
Locomotor	564	577	569	21	18	19
Any disability	461	421	444	79	143	106

Source: NSS, 2002, Statement 13

Contrary to the perception of urban bias in the levels of literacy, the current enrolment ratio per 1000 disabled persons

Table 6

Per 1000 Distribution of Disabled Persons by Broad Usual Activity Status for Each Sex and Sector

All-India

	Disabled Persons Per 1,00,000 Persons								
	Rural			Urban			Rural + Urban		
Type of Disability	Employed	Unemployed	Out of Labour Force	Employed	Unemployed	Out of Labour Force	Employed	Unemployed	Out of Labour Force
(1)	(2)	(3)	(4)	(5)	(6)	(7)	(8)	(9)	(10)
Male									
Mental retardation	89	0	911	58	1	941	81	1	919
Mental illness	199	2	799	99	4	897	176	2	821
With blindness	139	4	857	193	5	802	149	4	847
With low vision	339	5	655	291	7	702	331	6	663
Hearing	530	4	466	347	17	635	492	6	501
Speech	391	7	602	249	16	734	356	9	635
Locomotor	387	11	602	404	22	574	391	14	595
All disabled	369	8	622	347	18	635	364	11	625
Female									
Mental retardation	20	0	980	5	1	994	16	0	984
Mental illness	59	0	941	15	0	985	49	0	951
With blindness	43	1	956	33	3	963	41	1	958
With low vision	73	0	927	51	0	949	69	0	931
Hearing	198	0	802	101	3	896	177	1	822
Speech	143	3	854	64	7	929	125	4	871
Locomotor	98	4	898	107	5	888	100	4	896
All disabled	109	2	889	87	4	909	104	3	893

Contd.

All-India

Type of Disability	Disabled Persons Per 1,00,000 Persons								
	Rural			Urban			Rural + Urban		
	Employed	Unemployed	Out of Labour Force	Employed	Unemployed	Out of Labour Force	Employed	Unemployed	Out of Labour Force
(1)	(2)	(3)	(4)	(5)	(6)	(7)	(8)	(9)	(10)
Persons									
Mental retardation	64	0	936	38	1	961	56	0	943
Mental illness	142	1	857	67	3	930	126	1	873
With blindness	88	2	910	103	4	893	91	2	907
With low vision	195	3	803	158	3	838	188	3	809
Hearing	374	2	624	229	10	761	343	4	653
Speech	290	5	705	178	13	809	263	7	730
Locomotor	279	9	712	289	15	696	282	10	708
All disabled	263	6	731	238	12	749	257	7	735

Source: NSS, 2002, Statement 14

in the ordinary school was higher in the rural than in the urban–475 and 444, respectively for the two sectors. The enrolment ratio was the highest among persons having locomotor disability and the lowest, as expected, among the mentally retarded, and also, higher among the boys than among the girls. In the case of enrolment in the special schools, although the pattern remained the same, it was reversed–about 11 per cent enrolled in the special schools in the urban as compared to even less than 1 per cent in the rural. The enrolment ratio is relatively higher among the blind and children with speech disability. However, the gender bias in the enrolment ratio is not prominent.

Living Arrangements of Disabled Persons: Information on living arrangement of the Disabled persons were collected to know whether they were living alone or with spouse only or with spouse and other members of the household. The results reveal that about 3 per cent of the disabled were living alone and it was 5 to 6 per cent among the visually disabled. These disabled persons did not have other members in the household to take care of them. Moreover, about 5 per cent of the disabled persons lived with their spouses only. But a large majority, about 92 per cent of the disabled, lived with their spouse and/or other members in the family. The results relating to the distribution of the disabled by living arrangement can be seen from Statement 17. The rural-urban differences are not prominent. However, a marginal difference is observed among the various types of disability.

Economic Disparities- Activity Status, Occupation

Usual Activity of the Disabled: Following standard international practice the disabled have been classified according to their "usual activity status" during the reference period of 365 days preceding the date of survey. Three major activity statuses are identified as:

Employed, Unemployed and Out of labour force: The distribution of disabled persons by their activity status, given in the column headings of Statement 14, shows that 26 per cent of the disabled persons were employed. The corresponding

Table 7

Number of Disabled Persons by Type of Living Arrangement Per 1000 Disabled Persons in Each Type of Disability

All-India

	Living Arrangement								
	Rural			*Urban*			*Rural + Urban*		
Type of Disability	*Living Alone*	*Living with Spouse Only*	*Living with Spouse and/ Others*	*Living Alone*	*Living with Spouse Only*	*Living with Spouse and/ Others*	*Living Alone*	*Living with Spouse Only*	*Living with Spouse and/ Others*
(1)	*(2)*	*(3)*	*(4)*	*(5)*	*(6)*	*(7)*	*(8)*	*(9)*	*(10)*
Mental retardation	3	4	992	1	3	995	3	4	993
Mental illness	31	44	922	19	32	945	29	42	927
With blindness	49	80	872	55	57	888	50	75	874
With low vision	61	97	840	47	50	902	59	88	851
Hearing	40	67	891	53	60	887	43	66	890
Speech	10	26	964	38	15	946	17	23	958
Locomotor	26	52	921	28	45	925	27	50	922
All disabled	31	55	914	33	44	922	31	52	915

Source: NSS, 2002, Statement 17

figures in rural and urban India were 26 and 24 per cent, respectively. Moreover, the proportion of employed among the disabled males was much higher than among the disabled females in both rural and urban areas. In fact, the proportion among the disabled males was 35 to 37 per cent and that among the disabled females was 9 to 11 per cent. The percentage of disabled persons seeking and/or available for work was higher in the urban areas (1.2) as compared to that in the rural areas (0.6). Examination of the said proportions by type of disability reveals that most of the mentally retarded remained out of labour force. The proportion of employed was lowest at 6 per cent among the mentally retarded while the rate was highest at 34 per cent among the persons having hearing disability. The proportion of unemployed was negligible except for the disabled males with speech and locomotor disability.

Most disabled persons in the rural areas were engaged in the primary sector whereas in urban areas, the tertiary sector followed by the secondary sector played the dominating role in employment generation so far as the disabled were concerned. The distribution pattern of workers by industry in the general population is to some extent observed among the disabled workers also. About 67 per cent and 73 per cent of the disabled male and female workers living in rural areas were engaged in the primary sector. On the other hand, the share of tertiary and secondary sector was about 89 per cent in the urban areas for male workers and 85 per cent for female workers. Substantial differences are also observed in the distributions in respect of type of disability.

Equity and Human Rights Issues

Extent of Physical Disability: For determining the extent of physical disability of a Disabled person, self-care, such as, ability to go to latrine, taking food, getting dressed, etc. were taken into account. Irrespective of whether or not a disabled person had 'single' or 'multiple' disability, they were classified into one of the four categories, viz., (i) those not able to take self-care even with aid/appliance, (ii) those able to take self-

Table 8

Prevalence and Incidence Rate of Visually (Per 1,00,000 Persons) Obtained from NSS 36th, 47th and 58th Round, All-India

All-India									
	36th Round (July–December, 1981)			*47th Round (July–December, 1991)*			*58th Round* (July–December, 2002)*		
Sector	*Male*	*Female*	*Persons*	*Male*	*Female*	*Persons*	*Male*	*Female*	*Persons*
(1)	*(2)*	*(3)*	*(4)*	*(5)*	*(6)*	*(7)*	*(8)*	*(9)*	*(10)*
Prevalence Rate									
Rural	444	670	553	471	548	525	276	326	296
Urban	294	425	356	263	346	302	163	228	194
Incidence Rate									
Rural	32	45	38	22	28	25	10	16	13
Urban	23	38	30	15	25	20	7	10	9

* *for persons of age 5 years and above*

Source: NSS, 2002, Statement 28

care only with aid/appliance. The degrees of disability referred to the above three categories are termed as (i) cannot function even with aid/appliance, (ii) can function only with aid/appliance, and (iii) can function without aid/appliance. There was another category of the disabled for whom the aid/appliance was neither available nor tried and this category alone was about 9 to 10 per cent of all the disabled. The distribution of the disabled by these categories, given in Statement 8 for each sex separately for rural and urban sectors of all-India reveals that among the disabled, about 13 per cent in both rural and urban India were observed to be severely disabled as they could not function even with aid/appliance. The corresponding percentage for males was 12 and for females a little higher at 15. On the other hand, about 60 per cent of the disabled were able to take self-care without any aid or appliances. In this category, the rural-urban differences are absent but a higher percentage of disabled males were capable to take self-care as compared to disabled females. The all-India pattern by and large is also reflected in most states.

Onset of Disability with respect to Work: Onset of disability in a person who was usually working may sometimes lead to loss of work or change of work. Information on whether the disabled person was working before the onset of disability was collected. For disabled persons of age 5 years and above, the proportion (per 1000 disabled) who were working before the onset of disability is given in Statement 16 for rural and urban India. The Statement reveals that about 37 per cent of the disabled (age 5 +) as a whole were working before the onset of disability. Among the males, the proportion was 41 per cent and among females, it was 32 per cent. The rural-urban difference exists and is tilted towards rural. As far as the type of disability is concerned, a very few among the mentally retarded were working before the onset of disability. This may be due to the fact that among them, a large proportion was born with mental retardation and therefore, they were unable to perform any economic activity. In this respect the persons with visual disability are found to

Table 9

Prevalence and Incidence Rate (Per 100,000 Persons) of Hearing Disability Obtained from NSS 36th, 47th and 58th rounds by Sex and Sector

All-India									
	36th Round (July–December, 1981)			*47th Round (July–December, 1991)*			*58th Round* (July–December, 2002)*		
Sector	*Male*	*Female*	*Persons*	*Male*	*Female*	*Persons*	*Male*	*Female*	*Persons*
(1)	*(2)*	*(3)*	*(4)*	*(5)*	*(6)*	*(7)*	*(8)*	*(9)*	*(10)*
Prevalence rate									
Rural	595	510	573	498	435	467	351	332	342
Urban	386	395	390	325	355	339	252	256	254
Incidence rate									
Rural	20	18	19	16	14	15	10	7	8
Urban	14	15	15	11	14	12	8	7	7

* *for persons of age 5 years and above*

Source: NSS, 2002, Statement 33

be affected most - the proportion among them being 54 to 60 per cent.

Mental Retardation and Mental Illness and their Causes

The National Sample Survey has provided the estimates of the prevalence rate separately for number of mentally retarded and mentally ill persons per 1, 00,000 persons. Statement 19 provides the prevalence rate for rural and urban sectors of all-India. It shows that about 94 persons per 1, 00,000 were mentally retarded and the corresponding rate was 105 for the mentally ill. The prevalence rate was higher for males in both rural and urban sectors, and among the mentally retarded and ill. For the mentally retarded the prevalence rate was higher among males (113 to 118) as compared to females (69 to 81). The corresponding figures for the mentally ill were 105 to 128 and 71 to 91. The rural–urban differences in the prevalence of mental retardation or of the mental illness were insignificant.

The principal cause of mental retardation was 'illness during childhood' (42 percent) followed by the 'head injury in childhood' (10 per cent). Cases of mental retardation due to 'pregnancy and birth related' was 3 per cent. About 2 per cent of the mentally retarded reported that the incidence was hereditary. It may be noted that for 23 per cent of the mentally retarded, the respondent was not aware of the probable cause of retardation. There are marginal variations in these proportions in respect of sex and residential status. Only nine percent out of total mentally ill persons reported 'illness during childhood' as the cause for their illness. And about 46 per cent reported reasons other than the listed ones' as the cause. The 'not known' cases were as high as 36 per cent, which is a reflection of the limitations of the data.

The distribution of mentally disabled persons by age at onset is given Statement 23 for rural and urban sector of India. Unlike the other disabilities, mental retardation is a phenomenon whose manifestation is observed since birth or at the very early ages of life. About 87 per cent of the mentally disabled reported to have the problem since their birth and about 8 per cent had it in the age group 0-4 years. For the mentally retarded females, about 90 per cent among them had the problem since their birth. An important feature observed among the mentally retarded is that the manifestation of disability is completed within the teen-ages. The rural and urban features indicated that the phenomenon of mental retardation since birth is much higher in the rural than in the urban. It is obvious that the mental retardation could be reduced if adequate health care was available for pregnant mothers and the children during their childhood. On the other hand, the problem of mental illness is associated with ageing. The possibility of onset of mental illness increases as one gets older. The trend and the possibility of onset over the ages is seen to be very steady for each sex and in both rural and urban areas.

Negative Attitudes-Negative attitudes held by the families of the disabled, and often the disabled themselves, deter disabled persons from taking an active part in the family, community or workforce. Those suffering from mental illness or mental retardation face the worst stigma and are subject to severe social exclusion

Challenges to Social Acceptance-People with disabilities are considered ineligible to marry those without disabilities unless "adjusted" by high dowry. Disabled girls are usually married to older men, leading to a higher incidence of widowhood. Showcasing success stories of people with disabilities can challenge these deep rooted negative perceptions.

Denial of Access- PWDs often do not have access to public buildings, transportation etc because of their disability, because they need the help of a care giver to take them to these places.

Preventable Causes- A large number of disabilities in India are preventable, including those arising from medical issues during birth, maternal conditions, malnutrition, as well as accidents and injuries. However, the health sector is yet to react more proactively to disability, especially in the rural areas.

Regional Disparities- There is great regional disparity. In general, states that lag in health services also lag in caring for the disabled. Those disabled from birth, women, and vulnerable are less likely to seek health care. Despite years of public intervention, only a few disabled people have access to aids and appliances

Lack of Education- Large number of children with disabilities are out of school. They are 4 to 5 times less likely to be in school than SC/ST children. If they do stay in school, they rarely progress beyond primary levels. This leads to lower employment and incomes. Education System has not responded to the special needs of the Disabled children.

Lack of Employment- Employment of PWD actually fell from 43% in 1991 to 38% in 2002, despite the country's economic growth. In the public sector, despite a 3% reservation since 2003, few posts were regarded as "suitable" for PWDs. The situation is worse in the private sector.

Conclusions and Policy Implications

- 8.4 % of rural households and 6.1% of urban households had at least one disabled.
- 1.8 % of the total population were disabled. The prevalence rate is greater in rural than in urban, and among males than among females.
- PWDs face disadvantages in matrimony, education and in employment. The paper has pointed some of the inequities faced by the PWDs.
- India has a progressive policy framework for Disabled including the passing of "*The Persons with Disabilities Act of 1995*". However few PWDs are aware of these.
- Social protection measures targeting the PWDs are needed and adequate resources be made available for them. Better Monitoring of the programmes meant for PWDs is essential.
- Reservations for PWDs in education, employment and poverty alleviation programmes should be implemented.

Table 10
Prevalence and Incidence Rate (Per 100,000 Persons) of Speech Disability Obtained from NSS 36th, 47th and 58th Rounds by Sex and Sector All-India

All-India

	36th Round (July–December, 1981)			*47th Round (July–December, 1991)*			*58th Round* (July–December, 2002)*		
Sector	*Male*	*Female*	*Persons*	*Male*	*Female*	*Persons*	*Male*	*Female*	*Persons*
(1)	*(2)*	*(3)*	*(4)*	*(5)*	*(6)*	*(7)*	*(8)*	*(9)*	*(10)*
Prevalence Rate									
Rural	379	228	304	333	208	273	254	184	220
Urban	342	207	279	285	182	237	228	154	193
Incidence Rate									
Rural	6	2	4	6	4	5	3	2	3
Urban	7	3	5	5	4	5	4	2	3

* *for persons of age 5 years and above*
Source: NSS, 2002, Statement 38

- Public-Private Partnerships with NGOs in implementing and monitoring programmes meant fof PWDs could be beneficial.

Annex-Definition of Disabilities in NSS

Disability: A person with restrictions or lack of abilities to perform an activity in the manner or within the range considered normal for a human being was treated as having disability. It excluded illness/injury of recent origin (morbidity) resulting into temporary loss of ability to see, hear, speak or move.

Mental Disability: Persons who had difficulty in understanding routine instructions, who could not carry out their activities like others of similar age or exhibited behaviours like talking to self, laughing/crying, staring, violence, fear and suspicion without reason were considered as mentally disabled for the purpose of the survey. The "activities like others of similar age" included activities of communication (speech), self-care (cleaning of teeth, wearing clothes, taking bath, taking food, personal hygiene, etc.), home living (doing some household chores) and social skills.

Visual Disability: By visual disability, it was meant, loss or lack of ability to execute tasks requiring adequate visual acuity. For the survey, visually disabled included (a) those who did not have any light perception-both eyes taken together and (b) those who had light perception but could not correctly count fingers of hand (with spectacles/contact lenses if he/she used spectacles/contact lenses) from a distance of 3 metres (or 10 feet) in good day light with both eyes open. Night blindness was not considered as visual disability.

Hearing Disability: This referred to persons' inability to hear properly. Hearing disability was judged taking into consideration the disability of the better ear. In other words, if one ear of a person was normal and the other ear had total hearing loss, then the person was judged as normal in hearing for the purpose of the survey. Hearing disability was judged without taking into consideration the use of hearing aids (i.e., the position for the person when hearing aid was not used).

Table 11
Prevalence and Incidence Rate (Per 100,000 Persons) of Locomotor Disability Obtained from NSS 47th and 58th Rounds by Sex and Sector

All-India

	36th Round (July–December, 1981)			*47th Round (July–December, 1991)*			*58th Round* (July–December, 2002)*		
Sector	*Male*	*Female*	*Persons*	*Male*	*Female*	*Persons*	*Male*	*Female*	*Persons*
(1)	*(2)*	*(3)*	*(4)*	*(5)*	*(6)*	*(7)*	*(8)*	*(9)*	*(10)*
Prevalence Rate									
Rural	1047	597	828	1345	784	1074	1274	804	1046
Urban	800	544	679	1170	728	962	1058	730	901
Incidence Rate									
Rural	64	42	53	64	42	53	58	40	49
Urban	61	47	54	64	39	52	60	43	52

Source: NSS, 2002, Statement 44

Persons with hearing disability might be having different degrees of disability, such as profound, severe or moderate. A person was treated as having 'profound' hearing disability if he/she could not hear at all or could only hear loud sounds, such as, thunder or understands only gestures. A person was treated as having 'severe' hearing disability if he/she could hear only shouted words or could hear only if the speaker was sitting in the front. A person was treated as having 'moderate' hearing disability if his/her disability was neither profound nor severe. Such a person would usually ask to repeat the words spoken by the speaker or would like to see the face of the speaker while he/she spoke or would feel difficulty in conducting conversations.

Speech Disability: This referred to persons' inabil ity to speak properly. Speech of a person was judged to be disordered if the person's speech was not understood by the listener. Persons with speech disability included those who could not speak, spoke only with limited words or those with loss of voice. It also included those whose speech was not understood due to defects in speech, such as stammering, nasal voice, hoarse voice and discordant voice and articulation defects, etc.

Locomotor Disability: A person with- (a) loss or lack of normal ability to execute distinctive activities associated with the movement of self and objects from place to place and (b) physical deformities, other than those involving the hand or leg or both, regardless of whether the same caused loss or lack of normal movement of body–was considered as disabled with locomotor disability. Thus, persons having locomotor disability included those with (a) loss or absence or inactivity of whole cr part of hand or leg or both due to amputation, paralysis, deformity or dysfunction of joints which affected his/her "normal ability to move self or objects" and (b) those with physical deformities in the body (other than limbs), such as, hunch back, deformed spine, etc. Dwarfs and persons with stiff neck of permanent nature who generally did not have difficulty in the normal movement of body and limbs was also treated as disabled.

References

Jeffery, Roger and Singal, Nidhi (2008): "Measuring Disability in India", *Economic and Political Weekly,* Vol. 43 No. 12 and 13 March 22-April 04, 2008.

Mander, Harsh (2008): "Living with Hunger: Deprivation Among the Aged, Single Women and People with Disability" *Economic and Political Weekly,* Vol. 43 No. 17 April 26-May 02, 2008.

Mehrotra, Nilika (2004): "Women, Disability and Social Support in Rural Haryana", *Economic and Political Weekly,* Vol. 39 No. 52 December 25-December 31, 2004.

Mishra, A.K and Gupta, Ruchika (2006): "Disability Index ", *Economic and Political Weekly,* VOL 41 No. 38 September 23 - September 29, 2006.

National Sample Survey, 2003, *Disabled Persons in India,* NSS 58tth round July–December 2002.

National Sample Survey, 2007, *Sarvekshana,* 91 Issue, Vol. XXVII No. 1 & 2 July 2007, New Delhi.

R.N. Pandey and A.L. Chatterjee* (2007): "An Integrated Summary of NSS 58th Round (July 2002-December 2002) On Disabled Persons in India", *Sarvekshana,* 91 Issue, Vol. XXVII No. 1 & 2 July 2007, New Delhi.

Vaidyanathan, K.E. (2008): "Disability in India: Measurement and Some Findings", Paper submitted for the IUSSP Conference, Marrakech, 2009.

World Bank, 2007, *People with Disabilities in India: From Commitments to Outcomes.* World Bank, Human Development Unit, South Asia Region, Washington DC.

SECTION - 2

Health and Nutrition Inequalities, Policies and Programmes

6

Food Security, Poverty and Health Status in India: An Outcome Evaluation Perspective

M.H. Suryanarayana

Introduction

The Eleventh Plan on food security does not seem to be based on careful presentation of facts and their appreciation. It suffers from a very simple methodological limitation that it interprets comments and recommends policies on issues concerned with deprivation with reference to estimates of mean-based averages and not distributional profiles. As is well known, mean is not a robust estimator of average for skewed distributions and hence, would represent largely changes in the upper percentiles for the case under review. In consequence, much of what is interpreted in the Plan document are fiction rather than fact and assessment. And the Plan review of the status of food security of the population and its policy recommendation seems to be misplaced and calls for a revision. Food security is an area, which has received wide attention in the wake of the recent food inflation across countries in the world. Hence, this paper seeks to highlight this issue with reference to the same data source as used in the Eleventh Plan.

Plan Perspective on Food Security

The Plan recognizes the importance of food security in order to improve, *inter alia*, what it calls "nutritional outcomes" for the poor and to facilitate quick recovery from illness (GoI, 2008; p. 128-148). In other words, food security is quite important as an answer to morbidity also. All the more so given the (i) observed decline in pre capita cereal production; and (ii) stagnant income levels of the poor. The document cites empirical details on nutritional outcome measures like low birth weight of newborn babies, weights and heights of adults, which are explained in terms of, *inter alia*, deficit in energy intake. It presents evidence to show that the rate of malnutrition as reflected in estimates of underweight children has not declined at all between 1998-99 and 2004-05 though the economy was growing at the rate of 6 per cent per annum.[1] Hence, the Plan calls for a review of issues relating to food security not simply in terms of cereal production and consumption but in terms of scope for improving nutritional outcome for the poor. While one may appreciate the Plan emphasis on assessing the situation with an integrated perspective on outcomes, it is also important to make factually correct assessments of the food economy from a distributional perspective, for the poor in particular, given its bearings on policy choice and implementation. Hence, the Plan perspective on the food security situation is provided below:

The Plan document provides information on changes in cereal consumption, consumption patterns and calorie intake since 1972/73, which is as follows:

(i) Cereals are a major source of energy intake for the Indian population. Per capita cereal consumption has declined in both rural and urban areas. Consumption of non-cereals has not increased to make up for this decline.

(ii) Reasons for this decline are stagnant incomes and declining budget shares for food. Between 1972-73 and 1987-88 and 2004-05, food share declined from 73 per cent to 64 per cent and finally to 55 per cent in rural India and from 65 per cent to 56 and to 43 per cent in urban India (GoI, 2008; p. 131).

(iii) In rural India, though the shares of other food items like milk and milk products, fish, egg & meat, and fruits and nuts increased, the increase has not been sufficient to make up for the loss in calories due to decline in cereal consumption. In urban India, the share in expenditure of other food items like milk and milk products, edible oils and sugar have declined.

(iv) As a result, average per capita calorie intake per diem decreased from 2221 kcals (1983) to 2153 (1993-94), 2149 (1999-2000) and to 2047 (2004-05 in rural India, that is, by eight per cent between 1983 and 2004-05; the corresponding estimates for urban India being 2089, 2071, 2156 and 2020 involving a reduction in calorie intake of 3.3. per cent.

(v) Average calorie intakes in both rural and urban areas have fallen increasingly short of the calorie norms for official poverty lines for the rural (2400 kcals) and urban (2100 kcals) India.

There is general tendency among experts and expert study groups to conclude with reference to the average estimates presented above that food insecurity and under-nutrition has increased in India. Of course, estimates by the poverty-line-calorie norms show that incidence of calorie deficiency is 90 per cent in rural India and 70 per cent in urban India. While experts use this kind of evidence to advocate universalization of the public distribution system (PDS), the Plan document recommends, given the prevailing inequities in distribution, that average calorie availability in the country should be at 'least 20% higher than the per capita requirement (i.e. 2100 calories for urban and 2400 calories for rural areas)' (GoI, 2008, p. 139).

As regards policies, the Plan document goes on to evaluate the PDS and concludes "*PDS seems to have failed in serving the second objective of making foograins available to the poor. If it had, the consumption levels of cereals should not have fallen on average–* as it has consistently over the last two decades" (GoI, 2008; p. 135). Observing that purchasing power is a serious constraint on household food security, the Plan review assesses the PDS in terms of rupees transferred as given by the difference between average market price and the PDS price and concludes that what matters is possession of ration and its type and not economic status of the household.

This kind of interpretations and policy recommendations raises several issues. How stagnant are the real incomes of the poor during the sample period under review? How meaningful are the interpretations of estimates of consumption budget shares at current prices? What do the estimates of quantities for different population groups suggest? How valid are the interpretations of such estimates for the total population? In other words, how valid is the interpretation that the PDS failure to deliver to the poor has accounted for the decline in cereal consumption on average? How valid are the exogenous norms for threshold levels of calorie intake worked out in the 1950s and 1960s, that is, almost half a century ago since when the economy has experienced structural and technological change and improvements? What have been the temporal changes in calorie intake across different decile groups? What do they mean? How far the self-perception of the population with reference to adequacy of food consumption corroborates such findings? How far these measures and interpretations are validated by estimates of final health outcome parameters? How reasonable is it to expect positive outcomes in health and nutrition in response to income increases? The following section examines these issues.

Review

Real Incomes and Budget Share Estimates

One important explanation put forward by the Eleventh Plan for the decline in average cereal consumption and hence, calorie intake of the population is stagnant real incomes. It even states: "Low and stagnating incomes among the poor has meant that low purchasing power remains a serious constraint to household food and nutritional security, even if food production picks up as a result of interventions in agriculture and creation of total infrastructure" (GoI, 2008, p. 128). But, real incomes as reflected in estimates of consumption at constant prices were not really stagnant during the sample period under review. We have examined this type of questions in detail using different deflators (Suryanarayana, 1995a). Among them, the results (relevant to the question under review) obtained using fractile-group-specific deflators based on representative price indices for rural and urban India have brought out the following: In rural India, the poorest three decile groups experienced higher (in percentage terms) increases in consumer expenditure than the whole population during the period 1970-71 and 1988-89. The consumption expenditure (at constant prices) for the rural population as a whole increased by 18.88 per cent; it increased by 32.02 per cent for the poorest and by 28.05 per cent for the second poorest decile group. As regards the urban sector, the corresponding increases for different decile groups were broadly the same, between 16.50 and 20.25 per cent. This is only a subset of the period under review in the Eleventh Plan. Hence, we present estimates for the poorest five-decile groups and the population as a whole in rural and urban India for the period considered in the Plan document (Table 1).

Table 1 provides estimates of decile group wise per capita consumer expenditure for rural and urban India for the different years cited in the Plan document.[2] The estimates at 1972-73 prices are obtained using deflators implicit in the poverty lines for the corresponding years. Unlike the estimates cited in the preceding paragraph, estimates presented in Table 1 are obtained using common deflators for all the decile groups in rural and urban India separately. These estimates show the cost of living for the poor household increased by about 785 per cent in rural India and 1040 per cent in urban India between the terminal years.[3] The estimates of averages for both rural and urban India show that real per capita

Table 1
Monthly Per Capita Consumer Expenditure (at 1972/73 prices) by Select Decile Groups: Rural and Urban India

Decile Group	*1972/73*	*1977/78*	*1983*	*1987/88*	*1993/94*	*1999/00*	*2004/05*	*Increase (%)between 1972/73 & 2004/05*	*Increase (%)between 1993/94 & 2004/05*
Rural All-India									
0-10	16.26	16.92	19.18	22.05	22.69	26.45	25.76	58.41	13.51
10-20	22.70	23.97	26.46	29.36	30.26	34.13	33.59	47.97	11.01
20-30	26.90	28.89	31.47	34.39	34.69	39.32	38.65	43.68	11.41
30-40	30.86	31.83	34.83	38.28	39.34	44.21	43.61	41.33	10.87
40-50	35.56	36.80	40.65	42.71	43.82	48.86	48.58	36.61	10.85
0-100	44.17	48.90	50.67	55.09	54.98	59.69	63.08	42.80	14.72
Urban All-India									
0-10	21.90	21.00	23.38	24.30	25.93	30.22	28.45	29.91	9.74
10-20	29.90	29.80	32.03	32.92	35.82	40.57	38.78	29.70	8.28
20-30	36.11	35.73	38.03	38.57	42.68	48.41	46.84	29.71	9.75
30-40	38.39	40.92	46.04	44.01	48.76	56.14	54.90	43.01	12.59
40-50	48.51	46.75	49.03	51.08	56.33	64.66	64.36	32.68	14.25
0-100	63.33	65.26	68.55	71.41	77.02	89.07	92.44	45.96	20.02

Source: Author's estimates based on corresponding NSS estimates at current prices (GoI, 1977, 1986a, 1986b, 1991, 1996, 2001a & 2006b) and deflators implicit in the official poverty lines. Poverty lines from 1977/78 till 2004/05 are GoI estimates and corresponding estimates for 1972/73 are from Tendulkar *et al.*, 1993).

consumption levels have increased by more than 40 per cent since 1972/73. The increases have been progressive in rural India in the sense that the poorest three decile groups enjoyed greater percentage increases in their real consumption than the population as a whole and hence, than the relatively better off. However, the increases in real consumption in urban India have been regressive.[4]

The Plan attributes the decline in calorie intake largely to changes in consumption patterns involving a decline in budget shares for cereals and other essential food items. The estimates of budget shares are at current price and that too for the total population by sector. Needless to say, the observed changes in consumption patterns based on estimates at current prices could reflect changes in relative prices rather than consumption patterns. Besides, the Plan has made little attempt to examine the structural changes underlying the estimates of budget shares on different broad groups of consumption. It is important to examine the changes in consumption patterns by population sub-groups in order to bring out differential behavioral changes. One such attempt (Suryanarayana 1995a) based on commodity-wise monthly per capita consumer expenditures at current as well as at constant prices for the period 1972-73 to 1988-89 has brought out the following:

(i) The budget share of the rural poorest decile group on cereals decreased from 62 per cent in 1972-73 to 43 per cent in 1988-89; a difference of 19 points. When the same is examined at constant prices, the decline is much less, that is from 59 per cent in 1972-73 to 51 per cent in 1988-89; a difference of only 8 points. Thus, changing relative prices have exaggerated the observed decline in the proportion of consumer expenditure on cereals.

(ii) Budget shares both at current and constant prices increased somewhat for the following commodity groups: (a) milk and milk products, (b) edible oils, (c) fruits, vegetables and nuts, (c) sugar, and (d) durables and miscellaneous goods & services. There was a real increase in the consumption of all these commodity groups, including cereals, for the rural poorest decile group.

(iii) For commodity groups like (a) meat, fish & eggs, (b) pan, tobacco and intoxicants, (c) clothing and footwear and (d) fuel and light, consumption shares at current prices increased but at constant prices decreased. Per capita monthly consumer expenditure at constant prices on these items by the rural poorest decile group actually fluctuated around a stationary level.

(iv) Total consumption at constant prices increased by 28 per cent between 1977-78 and 1988-89. The commodities which largely accounted for this increase are (i) cereals and cereal substitutes (6.82 per cent), (ii) fruits, vegetables and nut (4.92 per cent) (iii) durables and miscellaneous goods & services (3.25 per cent) followed by (iv) edible oils (2.93 per cent), (v) beverages and refreshments (2.30 per cent), (vi) milk and milk products (1.76 per cent), (viii) pan, tobacco and intoxicants (1.72 per cent), (ix) fuel & light (1.37 per cent), (x) pulses (1.32 per cent) and (xi) sugar (1.04 per cent). For items like (a) salt & spice, (b) meat, fish & eggs and (c) clothing and footwear, there was virtually no increase in consumer expenditure. In sum, the consumption basket of the poorest decile group seems to have improved in terms of quality and diversity.

(v) One finds a similar profile for other decile groups and also for the entire population in the rural sector but with a difference: Cereal consumer expenditure declined for all the decile groups except the poorest two. As regards the rural population as a whole, total consumption increased by 5.99 per cent. The commodities which accounted for this increase are (i) fruits and vegetables (3.31 per cent) followed by (ii) beverages and refreshments (2.07 per cent), (iii) edible oils (1.40 per cent) and (iv) milk and milk products (1.25 per cent).

(vi) The story for the urban sector is no different. While the proportion of expenditure on cereals at current prices by the poorest decile group decreased from 49 per cent in 1970-71 to 34 per cent in 1988-89 involving a difference of 15 points, that at constant prices also declined but from 49 per cent in 1970-71 to 40 per cent in 1988-89 with a difference of 9 points. Total consumption at constant prices increased by 14.12 per cent for this decile group during the second period. This was largely accounted for by (i) durables and miscellaneous goods and services whose consumption increased by 4.16 per cent followed by (ii) milk & milk products (2.56 per cent), (iii) edible oils (2.51 per cent) and (iv) fruits, vegetables and nuts (1.45 per cent). These four commodity groups accounted for bulk of the increases in total real consumption for other decile groups and also for the whole urban population.

The estimates at constant price discussed above, though careful, do not exhaust the entire period under review. Hence, one option could be to examine changes in terms of cereal consumption (expenditure as well as quantities consumed) and calorie intakes. This would lead us to a review of changes in cereal consumption basket in India in the following section.

Cereal Consumption

Consistent with the observed increases in per capita total consumer expenditures at constant prices, given the generally low levels of consumption, one would expect increases in cereal consumption expenditure to be a priority. However, cereal expenditure declined for all but the poorest decile group in both rural and urban all-India. Generally the percentage decrease in cereal expenditure was higher for the richer decile groups in both the sectors (Table 2). This would call into the question the Plan observation that low purchasing power is a constraint on household food security and with limited purchasing power household could not diversify their consumption basket. This is all the more so for the following reasons:

Table 2

Monthly Per capita Cereal Consumption Expenditure (at current prices): Rural & Urban All-India

	Rural-All-India				*Urban-All-India*			
	1972/73	*2004/05*			*1972/73*	*2004/05*		
Decile Group	*At Current Prices*	*At Current Prices*	*At 1972/73 Prices*	*Increase (%) at Constant Prices*	*At Current Prices*	*At Current Prices*	*At 1972/73 Prices*	*Increase (%) at Constant Prices*
0-10	9.75	75.18	11.17	14.59	10.085	80.45	11.14	10.46
10-20	13.04	87.49	12.30	-5.64	12.699	90.36	12.21	-3.886
20-30	14.81	91.99	13.03	-12.00	14.106	96.04	12.89	-8.594
30-40	16.33	95.72	13.65	-16.39	14.580	99.96	12.93	-11.34
40-50	17.75	99.29	14.27	-19.62	15.672	105.64	13.61	-13.16
50-60	18.53	102.68	14.74	-20.46	15.861	108.62	13.50	-14.91
60-70	20.18	107.20	14.95	-25.93	16.620	113.21	13.86	-16.59
70-80	21.08	111.65	15.21	-27.87	16.711	118.44	13.86	-17.09
80-90	23.46	114.49	15.79	-32.71	16.779	122.92	13.74	-18.12
90-100	26.78	128.40	16.62	-37.92	16.588	133.76	13.61	-17.96
All	18.17	101.41	14.28	-21.42	14.970	106.94	13.20	-11.81

Note: Estimates of per capita cereal consumer expenditure at 1972/73 prices are obtained using deflators based on unit values for total cereals for the years 1972/73 and 2004/05.

Source: Decile group wise estimates of cereal consumption obtained by linear interpolation from the NSS tables in GoI (1977 & 2006b).

Both in rural and urban India, the brunt of cereal inflation has been the minimum on the poorest decile group (Table 3). Relative prices have changed. Though prices have increased, coarse cereals continue to be the cheapest among cereal grains (Table 3). Still both the poor and the rich have reduced their consumption of coarse cereals with the difference that the poorer decile groups in both rural and urban all-India have substituted coarse cereals by superior cereals. The net result is that only the poorest decile group enjoyed an increase (about 10 per cent) in total cereal consumption in rural and urban all-India (Table 4). Accordingly, estimates of average per capita cereal quantities consumed for the total population show a decline in both rural and urban India during sample period under consideration (Table 5). A profile across decile groups of population shows that the decline in average per capita cereal consumption for the total rural and urban population has largely been due to a pronounced decline in cereal consumption of the top decile groups. These findings do not at all corroborate the kind of explanations provided by the Plan for the observed decline in cereal consumption. At a time when the PDS meets the household's cereal requirements only to a partial extent and the open market prices, levels as well as spread across space or seasons, themselves are determined substantially by state interventions (Suryanarayana 1995b), the Plan estimates and interpretation of income transfers through the PDS (to promote food security) in terms of differences between open market and PDS prices make as little sense as castles of cigarette packs for the homeless.

Changes in the composition of the consumption basket mentioned above could reflect partly changing tastes, consumer responses to changing relative prices and their substitution effects on consumer choices but largely changing production and supply conditions. Under the new agricultural growth strategy, benefiting largely wheat and rice, crop composition of food grains has changed considerably in favor of superior cereals. Structural changes in the rural economy involving a decline in coarse cereal availability and changes

Table 3
Unit Values of Cereals by Decile Group of Population: Rural & Urban All-India

	Unit Values								Increase (%) in Unit Values between 1972/73 and 2004/05			
	1972/73				2004/05							
Decile Group	Rice	Wheat	Cereals	Total	Rice	Wheat	Cereals	Total	Rice	Wheat	Cereals	Total
Rural India												
0-10	1.28	1.04	0.89	1.07	7.85	6.61	5.72	7.22	515.27	533.31	545.64	573.23
10-20	1.27	1.00	0.92	1.08	8.47	6.97	6.19	7.71	565.46	598.51	572.05	611.29
20-30	1.30	1.01	0.94	1.11	8.68	7.05	6.30	7.84	566.04	598.28	567.61	605.90
30-40	1.32	1.03	0.98	1.14	8.91	7.11	6.37	7.98	575.77	592.49	552.35	601.12
40-50	1.36	1.04	1.01	1.17	9.13	7.18	6.48	8.15	573.32	592.32	543.06	595.93
50-60	1.37	1.04	1.03	1.19	9.30	7.24	6.72	8.28	576.92	595.49	554.23	596.70
60-70	1.35	1.04	1.05	1.18	9.60	7.35	6.76	8.48	611.87	606.05	542.79	617.21
70-80	1.36	1.04	1.06	1.19	9.88	7.44	6.86	8.72	628.32	613.70	546.85	634.21
80-90	1.47	1.05	1.08	1.24	10.32	7.59	7.10	8.97	600.87	620.12	560.04	625.27
90-100	1.67	1.03	1.06	1.26	11.31	8.06	8.19	9.73	579.33	686.43	671.99	672.34
All	1.39	1.03	1.01	1.18	9.37	7.32	6.60	8.35	575.65	607.94	556.34	610.22
Urban India												
0-10	1.37	1.00	1.03	1.15	8.94	7.85	7.39	8.33	552.48	686.07	620.85	622.23
10-20	1.40	1.04	1.11	1.21	9.69	8.21	7.94	8.94	592.20	687.77	618.35	640.36
20-30	1.45	1.07	1.17	1.26	10.18	8.59	8.32	9.36	601.06	699.66	608.51	644.87
30-40	1.47	1.08	1.20	1.27	10.85	8.76	9.03	9.84	637.94	708.25	650.84	673.27

Contd.

Decile Group	Per Capita Cereal Consumption (Kg Per Month) 1972/73 Rice	Wheat	Coarse Cereals	Total	2004/05 Rice	Wheat	Coarse Cereals	Total	Increase (%) between 1972/73 and 2004/05 Rice	Wheat	Coarse Cereals	Total
60-70	5.48	5.32	1.35	12.15	4.84	4.90	0.40	10.13	-11.75	-7.97	-70.16	-16.59
70-80	5.47	5.41	1.22	12.09	4.94	4.69	0.39	10.03	-9.58	-13.26	-67.68	-17.09
80-90	5.34	5.56	0.93	11.84	4.72	4.65	0.32	9.69	-11.73	-16.34	-65.32	-18.12
90-100	4.86	5.79	0.77	11.43	4.34	4.78	0.25	9.37	-10.73	-17.42	-67.58	-17.96
'All	4.94	4.82	1.56	11.32	4.85	4.65	0.48	9.98	-1.76	-3.61	-68.97	-11.81

Source: Author's estimates based on GoI (1977, 2006b).

in labour markets could have accounted for some decline in total cereal consumption of the rural poorer decile groups.[5] In sum, the share of wheat in the cereal basket increased and that of coarse cereals decreased in both rural and urban sectors. Thus, there have been some qualitative improvements in the consumption patterns of the population.

Calorie Intake

As rightly observed in the Plan document, with the decline in average cereal consumption, a decline in average calorie intake would follow unless accompanied by compensating increases in non-cereal consumption. The story based on averages would conceal rather than reveal any insight about the dynamics of the ongoing development process. For instance, though cereal consumption increased only for the poorest decile group (Table 5), per capita calorie intake has generally increased for the bottom two decile groups in rural and bottom three decile groups in urban all-India. This would suggest that there have been compensating increases in non-cereal consumption for the bottom two/three decile groups of the rural/urban population. Still their calorie intakes fall short of the norms used for defining the poverty lines. On the other hand, top decile groups have reduced their cereal consumption and hence, calorie intake by choice. The decline in the calorie intake of the richer sections could be explained in terms of changing consumption patterns in favor of non-calorie food and non-food items at the expense of calorie intake. The poor too seem to have opted for some diversification in consumption providing a more nutritious diet though not adequate energy (Surynarayana 1995a). The combined impact of these two diverse patterns of changes is that estimates of incidence of calorie deficiency by the conventional calorie norms for the total (rural and urban combined) population turns out to be higher about 80 per cent for India.

The calorie norms cited above have been worked out in the 1950s/1960s and hence, may be outdated and irrelevant with improvements in modes of production and standard of living. This could be the reason for voluntary reductions in

Table 5
Estimates of Per Capita Cereal Consumption: Rural & Urban All-India

(Kg Per 30 Days)

	Rural All-India					*Urban All-India*				
Decile Group	*1972/73*	*1983*	*1993/94*	*1999/2000*	*2004/05*	*1972/73*	*1983*	*1993/94*	*1999/2000*	*2004/05*
0-10	9.08	10.35	10.53	10.49	10.16	8.75	9.19	9.53	9.57	9.66
10-20	12.03	12.45	12.09	11.65	11.08	10.52	10.46	10.64	10.30	10.11
20-30	13.32	13.38	12.65	12.30	11.44	11.23	10.98	10.80	10.80	10.26
30-40	14.35	13.94	13.22	12.59	11.71	11.46	11.34	10.93	10.67	10.16
40-50	15.15	14.78	13.40	12.92	11.89	11.84	11.49	11.03	10.87	10.28
50-60	15.60	15.29	13.77	13.09	12.11	11.90	11.88	10.96	10.78	10.13
60-70	17.07	15.66	14.12	13.43	12.34	12.15	12.12	11.02	10.74	10.13
70-80	17.75	16.34	14.46	13.54	12.50	12.09	12.12	10.80	10.60	10.03
80-90	18.96	17.41	14.65	13.81	12.45	11.84	12.08	10.77	10.62	9.69
90-100	21.26	19.40	15.52	14.18	15.81	11.43	12.16	10.31	10.06	9.37
All	15.46	14.90	13.44	12.80	12.15	11.32	11.38	10.68	10.50	9.98

Source: Decile group wise estimates of cereal consumption obtained by linear interpolation from the NSS tables in GoI (1977, 1986a, 1989a, 1991, 1996, 2001a, & 2006b).

cereal consumption and calorie intake of the richer decile groups. This would raise a question on the relevance of the calorie norms for food security estimates. In other words, the NSS estimates of consumer expenditure, cereal consumption and calorie intake by decile groups provide little evidence to corroborate the hypothesis that "low and stagnant incomes" have proved a constraint on household food and nutritional security. Instead, they call into question (i) the relevance of calorie norms proposed half a century back for a scenario when modes of production were very dissimilar to the one obtaining at present and (ii) the policy recommendation of the Plan to increase average calorie intake by 20 per cent or if the calorie norms are still valid, they call for consumer education to guide choice of nutritious diets and healthy consumption habits.

In sum, it would not make sense to verify issues related to food security with reference to outdated exogenous norms. Instead, it is high time we revise the cereal and calorie norms for defining food security. However, it is important to examine how valid is the case for revising the norms for food security. One option could be to verify in terms of self-perception regarding adequacy of food consumption, which is done in the following section.

Perceptions on Food Adequacy

Since its 38th round (1983), the National Sample Survey Organization has periodically asked what are called probing questions like whether the household gets two square meals a day through out the year. Such questions were asked during the 38th (1983), 50th (1993-94) and the 61st (2004-05) rounds. Till the 55th round, the investigator asked direct question to the household. In 1983, 81 per cent of the rural households reported adequate food consumption (two square meals a day); this percentage increased to 95 in 1993-94, 96 in 1999-2000 and to 97 in 2004-2005 (Table 7). In the urban sector, corresponding number increased from 93 per cent in 1983 to 99 percent in 1999-2000 and 2004-2005. In sum, this piece of evidence corroborates the perception that the population is well fed.

Table 6

Estimates of Energy Intake: Rural & Urban All-India (Kilocalories Per Capita Per Diem)

	Rural All-India						*Urban All-India*					
Decile Group	*1972/73*	*1983*	*1993/94*	*1999/2000*	*2004/05*	*Change (%)***	*1972/73*	*1983*	*1993/94*	*1999/2000*	*2004/05*	*Change (%)***
0-10	1192.09	1356.31	1460.12	1491.48	1480.52	24.20	1298.70	1331.76	1443.50	1520.88	1510.50	16.31
^10-20	1591.90	1681.80	1731.32	1730.52	1681.42	5.62	1575.94	1588.29	1702.40	1731.16	1687.67	7.09
20-30	1783.40	1847.86	1850.00	1865.30	1800.00	0.93	1745.94	1724.00	1803.48	1912.56	1833.00	4.99
30-40	1944.00	1952.00	1971.66	1955.22	1882.45	-3.17	1802.18	1861.19	1896.79	1970.46	1856.41	3.01
40-50	2115.04	2111.53	2056.48	2049.15	1958.95	-7.38	1980.00	1912.41	1992.81	2092.92	1944.62	-1.79
50-60	2210.00	2229.56	2156.34	2170.62	2044.32	-7.50	2035.48	2046.00	2074.64	2189.89	2024.00	-0.56
60-70	2451.41	2322.00	2275.17	2287.78	2158.00	-11.97	2266.00	2221.13	2186.00	2297.00	2111.12	-6.83
70-80	2581.40	2506.92	2410.00	2403.00	2290.00	-11.29	2382.13	2294.20	2296.74	2467.69	2209.00	-7.27
80-90	2929.00	2779.53	2584.72	2582.54	2376.40	-18.87	2658.75	2500.71	2470.50	2536.00	2343.04	-11.87
90-100	3861.77	3422.49	3034.19	2954.39	2797.94	-27.55	3324.88	3410.30	2843.14	2841.53	2680.64	-19.38
All	2266.00	2221.00	2153.00	2149.00	2047.00	-9.66	2107.00	2089.00	2071.00	2156.00	2020.00	-4.13

** Change refers to changes between 1972/73 and 2004/05.

Source: Authors' estimates based on GoI (1983, 1989b, 1996b, 2001c & 2007c)

Table 7

Percentage Distribution of Households by Food Availability Status

Sector/Round	% of Households				
	Getting Enough Food Everyday throughout the Year	Not Getting Enough Food Everyday: Some Months of the Year	Not Getting Enough Food Everyday: All Months of the Year	Not Recorded	All
Rural All-India					
NSS 61st round(July 2004-June 2005)	97.4	2.0	0.4	0.2	100
NSS 55th round(July 1999-June 2000)	96.2	2.6	0.7	0.5	100
NSS 50th round(July 1993-June 1994)	94.5	4.2	0.9	0.4	100
NSS 38th round(Jan – Dec 1983)	81.1	16.2	2.4	0.3	100
Urban All-India					
NSS 61st round(July 2004-June 2005)	99.4	0.4	0.1	0.1	100
NSS 55th round(July 1999-June 2000)	98.6	0.6	0.3	0.4	100
NSS 50th round(July 1993-June 1994)	98.1	1.1	0.5	0.3	100
NSS 38th round(Jan – Dec 1983)	93.3	5.6	0.8	0.3	100

Source: GoI (2001, p.16 & 2007b; p. 22)

The NSS findings presented in the preceding paragraph would raise the question as to whether cereal/calorie shortfall is a question of voluntary choice or involuntary. As the preceding findings show, cereal consumption and calorie intakes of the richer decile groups have declined by choice. If the corresponding limits were to be the norm, then, after appropriate normalization, only about 30 per cent of the rural and 40 per cent of the urban population were food insecure and these macro estimates of food insecurity fell well in the neighborhood of the poverty estimates (Suryanarayana and Dimtri, 2005). Contrary to the Plan call for increasing average calorie intake by 20 per cent in rural and urban areas, there is a need for a downward revision.

Perceptions on Food Security and Morbidity

Given the Plan emphasis on an integrated perspective on food security and health outcomes, the preceding discussion would raise a number of issues: What would be the appropriate calorie norm for food security? Should one consider objective estimates of food consumption relative to exogenous outdated norms? Could one base one's judgment on subjective perceptions of adequacy of food consumption and morbidity? How do we verify these questions? How far measures of association would validate these measures? What is the evidence?

Some relevant information is provided in Tables 8 to 10. The estimates of association as measured by rank correlation coefficients are presented in Table 11. The estimates of association do not make much sense. For instance, cross sectional evidence on rural household perceptions on adequate food consumption co vary inversely with estimates of per capita calorie intake across states while the association is observed to be positive for the urban sector. Consistent with this finding, household perception on food adequacy bears significant positive association with incidence of calorie deficiency (with reference to alternative norms) in the rural sector and simple negative association in the urban sector. Only sensible estimate of association pertains to the ones

Table 8 (a)
Measures of Nutritional Status Across States: 2004-2005

	Rural Sector							
	% Expenditure on		*Per Capita Per Day Intake of*			*Per Consumer Unit Per Day Intake of*		
	Food	*Cereals*	*Calorie(Kcal)*	*Protein(gm)*	*Fat(gm)*	*Calorie(Kcal)*	*Protein(gm)*	*Fat(gm)*
Andhra Pradesh	55.2	19.4	1995	49.8	33.5	2475	61.8	41.6
Assam	66	24.8	2067	52.7	26.7	2515	64.1	32.4
Bihar	64.8	27.1	2049	57.8	28.4	2560	72.3	35.5
Chhatisgarh	56.2	27.2	1942	47.4	19.9	2424	59.2	24.8
Gujarat	58	13.3	1923	53.3	50.9	2380	65.9	63
Haryana	48.6	8.6	2226	69.6	55.4	2738	85.6	68.1
Jharkhand	61.9	27.2	1961	51.2	22.8	2440	63.8	28.4
Karnataka	55.7	16.5	1845	48.8	33.9	2276	60.2	41.8
Kerala	45	11	2014	55.4	40.8	2549	70.1	51.6
Madhya Pradesh	52.9	18.1	1929	58.8	35.1	2386	72.7	43.4
Maharashtra	51.7	14.5	1933	55.7	41.5	2405	69.3	51.6
Orissa	61.6	28.3	2023	48.3	17.8	2512	59.9	22.1
Punjab	49.2	8.8	2240	66.7	58.7	2763	82.3	72.5
Rajasthan	54.8	14.5	2180	69.6	50.9	2714	86.7	63.3
Tamilnadu	52.4	15.5	1842	44.9	29.6	2294	55.9	36.9
Uttar Pradesh	53.6	17.6	2200	65.9	37.5	2743	82.1	46.8
West Bengal	58.7	23.4	2070	52	26.5	2545	64	32.6
All	55	18	2047	57	35.5	2540	70.8	44
Upper quartile			2070	58.8	41.5	2560	72.7	51.6

Source: GoI (2007a; p. 44).

Table 8(b)

Measures of Nutritional Status across States: 2004-2005

	Rural Sector							
	% Expenditure on		*Per Capita Per Day Intake of*			*Per Consumer Unit Per Day Intake of*		
	Food	*Cereals*	*Calorie(Kcal)*	*Protein(gm)*	*Fat(gm)*	*Calorie(Kcal)*	*Protein(gm)*	*Fat(gm)*
Andhra Pradesh	41.6	12.2	2000	50.9	43.2	2449	62.4	52.9
Assam	49.5	13.6	2143	55.9	36.8	2593	67.6	44.5
Bihar	51.1	17.2	2190	62.2	40.4	2683	76.1	49.5
Chhatisgarh	39	12.1	2087	53.9	37.2	2550	65.9	45.4
Gujarat	44.9	8	1991	57.3	63.5	2436	70.1	77.7
Haryana	41.4	6.9	2033	60.5	54.4	2487	74	66.6
Jharkhand	46.9	13.4	2458	69.5	53.8	3013	85.2	65.9
Karnataka	43.2	11.1	1944	52.2	43.3	2385	64	53.1
Kerala	40	8.4	1996	56.7	44.9	2534	72	57.1
Madhya Pradesh	38.9	9.8	1954	58.2	43.4	2397	71.4	53.2
Maharashtra	40.4	8.4	1847	52.1	50.1	2261	63.8	61.3
Orissa	49.9	16.8	2139	55.2	28.3	2596	67	34.4
Punjab	37.6	6.4	2150	63.4	61	2614	77	74.2
Rajasthan	41.6	9.6	2116	64	56.4	2586	78.2	69
Tamilnadu	42.7	10.3	1935	49.2	41.1	2394	60.8	50.8
Uttar Pradesh	45	11.4	2124	65.1	46.1	2598	79.7	56.4
West Bengal	43.4	11.3	2011	55.1	39.1	2467	67.6	48
All	42.5	10.1	2020	57	47.5	2475	69.9	58.2
Upper quartile			2139	62.2	53.8	2596	76.1	65.9

Source: GoI (2007a; p. 44).

Table 9

Incidence of Calorie Deficiency With Reference to Alternative Norms: 2004-05

	Rural Sector		*Urban Sector*	
	Incidence of Calorie Deficiency w.r.t Norm (per capita per diem) of		*Incidence of Calorie Deficiency w.r.t Norm of*	
	2100 Kcals	*2400 Kcals*	*2030 Kcals*	*2100 Kcals*
Andhra Pradesh	73.92	93.14	60.77	64.66
Assam	61.28	93.60	47.23	55.42
Bihar	62.06	87.74	43.39	47.44
Gujarat	82.22	93.17	53.94	72.20
Haryana	51.37	71.50	63.35	70.66
Karnataka	84.50	97.06	67.08	76.99
Kerala	71.15	84.89	60.45	64.90
Madhya Pradesh	76.25	82.43	66.38	71.24
Maharashtra	70.51	78.36	83.18	89.39
Orissa	64.94	85.55	45.70	52.42
Punjab	51.54	75.45	51.83	56.00
Rajasthan	57.36	80.41	48.27	60.73
Tamil Nadu	84.62	95.75	71.29	75.94
Uttar Pradesh	52.9	76.55	38.84	41.18
West Bengal	62.65	87.22	56.43	72.98
All India	64.9	90.73	60.78	68.67

Source: Author's estimates (without any normalization for age-gender-activity parameters) based on GoI (2006b & 2007c)

Table 10
Morbidity Profile Across States

Major State	*Rural*			*Urban*		
	PAP	*PPC*	*IMR*	*PAP*	*PPC*	*IMR*
Andhra Pradesh	90	36	71	114	47	35
Assam	82	58	73	83	48	38
Bihar	53	32	62	63	30	50
Chhattisgarh	69	38	-	72	31	-
Delhi						
Gujarat	69	29	68	78	29	37
Haryana	95	48	65	87	43	51
Himachal Pradesh	87	26	-	59	19	-
Jammu & Kashmir	70	30	-	78	34	-
Jharkhand	33	21	-	50	21	-
Karnataka	64	32	65	57	20	25
Kerala	255	103	11	240	100	8
Madhya Pradesh	61	32	90	65	36	56
Maharashtra	93	44	52	118	50	34
Orissa	77	49	91	54	30	56
Punjab	136	61	55	107	44	35
Rajasthan	57	23	81	72	27	55
Tamil Nadu	95	54	50	96	49	32
Uttaranchal	52	31	-	65	25	-
Uttar Pradesh	100	55	83	108	55	58
West Bengal	114	56	52	157	62	36
India	88	45	69*	99	44	40*

Notes:
(i) PAP: Number (per 1000) of persons reporting ailment for 2004-05
(ii) PPC: Number (per 1000) of persons reporting commencement of any ailment during the last 15 days for 2004-05
(iii) IMR: Infant mortality rat estimated for 2002 through the Sample Registration Scheme of the Office of the Registrar-General of India
Source: GoI (2006a)

Table 11
Correlation Matrix: Rural and Urban Sectors (2004-05)

Rural Sector

Variables	*Per CapitaCalorie Intake*	*Cal. HCR_ 2100*	*Cal. HCR_2400*	*Food. Avail. Status*	*PAP*	*PPC*	*IMR*
Per capita calorie intake	1.00	(-) 0.98(0.0000)	(-) 0.70(0.0039)	(-) 0.51(0.0517)	(-) 0.14	0.09	(-) 0.10
Cal. HCR_ 2100	(-) 0.98(0.0000)	1.00	0.72(0.0026)	0.56(0.0297)	(-) 0.23	(-) 0.30	(-) 0. 18
Cal. HCR_ 2400	(-) 0.70(0.0039)	0.72(0.0026)	1.00	0.79(0.0004)	(-) 0.34	(-) 0.18	(-) 0.09
Food. Avail. Status	(-) 0.51(0.0517)	0.56(0.0297)	0.79(0.0004)	1.00	(-) 0.14	0.09	(-) 0.10

Urban Sector

Variables	*Per capitaCalorie intake*	*Cal. HCR_ 2030*	*Cal. HCR_ 2100*	*Food. aAvail. Status*	*PAP*	*PPC*	*IMR*
Per capita calorie intake	1.00	(-) 0.88(0.0000)	(-) 0.89	0.39	(-) 0.21	(-) 0.11	0.50(0.0562)
Cal. HCR_ 2030	(-) 0.88(0.0000)	1.00	0.90(0.0000)	(-) 0.33	0.23	0.10	(-) 0.60(0.0174)
Cal. HCR_ 2100	(-) 0.89	0.90(0.0000)	1.00	(-) 0.32	0.21	0.04	(-) 0.61(0.0165)
Food. Avail. Status	0.39	(-) 0.33	(-) 0.32	1.00	(-) 0.18	0.04	(-) 0.19

Notes:

(i) Cal. HCR_2030 denotes percentage of population with per capita calorie intake per diem less than 2030 kcals

(ii) Cal. HCR_2100 denotes percentage of population with per capita calorie intake per diem less than 2100 kcals

(iii) Cal. HCR_2400 denotes percentage of population with per capita calorie intake per diem less than 2400 kcals

(iv) Food availability status refers to percentage number of households reporting adequate food consumption through out the year.

(v) Figures in parentheses are p-values, which are reported only for estimates, which are significant at least at a 10-per cent level.

Source: Author's estimates based on the NSS data

between calorie intake and incidence of calorie deficiency in both rural and urban sectors. Other measures of association between subjective and objective measures of food security and alternative measure of morbidity/health consciousness are insignificant for the rural sector. As regards the urban sector, either they are insignificant or do not make any sense. For instance, association between incidence of calorie efficiency and infant mortality is significant and inverse implying that higher the incidence of calorie deprivation lower is incidence of infant mortality, which is absurd.

While food security *per se* is important to promote good health outcomes, the latter depend crucially on other important factors like biology, choice and environment. Most important is to recognize prevalence of morbidity rates across sates, which definitely would affect the utilization of nutrients consumed. In this context, programmes to reform the health sector in India, which included *inter alia* user charges for services in public health facilities to the non-poor in particular since the early 1990s (GoI 2007d; p. 221) might have also affected health outcomes adversely.

In sum, it is important to distinguish between input and outcome measures; the process is not instantaneous to generate contemporaneous correlations; instead, there would be lags also. There is limited scope for cross-sectional/time series comparisons between incomes/growth rates, malnutrition and health outcomes. It is important to take a holistic perspective on this issue.

Conclusions

This study reviews the basis for such assessments in terms of disaggregate analysis of changes in consumer expenditures and consumption patterns by decile groups in rural and urban India. The assessment is carried out after appropriate consumption-basket specific price adjustments for estimates of nominal consumption and in terms of changes in physical quantities with reference to the observed structural changes in the economy. The study brings out that real consumption expenditure of all the decile groups, the bottom three decile groups in particular, increased since the mid-70s. It shows that current price estimates of budget shares, as is well known, exaggerate changes in consumption pattern and analysis based on averages for the population could be misleading. Per capita cereal expenditures of the bottom decile groups in rural India increased. However, this was not accompanied by corresponding increases in quantities of cereal consumption because of structural changes in the economy. With casualization and hence, monetization of the labour market, there has been a progressive increase in the dependence of the poor households, landless labour in particular, on the commodity market. With changes in cereal production patterns and hence availability in favour of superior cereals, these households had to shift their consumption in favour of superior but costlier rice and wheat, which are inferior to coarse cereals in terms of calorie content. As a result, cereal consumption and hence, calorie intake has not increased to a commensurate extent. On the other hand, with changes in infrastructure and technology, average energy requirements seem to have declined calling for reduced calorie intake. This could be one major reason for the observed trend decline in average calorie intake of the richer decile groups in rural and urban India. Therefore, estimates of incidence of calorie deficiency with reference to outdated norms show a trend increase. Hence, there is a need for revising downward the calorie norms consistent with the converging pattern of changes in calorie intake in across decile groups in rural and urban India.

The case for such an approach is validated by the survey finings which show that the percentage number of rural and urban households reporting adequate food consumption through out the year has increased since 1983 and has reached almost 98 per cent. This would raise the question regarding an appropriate norm and strategy for food security. Should one measure it in terms of objective estimates of calorie intake with reference to an exogenous norm or subjective perceptions on adequate food consumption? The limited evidence in terms of bivariate correlations between subjective and objective estimates food consumption, and measures of health status do not provide any unambiguous answer. The estimates are either weak or perverse, which could be because of the lags and simultaneous interaction of a host of variables in determining these outcomes.

References

Government of India (1977): "Survey Results: Consumer Expenditure: NSS, 27th Round (October1972- September 1973)", *Sarvekshana: Journal of he National Sample Survey Oganisation*, Department of Statistics, Ministry of Planning, pp. S287-S436.

Government of India (1983): "A Note on Per Capita Per Diem Intake of Calories, Protein and Fat based on the Data Collected in the Household Survey on Consumer Expenditure, NSS 27th Round: October 1972 - September 1973', *Sarvekshana*, Vol. VI, Nos. 3-4, 1983.

Government of India (1986a): "Some Results on the Second Quinquennial Survey on Consumer Expenditure: National Sample Survey Thirty-second round (July '77-June '78)", *Sarvekshana*, Vol. IX, No. 3, pp. S51-S184.

Government of India (1986b): "A Report on the Third Quinquennial Survey on Consumer Expenditure: National Sample Survey. Thirty-eighth round (January-December 1983)", *Sarvekshana*, Vol. IX, No. 4, pp. S1-S102.

Government of India (1989a): "Results on Per Capita Consumption of Cereals for Various Sections of Population: NSS 38th round (1983)", *Sarvekshana*, Vol. XIII, No. 2, pp. S1-S176.

Government of India (1989b): "Results on Per Capita and Per Consumer Unit Per Diem Intake of Calorie, Protein and Fat and Perceptions of the People on Adequacy of Food", *Sarvekshana*, Vol. XIII, No. 2, Issue No. 41, pp. S177-S258.

Government of India (1991): "Results of the Fourth Quinquennial Survey on Consumer Expenditure (sub-sample 1): NSS 43rd round (July 1987-June 1988)", *Sarvekshana*, Vol. XV, No. 1, pp.

Government of India (1996a): *Level and Pattern of Consumer Expenditure. 5th Quinquennial Survey 1993-94*, Report No. 402, National Sample Survey Organisation, Department of Statistics, New Delhi.

Government of India (1996b): *Nutritional Intake in India NSS 50th Round July 1993-June 1994 Fifth Quinquennial Survey on Consumer*

Expenditure, Report No. 405, National Sample Survey Organisation, Department of Statistics, New Delhi.

Government of India (2001a): *Level and Pattern of Consumer Expenditure in India 1999-2000 NSS 55th Round July 1999–June 2000*, Report No. 457 (55/1.0/3), National Sample Survey Organisation, Ministry of Statistics & Programme Implementation, New Delhi.

Government of India (2001b): *Reported Adequacy of Food Intake in India 1999-2000 NSS 55th Round (July 1999-June 2000)*, Report No. 466(55/1.0/7), National Sample Survey Organisation, New Delhi.

Government of India (2001c): *Nutritional Intake in India 1999-2000 NSS 55th Round (July 1999-June 2000)*, Report No. 471(55/1.0/9), National Sample Survey Organisation, New Delhi.

Government of India (2006a): *Morbidity, Health Care and the Condition of the Aged NSS 60th Round (January-June 2004)*, Report No. 507(60/25.0/1), National Sample Survey Organisation, New Delhi.

Government of India (2006b): *Level and Pattern of Consumer Expenditure, 2004–2005, NSS 61st Round (July 2004 – June 2005)*, NSS Report No. 508(61/1.0)/1), National Sample Survey Organisation, Ministry of Statistics and Programme Implementation, New Delhi.

Government of India (2007a): *Perceived Adequacy of Food Consumption in Indian Households 2004-2005 NSS 61st Round (July 2004-June 2005)*, Report No. 512(61/1.0/5), National Sample Survey Organisation, New Delhi.

Government of India (2007b): *Poverty Estimates for 2004-05*, Press Information Bureau, New Delhi, India.

Government of India (2007c): *Nutritional Intake in India 2004-2005 NSS 61st Round (July 2004-June 2005)*, Report No. 513(61/1.0/6), National Sample Survey Organisation, New Delhi.

Government of India (2007d): *Economic Survey 2006-2007*, Ministry of Finance, New Delhi.

Government of India (2008): *Eleventh Five Year Plan 2007-12 Volume II Social Sector*, Planning Commission, Oxford University Press, New Delhi.

Suryanarayana, M.H. (1995a): "Growth, Poverty and Levels of Living: Hypotheses, Methods and Policies", *Journal of Indian School of Political Economy*, Vol. 7, No. 2, pp. 203-255.

Suryanarayana, M.H. (1995b) "PDS: Beyond Implicit Subsidy and Urban Bias", *Food Policy*, Vol. 20, No. 4, pp. 259-278.

Suryanarayana, M.H. and Dimitri Silva (2005): "Is Targeting the Poor a Penalty on the Food Insecure? Poverty and Food Insecurity in India", *Journal of Human Development*, Vol. 8, No. 1, pp. 89-107.

Tendulkar, Suresh D., K. Sundaram and L.R. Jain (1993): *Poverty in India, 1970-71 to 1988-89*, ARTEP Working Papers, International Labour Organisation, Asian Regional Team for Employment Promotion, New Delhi.

Footnotes

1. Here again the focus only on average outcome without considering distribution of crucial variables like income would be misleading. Further, health outcomes in response to changes in income cannot be instantaneous; instead it would be a dynamic response involving considerable time lag.
2. This is also because the NSS distribution estimates for the post-1970s are comparable (Suryanarayana 1995a).
3. Not reported here but are available with the author for verification.
4. It may be noted that the estimates (Table 1) (a) are not comparable in a strict sense to those cited in the preceding paragraph because of differences in the base year and, most importantly, differences in methods of deflation; and (b) the extent of increase in real consumption was less for the poor then for the average in both rural and urban all-India.
5. For further empirical details, see Suryanarayana (1995).

7

Poverty Alleviation and Human Development in India: Approaches and Achievements

Ulimiri V. Somayajulu, Tilak Mukherji

Introduction

Poverty in India is widespread as it is estimated to have a third of the world's poor. According to the Planning Commission of India, 28% of the population was living below the poverty line in 2004–2005, down from 51% in 1977–1978, and 36% in 1993-1994 (Planning Commission, 2007). According to the World Bank's estimate, 42% of the country's population were below the international poverty line of $1.25 a day (PPP, in nominal terms Rs. 21.6 a day in urban areas and Rs 14.3 in rural areas); having reduced from 60% in 1980(World Bank, 2005, 2006). Although Indian economy has grown steadily over the last two decades, its growth has been uneven across different social and economic groups, geographic regions, and rural and urban areas. During 1999 - 2008, Gujarat (8.8%), Haryana (8.7%) and Delhi (7.4%) recorded higher annual growth rates than Bihar (5.1%), Uttar Pradesh (4.4%), and Madhya Pradesh (3.5%). Poverty rates in rural Orissa (43%) and rural Bihar (41%) are among the world's most extreme.

The India State Hunger Index 2008 compiled by the International Food Policy Research Institute (IFPRI) indicates the best nutritional situation in Punjab, while severe malnutrition in Madhya Pradesh is comparable to that of Ethiopia or Sudan. India has a higher rate of malnutrition among children under the age of three years (46% in 2007) than any other country in the world (The Times, 2007).

Despite significant economic progress, one fourth of the nation's population earns less than the government specified poverty threshold of Rs 12 per day (approximately USD $0.25). Official figures estimate that 28% of Indians lived below the national poverty line in 2004-2005. National Commission for Enterprises in Unorganised Sector (NCEUS, 2007) found that 77% of Indians, or 836 million people, lived on less than Rs 20 (approximately USD $0.50 nominal; $2 PPP) per day.

As per 2001 Census, 36% of Indian households availed banking services, 35% owned a radio or transistor, 32% own television, 9% own phone, 44.% own bicycle, 12% own scooter, motorcycle or a moped, and 3% own car, jeep or van; 35% of households had none of these assets. According to Department of Telecommunications of India, the phone density has reached 33% by Dec 2009 and has an annual growth of 40% (TCPO, 2007)

Objective and Data Sources

The objectives of this paper are a) To review the approaches initiated by the Government of India for poverty alleviation and b) to understand the achievements up to now through these programmes. This paper uses the reports prepared by Planning Commission (2006, 2007) and Eleventh Five Year plan (2007-2012) and other secondary sources.

Approaches to Alleviate Poverty

Since 1950s, Indian government and non governmental organisations have initiated several programmes to alleviate poverty, including subsidising food and other necessities, increased access to loans, improving agricultural techniques and price support, and promoting education and family planning. These measures have helped in eliminating famines, cut absolute poverty levels by more than half, and reduced illiteracy and malnutrition. However, since the mid 1990s, 30 million people have been added to the ranks of the hungry and 46% of children are underweight.(Planning Commission, 2007a).

Since the early 1950s, Government of India has initiated, sustained, and refined various schemes/programmes to help the poor attain self sufficiency in food production. The most important initiative has been the supply of basic commodities, particularly food at controlled prices, available throughout the country as poor spend about 80% of their income on food.

Table 1
Poverty Alleviation Programmes

Type	*Programme*
Self Employment	Swarnjayanti Gram Swarozgar Yojana (SGSY)
	Jawahar Gram Samridhi Yojana (JGSY)
Wage Employment	Employment Assurance Scheme (EAS)
	Sampoorna Gramin Rozgar Yojana (SGRY)
	Sampoorna Gramin Rozgar Yojana (SGRY)
Food Safety	Food for Work Programme
Social Security	National Social Assistance Programme(NSAP)
	National Old Age Pension Scheme (NOAPS)
	Annapurna
	National Family Benefit Scheme (NFBS)
	National Maternity Benefit Scheme (NMBS)

Eradication of poverty in India is generally only considered to be a long term goal. Poverty alleviation is expected to make better progress in the next 50 years than in the past, as a trickle down effect of the growing middle class. Other initiatives such as increasing focus on education, reservation of seats in government jobs and increasing empowerment of women and economically weaker sections of society, are also expected to contribute to the alleviation of poverty. It must be stated that it is incorrect to say that all poverty reduction programmes have failed. This is evident from the growth of the middle class (which was virtually non existent at the time of India's independence in 1947) indicating economic prosperity has indeed been very impressive in India, but the distribution of wealth is not at all even (Naresh C Saxena and Jayanti S Ravi).

The poverty alleviation programmes can broadly be classified as self employment programmes, wage employment programmes, food safety programme and social security programmes.

Poverty Alleviation Programmes in Rural India

Poverty alleviation remains a major challenge for the Government in spite of steady decline in rural poverty over the last two decades. Acceleration of economic growth, with a focus on sectors which are employment intensive, facilitates the removal of poverty in the long run. There is a need to complement these programmes with a focus on provision of basic services for improving the quality of life of the people and direct intervention in the form of targeted poverty alleviation programmes. While growth continues to be the prime mover, poverty alleviation programmes supplement the growth efforts and protect the poor from destitution, sharp fluctuations in employment and incomes and social insecurity. The specifically designed poverty alleviation programmes for generation of both self employment and wage employment in rural areas have been redesigned and restructured in order to enhance their efficacy/impact on the poor and improve their sustainability(Yesudian, 2007).

Swarnjayanti Gram Swarozgar Yojana (SGSY)

The self employment programme of Swarnjayanti Gram Swarozgar Yojana (SGSY), launched on April 1, 1999, was conceived keeping in view the strengths and weaknesses of the earlier schemes of Integrated Rural Development Programme (IRDP) and Allied Programmes along with Million Wells Scheme (MWS). The objective of restructuring was to make the programme more effective in providing sustainable incomes through micro enterprises. The SGSY laid emphasis on the following:

- Focussed approach to poverty alleviation
- Capitalising advantages of group lending
- Overcoming the problems associated with multiplicity of programmes

SGSY is conceived as a holistic programme of micro enterprises covering all aspects of self employment viz. organisation of the rural poor into Self Help Groups (SHGs) and their capacity building, planning of activity clusters, infrastructure build up, technology, credit and marketing. Micro enterprises in the rural areas are sought to be established by building on the potential of the rural poor. The programme aimed at bringing the existing poor families above the poverty line.

Under the SGSY, the focus was on vulnerable sections among the rural poor with SCs/STs accounting for 50%, women 40% and the disabled 3% of the beneficiaries. The list of BPL households, identified through BPL census, duly approved by the Gram Sabha forms the basis for assistance to families under SGSY. The beneficiaries (also called Swarozgaris) could be individuals or groups. While the identification of individual beneficiaries was made through a participatory approach, the programme laid emphasis on organisation of poor into SHGs and their capacity building. The SHGs consist of 10 to 20 persons. Involvement of women members in each SHG was encouraged and at the block level it is stipulated that, at least half of the groups would be exclusively women's groups. For providing a revolving fund to the SHGs, the DRDAs could use 10 per cent of the allocation under SGSY.

Under SGSY, micro enterprises in the rural areas were set up with an emphasis on the 'cluster' approach. Four to five key activities were identified in each block based on the resource endowments, occupational skills of the people and availability of markets and these activities were implemented preferably in clusters so that backward and forward linkages could be effectively established. The key activities were to be selected with the approval of the Panchayat Samiti at the block level and DRDAs/Zila Parishad at the district level. SGSY adopted project approach with project reports prepared for each key activity in association with banks and financial institutions.

The SGSY was a credit cum subsidy programme, with credit as the critical component and subsidy as a minor and enabling element and envisaged greater involvement of banks and promotion of multiple credit rather than a one time credit injection. Subsidy under SGSY was provided at 30% of the project cost, subject to a maximum of Rs.7500. In respect of SCs/STs, it was 50% subject to a maximum of Rs.10,000. For groups, the subsidy was 50% subject to a ceiling of Rs.1.25 lakh. There was no monetary limit on subsidy for irrigation projects. Subsidy under SGSY is back ended to ensure proper utilisation of funds by the target group.

Since proper infrastructure is essential for the success of micro enterprises, 20% (25% in the case of North Eastern States) of SGSY allocation for each district will be set apart under SGSY Infrastructure Fund for this purpose. Since SGSY laid emphasis on skill development through well designed training courses, the DRDAs were allowed to set 10% of the SGSY allocation apart on training to be maintained as SGSY Training Fund to be utilised to provide both orientation and training programmes to Swarozgaris. For this purpose, training facilities of polytechnics, Krishi Vigyan Kendras, Khadi and Village Industries Boards, State Institutes of Rural Development, Extension Training Centres, reputed voluntary organisations and departmental training institutes were utilised. The programme also sought to ensure upgradation of the technology in the identified activity clusters and for promoting marketing of the goods.

About 15% of the funds under SGSY were set apart, at the national level, for projects having a far reaching significance to be taken up in conjunction with other Departments or semi government or international organisations. The SGSY was implemented by the District Rural Development Agencies (DRDAs) through the Panchayat Samitis with the process of planning, implementation and monitoring involving coordination with banks and other financial institutions, PRIs, NGOs as well as technical institutions in the district. Hence, the implementation of SGSY called for integration of various agencies - DRDAs, banks, line departments, Panchayati Raj Institutions (PRIs), Non Governmental Organisations (NGOs) and other semi government organisations.

Funds under the SGSY were shared by the Centre and the States in the ratio of 75:25. The Central allocation was distributed in relation to the incidence of poverty in the State. Additional parameters like absorption capacity and special requirements were also considered.

In 1999-2000 (up to February, 2000) an expenditure of Rs.804.23 crore was incurred under the scheme as against the total allocation of Rs.1467.73 crore. During this period, more than 3.40 lakh self help groups were assisted. A Central outlay of Rs.1000.00 crore was provided for the scheme in 2000-01.

Jawahar Gram Samridhi Yojana (JGSY)

The Jawahar Rozgar Yojana (JRY) was recast as the Jawahar Gram Samridhi Yojana (JGSY) with effect from April 1, 1999 to impart a thrust to creation of rural infrastructure. The JGSY was implemented as a CSS with funding in the ratio of 75:25 between the Centre and the States.

The primary objective of JGSY was creation of demand driven community village infrastructure including durable assets at the village level and assets to enable the rural poor to increase the opportunities for sustained employment. The secondary objective was generation of supplementary employment for the unemployed poor in the rural areas. The wage employment under the programme was given to Below Poverty Lines (BPL) families.

While there was no sectoral earmarking of resources under JGSY, 22.5% of the annual allocation was to be spent on individual beneficiary schemes for SCs/STs and 3% was to be utilised for creation of barrier free infrastructure for the disabled. All works that result in creation of durable productive community assets were to be taken up under the programme as per the felt need of the area/people by the village panchayat. These included creation of infrastructure for SCs/STs habitations, infrastructure support for SGSY, infrastructure required for supporting agricultural activities in the village, community infrastructure for education and health, roads and other social, economic and physical infrastructure.

The wages under the programme were either the minimum wages notified by the States or higher wages as fixed by the States through the prescribed procedure. The wage material ratio of 60:40 was made flexible so as to enable the building up of demand driven rural infrastructure. However, efforts may be made to ensure that labour intensive works were taken up with sustainable low cost technology.

Under the programme, village panchayats had the sole authority for preparation of the Annual Action Plan and its implementation, accepted by the Gram Sabha. The Gram Sabha was empowered to approve schemes/works. Completion of the incomplete works was to be given priority over new works and works which could not be completed within two financial years were not included. At the village level, the entire work relating to coordination, review, supervision and monitoring of the programme was the responsibility of the village panchayat. The village panchayats had the power to execute works/schemes upto Rs.50,000 with the approval of the Gram Sabha. Social audit was also undertaken by the Gram Sabha and at the village level, monitoring and vigilance committees were set up to oversee and supervise the works/schemes undertaken.

At the district level, the DRDAs/Zilla Parishads and at the intermediate level the Panchayat Samitis had the overall responsibility for guidance, coordination, supervision, periodical reporting and monitoring the implementation of the programme. Village Panchayats were allowed to spend up to a maximum of 7.5% of the funds or Rs.7500/- whichever was less during a year on the administrative contingencies and for technical consultancy. The village panchayat was permitted to spend up to a maximum of 15% on maintenance of the public assets created within its geographical boundary.

Since the entire funds were to be utilised by the village panchayats under JGSY, the Innovative JRY has been discontinued.

The primary objective of the JGSY had undergone a change from employment generation to rural infrastructure. As such, the States have taken time to adjust their monitoring mechanism as per the new monitoring parameters from employment generation to number of works undertaken/ completed. During 1999-2000, 5.84 lakh works were completed as against a target of 8.57 lakh works. An expenditure of Rs.1841.80 crore was incurred during 1999-2000 as against a total allocation of Rs.2209.24 crore. A Central outlay of Rs.1650.00 crore was earmarked for JGSY for the year 2000-01.

Employment Assurance Scheme (EAS)

The Employment Assurance Scheme (EAS) was launched on 2nd October, 1993 in 1772 identified backward blocks of 257 districts situated in drought prone, desert, tribal and hill areas where the Revamped Public Distribution System (RPDS) was in operation. The programme was subsequently extended to more blocks and thereafter was universalized covering all the 5448 rural blocks of the country. The EAS was restructured w.e.f. 1999-2000 to make it the single wage employment programme. While the basic parameters have been retained, the scheme has become an allocative scheme instead of demand driven and a fixed annual outlay was to be provided to the States. The programme was implemented as a CSS on a cost sharing ratio of 75:25 between the Centre and States.

The primary objective of the EAS was creation of additional wage employment opportunities during the period of acute shortage of wage employment through manual work for the rural poor living below the poverty line. The secondary objective was creation of durable community, social and economic assets for sustained employment and development. EAS was open to all the needy rural poor living below the poverty line. A maximum of two adults per family were provided wage employment. While providing employment, preference was given to SCs/STs and parents of child labour withdrawn from hazardous occupations below the poverty line.

The programme was implemented through the Zilla Parishads (DRDAs in those States where Zilla Parishads do not exist). The list of works was finalised by the Zilla Parishad in consultation with the Members of Parliament. In areas where Zilla Pasrishads are not in existence, a Committee consisting of MLAs, MPs and other public representatives was constituted for selecting the works. Gram Sabhas were informed about the details of works taken up under the scheme. The EAS was in operation at district/Panchayat samiti level throughout the country, but works were to be taken up in only those Panchayat samitis/districts where there was a need for creating additional wage employment. About 70% of the funds allocated for each district were allocated to the Panchayat Samitis and 30% were reserved at the district level and are to be utilised in the areas suffering from endemic labour exodus/areas of distress. Diversion of funds from one district to another and from one Panchayat to another was not permitted. Work would not be taken up under EAS if the demand for wage employment can be fulfilled through other plan or non-plan works. Only labour intensive works of productive nature which create durable assets were to be taken up under the scheme. About 80% of the funds were released to the district as per normal procedure and the remaining 20% were to be released as an incentive only if the States had put in place elected and empowered Panchayati Raj Institutions (PRIs).

Priority was given to the works of soil and moisture conservation, minor irrigation, rejuvenation of drinking water sources and augmentation of ground water, traditional water harvesting structures, works related to watershed schemes (not watershed development), formation of rural roads linking villages with other villages/block headquarters and roads linking the villages with agricultural fields, drainage works and forestry.

Zilla Parishads/Panchayat Samitis were permitted to spend up to a maximum of 15% on maintenance of assets created under this scheme. Funds available from other sources like cooperatives, market committees or other institutions/ departments could be dovetailed with EAS funds for similar purposes. The wage material ratio of 60:40 was to be strictly implemented and for this purpose, the block would be the unit of consideration. Payment of wages was at the minimum wage rate fixed by the States and higher wages to the extent of 10% of the total wage component could be paid to the skilled persons.

Table 2 gives the financial and physical performance of the various poverty alleviation schemes during the 8th and 9th plan period. During 1999-2000, a total allocation of Rs.2431.46 crore was made under EAS and an expenditure of Rs.1998.26 crore was incurred. As against the target of 4091.63 lakh mandays, 2566.39 lakh mandays were generated. A Central outlay of Rs.1300.00 crore was provided for EAS for 2000-01.

SHGs are considered as appropriate grass root level institutions for attacking multiple deprivation. The number of SHGs which is about 4 million–is increasing at an encouraging pace drawing support from the central and state governments, NABARD, banks and NGOs. The SHGs are supported for taking up income generating activities.

Food for Work Programme

The Food for Work programme was started in 2000-01 as a component of the EAS in eight notified drought affected states of Chattisgarh, Gujarat, Himachal Pradesh, Madhya Pradesh, Orissa, Rajasthan, Maharashtra and Uttarakhand. The programme aimed at augmenting food security through wage employment. Food grains are supplied to the states free of cost. However, lifting of food grains for the scheme from Food Corporation of India (FCI) godowns had been slow. Against an allocation of 35.31 lakh tonnes of food grains, only 21.26 lakh tonnes were lifted by the target states up to January 2002.

Table 2

Financial and Physical Performance of Poverty Alleviation Programmes IRDP / SGSY, JRY / JGSY and EAS During Eighth and Ninth Plan–Year wise (Rs. Crores)

Plan Period	Year	IRDP/ SGSY			JRY/ JGSY			EAS		
		Total Allocation (Centre+ State)	*Total Expen-diture*	*Lakh Families Swaroz-garies*	*Total Allocation (Centre + State)*	*Total Expen-diture*	*Emplo-yment in Lakh Mandays*	*Total Allocation (Centre + State)*	*Total Expen-diture*	*Emplo-yment in Lakh Mandays*
Eighth Plan	1	2	3	4	5	6	7	8	9	10
	1992-1993	662.22	693.88	20.69	3169.05	2709.59	7821.02	0.00		
	1993-1994	1093.43	956.65	25.39	4059.42	3878.71	10258.4	0.00	183.75	494.74
	1994-1995	1098.22	1008.31	22.15	4376.92	4268.33	9517.07	0.00	1235.45	2729.56
	1995-1996	1097.21	1077.16	20.89	4848.70	4466.91	8958.25	0.00	1720.61	3465.27
	1996-1997	1097.21	1131.68	19.24	2236.79	2163.98	4006.32	0.00	2160.41	4030.02
Total		5048.29	4867.68	108.36	18690.88	17487.52	40561.06	0.00	5300.22	10719.59
Ninth Plan										
	1997-1998	1133.51	1109.54	17.07	2499.21	2439.38	3955.89	2460.48	2904.97	4717.74
	1998-1999	1456.28	1162.28	16.77	2597.03	2525.48	3766.41	2485.15	2882.18	4279.36
	1999-2000	1472.34	959.86	9.34	2205.58	2032.45	2683.08	2431.46	2182.61	2786.17
	2000-2001	1332.50	1116.27	10.30	2192.96	1929.23	2683.17	2082.27	1861.11	2183.92
	2001-2002	774.50	555.15	6.25	2493.01	699.07	860.79	1730.92	530.92	666.27
Total		6169.13	4716.17	56.92	11687.93	9625.61	13949.34	11190.28	10361.79	14633.46

Source: Ministry of Rural Development, http://www.rural.nic.in

Sampoorna Gramin Rozgar Yojana (SGRY)

JGSY, EAS and Food for Work Programme, aimed at the creation of employment opportunities in the rural areas and they were revamped and merged under the new Sampoorna Gramin Rozgar Yojana (SGRY) scheme from September 2001. The basic aim of the scheme continued to be generation of wage employment, creation of durable economic infrastructure in rural areas and provision of food and nutrition security to the poor. The amalgamation of the earlier schemes led to an augmentation of resources for this programme. The works taken up under the programme were labour-intensive and the workers were paid the minimum wages notified by the states. Payment of wages was done partly in cash and partly in kind - 5 kg of food grains and the balance in cash. The Centre and the states shared the cost of the cash component of the scheme in the ratio of 75:25. An allocation of Rs. 3750 crore was made for the programme in 2001-02.

A review of various wage employment programmes during the Ninth Plan revealed that there has been a considerable reduction in terms of allocation as well as in employment generation. This was largely due to changes in allocation for rural development schemes during the plan period. The allocation by both the Centre and the states under JRY went down from Rs. 18,691 crore in the Eighth Plan to Rs. 11,688 crore in the Ninth Plan.

National Social Assistance Programme (NSAP)

The NSAP was launched with effect from 15th August, 1995 as a 100 per cent Centrally Sponsored Scheme with the aim to provide social assistance benefit to poor households in the case of old age, death of primary breadwinner and maternity. This represents a significant step towards the fulfillment of the Directive Principles in Articles 41 & 42 of the Constitution. The programme supplements the efforts of the State Governments with the objective of ensuring minimum national levels of well being and the Central assistance is an addition to the benefit that the States are already providing on Social Protection Schemes or may provide in future. The provision of Central assistance seeks to ensure that social protection to beneficiaries is uniformly available.

The main features of the three components of the NSAP (i) National Old Age Pension Scheme (NOAPS), (ii) National Family Benefit Scheme (NFBS) and (iii) National Maternity Benefit Scheme (NMBS) are briefly discussed below:

National Old Age Pension Scheme (NOAPS)

Old age pension of Rs.75 per month, per beneficiary is provided to person of 65 years and above who is a destitute in the sense of having little or no regular means of subsistence from his/her own sources of income or through support from family members or other sources. In order to determine destitution, the criteria, if any, currently in force in the States/UTs may also be followed.

National Family Benefit Scheme (NFBS)

A sum of Rs.10,000 is provided in the case death of primary breadwinner due to natural or accidental causes. The family benefit is paid to such surviving member of the household of deceased who, after local enquiry, is determined to be the Head of the household. The primary breadwinner is defined as a member, whose earnings contribute substantially to the household income and who is more than 18 years and less than 65 years of age. The bereaved household should qualify as a BPL according to the criteria prescribed by the Government of India.

National Maternity Benefit Scheme (NMBS)

A lump sum cash assistance of Rs.500 was provided to pregnant women of households below the poverty line up to the first two live births provided they are of 19 years and above. The maternity benefit was to be disbursed in one installment, 12-8 weeks prior to the delivery. In case of delay it can be disbursed to the beneficiary even after the birth of the child.

The NSAP was implemented by the State/UT Governments with assistance from Panchayats and municipal functionaries. Each State/UT had a nodal department identified for implementing the scheme. In the districts, there were District Level Committees on NSAP.

The Gram Panchayats/Municipalities had an active role in identification of beneficiaries under the NSAP. The State Governments communicate targets for the three components of NSAP to Panchayats/municipalities so that identification of beneficiaries could suitably be made by Gram Panchayats/Neighbourhood/Mohalla Committees in line with these targets. In case of cash disbursement, the payments were to be made in public meetings preferably of Gram Sabha meetings in villages, and of neighbourhood/mohalla committees in urban areas. The Panchayats/Municipalities were responsible for disseminating information about NSAP and the procedures for obtaining benefits under it. In this task, the Panchayats and Municipalities were encouraged to seek the involvement/cooperation of voluntary agencies to the extent possible for identifying beneficiaries and persuading them to avail of the benefits intended for them.

The NSAP also provides opportunities for linking social assistance packages to anti poverty programmes and schemes for provision of basic needs e.g. the old age pension could be linked to medical care and other benefits for the old and poor, family benefit beneficiaries could be assisted under SGSY while maternity assistance could be linked with maternal and child care programmes.

Table 3 gives the financial and physical performance of NSAP. As against an allocation of Rs.767.05 crore made under NSAP during 1999-2000, an expenditure of Rs.596.99 crore was incurred up to December, 1999. A Central allocation of Rs.715.00 crore had been earmarked for the scheme in 2000-01.

Annapurna

In 1999-2000, the Government had announced the launching of a new scheme 'Annapurna' to provide food security to those indigent senior citizens who are not covered under the Targeted Public Distribution System (TPDS) and who have no income of their own and none to take care of them in the village. 'Annapurna' would provide 10 kg. of food grains per month

Table 3
Financial and Physical Performance under National Social Assistance Programme

(in Rs Crores)

	NOAPS		*NFBS*		*NMBS*	
Year	*Expenditure*	*No. of Beneficiaries*	*Expenditure*	*No. of Beneficiaries*	*Expenditure*	*No. of Beneficiaries*
1995-96	109.88	2,937,677	43.44	2,84,260	24.50	6,57,891
1996-97	319.55	4,760,327	92.00	1,66,090	52.63	1,282,025
1997-98	365.19	5,087,830	130.56	2,18,456	54.70	1,557,292
1998-99	467.15	5,080,821	188.02	2,66,411	70.43	1,562,072
1999-00	456.25	5,017,542	194.98	2,15,815	73.40	1,299,719
2000-01	476.66	5,148,226	200.93	2,02,999	83.90	1,456,079
2001-02(P)	362.08	5,052,568	97.96	1,04,298	Transferred to Ministry of Health and Family Welfare	

Source: Ministry of Rural Development, http://www.rural.nic.in

free of cost to all such persons who are eligible for old age pensions but are presently not receiving it and whose children are not residing in the same village. The Gram Panchayats would be required to identify, prepare and display a list of such persons after giving wide publicity. A Central allocation of Rs.100 crore was earmarked for the scheme in 2000-01.

Rural Housing–Indira Awaas Yojana (IAY)

In the Ninth Plan, the Special Action Plan for Social Infrastructure identified 'Housing' as one of the priority areas. It aimed at providing 'Housing for All' and facilitated construction of 20 lakh additional dwelling units, of which 13 lakh dwelling units were to be constructed in rural areas. The composite housing strategy for the Ninth Plan was a multipronged strategy which got operationalised w.e.f. 1999-2000. The salient features of the strategy under Action Plan are given below.

The Indira Awaas Yojana (IAY) would continue to be major scheme for construction of houses to be given to the poor, free of cost. However, an additional component - conversion of unserviceable kutcha houses to semi pucca houses- had been added. From 1999-2000, the criteria for allocation of funds to States/UTs under IAY has been changed to 50% poverty ratio and 50 % housing shortage in the State. The criteria for allocation of funds to a district in a State had been changed to the SC/ST population and housing shortage, with equal weightage to each of them.

A Credit cum Subsidy Scheme for rural housing had been launched from 1.4.1999 which would target a rural family having annual income up to Rs.32,000. The subsidy portion would be restricted to Rs.10,000/- and loan amount to Rs.40,000/-. The loan portion would be disbursed by the commercial banks, housing finance institutions etc.

Equity support by the Ministry of Rural Development (MORD) to Housing and Urban Development Corporation (HUDCO) had been increased to improve the outreach of housing finance in rural areas. In addition, an Innovative Scheme for Rural Housing and Habitat Development and Rural

Building Centres (RBCs) had been introduced to encourage innovative, cost effective and environment friendly solutions in building/housing sectors in rural areas.

A National Mission for Rural Housing and Habitat had been set up to address the critical issues of 'housing gap' and induction of science and technology inputs into the housing/construction sector in rural areas.

Samagra Awaas Yojana, a comprehensive housing scheme, was launched in 1999- 2000 on pilot project basis in one block in each of 25 districts of 24 States and in one Union Territory with a view to ensuring integrated provision of shelter, sanitation and drinking water. The underlying philosophy was to provide for convergence of the existing rural housing, sanitation and water supply schemes with special emphasis on technology transfer, human resource development and habitat improvement with people's participation. The existing schemes of housing, drinking water and sanitation would follow the normal funding pattern.

However, a Special Central Assistance of Rs 25.00 lakh would be provided for each block for under taking overall habitat development and IEC works with 10% contribution coming from the people. In 1999-2000 (up to February, 2000), Rs.1438.39 crore was spent and 7.98 lakh dwelling units were built under the IAY. In the Annual Plan 2000-01, the Central outlay of Rs.1710.00 crore was provided for Rural Housing.

Area Development Programmes

The Drought Prone Area Programme (DPAP), Desert Development Programme (DDP) and Integrated Wastelands Development Programme (IWDP) were being implemented with effect from 1.4.1995. The main features of this strategy include :

- Area development programmes to be implemented exclusively on watershed basis.
- Programmes and activities to be confined to the identified watershed of about 500 hectares and are to be executed on a project basis spanning over a period of four to five years

- Watershed project to cover a village, as far as possible
- Elaborate institutional mechanism at various levels clearly defined for effective participation of the local people and the PRIs in all stages of project management
- DRDA/ZP to be the nodal Government agency at the district level to act as a facilitator and provider of finances and technical assistance to the people's orgasnisations executing the watershed projects

Drought Prone Area Programme (DPAP)

DPAP aimed at minimising the adverse effects of drought on production of crops and livestock and productivity of land, water and human resources ultimately leading to the drought proofing of the affected areas. It also aimed at promoting overall economic development and improving the socio-economic conditions of the resource poor and disadvantaged sections inhabiting the programme areas. The DPAP was in operation in 947 blocks of 161 districts in 13 States. Under DPAP, Rs.89.44 crore was spent during 1999-2000. For 2000-01, the Central outlay of Rs.190.00 crore was provided for DPAP as against Rs.95.00 crore in 1999-2000.

Desert Development Programme (DDP)

DDP was envisaged as an essentially land based activity and conceived as a long term measure for restoration of ecological balance by conserving, developing and harnessing land, water, livestock and human resources. The main objectives of this programme were: (i) combating drought and desertification; (ii) encouraging restoration of ecological balance; (iii) mitigating the adverse effects of drought and adverse edaphoclimatic conditions on crops and livestock and productivity of land, water and human resources; (iv) promoting economic development of village community; and (v) improving socio economic conditions of the resource poor and disadvantaged sections of village community viz; asset less and women.

Under DDP, Rs.49.22 crore was spent during 1999-2000. In the Annual Plan 2000-01, the Central outlay of Rs.135.00 crore was provided for DDP vis-à-vis Rs.85.00 crore in 1999-2000.

Under DPAP and DDP, funds were directly released to DRDAs/Zilla Parishads for implementation of the programme. From 1999-2000, the funding pattern under these programmes were changed to 75:25 cost sharing basis between the Centre and the States.

Integrated Wastelands Development Programme (IWDP)

IWDP has been under implementation since 1989-90 wherein wastelands are being developed with the active participation of stakeholders i.e. user groups, self help groups and PRIs. Here, the projects are sanctioned in favour of DRDAs/ZPs for the period of five years. The projects are implemented through the Project Implementing Agencies (PIAs) which can be a Line Department or a reputed NGO having sufficient experience in the field of watershed development. The programme is implemented all over the country.

IWDP is a 100% Central Sector scheme with the cost norm being Rs.4000 per hectare. The basic objective of this scheme is to take up integrated wastelands development based on village/micro watershed plans. The stakeholders prepare these plans after taking into consideration land capability, site conditions and local needs. The scheme also helps in generation of employment in rural areas besides enhancing people's participation in the wastelands development programmes at all stages. This leads to equitable sharing of benefits and sustainable development.

The major activities taken up under the scheme are: (i) soil and moisture conservation measures like terracing, bunding, trenching, vegetative barriers etc; (ii) planting and sowing of multi purpose trees, shrubs, grasses, legumes and pasture land development; (iii) encouraging natural regeneration; (iv) promotion of agro forestry and horticulture; (v) wood substitution and fuel wood conservation measures; (vi) measures needed to disseminate technology; training, extension and creation of greater degree of awareness among the participants; and (vii) encouraging people's participation.

About 247 IWDP projects in 25 States with a total outlay of Rs.778.12 crore to treat total project area of 15.98 lakh hectare were sanctioned before March 31, 1999. Thirty nine projects covering an area of 3.83 lakh hectare were approved by the Project Sanctioning Committee. For Annual Plan 2000-01, the Central outlay was enhanced to Rs.480.00 crore vis-à-vis Rs.82.00 crore in 1999-2000.

In pursuance to the Government decision to bring the unification of multiplicity of Wasteland Development Programmes of different Ministries/Departments, within a framework of 'Single National Initiative', the common guidelines for implementation of watershed projects/ programmes by the Ministry of Rural Development and Ministry of Agriculture have been evolved and an effort is being made to bring them under one umbrella/Ministry.

MNREGA

Launched in February 2006, the programme, recently renamed the Mahatma Gandhi NREGA, gets the most government money among social welfare schemes, with an allocation of Rs39,100 crore in the year ending 31 March. The Mahatma Gandhi National Rural Employment Guarantee Act, 2005, (MGNREGA) was enacted on 7th September 2005 as " *An Act to provide for the enhancement of livelihood security of the households in rural areas of the country by providing at least one hundred days of Guaranteed wage employment in every financial year to every household"*

The objectives of MGNREGA are:

- Providing wage employment opportunities
- Creating sustainable rural livelihoods through regeneration of the natural resource base i.e. augmenting productivity and supporting creation of durable assets
- Strengthening rural governance through decentralisation and processes of transparency and accountability

Table 4
Mahatma Gandhi National Rural Employment Guarantee Act (MGNREGA)-Performance, 2009-10 and 2010-11

	2009-10	*2010-11*
Employment provided to households	4.62 crores	3.71 crores
Person days (in crore)		
Total	226.67	124.98
SCs	67.46 (30%)	28.34 (23%)
STs	49.27 (22%)	21.33 (17%)
Women	110.7 (49%)	75.31 (60%)
Total works taken up	38.07 lakhs	64.68 lakhs
Works completed	14.79 lakhs	1.93 lakhs
Works in progress	23.28 lakhs	62.68 lakhs

*Source:*_ http://nrega.nic.in

MGNREGA pioneers the Government's of radicalization of State welfare policies, foregrounding its development obligations as citizen rights. The most significant feature of the MGNREGA is that it vests the country's rural communities with rights to demand employment and binds the Government to time bound legal guarantees to honour and fulfill the demand. The implementation of the Act has yielded encouraging results, despite uneven performance across the country, in augmenting employment, increasing wage earnings, stemming distress migration, enhancing productivity and promoting equity, specially gender equity. This Act for unskilled manual labour is ushering in a new era of technology and financial inclusion for rural communities. MGNREGA, designed primarily as a social safety net has the potential to transform rural India into a more productive, equitable, connected society.

Realising the vision of the Act necessitates the development of a comprehensive strategic framework and a time bound Plan of Action to strengthen existing delivery systems and enhance people's capacity to enforce their rights this is a challenging task as it confronts legacy behaviour, structural hierarchies, historical dependencies, and a nexus of vested interests that resist progressive change. This is further aggravated by multiple deprivations and unequal dependencies of rural communities. Several basic conditions on which the legal provisions are expected to be enforced are usually missing generating the dual challenge of creating systems for implementation and compelling existing systems to deliver against guaranteed mandates. It is like making the road while hitting it, running.

Therefore, fulfilling the radical rights based vision of MGNREGA requires delineating a clear strategic framework drawn from the stated goals of the Act and drawing up a detailed time bound plan of action for its implementation. Such a plan requires innovative thinking as there is no precedence to many of the right based instruments intrinsic to its design. The strategic framework has to have components that strengthen the existing delivery systems as well as to evolve new structures and reengineer process.

Based on implementation experience and feed back, the broad components of the strategic framework can be organised as two broad sets, the first related to the sequence of processes mandated by law and the second related to the management systems expected to implement those processes. The first focuses on facilitating demand based processes and the second strengthening the supply side systems to respond effectively to the demand. Though admittedly, dichotomies of supply and demand are not adequate ways of describing the participatory inter related manner in which the agencies are expected to act, and it is in fact hoped that the strategic framework of action will help realise the vision of collective and collaborative ownership of rights and obligations.

Components related to strengthening legal processes and entitlements include: Social Mobilisation, Planning, Works management, Asset creation, Wage payment, Transparency and Public accountability, Grievance redressal.

Components related to strengthening management systems to ensure that the processes mandated by the Act include: Augmenting human resources, Training all stakeholders, Evolving new structures and processes where needed, Using ICT enabled processes, Strengthening monitoring and review systems, Regular independent research and evaluation, Incentivising performance and Encouraging knowledge sharing

The strategic framework has been converted into a Plan of Action for the fiscal year 2010-2011.Outcomes expected in the implementation of the strategic framework are:

- building capacity of the system to deliver a legal guarantee
- developing capabilities of the people to demand rights
- identifying issues to leverage the Act to make it an instrument for integrated, sustainable development.

Achievements

According to the Planning Commission of India, population below poverty line reduced from 51% in 1977–1978, to 36% in 1993-1994 and further to 28% in 2004-05. According to the World Bank, 42% of India's population in 2005 was below the international poverty line of $1.25 a day (PPP, in nominal terms Rs. 21.6 a day in urban areas and Rs 14.3 in rural areas); against 60% in 1980.

The World Bank estimates that 456 million Indians (42% of the total Indian population) live under the global poverty line of $1.25 per day (PPP). Thus India is home to one third of the global poor. There is significant decline in poverty from 60% in 1981 to 42% in 2005, along with increase in income inequality (Gini coefficient of 32.5 during 1999- 2000).

The Planning Commission of India estimates (on the basis of 61st round of the National Sample Survey (NSS) with the criterion used being monthly per capita consumption expenditure below Rs. 356.35 for rural areas and Rs. 538.60 for urban areas) indicate decline from 51% in 1977–1978 to 36% in 1993-1994 and to 28% in 2004–2005. Three fourth of the poor in India are in rural areas, most of them are daily wagers, self employed householders and landless labourers.

1950 to mid 1970s: In 1951, 47% of India's rural population was below the poverty line. The proportion went up to 64% in 1954-55; it came down to 45% in 1960-61 but it went up to 51% in 1977-78

Mid-1970s to 1990: Poverty declined significantly between the mid-1970s and the end of the 1980s with the decline being more pronounced between 1977-78 and 1986-87, with rural income poverty declining from 51% to 39%. It declined to 34% by 1989-90. Urban income poverty reduced from 41% in 1977-78 to 34% in 1986-87, and further to 33% in 1989-90.

After 1991: This post economic reform period had setbacks as well as progress. Rural income poverty increased from 34% in 1989-90 to 43% in 1992 and then fell to 37% in 199394. Urban income poverty went up from 33% in 1989-90 to 34% in 1992 and declined to 32% in 1993-94. NSS data for 1994-95 to 1998 show little or no poverty reduction, and indicate that till 1999-2000 rural poverty increased during the post reform period. The official estimate of poverty for 1999-2000 was 26%, indicating decline that led to much debate and analysis. This was attributed to the adoption of new methodology adopted by NSS leading to higher estimated mean consumption and also an estimated distribution that was more equal than in past NSS surveys.

The NSS for 2004- 2005, which is comparable to the surveys before 1999-2000 shows poverty at 28% in rural areas, 26% in urban areas and 28% for the country as a whole, using Uniform Recall Period Consumption. The corresponding figures using the Mixed Recall Period Consumption method was 21.8%, 21.7% and 21.8% respectively. These indicate poverty decline after 1998, although it is still being debated whether there was any significant poverty reduction between 1989-90 and 1999-2000. These suggest that most of the decline in rural poverty during 1993-94 to 2004-05 occurred after 1999-2000. Table 5 gives the official poverty estimates provided by NSS.

Poverty has decreased significantly since reforms were started in the 1980s. After the liberalisation process and moving away from the socialist model, India is adding 60 to 70 million people to its middle class every year. Analysis by, Marvin J. Cetron, founder of "Forecasting International" indicates that an estimated 390 million Indians belong to the middle class; one third of them have emerged from poverty in the last ten years. At the current rate of growth, a majority of Indians will be middle class by 2025. Literacy rates have risen from 52% to 65% during the initial decade of liberalisation (1991-2001).

Table 5
Official Poverty Rates–NSS

Year	*Round*	*Uniform Poverty Rate (%)*	*Mixed (%)*	*Poverty Reduction Per Year(%)*	*Mixed Reduction (%)*
1977-78	32	51.3			
1983	38	44.5			
1987-88	43	38.9		1.3	
1993-94	50	36.0		1.2	
1999-00	55		26.9	0.5	
2004-05	61	27.5	21.8	0.8	1.0

Source NSS Reports, http://www.mospi.nic.in

While total overall poverty in India has declined, the extent of poverty reduction is often debated. While there is a consensus that there has not been increase in poverty between 1993-94 and 2004-05, it is not clear if one considers other non-pecuniary dimensions (such as health, education, crime and access to infrastructure). With the rapid economic growth that India is experiencing, it is likely that a significant fraction of the rural population will continue to migrate toward cities, making the issue of urban poverty more significant in the long run.

Though absolute poverty may not have increased, India remains at a abysmal rank in the UN Human Development Index. India is positioned at 132ond place in the 2007-08 UN HDI index. It is the lowest rank for the country in over 10 years. In 1992, India was at 122ond place. The situation has become worse on critical indicators of overall well-being such as the number of people who are undernourished (India has the highest number of malnourished people, at 230 million, and is 94th of 119 in the world hunger index), and the number of malnourished children (43% of India's children under 5 are underweight (BMI<18.5), the highest in the world) as of 2008.

Nicholas Stern, Vice President of the World Bank, argues that increasing globalisation and investment opportunities have contributed significantly to the reduction of poverty in the country. A study by the McKinsey Global Institute found that in 1985, 93% of the Indian population lived on a household income of less than Rs 90,000 a year, or about a dollar per person per day; by 2005 that proportion reduced to 54%. More than 103 million people moved out of desperate poverty in the course of one generation in urban and rural areas as well. The projections indicate that if India can achieve 7.3% annual growth over the next 20 years, 465 million more people will be lifted out of poverty. Rural India has benefited from this growth as extreme rural poverty declined from 94% in 1985 to 61% in 2005, and it is expected to drop to 26% by 2025. The report concludes that *India's economic reforms and the increased growth that has resulted have been the most successful anti-poverty programmes in the country.*

Poverty and Employment

The strategy of doubling the rate of growth of agriculture is expected to reduce poverty further if a steady expansion of schemes aimed at supporting incomes and welfare of poorer sections, viz., National Rural Employment Guarantee, Bharat Nirman, National Rural Health Mission, etc. is achieved. It is evident that a greater stress is laid on agricultural growth for overall development. To provide gainful employment, the XI plan would be paying special attention to labour intensive manufacturing sectors such as food processing industry, textiles, small and medium enterprises (SMEs), tourism and construction apart from focusing on employment generating schemes that yield results in the short term

Concluding Remarks

India has made some progress in the reduction of income poverty. Yet, as many as 280 million persons are living below the poverty line. According to UNDP's Human Development Report, 2003 (UNDP, 2003), India has the largest number of poor among the countries of the world and is home for one fourth of the world's poor. A large number of hard core poor are located in remote and inaccessible areas. The problem of poverty alleviation is becoming far more difficult than in the past, since those who were near the poverty line might have crossed it, but leaving much below the line as the hardcore.

The regional differences in poverty reduction are found to be substantial. The decline in state's incidence of poverty ranged between 12-50 % points in rural areas during 1973-2000 and 20-40% points in urban areas. The inter state variations in the rural poverty reduction are attributed to the variations in their agricultural productivity improvement. Initial endowments of physical infrastructure and human resources did contribute to the inter state variations in the performance. Andhra Pradesh which had benefited from the green revolution and Kerala and West Bengal which had implemented land reforms, experienced significant decline in the rural poverty ratio. Despite that, the rural poverty level was higher in West Bengal in 1999-00 than that of All India, because of extremely high poverty level in the first phase. Assam, Bihar, Madhya Pradesh, Orissa and Uttar Pradesh have higher incidence of poverty as well as poor record in poverty reduction.

Poverty alleviation programmes should go beyond their present minimal concerns of providing safety nets. There should be a substantial investment in human resource development for enhancing people's capabilities. Along with this, there should be attempts to create more economic space for the poor by equipping them with assets and skills for livelihood outside agriculture. The poverty alleviation programmes are mainly top down ventures with dependence on the bureaucracy, though there have been some efforts towards strengthening the participation of the people through PRI and Self Help Groups (SHGs) in the planning and implementation of the programmes. Development alternatives need to be explored and concerted efforts and higher levels of public expenditures on health, education and other basic needs are urgently needed to break the poverty trap.

Broad based inclusive growth is the best solution with people centered decentralization with participatory institutional structures so that the social capital of the poor gets enlarged and make them partners in socio economic transformation of the Indian economy. Other measures needed include development of human resources of the poor and transfer of eco-friendly, cost effective technologies to rural areas are some of the pre-requisites.

References

Naresh C. Saxena and Jayanti S. Ravi Rural Poverty Reduction through Centrally Sponsored Schemes, Paper presented for discussion in the National Advisory Council, Government of India, http://www.nac.nic.in

National Commission for Enterprises in the Unorganised Sector (2007): Report on Work and Promoting Social Security Programmes, New Delhi.

Planning Commission (2006): Report of the XI Plan, Planning Commission, Govt of India, New Delhi.

Planning Commission (2007): Poverty Estimates for 2004-05 Planning Commission, Govt of India, New Delhi.

Planning Commission (2007a): Poverty Alleviation in Rural India–Strategy and Programmes, Planning Commission, Govt of India, New Delhi.

Town and Country Planning Organisation (2001): Households Availing Banking·Services in India TCPO, Ministry of Urban Affairs http://www.urbanindia.in

The Times (2007): Indian Children Suffer More Malnutrition than in Ethiopia http://www.timesonline.co.uk

UNDP (2003): Human Development Report, http://www.hdr.undp.org

World Bank (2005): New Global Poverty Estimates–What It Means for India ? http://www.worldbank.org

World Bank (2006): Inclusive Growth and Service Delivery : Building on India's Success, http://www.worldbank.org

Yesudian (2007): *Poverty Alleviation Programmes in India: A Social Audit* in Indian J Med Research 126, October 2007

8

Economic Status and In-equalities in Child Health: A Glimpse into NFHS-3 Tamil Nadu Data

M. V. Vaithilingam

Introduction

Health is one of the important and indispensable aspects of development in human society. The widely accepted definition of health given by WHO in its preamble is that it is 'a state of complete physical, mental and social well-being and not merely an absence of disease or infirmity.' In recent years, this statement has been amplified to include the ability to lead a 'socially and economically productive life.' The operational definition of health says that it is 'a condition or quality of the human organism expressing the adequate functioning of the organism in given conditions, genetic or environmental.' Maternal and child health refers to the promotive, preventive, curative and rehabilitative health care for mothers and children. It includes the sub-areas of maternal health, child health, family planning, school health, handicapped children in special settings such as day care (Park, 2002). Inequalities in socio-economic conditions of the people hamper for health and development in general. The child health is more affected due to poor economic conditions of the parents. Economic condition of an individual determines his/her health as of his/her education and employment opportunities. Good economic condition of a couple plays a significant role, more importantly, in improving and sustaining the health of their children. (concerned studies) On the same line, this study tries to examine the economic status and its relationship with child health.

Literature Review

Child health and early childhood mortality vary by various factors, especially, more of economic ones. The level of household economy has significant impact on child health. Wagstaff (2000) identified significant inequality in child mortality in his cross-country study, and opined that unequal access to financial resources as one of the major barriers impeding access to preventive as well as curative health services. Condliffe and Charles (2008) using cross-sectional data, found a positive relationship between children's health and income, with income's protective effect increasing with age. Female foeticide is one of the serious problems throughout the country affecting both rich and poor, with a recent report indicating that the worst sex ratios are found in the richest, best educated areas in India (Economist, 2010).

Malnutrition among children results anaemia mostly due to parents' poor economic condition. Anemia is defined as 'a condition in which the hemoglobin content of blood is lower than normal as a result of a deficiency of one or more essential nutrients, regardless of the cause of such deficiency (WHO, 1968). By far the most frequent cause of nutritional anaemia is iron deficiency, and less frequently folate or vitamin B12 (WHO, 1975). The incidence of anaemia is highest among women and young children, varying between 60 to 70 percent. Recent surveys indicate that in rural India, anaemia is much more widespread that hitherto believed, even among men. Iron deficiency can arise either due to inadequate intake or poor bioavailability of dietary iron or due to excessive losses of iron from the body. Women loose a considerable amount of iron especially during menstruation. Some of the other factors leading to anemia are malaria and hookwarm infestations. In addition mothers who have children born at close intervals become anaemic due to the additional demands of the rapid pregnancies and the loss of blood in each delivery. In some areas of India, it has been shown that folate deficiency anaemia affects 25-50 percent of pregnant women attending hospital clinics. Present evidence suggests that a high prevalence of folate deficiency anaemia in pregnancy is a universal phenomenon and is associated with the economically underprivileged (Layrisse, Roche, Baker, 1976).

Antenatal care (ANC) is the 'care before birth' to promote the well-being of mother and fetus, and is essential to reduce maternal mortality and morbidity, low-weight births and perinatal mortality However, the content and quality of antenatal care and the availability of effective referral and essential obstetric care are important for antenatal care to be effective. The access and utility of antenatal care is influenced by the economic condition of the families. Most of the studies in India (Bhatia and Cleland, 1995; Navaneetham and Dharmalingam, 2002; Palikadavath, Foss, and Stones, 2004; Ram and Singh, 2006) and in other developing countries (Becker, David, and Ronals, 1993; Magadi, Madise and Rodrigues, 2000; Celik and Hotchkiss, 2000) have attributed socio-economic differentials in antenatal care utilization to a combination of poor access to health services, low education level and poor demand. Some studies, however, have suggested poor quality, unfriendly treatment and less information sharing by health providers to the poor and disadvantaged women (Haddad, Fournier and Machouf, 1998; Schuler and Hossain, 1998; Barber, Bertozzi and Gerler, 2007). These studies also suggested that the perception of poor quality of care may lead to under-utilization of health services by the poor women. Rani, Bonu and Harvey (2004) found significant socio-economic differentials in the quality of care in both north and south India, but were more glaring in north India. A significantly positive relationship was observed between the quality and utilization of antenatal care in the rural areas.

Vaccination plays an important role in child health and survival. The level of immunization sometimes depends on the level household income. Koenig, et al. (2001) found that unvaccinated children from poor households in Bangladesh are over three times more likely to die than vaccinated children from better-off households and that immunization can reduce this risk to just over 1.5 times higher. Immunization is affordable and relatively easy to roll-out even in developing countries. A study in Nigeria (Gage et al., 1997) found that income of the households exerts considerable influence on child survival, particularly in the early years of life and likelihood of a child getting immunized increase with the economic status of the household. A recent work found full vaccination rates to be about four times higher in the richest quintile than the poorest, and observed similar patterns for medical treatment of acute respiratory infections. Probability of child deaths was also found to be inversely related with household wealth status (Rustein and Johnson, 2004).

Nutrition has major effect on health. The intake of children and their health are mostly influenced by the economic condition of the parents. Nutrition refers to the availability of energy and nutrients to the body's cells in relation to body requirements. Malnutrition refers to any balance in satisfying nutrition requirements. Malnutrition among children is often caused by the synergic effects of inadequate or improper food intake, repeated episodes of parasitic or other childhood diseases such as diarrhea, and improper care during illness (Pelletier, 1994; Ruzicka and Kane, 1985). Malnutrition is often cited as an important factor contributing to high morbidity and mortality among children in developing countries (Sommer and Loewenstein, 1975; Chen, et al., 1980; Vella et al., 1992; Santhanakrishnan and Ramalingam, 1987; Briend et al., 1988). Some studies (Larrea, and Kawachi, 2005; Hong, Banta and Betancourt, 2006) have identified poverty as the chief determinant of malnutrition in developing countries that perpetuates into intergenerational transfer of poor nutritional status among children and prevents social improvement and equity. Some analytical studies (Strauss and Thomas, 1998;

WHO, 1999) state that the two-way causality of poverty and under nutrition seems to pose a very significant pretext for malnutrition in India like other developing nations, where poverty and economic insecurity, coupled by constrained access to economic resources permeate malnourishment among the children. Growing evidence suggests that in India the gap in prevalence of underweight children among the rich and the poor households is increasing over the years with wide regional differentials (Pathak, 2009).

Objectives

The objectives of the study are: (1) to understand the level of child health indicators in Tamil Nadu in comparison with national averages; and (2) to examine the differentials of child health indicators by wealth index in Tamil Nadu.

Data Sources

This study uses data from National Family Health Survey (NFHS) 3 (2005-2006).[1] NFHS 3 deals with information on various socio-economic, demographic and health aspects including child health such as early childhood mortality, children suffering from acute respiratory infection (ARI), fever, diarrhea and anemia, antenatal care, vaccination coverage, breastfeeding, and nutritional status.[2] The wealth index[2] has been developed and tested in a large number of countries in relation to inequalities in household income, use of health services, and health outcomes (Rustein, et al. 2000). It is an indicator of the level of wealth that is consistent with expenditure and income measures (Rustein, 1999). The wealth index was constructed using household asset data and housing characteristics. Each household asset is assigned a weight (factor score) generated through principal component analysis, and the resulting asset scores are standardized in relation to a normal distribution with a mean of zero and standard deviation of one (Gwatkin, et al. 2000). Each household is then assigned a score for each asset, and the scores were summed for each household. Individuals are ranked according to the score of the household in which they reside. The sample is then divided into quintiles, i.e., five groups with an equal number of individuals in each. Bivariate analysis has been carried out to study the economic inequalities with selected child health indictors. The child health indicators selected for this study are: (1) early childhood mortality rates; (2) percentage of children (age <5 years) who had symptoms of acute respiratory infection (ARI); (3) percentage of children (age 6-59 months) classified as having anemia; (4) percentage of women who had live births by doctor or ANM/Midwife/Nurse who provided antenatal care during pregnancy; (5) percentage of children age 12-23 months who received specific vaccines (DPT 3 and Polio; (6) percentage of children with vaccination card seen; and (7) percentage of children under five years classified as malnourished according to three anthropometrical indices of nutritional status such as (a) stunted (weight-for-age), (b) wasted (weight-for-height), and (c) underweight (weight-for-age).

Results and Discussion

The data on various child health indicators in relation with household wealth index in Tamil Nadu are discussed under: (1) Differentials in Early Childhood Mortality across Households' Wealth Index; (2) Differentials in ARI among Children across Households' Wealth Index; (3) Differentials in Anemia among Children across Households' Wealth Index; (4) Differentials of Antenatal Care Provider (ANC) across Households' Wealth Index; (5) Differentials of Vaccination Coverage across Households' Wealth Index; and (6) Differentials of Nutritional Status among Children Households' Wealth Index.

Differentials in Early Childhood Mortality Across Households' Wealth Index

Mortality rates are good indicators to measure the level of health and health care in different countries. They also help in assessing the overall socio-economic development of a country and correlate well with certain economic variables such as gross net domestic product (GNP). Medical and social progress has substantially reduced mortality in childhood. It has become customary to consider mortality in and around infancy in a number of time periods convenient from both the analytical and programmatic point of view such as: (a) perinatal period (from 28 weeks of gestation to after 7 days of birth); (b) early neonatal period (upto 7 days after birth); (c) late neonatal period (from 7 days to 28 days after birth); (d) neonatal period (upto 28 days after birth); and (e) post-neonatal period (from 28 days to one year after birth) (Park, 2002).

The early childhood mortality rates in Tamil Nadu seem to be significantly lower than the national averages. For example, the under-five mortality rate in Tamil Nadu (45 child deaths per 1000 live births) is 29 percent points less than the national average (74 child deaths per 1000 live births) followed by infant mortality rate (20 percent points, 38 and 57 respectively), neonatal mortality rate (14 percent points, 26 and 39 respectively), child mortality (< 4 years) (11 percent points, 8 and 18 respectively), and post-neonatal mortality (8 percent points, 18 and 11 respectively). The infant and under-five mortality rates are more among households with lower wealth quintiles and less among households with higher wealth quintiles (Table 1).

Differentials in ARI among Children Across Households' Wealth Index

Infections of the respiratory tract are perhaps the most common human ailment. While they are a source of discomfort, disability and loss of time for most adults, they are a substantial cause of morbidity and mortality in young children and the elderly. Many of these infections run their natural course in older children and in adults without specific treatment and without complications. However, in young infants, small children and in the elderly, or in persons with impaired respiratory tract reserves, it increases the morbidity and mortality rates. Childhood illness in terms of percentage of children (age <5 years) who had acute respiratory infection, fever, and diarrhea by wealth index in the last two weeks preceding the survey are discussed.

Table 1

Neonatal, Post Neonatal, Infant, Child, and Under-five Mortality Rates for the 10-year Period Preceding the Survey by Wealth Index, Tamil Nadu and India, 2005-2006

Tamil Nadu/ India	*Wealth Index*	*Neonatal Mortality (NN)*	*Postneonatal Mortality* (PNN)*	*Infant Mortality* $({}_1q_0)$	*Child Mortality* $({}_4q_1)$	*Under-Five Mortality* $({}_5q_0)$
Tamil Nadu	Lowest	(31.2)	(21.9)	(53.2)	(13.3)	(65.7)
	Second	31.8	23.5	55.3	14.0	68.5
	Middle	33.6	8.3	41.9	8.2	49.8
	Fourth	15.9	4.9	20.8	1.5	22.3
	Highest	16.7	6.5	23.2	4.2	27.3
	Total	26.3	11.4	37.7	7.6	45.0
India	Total	39.0	18.0	57.0	18.4	74.3

Note: Total includes births to women belonging to other religions and births to women with missing information on caste/tribe, who are not shown separately. ( ) Based on 250-499 unweighted cases. *Computed as the difference between the infant and neonatal mortality rates. NN= Neonatal mortality- the probability of dying in the first month of life; PNN- Postneonatal mortality- the probability of dying after the first month of life but before the first birth day; ${}_1q_0$ infant mortality- the probability of dying before the first birth day; ${}_4q_1$- the probability of dying between the first and fifth birth days; and ${}_1q_0$- the probability of dying before the fifth birthday.

It was found that all these indicators seem to be less pronounced in Tamil Nadu (34% of children with symptoms of ARI, 9% of children with fever, and 5% of children with any diarrhea) compared to the national averages (6%, 15% and 9% respectively). Four percent of children under-five had symptoms of ARI (cough accompanied by short, rapid breathing which was chest-related considered a proxy for pneumonia). Nine percent of children under age five were reported to have had fever in the last two weeks preceding the survey. Five percent of children had diarrhea in the last two weeks preceding the survey. The percentage of children (age (< 5 years) who had symptoms of acute respiratory infection is more among lower wealth quintiles (8% of children with symptoms of ARI, 13% of children with fever, and 5% of children with any anemia in lowest wealth quintile) and less among higher wealth quintiles (0.8%, 8%, 5% respectively in highest wealth quintile) (Table 2).

Table 2
Percentage of Children (age <5 years) Who had Symptoms of Acute Respiratory Infection (ARI), Fever and Diarrhea in the Last Two Weeks Preceding the Survey by Wealth Index, Tamil Nadu and India, NFHS 3 (2005-2006)

Tamil Nadu/India	*Wealth Index*	*Children with Symptoms of ARI (%)*	*Children with Fever (%)*	*Children with Any Diarrhea (%)*
Tamil Nadu	Lowest	7.6	13.4	5.3
	Second	4.9	6.6	5.1
	Middle	4.7	11.2	6.5
	Fourth	1.7	6.5	4.9
	Highest	0.8	8.0	4.5
	Total	3.7	9.1	5.4
India	Total	5.8	14.9	9.0

Note: Symptoms of ARI (cough accompanied by short, rapid breathing which was chest-related) considered a proxy for pneumonia.

Differentials in Anemia among Children Across Households' Wealth Index

Anemia is one of the major health problems in India, especially, among women and children. Anemia can result in maternal mortality, weakness, diarrhea, diminished physical and mental capacity, increased morbidity from infectious diseases, perinatal mortality, premature delivery, low birth weight, and (in children) impaired cognitive performance, motor development, and scholastic achievement.

It was found that children with anemia seem to be less in Tamil Nadu (children suffering from anemia status by hemoglobin level: mild 27%, moderate 35%, severe 3% and any 64%) compared to the national averages (26%, 40%, 3% and 70% respectively). More or less, the percentage of children age 6-59 months classified by having anemia by wealth index is more for children belonging to lower wealth quintiles (23%, 39%, 2%, and 64% respectively in lowest wealth quintile) and less among higher wealth quintiles (26%, 25%, 0.2%, 52% respectively in highest wealth quintile) (Table 3).

Table 3
Percentage of Children Age 6-59 Months Classified as Having Anaemia by Feed by Wealth Index, Tamil Nadu and India, NFHS 3 (2005-2006)

Anemia Status by Hemoglobin Level

Tamil Nadu/ India	*Wealth Index*	*Mild (10.0-10.9 g/dl)*	*Moderate (7.0-9.9 g/dl)*	*Severe (<7.0 g/dl)*	*Any Anemia (<11.0 g/dl)*
Tamil Nadu	Lowest	23.4	38.9	1.9	64.2
	Second	27.2	34.5	5.7	67.4
	Middle	27.8	37.4	3.4	68.6
	Fourth	28.1	34.7	1.5	64.3
	Highest	26.2	25.3	0.2	51.7
	Total	27.1	34.6	2.6	64.2
India	Total	26.3	40.2	2.9	69.5

Note: Table is based on children who stayed in the household the night before the interview. Prevalence of anemia, based on hemoglobin levels, is adjusted for altitude using the CDC (Centres for Disease Control) formula, 1998. Recommendations to prevent and control iron deficiency in the United States, Morbidity and Mortality Weekly Report 47 (RR 3): 1-29). Hemoglobin levels are shown in grams per deciliter (g/dl). Total includes children belonging to other religions and children with missing information on mother's anemia status, who are not shown separately.

Differentials of Antenatal Care Provider (ANC) Across Households' Wealth Index

Antenatal care is the care of the woman during pregnancy. The primary aim of antenatal care is to achieve at the end of a pregnancy a healthy mother and a healthy baby. Ideally this care should begin soon after conception and continue throughout pregnancy. In some countries, notification of pregnancy is required to bring the mother in the prevention care cycle as early as possible. Ideally, the mother should attend the antenatal clinic once a month during the first 7 months; twice a month, during the next month; and thereafter once a week, if everything is normal. A high proportion of mothers in India are from lower socio-economic group and many of them are working women. Attendance at the antenatal clinic may mean loss of daily wages (VHAI, 1974). Consequently, it is difficult for them to attend the antenatal clinic so often. In this case, a minimum of 3 visits covering the entire period of pregnancy should be the target as: first visit at 20 weeks or as soon as the pregnancy is known; second visit at 32 weeks; and third visit at 36 weeks. Further visits may be made if justified by the condition of the mother. At least one visit should be paid in the home of the mother.

Table 4
Percent Distribution of Women Who Had a Live Birth in the Five Years Preceding the Survey by Antenatal Care (ANC) Provider During Pregnancy for the Most Recent Live Birth by Wealth Index, Tamil Nadu and India, 2005-2006

Tamil Nadu/ India	*Wealth Index*	*Doctor*	*ANM/ Nurse/ Midwife/ LHV*	*Anganwadi/ ICDS Worker*	*No One*	*Total*
Tamil Nadu	Lowest	74.5	22.2	0.8	2.5	100.0
	Second	72.9	21.9	2.9	2.3	100.0
	Middle	79.8	17.6	1.0	1.6	100.0
	Fourth	89.3	10.3	0.4	0.0	100.0
	Highest	95.6	3.9	0.4	0.1	100.0
	Total	83.6	14.3	1.0	1.1	100.0
India	Total	50.2	23.0	1.6	25.2	100.0

Note: If more than one source of ANC was mentioned, only the provider with the highest qualification is considered in this tabulation. Total includes women belonging to other religions, who are not shown separately. ANM= Auxiliary Nurse Midwife; LHV= Lady Health Visitor; ICDS=Integrated Child Development Services.

Table 4 presents percentage distribution of women who had a live birth in the last five years preceding the survey by antenatal care provider during pregnancy for the most recent live birth by wealth index. Almost all mothers in Tamil Nadu (99%) received at least 3 antenatal care visits for their last birth, the highest level in India. Among women who gave birth in the five years preceding the survey, almost all (98%) received ANC from a health professional (84% from a doctor and 14% from an ANM/nurse/midwife/LHV) for their last birth. As antenatal care in Tamil Nadu is almost universal, there are almost no differences in the percentage receiving antenatal care in different population groups. The percentage of women who had a live birth by ANC by doctor is 33 percentage points more than the national average. The percentage of women who had a live birth by ANC provider-doctor and NM/Nurse/Midwife/LHV is more among women belonging to the households with higher wealth quintiles (96% and 4% respectively in highest wealth quintile) and less among women belonging to the households with lower wealth quintiles (75% and 22% respectively in lowest wealth quintile).

Differentials of Vaccination Coverage Across Households' Wealth Index

The vaccination of children against six serious but preventable diseases (tuberculosis, diphtheria, pertussis, poliomyelitis and measles) has been an important intervention in the Child Survival and Safe Motherhood Programme of the Government of India (Government of India, 1994). For immunizing infants, the preparation of choice is DPT. Firstly, because the infant can be immunized simultaneously against three diseases, viz., Diphtheria, Pertussis and Tetanus which is a great gain administratively. Secondly the Pertussis component in DPT vaccine enhances the potency of the Diphtheria Toxoid. There are two types of DPT vaccine- plain and absorbed. Absorption is usually carried out on a mineral carrier like aluminum phosphate or hydroxide. Studies have shown that absorption increases the effectiveness of the vaccine. The contents per dose vary according to the manufacturer. The plain (DPT) vaccine can be used as a booster.

The full vaccination coverage in the state is almost twice (81%) the national average (44%), the highest among all the states in India. All the children have received at least some vaccinations. Almost all children have received a BCG vaccination (99.5%). Ninety-six percent of children have received the recommended three doses of DPT and 88 % have received at least the recommended 3 doses of polio vaccine. Ninety-three percent of children have been vaccinated against measles. Percentage of children age 12-23 months who received DPT 3, Polio 3 and percentage of children with a vaccination card seen are less among children belonging to households with lower wealth quintiles and more among children belonging to households with higher wealth quintiles (Table 5).

Differentials of Nutritional Status Among Children Households' Wealth Index

The calculation of the three indices of child malnutrition involves comparison with an international reference population as recommended by the World Health Organization (Dibley et al., 1987). The justification for use of a reference population is the empirical finding that well-nourished children in all populations follow very similar growth patterns (Habicht et al., 1974). The Nutrition Foundation of India (NFI) has concluded that the WHO standard is applicable to Indian children (Agarwal et al., 1991).Malnutrition is an underlying cause of many child deaths and plays an important role in children's life chances. About 17% (DHS, 2005-2006) of children below five years suffer from acute malnutrition in India. The problem is very alarming in households belonging to the lowest wealth quintile where 21% of under-five children (12% in the richest households, are stunted, which has long-term consequences for children's physical and mental development.

Table 6 presents percentage of children under five years classified as malnourished according to three anthropometrical indices of nutritional status: stunted (height for age), wasted (weight for height) and underweight (weight for age) by wealth index in Tamil Nadu. Almost one-third (31%) of children under age five in Tamil Nadu are stunted (low height for age), or too short for their age, which indicates that they have been undernourished for some time. Twenty-two percent are wasted (low weight for height), and underweight (low weight for age), or too thin for their height, which may result from inadequate recent food intake or a recent illness. Thirty percent are underweight, which takes into account both chronic and acute under nutrition. All the three measures of children's malnourishment seem to be significantly low in Tamil Nadu than the national averages (48%, 20%, and 43% respectively). These measures are negatively associated with wealth quintiles.

Table 5

Percentage of Children Age 12-23 Months Who Received Specific Vaccines at Any Time Before the Survey (According to a Vaccination Card or the Mother's Report), and Percentage with Vaccination Card Seen by the Interviewer by Wealth Index, Tamil Nadu and India, NFHS 3 (2005-2006)

Tamil Nadu/ India	Wealth Index	BCG	DPT 1	DPT 2	DPT 3	Polio* 0	Polio* 1	Polio* 2	Polio* 3	Measles	All Basic Vaccinations**	Children with a Vaccination Card Seen
Tamil Nadu	Lowest	*	*	*	*	*	*	*	*	*	*	*
	Second	(97.5)	(92.9)	(92.9)	(92.9)	(89.7)	(97.5)	(97.5)	(85.1)	(90.4)	(75.5)	(32.9)
	Middle	100.0	100.0	98.7	94.8	97.5	100.0	97.6	87.9	91.6	81.4	32.8
	Fourth	99.5	100.0	98.0	94.6	93.6	99.9	95.8	90.9	95.4	85.4	39.6
	Highest	100.0	100.0	98.8	98.8	96.4	100.0	92.2	90.2	90.4	80.0	56.9
	Total	99.5	98.9	97.7	95.7	94.5	99.6	96.3	87.8	92.5	80.9	36.9
India	Total	78.1	76.0	66.7	55.3	48.4	93.1	88.8	78.2	58.8	43.5	37.5

* Polio 0 is the polio vaccine given at birth. ** BCG, measles, and three doses each of SPT and polio vaccine (excluding polio vaccine given at birth). ( ) Based on 25-49 unweighted cases.

Table 6

Percentage of Children Under Age Five Years Classified as Malnourished According to Three Anthropometric Indices of Nutritional Status: Height-for-Age, Weight-for-Height, and Weight-for-Age by Wealth Index, Tamil Nadu and India, NFHS 3 (2005-2006)

		Underweight (Height-for-age)			*Wasted (Weight-for-height)*				*Stunted (Weight-for-age)*			
Tamil Nadu/ India	*Wealth Index*	*Below-3 SD(%)*	*Below-2 SD(%)*	*Z Score (SD) (Mean)*	*Below-3 SD (%)*	*Below-2 SD (%)*	*Below + SD (%)*	*Z Score (SD) (Mean)*	*Below-3 SD (%)*	*Below-2 SD (%)*	*Below + SD (%)*	*Z Score (SD) (Mean)*
Tamil Nadu	Lowest	15.3	40.1	-1.3	11.0	27.7	0.7	-1.3	9.5	43.1	2.7	-1.6
	Second	15.8	37.7	-1.3	12.0	31.4	6.4	-1.1	11.9	38.0	2.1	-1.5
	Middle	13.7	35.4	-1.2	10.7	22.0	3.0	-1.1	7.1	34.1	1.7	-1.5
	Fourth	8.8	28.3	-1.0	7.2	20.4	3.8	-1.0	3.5	26.7	1.7	-1.2
	Highest	1.1	13.2	-0.5	3.6	13.4	4.1	-0.6	2.6	9.2	2.1	-0.7
	Total	10.9	30.9	-1.1	8.9	22.2	3.6	-1.0	6.4	29.8	1.9	-1.3
India	Total	23.7	48.0	-1.9	6.4	19.8	1.5	-1.0	15.8	42.5	0.4	-1.8

Note: Table is based on children who stayed in the household the night before the interview. Each of the indices is expressed in standard deviation units (SD) from the median of the 2006 WHO International Reference Population. Table is based on children with valid dates of birth (month and year) and valid measurements of both height and weight. Total includes children belonging to other religions and children with missing information on size at birth, who are not shown separately.

Conclusions

Most of the child health indicators in the state seem to be desirably good for higher wealth index categories and significantly higher than the national averages. Among various child health indicators, infant and under-five mortality, acute respiratory infection, prevalence of anemia, and percentage of children who are underweight, wasted and stunted are found to be negatively associated with wealth quintiles; and antenatal care by doctor and ANM/Nurse/Mid-wife/Local health visitor, vaccination coverage (DPT 3 and Polio 3), and children with vaccination card seen are found to be positively associated with wealth quintiles. The government and non-government organizations which are specific to child health need to strive for employment generation among families with low levels of income. As most of the child health indicators are desirably good with families of higher level income, there is possibility of improving and sustaining child health indicators.

References

Agarwal, K.N. and Agarwal, D.K., Benakappa, D.G., Gupta, S.M., Khanduja, P.C., Khatua, S.P., Ramachandran, K., Udani, P.M., and Gopalan, C. (1991): *Growth Performance of Affluent Indian Children (under-fives): Growth Standard for Indian Children*. New Delhi : Nutrition Foundation of India.

Barber, S.L., Bertozzi, S.M., and Gerler, P. (2007): Variation in Prenatal Care Quality for the Rural Poor in Mexico. *Health Afford* 26: 310-323.

Becker, S., David, H.P., Ronald, H.G. (1993): Determinants of Use of Maternal and Child Health Servires in Metro Cebu. *Philippines Health Transition Review* 3: 77-89.

Bhatia, J.C. and Cleland, J. (1995): Determinants of Maternal Care in a Region of South India. *Health Transition Review* 5: 127-142..

Briend, A., Wojtyniag, B., and Rowland, M.G.M. (1988): *Breastfeeding, Nutritional Status, and Child Survival in Rural Bangladesh. British Medical Journal* 296 (6626) : 879-82.

Celik, Y. and Hotchkiss, D.R. (2000): Socio-economic Determinants of Maternal Health Care Utilisation in Turkey. *Social Science Medicine* 50: 1797-1806.

Chen, L.C., Chowdhury, K.M.A., and Huffman, S.L. (1980): Anthropometric Assessment of Energy-Protein Malnutrition and Subsequent Riks of Mortality Among Pre-school-aged Children. *American Journal of Clinical Nutrition* 33 (8) : 1836-45.

Condliffe, Simon, and Charles R. Link (2008): Relationship Between Economic Status and Child Health: Evidence from the United States. *American Economic Review* 98 (4): 1605-1618.

Demographic and Health Surveys (2005-2006): Bangladesh and India DHS Survey Data. Measure DHS Online (retrieved from *http://www.statcompiler.com*)

Dibley, M.J., Staehling, N.W., and Trowbridge, F.L. (1987): Interpretation of z-Score Anthropometric Indicators Derived from the International Growth Reference. *American Journal of Clinical Nutrition* 46 (5) : 749-62.

Economist (2010), *Gendercide* (Opinion Piece), 6 March.

Gage, A. J., Sommerfelt, A. E., Piani, A. L. (1997), Household Structure and Childhood Immunization in Nizer and Nizeria, *Demography* 34: 295-309.

Government of India (1994): *National Child Survival and Safe Motherhood Programme*. New Delhi: Maternal and Child Health Division, Department of Family Welfare, Ministry of health and Family Welfare.

Habicht, J.P., Martorell, R.,Yarbrough, C., Malina, R.M., Klein, R.E. (1974): Height and Weight Standard for Pre-school Children: How Relevant Are Ethinc Differences in Growth Potential? *Lancet* 1 (7858): 611-4.

Haddad, S., Fournier, P. and Machouf, N. (1998): What does Quality of Care Mean to lay People? Community Perceptions of Primary Health Care Services in Guinea. *Social Science Medicine* 47: 381-381.

International Institute for Population Sciences (IIPS), (2007): *National Family Health Survey (NFHS-3), 2005-2006, India*. Mumbai: IIPS.

International Institute for Population Sciences (IIPS), (2008): *National Family Health Survey (NFHS-3) 2005-2006, Tamil Nadu*. Mumbai: IIPS.

Gwatkin, D.R., Rustein, S., Johnson, K., Pande, R.P., and Wagstaff, A. (2000): *Socio-economic Differences in Health, Nutrition and*

Poverty (HNP/Poverty Thematic Group of the World Bank). Washington, D.C.: The World Bank.

Larrea, C. and Kawachi, I. (2005): Does Economic Inequality Affect Child Malnutrition? The Case of Equador. *Social Science and Medicine* 60 (1): 165-178.

Hong, R., Banta, J.E., Betancourt, J.A. (2006): Relationship Between Household Wealth Inequality and Chronic Childhood Under-nutrition in Bangladesh. *International Journal for Equity in Health* 5: 15.

Layrisse, M., Roche, M., and Baker, S.J. (1976): Nutritional Anemias. In: *Nutrition in Preventive Medicine (WHO Monograph No. 62).* WHO: Geneva.

Magadi, M.A., Madise, N.J., and Rodrigues, R.N. (2000): Frequency and Timing of Antenatal Care in Kenya: Explaining the Variations Between Women of Different Coimmunities. *Social Science Medicine* 51: 551-561.

Ministry of Health and Family Welfare (MoHFW) 2005, *Annual Report 2004-2005.* New Delhi: MoHFW.

National Institute of Nutrition (NIN) (1989), *Nutrition.* Hyderabad: NIN.

Navaneetham, K and Dharmalingam, D. (2002): Utilisation of Maternal and Health Services in Southern India. *Social Science Medicine* 55: 1849-1869.

Pallikadavath, S., Foss, M., and Stones, R.W. (2004): Antenatal Care provision and Inequality in North India. *Social Science Medicine* 59: 1147-1158.

Park, K. (2002): *Park's Textbook of Preventive and Social Medicine.* Jabalpur: Banarsidas Bhanot.

Pathak, K.P. (2009): *Socio-economic Inequality in Malnutrition in India, 1992-2005.* Paper presented at the Annual Meeting of the Population Association of America (PAA) at Detroit, Michigan, USA, 29 April- 2 May.

Pelletier, D.L. (1994): Relationship Between Child Anthropometry and Mortality in Developing Countries : Implications for Policy, Programmes and Future Research. *Journal of Nutrition Supplement* 124 (10S) : 2047S-2081S.

Ram, F and Singh, A. (2006): Is Antenatal Care Effective in Improving in Maternal Health in Rural Uttar Pradesh? Evidence from A

District-Level Household Survey. *Journal of Bio-social Science* 38: 433-448.

Rani, Manju, Bonu, Sekhar and Harvey, Steve (2004): Differentials in the Quality of Antenatal Care in India. *International Journal for Quality in Health Care* 20 (1) : 62-71.

Rustein, S. (1999): *Wealth Versus Expenditure: Comparison Between the DHS Wealth Index and Household Expenditures in Four Departments of Guatemala.* Calverton, Maryland: ORC Macro.

Rustein, S., Johnson, K., and Gwatkin, D. (2000): "Poverty, Health Inequality, and Its Health and Demographic Effects", Paper presented at the 2000 Annual Meeting of the Population Association of America, Los Angeles, California.

Rustein, Shea O. and Johnson, K. (2004): DHS Wealth Index. *DHS Comparative Rports 6.* USA: ORC Macro Maryland.

Ruzicka, L.T., and Kane, P. (1985): *Nutrition and Child Survival in South Asia.* In Srinivasan, K. and Mukerji, S., eds. Dynamics of Population and Family Welfare. Mumbai: Himalaya Publishig House.

Santhanakrishnan, B.R., and Ramalingam, R. (1987): Risk Factors of Mortality in Children with Diarrhoeal Disease in Madras, India. *Journal of Diarrhoeal Disease Research* 5 (1): 36-39.

Schuler, S.R., and Hossain, Z. (1998): Family Planning Clinics Through Women's eyes and Voices: A Case Study from Rural Bangladesh. *International Family Planning Perspectives* 24: 170-175.

Somner, A. and Loewenstein, M.S. (1975): Nutritional Status and Mortality: A Prospective Validation of the QUAC Stic. *American Journal of Clinical Nutrition* 28 (3): 287-292.

Vella, V., A. Tomkins, Borghesi, A., Migliori, G.B., B.C. Adriko, and E. Crevatin (1992): Determinants of Child Nutrition and Mortality in North-West Uganda. *Bulletin of the World health Organization* 70 (5): 637-643.

Voluntary Health Association of India (VHAI) (1974): *Health Care of Children Under Five.* New Delhi: VHAI.

Wagstaff, A. (2000): Poverty and Health Care Inequalities, *Bulletin of the World health Organisation 80 (2).*

World Health Organisation (WHO) (1968): *Nutritional Anemias: Report of A WHO Scientific Group.* (Technical Report Series Number 405). WHO: Geneva.

World Health Organisation (WHO) (1975): *Control of Nutritional Anema with With Special Reference to Iron Deficiency: Report of A WHO Scientific Group*. (Technical Report Series Number 580). WHO: Geneva.

Footnotes

1. The earlier two rounds of NFHS were during 1992-1993 and 1998-1999. These surveys were conducted under the guidance and support of the Ministry of health and Family Welfare, Government of India. The International Institute for Population Sciences (IIPS) was designated as the nodal agency for the surveys. The United States Agency for International Development (USAID), United Kingdom Department for International Development (DFID), the Bill and Melindia Gates Foundation, UNICEF, UNFPA, and the Government of India provided funding for these surveys. The Macro International, Maryland, USA provided technical assistance for these surveys. The National AIDS Control Organization (NACO) and the National AIDS Research Institute (NARI), Pune extended assistance for the HIV component of the surveys.
2. The wealth index in NFHS 3 is based on 33 assets and housing characteristics: (1) Household electrification; (2) Type of windows; (3) Drinking water source; (4) Type of toilet facility; (5) Type of flooring; (6) Material of exterior walls; (7) Type of roofing; (8) Cooking fuel; (9) House ownership; (10) Number of household members per sleeping room; (11) Ownership of a bank or post-office account; (12) Ownership of a mattress; (13) Ownership of a pressure cooker; (14) Ownership of a chair; (15) Ownership of a cot/bed; (16) Ownership of a table; (17) Ownership of an electric fan; (18) Ownership of a radio/transistor; (19) Ownership of a black and white television; (20) Ownership of a colour television; (21) Ownership of a sewing machine; (22) Ownership of a mobile telephone; (23) Ownership of any other telephone; (24) Ownership of a computer; (25) Ownership of a refrigerator; (26) Ownership of a watch or clock; (27) Ownership of a bicycle; (28) Ownership of a motorcycle or scooter; (29) Ownership of an animal-drawn cart; (30) Ownership of a car; (31) Ownership of a water pump; (32) Ownership of a thresher; and (33) Ownership of a tractor.

9

Depletion of Resources and It's Impact on Food, Nutrition and Health: An Anthropological Observation

Samar Kumar Biswas and Somenath Bhattacharjee

Introduction

The term ecology was first defined by Ernst Haeckel in 1866 as "the science of relations between organisms and their environment" (Bramwell, 1989:.40). Human societies have an ongoing contact with and impact on the land, climate, plant and animal species in their vicinities and these elements of their environment have reciprocal impacts on them. The environment of human beings lies in their surroundings of land, air, water, forest and the substratum beneath the Earth's surface. These components of natural environment provide the fundamental resources to human beings for their survival. The well adaptable and well suitable environment is the prime source for the fulfillment of all of their basic needs. These mostly depend on the nature in a diversified manner and their way of accumulation reflects the culture of the human being. Ultimately the economic, social, political, religious entities of human being are closely related with natural resources and it is the habitation of human being in complete sense.

Among the total population of India, 8.20 percent are the tribal people (Census, 2001) and they have their own means of livelihood and traditional and cultural practices. They are dwelling in the high hills, isolated forest covered region and they are far from regular conveniences of communications and urban attractions. Their entire livelihood is very much dependant on the forest based natural products. The people collect their food from the environment and they primarily consume fruits, roots and tubers from the locally available plants. There are a number of water resources which provide them fish and other aquatic animals as a source of animal protein. Meanwhile, being closely associated with forest and environment, the people are very much dependant on the natural products for their clothing. For this purpose they collect the raw materials from their surroundings and weave it by their own hands. They collect the fuel from their surroundings. Further, they collect wood, bamboo and other raw materials from the forests to build the houses. The religious aspects deserve a special attention in the livelihood of the human society. The people of the tribal societies are primarily animists. Being closely associated with the nature, they have a number of deities related with their forest and environment. Apart from nature as a whole the people of simple societies have also cognated themselves with the animals and plants in the form of totem (Vidyarthi, 1977:236-244). They believe to be the descendants of the totemic plants and animals and forbid to kill them or to harm them in any sort. In the simple societies, all of the community members have an equal access over the natural products, land and resources. Among them the struggle and competition regarding the survival is almost absent. Thus, the society, environment and culture altogether form an interwoven network in the tribal societies which secures their livelihood.

Inter-relationship between Environment and Health

Every culture, irrespective of its simplicity and complexity has its own beliefs and practices concerning diseases. It is to be mentioned here that the disease and treatment particularly in the simple societies cannot be properly understood in isolation. Health and treatment are very much connected with the environment, particularly the forest ecology. The study of health problems deserves a special attention in the situation of rural poverty and particularly that of tribals. It is primarily due to the fact that the tribal communities are backward, living in isolated or remote areas where modern health facilities are not available. Naturally, the health situation of these communities would deserve a special attention both to understand the problem and to find out the solution (Chaudhuri, 2003:17-18). It may be pointed out that health, disease and treatment particularly in tribal societies cannot be properly understood in isolation. Health and treatment are very much connected with the environment, particularly the forest ecology. The health care system and traditional treatment are based on their deep observation and understanding of nature and environment (Chaudhuri, 2003:22-23). The tribals and other indigenous people use a number of plants and animal resources for different types of diseases and in this regard they have their indigenous knowledge which is carried out from generation after generation. Forest is the main source for them to collect the medicinal plants.

But today due to the pressure of several global forces, the tribal land, forest and natural resources particularly the medicinal plants are getting alienated in a diversified manner at a very faster rate. The depletion of natural resources is telling upon their fundamental human rights of food and nutritional security as well as traditional health care practices. These issues have been observed on a primitive tribal group and on a section of numerically dominant scheduled caste (previously the tribal Koch) group of North Bengal. The primary data were collected through intensive field work and case studies were taken on the disease affected people.

Resource Depletion and Its Effect on Health

Health Situation of the Totos

According to the Ministry of Tribal Affairs, Government of India, there are 75 Primitive Tribal Groups in 17 states and 1 union territory in India with a population of approximately 25 lakh (Census, 2001). At present in West Bengal there are three Primitive Tribal Groups and the Toto is one of them. Presently the Totos live in a small hill area at the foothills of the Himalayas just to the south of the border line between Bhutan and West Bengal, named as "Toto Para" village under Madarihat police station of Jalpaiguri district in West Bengal. They are living in this area since the middle of the 18th century. The whole area of the mouza comprising of about 3.12 square miles was recorded in the name of *Toto Mondal* or chief on behalf of the whole community during the first settlement operation conducted by Sunders in 1889-1894. During the field study in 2006, there were total 270 families with a population of 1300 including 685 male and 615 female. In Toto Para they resided in six different hamlets namely- *Dhumchi Gaon, Puja Gaon, Mitrang Gaon, Subba Gaon, Mandal Gaon and Panchayat Gaon* (Biswas and Bhattacharjee, 2008: 200-218).

The foremost characteristic regarding the economic perspective of Totos was, its close affinity with the environment. Forest was the main source for their sustenance and generation of cash income. Their forest based economy was mainly dependant on hunting, food gathering, collection of minor forest produce, collection of fuel, pastoralism, collection of fodder and construction materials etc. Earlier the Totos were primarily dependant on forest collection and Jhum cultivation. But during the study it was revealed that they were primarily dependant on plough cultivation by using simple technological devices. Generally they did not sell their crop; they produced it for their own consumption. However, they were unable to produce the seasonal food crops to large extent which could meet their demands. In this regard, they mostly had to depend on forest to collect jungle fruits, roots, tubers, leaves, mushrooms etc. to meet their seasonal shortage of food stuff. Previously a number of small streamlines went through the Toto Para region. The people collected different types of fishes and snails from those and it was their prime source of animal protein without any financial expenditure.

Earlier a huge area of this land with laterite soil was under orange plantation and orange was their prime cash earner. With these oranges they used to do *Angdaita* or trade tour to Bhutan. In old days they used to cultivate lac worm in the demarcated *Sirish* trees of the forest. Previously the Toto Para was with good quality of bamboo bushes in its adjacent forest areas. They used to construct their huts and houses from bamboo, bushes, wood, grass, leaves etc. available from forest. Moreover by selling the bamboos they could purchase their daily means of livelihood. In this regard the livelihood of the Totos was very much dependant on forest. However, the continuous influx of the outsiders and the rapid environmental degradation affected the livelihood of the Totos.

The rapid population explosion had forced the people to migrate from one place to another in search of basic amenities for livelihood. This had affected a lot to the tribal groups and the Totos of Toto Para were not an exception. For the fulfillment of basic needs, people from both nearer and distant provinces gradually came here and started to live permanently. According to the official estimate in 2003, among the total families of Toto Para, 74 percent families belonged to the Non Toto community (Biswas and Bhattacharjee, 2008: 252-271). In earlier, total 1996.76 acres of land was recorded in the name of Toto Mondal or chief on behalf of the whole community. But in 1969 a greater portion of land was recorded as vested due to unknown reason and during the study the Totos had only 343 acres of land. So, the Totos became both landless and resourceless within their own territory. Meanwhile, officially the forest in India covers an area of 7, 43,584 sq.km. Between 1951 to 1980 India had lost 4.3 million hectars of forestland which means 1, 40,000 hectars annually and it was converted to non forest uses (De, 2005:83). The total area of West Bengal is 88,752 sq. km. At present in West Bengal the forest are is only 13.38 percent and in North Bengal it is 14.13 percent. The Totos are residing in the Jalpaiguri district which covers 28.75 percent forest of its entire territory and this area also came under the effect of deforestation.

There is no doubt that with the decrease of forest area it became extremely difficult for the Totos to collect their daily necessities. In the past the low altitude region of the hillocks was covered with dense forest. A huge area of this land with laterite soil was under orange plantation upto 1930's. But afterwards there took place rapid deforestation for settled agriculture and in this regard the orchards were unable to tolerate the sunlight directly. Again due to deforestation, the humus formation which was good for the growth of orange orchards got affected seriously. Most probably it was the major cause for drop in orange orchards. Earlier, the Totos used to cultivate lac-worm and the *Pipuls* in the demarcated Sirish trees. But due to rapid deforestation, it went into abundance and the lac industry is now forgotten by them. Earlier there was a great importance of the bamboos in the socio-economic life of the Totos. But due to rapid commercialization, the Non Toto bamboo traders rapidly started to cut down the bamboo bushes for direct monetary exchange and as a result there was not a single bamboo bush in the village during the study. It had worsely affected to their household construction. Due to continuous deforestation the traditional economic pursuits of the Totos were almost on the way of abolishment and it had forced the people in the grief passage of poverty. They had to face all sorts of inconveniences to manage their common minimum livelihood and in this regard most of the concerned families had to go outside from their territory.

During the study it was revealed that more than 57 percent of the Toto families had to depend on Bhutan for their common minimum livelihood. But inspite of their hard work, 86 percent of their families could not earn more than Rs. 2000/- per month. Ultimately to manage the basic amenities they were getting enmeshed in the web of indebtedness. Their poverty forced them to take the loans or advances *(Dadan)* from *Mahajans* (money lenders). The concerned money lenders give them money under various terms and conditions which are commonly known as the *Thika* system. The Totos were unable to understand the clever motive of the Mahajans and ultimately they had to lose their personal belongings.

With the gradual increase of indebtedness as well as poverty, massive deforestation and alienation of both grazing and agricultural land, their crop production, animal husbandry and forest collection were severely affected. The adequate nutritional requirement was being seriously hampered and the scarcity of resources led to food crisis. The outsiders gradually started to settle down in different areas of the Toto Para village and it seriously hampered the natural flows of the streams. The entire situation had ultimately resulted in change from the abundance of fishes and snails to scarcity of the same.

Due to rapid decrease of the grazing land, the scope of animal husbandry became difficult to manage. The milk and other edible products were a good source of animal protein for the Totos. But with the continuous decrease of domestication their need of food and nutrition were unable to meet up with the requirements. On the other hand their acute economic scarcity hindered them to purchase the market based food products. It is to be mentioned here that the Totos depended on different cereals during different parts of the year. It could hardly cover up seven to eight months of the year and for the remaining period they had to supplement their diet by roots and tubers collected from the jungle. But the scarcity of natural resources had prevented this oppurtunity and often they had to face the crisis of food. The overall situation created an acute crisis of nutrition among the people. Even they could not afford nutritious diet to their pregnant women. As a result, there was a high risk that the malnourished mother may give birth to malnourished child. Further, in the Toto society the ailment related with the various diseases were deeply associated with the forest ecology. They had an intimate knowledge about the local environment and its various floras which had medicinal importance for them.

Earlier they were totally dependant on folk medicine and the medicinal plants were collected from forest. These people had a deep psychological faith on their traditional healers.

But due to massive deforestation and environmental degradation these resources gradually became scarce. As a result the traditional healers had to face all sorts of inconveniences to collect various herbal plants and other medicinal resources. Moreover infrequent communication from the nearest urban center and severe economic scarcity had prevented them to avail the western medical treatment. Ultimately they had a very little oppurtunity of treatment and various diseases like malaria, anemia, dysentery, pneumonia, gastric, skin diseases and tuberculosis could be noticed among the studied people. The environmental degradation and its adverse impact on their food and nutritional resources had made them vulnerable to a number of diseases. Moreover unavailability of the local medicinal resources was leading to illness and diseases.

Health Situation of Stone Crushers of Balasan Colony

The study area North Bengal is located in the Northern region of West Bengal. The entire region is famous for its diversified landscape and rich ethnic diversity. Among the different ethnic groups of North Bengal, the Rajbanshis are one of the early settlers and numerically dominant Scheduled Caste group of this region. Previously they were the tribal Koch but gradually through Brahmanism they got the status of caste population (Doshi and Jain, 1999). It is to be mentioned here that their early settlements were both in North Bengal and Bangladesh. They were entirely rural people and settled agriculture was their prime economic pursuit. Their only property was the cultivable land. They had a very close affinity with the surrounding nature.

These people were totally dependant on environmental resources to fulfill their requirements of common minimum livelihood. From the surrounding forests, they could collect their fuel and the raw materials related with their household constructions. They produced the crops mostly for their own consumption. On the other hand, they had the oppurtunity to cultivate different types of vegetables in their kitchen garden which would provide them the subsidiary item along with the prime staple food. In the villages they had a number of ponds and adjacent rivers and form these water bodies, they could easily catch the fish for their consumption. Meanwhile along with the agricultural land there were plentiful of grazing land and abundant source of animal fodder. It provided them ample oppurtunity for domestication. With the milk and other products of the domesticated animals they could easily fulfill their requirement of animal protein in their diet. From the surrounding environment they collected a number of medicinal plants for their ailment from various diseases. Thus the natural resources were the prime sources to fulfill their daily essentialities. Though they were not economically wealthy, they never faced any scarcity to persist the common minimum livelihood. But the entire scenario got changed after 1971.

In this period there was a severe political unrest and communal violence in Bangladesh. Being numerically minor the concerned people were forced to get displaced from their land and they had to leave their stable economic pursuit. They became almost roofless and resourceless as they migrated to different districts of North Bengal in the Indo Bangladesh border. A huge section of them got settled in the adjacent areas of Siliguri town and in the contemporary period it was emerging out as the largest urban center of North Bengal. The Balasan River was in close vicinity from this town. The said river in its flow from the high hill regions carried huge amount of natural resources like stones, boulders and sand. These resources served as the essential raw materials for the construction works. The studied people who were in desperate need for any means of survival and resettlement, readily took this opportunity and they started to collect and break up the stones and boulders according to the requisite shape and sizes required for the urban constructions. In this regard they got involved in a new occupational pursuit i.e. the stone based occupation. Moreover the vested land of Balasan river bed provided them a scope of resettlement by their own local adjustment and local political influence. In this way the studied settlement of Balasan Colony was established. But during the study it was noticed that they were undocumented and they had no administrative authorization of their settlement. This study was carried out among 200 families who were dependant on stone crushing occupation either primarily or secondarily (Biswas and Bhattacharjee, 2008:217-230). The said occupation was totally free from any kind of age and gender biasness because all the family members here worked together. It required only had manual labour and it was proportionately related with their income. It had forced the people to work in any climatic condition throughout the entire day.

Even most of the families gave their prior emphasis to the labour work inspite of the household particulars. Moreover in most of the families the children also had to work to meet up with the daily requirements. Thus the entire family had to work as a production unit. But inspite of their hard manual labour for ten to twelve hours in a day they had low income. Most of the families had an earning of only Rs. 2000/- per month and with this low income it became quite disproportionate for them to fulfill the common minimum livelihood in terms of food, shelter etc. of their 5 membered families. After their resettlement in a new environmental background they had no scope to pursue their traditional agricultural occupation. On the other hand, the land of this area was totally filled up with stone and sand which had restricted their scope of kitchen gardening. As a result they had no oppurtunity to accumulate their food resources from the environment as it was earlier. Moreover the concerned people had no scope to catch fishes from the Balasan river. Further, with the unavailability of agricultural land the grazing land also became scarce and it had reduced the scope of domestication for them. Ultimately the studied people were debarred to manage any sort of animal protein in their daily diet. They had to depend on the expensive market based products for their food. But with the low levels of income they became hardly capable to accumulate rice, pulses and one item of vegetables as their diet twice in a day. Consumption of expensive market based animal protein was a mere dream to them. With this quite less nutritive food they had to do hard manual labour throughout the entire day. It is to be mentioned here that scarcity of resources had hindered the studied families to provide nutritive food to their pregnant women. Moreover, the pregnant women also had to get involved with the stone crushing work to accumulate a fold of rice.

As a result, the hard manual labour during the pregnancy period and provision of less nutritive food might have resulted the fact that the concerned women were quite malnourished and often they had given birth to malnourished children (Biswas and Bhattacharjee, 2007: 182-202). Moreover lack of purified drinking water, lack of scientific sanitation and poor household construction were an added criterion to their poverty. Their hard manual labour, malnutrition and lack of proper livelihood infrastructure had made them vulnerable to a number of diseases like diarrhoea, anemia, dysentery, tuberculosis, frequent fever with cold and cough, menstrual cycle related problems etc. In their traditional society they had a deep psychological faith on their traditional medicine man and magico-religious healers. But now their traditional healers had to face all sorts of inconveniences to provide their treatment because they had a very little oppurtunity to collect the required medicinal plants from their surroundings. Often they had to go to a long distance to collect those and in view of this they demanded high fees. But the poor people were unable to fulfill their demand and in a number of cases they were unable to get the medication from their traditional healers. On the other hand, economic scarcity had hindered them to avail the western medicinal treatment. Ultimately they mostly sought the medical treatment from the local quacks for a quick recovery. They had no scope to redress their poor health condition, due to their inability to avail proper clinical diagnosis for the financial constraints as well as lack of convenient environment related with their livelihood. Ultimately the scarcity of environmental resources had forced the studied people to face a serious challenge related with the food, nutrition and health situation in a complete sense.

General Observation

Environment is deeply interrelated with the livelihood of the human being. It is the prime source for them to accumulate the raw materials related with daily requirements. They had a deep association with the nature and they utilized the natural resources proportionately to their requirements. They had a strong faith that the surrounding environment was their prime source of survival. The geographical isolation had been helpful for the people to execute their own social and cultural heritages in the lap of nature. The natural resources were helpful for them to redress their hunger; although they were not economically rich but the fruits, roots, tubers whatever they collected from the forest could easily meet up with their requirements.

However, due to the pressure of several global forces, their territorial isolation and own means of livelihood had to face a number of inconveniences. In the case of the Totos, the outsiders came and gradually got started to settle down on their land. Moreover, they indiscriminately started to use the natural resources for their own vested interest. As a result, the indigenous people were completely debarred from the rights over their land and resources. The scarcity of natural resources had seriously violated their fundamental human rights over the food and nutrition. It is because of the fact that the environment was the prime source for the Totos to collect their food. But its gradual destruction had limited their oppurtunity over its access. On the other hand their economic scarcity had hindered them to purchase expensive market based products.

Further, the environmental resources were the prime raw materials for them to build up the shelters. But its gradual destruction had seriously violated over their fundamental rights of properly constructed shelter. Scarcity of food might have told upon their nutrition and it probably had made them vulnerable to a number of diseases. Meanwhile, the concerned people were depended on a number of medicinal plants around their surroundings for their ailment. But the rapid environmental degradation had seized this oppurtunity from them. On the other hand, they had no adequate scope to avail the western medicinal treatment. In this way the environmental degradation and scarcity of natural resources had violated their rights to health. Further, among the stone crushers of Balasan colony, it was noticed that they had their own settlement and stable economic pursuit of settled agriculture. They had a close affinity with the nature and their daily livelihood was deeply interwoven with the natural resources. But due to severe political turmoil they were forced to get migrated and their interaction with the nature had been broken up. They were exposed in a new and distinct ecological set up. In a new environmental condition they had no oppurtunity to avail their food resources from the surroundings. Even they had no authority over their settlement because they were mostly undocumented. Thus lack of adequate authorization had debarred them from the fundamental rights of their shelter. Again, due to scarcity of natural resources their food and nutrition became depended on market based products. But their economic fragile had hindered them to fulfill the adequate requirements. As a result the shift over of environmental circumference and almost complete absence of floral and faunal resources had violated their fundamental rights of food and nutrition. To conduct the hard manual labour they were in a need of food and nutrition but they had no scope for it. It had made them vulnerable to a number of diseases. Meanwhile the scarcity of medicinal plants had reduced the scope of their traditional medical practices. On the other hand their poverty had hindered them from the western medical accessibilities and for a quick remedy they were mostly depended on the local quacks without any proper diagnosis. Ultimately their fundamental rights over health had been seriously violated and it was going on from one generation to the other.

From the overall discussion, it can be summarized that, environment is the fundamental aspect of survival for human being. The daily livelihood of the studied people was quite secured in the lap of nature. Afterwards, due to several causes and particularly due to the exploitative attitude of the human being the indigenous people and the early settlers had lost the access of their own land and natural resources. It had severely told upon their fundamental aspects of human rights and their livelihood was exposed in front of a serious challenge. Their insecurity of livelihood was a community matter and even a child had to take birth in an insecured circumstances. The depletion of environment and its resources had told upon their rights of survival and ultimately the time will tell us about their existence in near future.

References

Barmwell, A. (1989): *Ecology in the 20th Century: A History.* New Heaven: Yale University Press.

Biswas, S. K., and S. Bhattacharjee (2007): "Health Situation Among the Stone Crushers of Balasan River Bed in Siliguri, West Bengal, India". In: *Health Environment Development and Other Essays: Anthropological Perspectives (Vol-5).* B. Chaudhuri and S. Chaudhuri (Eds.). New Delhi: Inter India Publication, pp.182-202.

Biswas, S.K. and S. Bhattacharjee (2008): "Misery of Displacement A Study of the Rajbansis of Tarijot Colony". In: *Voice of Dalit.* S. Samel (Ed), New Delhi: MD Publications, pp. 217-230.

Biswas, S. K. and S. Bhattacharjee (2008): "The Totos in Transition". In *Primitive Tribal Groups in India: Tradition, Development and Transformation.* R.M.Sarkar(Ed), New Delhi: Serials Publication, pp. 200-218.

Biswas, S. K. and S. Bhattacharjee (2008): "Impact of Ecological and Environmental Change on a Primitive Tribe". In *Demography, Economic Inequality, Women and Other Essays.* V.B.Jugale (Ed), New Delhi: Serials Publication, pp. 252-271.

Census of India. (1991): New Delhi: Government of India.

Census of India. (2001): New Delhi: Government of India,

Chaudhuri, B. (2003): *Health, Forest and Development: The Tribal Situation.* New Delhi: Inter-India Publication.

De, S. (2005): *Participatory Forest Management and Democratic Decentralisation in India: Focus on the Pioneer State,* Siliguri: N. L. Publishers.

Doshi, S.L. and P.C. Jain (1999): *Rural Sociology*, Jaipur, Rawat Publication.

Vidyarthi, L.P. and B.K. Rai (1977): *The Tribal Culture of India. New Delhi,* Concept Publishing.

10

Initial Breastfeeding: Patterns and Differentials in Selected South Asian Countries

M.S.R. Murthy, Venkata Putcha

Introduction

Initial breastfeeding has a cultural connotation in South Asia. Usually mothers start breast feeing their infants after three days. Women have a misconception that the first milk, colostrums, is hard to be digested by new born infants. Honey and honey water was given by elders to infants after birth until three days. With the exposure to media women have started giving milk to infants within an hour of birth. "Breast milk contains exactly the nutrients that the infant needs, helping the infant's development, with breast-fed children performing better on intelligence tests than formula-fed children".

A study conducted in West Bengal of India (Bandhopadhya 2009) has focused on pollution of mothers after delivery which is called as birth pollution. Birth Pollution prevents mothers from social mingling with others. It may be for seven days or more. Most of the mothers discarded colostrums.

A study in Nepal has shown that a small proportion of infants (3.4 per cent) were breast fed within one hour of birth, and 56.6% were breast-fed within 24 h of birth. (Mullany et al 2008). These studies in south Asia have not considered changes in initiation of breastfeeding overtime.

Pakistan has a strong breastfeeding culture. The National Nutrition Survey 2001-2002 found that 96.3 per cent of one month old infants were breastfed. Exclusive breastfeeding rates, however, were not optimal, with rates of 52.2 per cent at four months and 50 per cent at six months. Among children older than 13 months, 60.7 per cent were still breastfed. (Arts, 2003)

It is hypothesised that breastfeeding initiation may increase overtime in the first hour after birth among couples due to several campaigns of breastfeeding and the celebration of breastfeeding weeks in many countries. A comparison of two time periods may show secular changes in breastfeeding practices. The authors have found this essential to see the changes in practices of couple due to many breastfeeding campaigns conducted in the past.

Methodology

The data provided by Demographic and health surveys of India, Pakistan, Nepal, and Bangladesh has been considered for the study, particularly births within three years preceding the survey.

DHS data of two time periods has been used for the countries chosen for the study: India (2005-06; 1998-99); Bangladesh (2007; 2004); Nepal (2006; 2001) and Pakistan (2006-07; 1990-91).

The tables have been prepared using table builder of DHS STAT compiler. The variables considered are: highest level of education of the respondent, wealth index, gender and residence differentials. These variables have been tabulated as percentage distribution of respondents in relation to breastfeeding initiated within one hour and within one day. No attempt has been made to use of test of significance.

Results and Discussion

The discussion has been made in different sections viz., Education level of the respondent, and wealth Index, residence and gender differentials have been considered. Birth order wise data is not available.

The sample women considered were: India: 33114; Pakistan: 5450; Nepal: 3260 and Bangladesh: 3589 for the periods 2005-06; 2007 and 2006 and 2007 respectively. The sample for the earlier survey was India: 32765; Pakistan: 3378; Nepal: 4096; and Bangladesh: 4119 for the periods 1999; 1991; 2001 and 2004 respectively. This analysis has been presented at two points: initiation of breastfeeding within one hour and within one-day.

Initiation of Breastfeeding Within One Hour by Mother's Education

The analysis has been made across two time periods in each country.

In the case of *Bangladesh,* differences have been found in the initiation of breastfeeding within one hour after birth. Around two-fifth of respondents belonging to illiterate, primary and secondary/higher have started breastfeeding within one hour after birth in 2007, whereas it was one-fifth (21), illiterate, one-fourth (25) primary and one-third (31) during 2004. The differences were quite distinct (Illiterate: 20; Primary: 17 percent; Secondary/higher: 10 percent).

In the case of *India,* small differences were noticed between 2006 and 1999. Around 14.3 percent (2007) in comparison to 13 percent (1999) of respondents belonging to Primary have breastfed their new born infants within one hour after birth. At primary level the differences were 4 percent between 2007 (22) and 1999 (18). At secondary/higher level the differences (7 percent) were prominent (2007: 29 and 1999: 22).

Nepal on the other hand recorded lesser differentials between the two time periods. Around one-third of respondents belonging to all educational levels at two time periods have breastfed their new born infants. It was better for illiterates at primary during 2006 than 2004. The difference was 1.6 percentage points. At primary level it was 3 percent in favour of 2006. It was 0.4 percentage points increase only at secondary/higher level.

In the case of *Pakistan* the earlier data available for the time periods were: 1991 and the latest was 2007. Hence marked improvement has been noticed. Around one-fifth of respondents have breastfed their new born infants during 2007. It was less than 10 percent during 1991.

Initiation of Breastfeeding within a Day by Mother's Education

The data for starting breastfeeding within one day shows that around three-fifths of respondents have breastfed their new born infants in Bangladesh at two time periods at all levels of education.

In the case of India, it was around two-fifth (38) in 2006 in comparison to 30 percent during 1999 at primary level of education. It was 8 percentage points in the case of Primary level (2006: 50 and 1999: 42 percent). The difference was slightly high at secondary/higher (8 percentage points) level (2006: 61 and 1999: 52).

In general Nepal has manifested high levels of breastfeeding status around 70 per cent and above. In general breastfeeding has improved during 2006 than 2001 at all levels of education.

On the other hand Pakistan lags behind in the initiation of breastfeeding within one day. Around one-fifth of respondents at all educational level have breastfed their new born infants during 2007 whereas it was below 10 percent during 1991. (Table 1)

Initiation of Breastfeeding Gender

There was a distinct improvement in breastfeeding status between two surveys in Bangladesh, India, and Pakistan whereas the differences were minimal in the case of Nepal.

In the case of *Bangladesh,* male differentials were less during 2007 and 2004. However, the differences between the two surveys were prominent around 15 percent (male: 14 and female: 16) within one hour of birth. Around two-fifth of respondents (2007) have breastfed their new born within one hour compared to one-fourth of respondents during 2004. Nevertheless, breastfeeding within a day showed that the differences were negligible.

Table 1
Per cent Distribution of Respondents by Level of Education of Respondent-India, Bangladesh, Pakistan and Nepal

Country Education	*Births Within Three Years Before the Survey*							
	Ever Breastfed		*Started Within 1 Hour*		*Started Within 1 Day*		*N Sample*	
Bangladesh	*2007*	*2004*	*2007*	*2004*	*2007*	*2004*	*2007*	*2004*
No education	98.6	98.1	40.7	21.1	83.4	82.4	856.0	1463
Primary	98.4	98.6	41.8	24.8	84.6	85.3	1112.0	1256
Secondary or Higher	98.5	98.2	40.4	30.5	84.7	87.6	1620.0	1400
Missing	100.0		0.0		100.0		1.0	
Total	98.5	98.3	40.9	25.5	84.3	85.1	3589	4119
India	*2006*	*1999*	*2006*	*1999*	*2006*	*1999*	*2006*	*1999*
No education	96.3	96.3	14.3	12.6	37.6	30.0	15989	17786
Primary	95.9	96.6	22.5	18.4	50.3	42.4	4628	5160
Secondary or Higher	96.7	96.6	29.3	22.3	61.0	51.7	12497	9809
Missing	100	100	100	23.0	100	69.9	1	10
Total	96.4	96.5	21.1	16.4	47.9	38.5	33114	32765
Nepal	*2006*	*2001*	*2006*	*2001*	*2006*	*2001*	*2006*	*2001*
No education	98.1	98.1	27.9	29.5	71.1	61.7	1859	2980
Primary	98.4	97.9	33.2	30.3	79.8	71.5	603	584
Secondary or Higher	98.9	97.7	39.3	38.6	83.6	73.1	799	532
Missing	98.3	98.0	31.7	30.8	75.8	64.6	3261	4096

Contd.

Country Education	Births Within Three Years Before the Survey							
	Ever Breastfed		*Started Within 1 Hour*		*Started Within 1 Day*		*N Sample*	
Pakistan	*2007*	*1991*	*2007*	*1991*	*2007*	*1991*	*2007*	*1991*
No education	93.7	95.5	22.5	9.4	55.3	24.8	3490	3164
Primary	93.5	94.5	22.5	5.8	55.8	20.7	836	397
Secondary or Higher	93.9	90.3	23.3	5.4	58.8	27.8	1123	517
Missing	93.7	94.8	22.7	8.6	56.1	24.8	5450	3378

However, *India* shows a different picture. Though male female differences were negligible there was a prominent increase between 2006 and 1999 surveys for the starting of breastfeeding within one hour and one day. Initiation of breastfeeding within one hour was around one-fifth of women only in 2006 in comparison to around 16 percent during 1999. Half Mothers have started breastfeeding within one day whereas two-fifth of mothers did the same in 1999.

Breastfeeding status was not better in *Nepal*. Around one-third of mothers have breastfed their male and female newborn infants within one hour for the two surveys (2006; 2001). The differences were marked in the case of initiation of breastfeeding within one day. Gender differences were at minimum at the previous survey compared to latest survey.

Pakistan presents an abysmal situation. Only one-fifth of mothers have initiated breastfeeding to their new born infants within one hour during 2007 survey. It was below 10 percent during 1991. It was half at initiation of breastfeeding within one day. It was one-fourth during 1991. A study among Pakistani citizens in Great Britain has showed similar results. How can a traditional society like Pakistan avoid breastfeeding? (Table 2)

Initiation of Breastfeeding by Residence

Rural and urban difference has been small in breastfeeding the infants within an hour in Bangladesh (urban: 39 Rural: 41.4) and Nepal (urban: 38 rural: 31), India (urban: 26.rural: 19) and Pakistan (urban: 22 rural: 23).

The differences have been minimal in the case of Bangladesh (urban: 86; rural: 84), Nepal (urban: 79; rural: 75), and Pakistan (urban: 59; rural: 55) compared to India (urban: 57; rural: 45) in the case of initiation of breastfeeding within a day. The values are better in Bangladesh and Nepal India and Pakistan. (Table 2)

Initiation of Breastfeeding within One Hour by Wealth Index

Wealth index has been prepared based on household gadgets and other valuables. A combined index has been prepared

Table 2

Per cent Distribution of Respondents by Gender Differentials of Children and Residence of Respondent-India, Bangladesh, Pakistan and Nepal

	Births Within Three Years Before the Survey							
Country	*Ever Breastfed*		*Started Within 1 Hour*		*Started Within 1 Day*		*N Sample*	
Bangladesh	*2007*	*2004*	*2007*	*2004*	*2007*	*2004*	*2007*	*2004*
Sex of the Child								
Male	98.1	98.1	40.9	26.3	84.9	85.3	1799	2063
Female	98.9	98.5	40.9	24.6	83.8	84.8	1790	2056
Residence								
Urban	98.9	98.2	38.9	23.8	86.0	85.4	761	813
Rural	98.4	98.3	41.4	25.8	83.9	85.0	2828	3307
Total	98.5	98.3	40.9	25.5	84.3	85.1	3589	4119
India	*2006*	*1999*	*2006*	*1999*	*2006*	*1999*	*2006*	*1999*
Sex of the child								
Male	96.0	96.3	21.5	16.6	48.7	38.9	17335	16997
Female	96.8	96.7	20.8	16.3	47.1	38.1	15780	15769
Residence								
Urban	96.5	96.5	26.5	19.9	57.0	46.6	8357	7267
Rural	96.3	96.4	19.3	15.4	44.9	36.2	24757	25499
Total	96.4	96.5	21.1	16.4	47.9	38.5	33114	32765

Contd.

Country	Births Within Three Years Before the Survey							
	Ever Breastfed		Started Within 1 Hour		Started Within 1 Day		N Sample	
Nepal	2006	2001	2006	2001	2006	2001	2006	2001
Sex of the child								
Male	98.6	97.8	32.4	31.2	77.4	64.1	1640	1990
Female	98.1	98.2	30.9	30.4	74.1	65.0	1621	2107
Residence								
Urban	98.6	97.4	37.7	36.4	78.5	73.2	388	248
Rural	98.3	98.1	30.9	30.4	75.4	64.0	2872	3848
Total	98.3	98.0	31.7	30.8	75.8	64.6	3261	4096
Pakistan	2007	1991	2007	1991	2007	1991	2007	1991
Sex of the child								
Male	93.3	94.7	21.9	8.3	55.8	23.9	2883	1753
Female	94.2	94.8	23.6	8.8	56.5	25.8	2566	1935
Residence								
Urban	93.5	94.2	22.2	5.7	58.8	27.1	1654	972
Rural	93.8	95.0	22.9	9.7	54.9	23.9	3796	2406
Total	93.7	94.8	22.7	8.6	56.1	24.8	5450	3378

which was divided into several categories. The values have been put on ordinal scale as: Lowest, Second, Middle, Fourth, and Highest.

Bangladeshi women have enhanced breastfeeding to two-fifth level during 2007 from a mere one-fourth to one-third during 2004. At lowest level of index it has improved from 18 percent to 42 percent whereas it improved from 24 percent to 40 percent at second level of wealth index. Middle level has increased from 27 percent to 42 percent on the other hand it improved from 32 to 44 at fourth level of index. Highest level of index has improved from 30 to 37.

In the case of *India,* the values area at low level in both the surveys compared to Bangladesh. The values of initiation of breastfeeding during 1999 were below one-fifth level (14 to 19) while the values ranged from 15 to 29 at 2006.

Nepal seems to be present at second place in this aspect after Bangladesh. Interestingly women belonging to lowest level of index are better placed (37 percent) during 2001 than other levels of index. During 2006 the values started at 27 percent to 39 percent.

Pakistan starts at 11percent and goes down as the index increases during 1991. It seems Pakistani elderly women impress the young mothers to avoid colostrums. However, the situation improved during 2007 but at one-fifth to one-fourth level.

Colostrum

Data on colostrums has been recorded for Pakistan and Bangladesh only. More than one-third proportion of Pakistani (35 per cent) women have given colostrum whereas it was two-fifth in the case Bangladesh. (Table not given)

Exclusive Breastfeeding Status

Data on exclusive status of women was available for two time periods for India and Nepal only. It was available for 2007 for Bangladesh and 1991 for Pakistan only. The data was provided for the infant ages 0-3; 4-6 and 7-9 months.

Table 3
Per cent Distribution of Respondents by Wealth Index- India, Bangladesh, Pakistan and Nepal Country Births Within Three Years Before the Survey

Country Wealth Index	*Births Within Three Years Before the Survey*							
	Ever Breastfed		*Started Within 1 Hour*		*Started Within 1 Day*		*N Sample*	
Bangladesh	*2007*	*2004*	*2007*	*2004*	*2007*	*2004*	*2007*	*2004*
Lowest	98.3	98.6	42.0	17.7	84.1	82.4	758	1029
Second	98.3	98.2	39.6	24.3	84.4	83.4	779	831
Middle	98.9	98.7	41.6	26.7	82.4	85.7	699	848
Fourth	98.4	98.2	43.7	32.4	87.0	87.2	94	717
Highest	98.5	97.7	37.3	29.6	84.0	88.0	659	695
Total	98.5	98.3	40.9	25.5	84.3	85.1	3589	4119
India	*2006*	*1999*	*2006*	*1999*	*2006*	*1999*	*2006*	*1999*
Lowest	96.9	96.4	15.4	14.0	39.2	31.6	8331	7622
Second	95.6	96.6	17.8	14.2	41.3	31.5	7432	7339
Middle	96.4	96.6	22.6	17.1	49.0	40.6	6518	6614
Fourth	96.6	96.5	25.5	19.0	55.6	45.2	6032	6281
Highest	96.3	96.3	28.9	19.3	62.4	48.1	4802	4910
Total	96.4		21.1		47.9		33114	32765

Contd.

Country Wealth Index	Births Within Three Years Before the Survey							
	Ever Breastfed		Started Within 1 Hour		Started Within 1 Day		N Sample	
Nepal	2006	2001	2006	2001	2006	2001	2006	2001
Lowest	99.1	98.4	26.6	36.8	81.7	76.4	820	1024
Second	98.8	97.9	34.8	31.7	72.2	62.3	684	886
Middle	97.3	97.6	30.6	24.6	71.2	51.8	660	851
Fourth	98.8	98.2	30.4	26.2	72.3	61.4	605	778
Highest	97.2	97.8	39.0	34.3	81.4	70.4	493	557
Total	98.3	98.0	31.7	30.8	75.8	64.6	3261	4096
Pakistan	*2007*	*1991*	*2007*	*1991*	*2007*	*1991*	*2007*	*1991*
Lowest	94.4	94.9	20.1	10.5	52.3	25.5	1266	763
Second	94.0	96.2	22.3	10.6	55.9	22.4	1144	826
Middle	92.1	94.7	22.7	8.8	55.9	23.7	1073	825
Fourth	95.2	94.8	25.5	7.0	58.0	24.0	1005	891
Highest	92.7	93.0	23.4	5.5	59.6	29.0	962	774
Total	93.7	94.8	22.7	8.6	56.1	24.8	5450	4078

For Infants of 0-3 Months

More than half (58 percent) of the women belonging to Bangladesh of 2007 have provided exclusive breastfeeding. Similarly more than half of India (58 percent; 2006 and 55 percent: 55 percent) whereas Nepal women have higher levels (70 percent: 2006 and 79 percent: 2001) for the two time periods. On the other hand only one-fifth (26.percent) of Pakistani women have given exclusive breastfeeding for the time period 1991. However, three-fifths (60 percent) of Pakistani have given breastfeeding and supplementary foods. The stage of 0-3 months of infants is formative period, hence they require exclusive breastfeeding. In this regard, Nepali women seem to have better knowledge than women of other countries.

For Infants of 4-6 Months

During this stage some women start weaning (initiation of supplementary feeding). Consequently breastfeeding has been declining with an increase in breastfeeding and supplementary status in all the countries under study. Around one half of women all countries under study have been giving breastfeeding and supplementary feeding together.

For Infants of 7-9 Months

There is a greater shift to breastfeeding and supplementary feeding together in all the countries under study. Most of the Bangladeshi women (92 percent: 2007) were in the stage followed by Nepal (87 percent: 2006 and 81 percent: 2001), India (75 percent: 2006 and 64 per cent: 1999) and Pakistan (62 percent: 1991). Scientifically weaning should take over exclusive breastfeeding during this stage with occasional breastfeeding. Exclusive breastfeeding may not provide required nutrients to infants at this stage. (Table 4)

Regional Comparison of India with Other Countries at 2006 Level

In general all women have breast fed their children. However, initiation of breastfeeding within an hour after birth varies.

Table 4
Breastfeeding (BF) Status of Infants

	Breastfeeding Status					
	Not BF	*Exclusive BF*	*BF and Plain Water*	*BF and Supplements*	*Total*	*Living Children*
Age 0-3 Months						
Bangladesh 2007	0.8	57.8	10.0	31.3	100	276
India 2005-06	2.0	58.3	20.3	19.4	100	3117
India 1998-99	2.0	55.2	22.7	20.1	100	3575
Nepal 2006	0.5	69.8	13.2	16.5	100	274
Nepal 2001	0	78.8	9.3	11.9	100	373
Pakistan 1990-91	3.6	26.2	9.9	60.4	100	509
Age 4-6 Months						
Bangladesh 2007	0.5	17.9	13.9	67.6	100	333
India 2005-06	2.5	23.3	25.3	48.9	100	2896
India 1998-99	2.2	27.3	27.6	42.9	100	2992
Nepal 2006	0	25.9	24.7	49.4	100	295
Nepal 2001	0.5	46.6	15.5	37.4	100	381
Pakistan 1990-91	9.9	17.7	13.1	59.3	100	368
Age 7-9 Months						
Bangladesh 2007	1.4	1.9	4.3	92.4	100	317
India 2005-06	4.2	6.3	14.7	74.7	100	2873
India 1998-99	5.0	10.0	21.6	63.5	100	2562
Nepal 2006	1.9	2.5	8.5	87.1	100	251
Nepal 2001	0.3	5.6	13.5	80.6	100	323
Pakistan 1990-91	7.8	13.5	16.3	62.3	100	328

Two-fifth (41 per cent) proportion of Bangladeshi women have breast fed their infants within an hour compared to other south Asian countries (India: 21; Pakistan: 23 and Nepal: 32). Certain states in India around Bangladesh such as Arunachal Pradesh (49., Assam (47), Manipur (54), Meghalaya (52), Mizoram (57), Nagaland (43), and Tripura (30) have corresponding figures with Bangladesh. Other states such as Kerala (53), Tamil Nadu (51), Himachal Pradesh (40), Orissa (51), Goa (56), and Maharashtra (47) have corresponding figures with Bangladesh.

A good proportion of Bangladeshi (84 per cent) and Nepal women (76 per cent) have breast fed their infants within one day compared to Indian (48) and Pakistani (56) women. New Delhi (60), Himachal Pradesh (68), Haryana (54), J and K (65), Uttaranchal (64), Orissa (76.9), Arunachal Pradesh (76), Assam (68), WB (66), Manipur (74), Meghalaya (79), Mizoram (78), Nagaland (67), Sikkim (81), Tripura (68), Goa (77), Maharashtra (70), Karnataka (66), Kerala (90) and Tamil Nadu (80) have manifested higher levels of breastfeeding within a day after delivery. (Table not given)

Conclusions

Initiation of breastfeeding within one has been promoted all over the globe through breastfeeding week campaigns. However, women have misapprehensions in providing breastfeeding within one-hour. Nevertheless Bangladesh and Nepal are in the forefront in this regard. India and Pakistan are lagging behind in this stance.

Exclusive breastfeeding for infants below six months was found among Bangladeshi and Nepali women. However, supplementary feeding with other milk and other foods has been more found in India and Pakistan than Bangladesh and Nepal. Wealth Index has shown more association with exclusive breastfeeding status in the Indian context than other countries. Vigorous international efforts in health related issues have in influenced programmes of health in Bangladesh and Nepal. However, supplementary feeding with other milk and other foods was prevalent in India and Pakistan. It shows infant nutrition has been differentially practiced in south Asian countries. Nevertheless, infant feeding is an important issue.

References

Arts Maaike. Infant Feeding in South Asia Earthquake Aftermath. Field Exchange on line Journal of Emergency Nutrition Network Issue 27 p. 3. 2006.

Bandyopadhyay Mridula (2009): Impact of Ritual Pollution on Lactation and Breastfeeding Practices in Rural West Bengal, India International Breastfeeding Journal 1 (2): 20-25.

Mullany Luke C., Joanne Katz., Yue M. Li., Subarna K. Khatry., Steven C. LeClerq. Gary L. Darmstadt., and James M. Tielsch (2008): Breast-Feeding Patterns, Time to Initiation, and Mortality Risk Among Newborns in Southern Nepal 1, 2 Journal of Nutrition 138: 599-603.

SECTION - III

Reproductive and Sexual Health, Poverty and Human Development

7

Poverty Alleviation and Human Development in India: Approaches and Achievements

[illegible] V. Somayajulu, Tilak Mukherji

Introduction

Poverty in India is widespread as it is estimated to have a third of the world's poor. According to the Planning Commission of India, 28% of the population was living below the poverty line in 2004-2005, down from 51% in 1977-1978, and 36% in 1993-1994 (Planning Commission, 2007). According to the World Bank's estimate, 42% of the country's population were below the international poverty line of $1.25 a day (PPP, in nominal terms Rs. 21.6 a day in urban areas and Rs. [illegible] in rural areas) [illegible], reduced from 60% in 1980 (World Bank, 2005, 2008). Although Indian economy has grown steadily over the last two decades, its growth has been uneven across different social and economic groups, geographic regions, and rural and urban areas. During 1999 - 2008, Gujarat (8.8%), Haryana (8.7%) and Delhi (7.4%) recorded higher annual growth rates than Bihar (5.1%), Uttar Pradesh (4.4%) and Madhya Pradesh (3.5%). Poverty rates in rural Orissa ([illegible]) and rural Bihar (41%) are among the world's most extreme.

11

Estimating AIDS Related Deaths in India: A Back-calculation Approach

Hemant Meitei, Manishankar K, Masayuki Kakehashi, Arni S.R. Srinivasa Rao

Introduction

By the end of March 2008 an estimated 22.7 lakhs HIV infected individuals in India (NACO, National AIDS Control Organization) [1]. Estimates of the size of AIDS and related deaths are of much significance for the advancement in prevention strategy and health care planning. HIV estimation has been a challenge to the Indian public health and various attempts have been made by the government of India. Despite the fact that HIV surveillance system has been in place the tracking of the HIV infected persons has not been fully put into its system. Due to the process of the transmission an HIV infected person is always looked with a sense of suspicion and stigma. As a result there is the infected persons do not come forward it its own. Therefore the challenge is mounting above the board. With the effort of the NACO the country is subdivided into high prevalence states where the prevalence of HIV is more than 1%. These states include Manipur Nagaland, Tamil Nadu, Andhra Pradesh, Karnataka and

Maharashtra. The recent experience highlights that the prevalence rate has been arrested to certain extent. Using the NFHS-3 estimation of the prevalence rate roughly there is about 2.5 million persons in India are infected with HIV by 2006. Deaths related to AIDS in India could have changed its pattern after introduction of Anti-retroviral Therapy (ART). In this article, we are interested to estimate AIDS deaths which were occurred before large scale ART introduction in India.

Objective

The focus of the work is to present the estimates of AIDS and AIDS deaths in India for the period 1986 to 2000 by using back calculation method.

Estimation Procedure

We recognize the difficulty in exact quantification of deaths occurred due to HIV (Human Immunodeficiency Virus) and AIDS. It is quite possible that thousands of deaths might have occurred at the national level during the past decade, though the crude deaths rates at the national level approximately remained uniform in the same period.

As HIV is associated with other opportunistic infections particularly TB it is more difficult to deal. Thus the estimation of death due to AIDS is more difficult. Besides these problems, the compliance of the general public to register death is also very poor in India more so in rural areas. Though NACO gives official number of deaths due to HIV/AIDS it is widely accepted that there is still underreporting of the number of deaths due to AIDS. Alternatively we have tried to arrive at number AIDS related deaths by using the back calculation method.

Fundamentally there is need to understand the progression of HIV to the state of full blown AIDS. This is important from the point of the management of treatment regime as well as the public health point of view. From the treatment point of view it is important to monitor the number of CD counts whereas from the point of public health the government has to take care of the progression to educate general population how to cope with the change in the lifestyle and maintaining a healthy practice through various ways such as taking healthy food, preventing from infections of other diseases.

Since the prevalence of HIV/AIDS is mainly among the productive age group any person dying from AIDS is very crucial because every death is accounted with the loss of life of the same person as well as it leaves a trail of miseries to the household in terms of direct cost due to expenditure made on the treatment and indirect costs of loss of productive activities accrued to this person. In case of married person it leads to the loss of the spouse at the prime time of life and also leaving the offspring as orphans.

Even though there is reported cases of AIDS related deaths by the NACO there is hardly observed data on the distribution of deaths by age pattern. Broadly it is among the population of 15-49 but NACO has recently documented that there is increasing number of death among older population (50 years and above) and children (less than 15 years)[1]. Therefore, it becomes imperative to have age specific deaths due to AIDS. After two decades of identification of HIV case in India the progress has been made in a comprehensive manner still there is need for improving. During the early phase when there was not much awareness of the HIV/AIDS among the general population and lack of adequate therapeutic management it has taken its toll.

From incubation point of view an HIV carrier has to take good and nutritious food and try to prevent from any kind of communicable infections. This is important since the immunity power is to be strengthened to prevent from infection. Taking this cue it is equally important to understand the length of the incubation period to travel from HIV status to the AIDS stage. The length of incubation is greatly affected by the immunity and environment to which an HIV positive person belongs. HIV positive people in poverty and children are more susceptible to shorter incubation period and they will contribute more to the number of deaths due to AIDS.

We designed a method to estimates AIDS deaths in India. This method matches HIV epidemic density estimated by back-calculation approach (BCA) [2,3] and national level HIV estimates generated by NACO [1] to estimate the under-reporting of AIDS. The proportions of under-reporting (or under-estimation or coverage rate) are applied to adjust the cumulative AIDS generated from BCA, and death numbers are estimated up to 2000. We also give projections for the near future. Given the reported number of AIDS cases and assuming the distribution for the incubation of AIDS (which is Weibull in this work), the Maximum Likelihood Estimation (MLE) technique which is statistically robust and asymptotically efficient is applied to estimate the parameters of the HIV infection density h(θ,s) at time s, in the equation 1.

$$a(\alpha,\beta,\theta,t) = \int_0^t h(\theta,s)F(\alpha,\beta,t-s)ds \qquad (2.1)$$

$F(\alpha,\beta,t)$ is the incubation distribution, where t is the incubation period, $a(\alpha,\beta,\theta,t)$ is cumulative AIDS cases at time t. The function $h(\theta,s)$ is assumed to be exponential. The incubation distribution parameters vary with mean, M (=9, 10 years) and standard deviation (SD=3,4,5,6 years). The combination of each mean value with the four standard deviations are used to select parameters (α,β) and detailed application of the BCA to project AIDS cases in India are explained (Projections of AIDS and Possible Implications in India, an unpublished manuscript submitted).

Annual reported HIV cases are more reliable in Japan than many other countries. We made an attempt to estimate parameters of incubation with the help of reported HIV and AIDS and the convolution equation (2.1).

$$A(\theta_K,\alpha_K,\beta_K,t) = \int_0^t h(\theta_k,s)F(\alpha_k,\beta_k,t-s)ds \qquad (2.2)$$

Where $A(t)$ is cumulative AIDS at time t, $h(\theta_k,s)$ is HIV incidence density function at s, $F(\alpha_k,\beta_k,t)$ is incubation distribution at t with α–scale andβ–*shape* parameters. k=1,2,3,4 for four subpopulations-male heterosexuals, male homosexuals, male unknowns and female.

Let the reported HIV cases h_i (i=1,2,3...□) in the time interval $[T_i, T_{i-1}]$, (i=1,2,3,...□) follow multinomial distribution with cell probabilities pi (i=1,2,3...□). Now, the parameter $□_k$ is estimated by maximizing the log-likelihood (*LL (H)*) given in equation (2.3).

$$LL(H) = \sum_{i=yr_1}^{yr_2} h_i \log p_i \tag{2.3}$$

where

$$p_i = \frac{\int_{T_i}^{T_{i+1}} h(\theta_k, s)ds}{\sum_{i=yr_1}^{yr_2} p_i}$$

The limits yr_1=year$_1$-1980, yr_2=year$_2$-1980 are determined, where year$_1$=1990 and year$_2$=1999 (i.e. reported HIV cases between 1990 and 1999 are responsible for the estimated HIV density) and 1980 is assumed to be the year prior to which no HIV infections. Hence, with the reported AIDS cases up to 1999 and the above estimated HIV density function, we estimated the parameters of the incubation distribution using the convolution equation (2.1). The parametric forms $h(\theta_k, s)$ and $F(\alpha_k, \beta_k, t)$ are exponential and two-parameter Weibull. Adjusting coverage rates explained in section 2.3 projects cumulative number of HIV and AIDS.

Coverage Rate and Adjusted Estimate

AIDS coverage rate (Co_k) explained here is used to adjust the HIV/AIDS estimate.

Adjusted HIV estimate

$$= \frac{C_k}{Co_k} \int_{T_o}^{T_i} h(\theta_k, s)ds \,\forall \{i = 1, 2, 3, \ldots \omega\} \; and \; \{k = 1, 2, 3, 4\}$$

Adjusted AIDS estimates

$$= \frac{C_k}{Co_k} A(\theta_k, \alpha_k, \beta_k, t) \,\forall\, \{k = 1, 2, 3, 4\}$$

$$C_k = \frac{\text{Cumulative } HIV \text{ Reported for k}^{\text{th}} \text{ subpopulation at time } T_\omega}{\int_0^{T_{\omega w}} h(\theta_k, s)ds}$$

where

$$Co_k = \frac{A(\theta_k, \alpha_k, \beta_k, T_\omega)}{\text{Cumulative } AIDS \text{ Reported for k}^{\text{th}} \text{ subpopulation at } T_\omega}$$

$$p_i = \frac{\int_{T_0}^{T_i} h(s)F(T_i - s)ds - \int_{T_0}^{T_{i-1}} h(s)F(T_{i-1} - s)ds}{\int_{T_0}^{T_\omega} h(s)F(T_\omega - s)ds} ; (i = 1, 2, 3 \ldots \omega)$$

p_i $h(t)$ and $F(t)$ are conditional probability, incidence density and incubation distributions.

Results

The NACO estimates of HIV infection as of mid 1998 ranges between 2.3 million (low) and 3.5 million (high) [1]. The corresponding period's BCA estimates of HIV infection with mean incubation period of 9 years (case I) ranges between 73,000 and 238,000 and with a mean of 10 years (case II) ranges between 103,000 and 370,000 for four sets[4] of plausible parameters. Considering NACO's range of estimates are standard, the proportions of under-estimation of HIV (coverage rates) for different setups given. (Table 1). We adjusted the cumulative AIDS obtained by BCA with these proportions for low and high estimates. Proportions of AIDS individuals who can afford life-prolonging therapies were meager during the past decade. The prevalent deaths in the each calendar year are calculated by taking median survival after attaining AIDS as one-year [5]. The entire analysis is carried out for cases I & II.

Table 1
Coverage Rates in India

	Set1	*Set2*	*Set3*	*Set4*
(Mean=9)				
Low	0.10337	0.06513	0.04401	0.03195
High	0.06793	0.04280	0.02892	0.02100
(Mean=10)				
Low	0.16073	0.09844	0.06410	0.04489
High	0.10562	0.06469	0.042212	0.02950

The coverage rates are better for mean=10, α= 11.0786; β=3.7138; θ=0.5144 (set 1) and worst coverage rates are located at mean=9, α=9.9928; β=1.5301, θ=0.5247 (set 4). We found two different scenarios are emerging from death estimates. If the coverage rate was better then there could be 85,000 to 130,000 cumulative number of deaths occurred up to 1999, and if the coverage rates were worst these figures ranges from 434,000 to 661,000. As per our design, the death number varies depending upon the degree of coverage rates. Importantly, the original BCA-AIDS estimates without adjusting for under-estimation is consistent with the reported cumulative AIDS that correspond to the former range above (See Table 2: Col 1 & Col 2) and same figures show poor consistency (See Table 2: Col 1 & Col 3) that correspondence to later range of death number. If we fix a mid-range of these above two estimated HIV ranges we suggest that, the actual figure of cumulative AIDS deaths up to 1999 in India lies towards the former range from the mid-range (i.e. towards the range obtained for consistent cases). The rapid increase in AIDS deaths can be attributed to severe HIV progression to AIDS. Tuberculosis is familiar opportunistic infection related with AIDS [5] and there were indications of tuberculosis linked AIDS deaths in India [6]. The present trend indicates steadiness of AIDS deaths in the near future is not expected. We restrict our analysis of AIDS deaths due to a little available information on under-reporting and survival of AIDS individuals in India. There is sufficient scope to improve and re-construct the deaths number provided the better estimates from HIV surveillance are available.

Table 2
Estimation of AIDS Cases and Deaths in India

	AIDS Number Cumulative							*AIDS Deaths*			
				Adjusted[1]		*Adjusted*[2]		*Prevalent*[1]		*Prevalent*[1]	
	*Reported**	*BCA*[1]	*BCA*[2]	*Low*	*High*	*Low*	*High*	*Low*	*High*	*Low*	*High*
Year	*(1)*	*(2)*	*(3)*	*(4)*	*(5)*	*(6)*	*(7)*	*(8)*	*(9)*	*(10)*	*(11)*
1986	5	9	23	55	84	724	1102	27	42	362	551
1987	14	14	23	85	129	717	1091	29	43	177	270
1988	25	29	41	181	275	1289	1961	76	116	556	845
1989	44	58	72	361	549	2266	3448	142	217	855	1301
1990	101	110	125	685	1042	3927	5976	271	413	1536	2337
1991	146	201	215	1251	1904	6744	10263	490	745	2604	3963
1992	286	357	368	2221	3380	11513	17520	866	1317	4455	6779
1993	538	621	626	3865	5882	19581	29797	1500	2282	7563	11509
1994	1061	1066	1061	6632	10091	33221	50554	2566	3905	12829	19523
1995	2152	1811	1798	11270	17150	56280	85644	4352	6623	21725	33060
1996	3040	3060	3043	19036	28967	95254	114952	7342	11172	36764	55946
1997	5148	5148	5148	32029	48740	161126	245192	12344	18784	62181	94623
1998	–	8642	8705	53765	81817	272454	414604	20711	31516	105137	159991
1999	–	14486	14716	901243	137145	460604	700920	34707	52814	177734	270464
2000	–	24261	24876	150942	229695	778585	1184803	58118	88440	300425	457169

* Reported cases for each year from 1986-89 were taken from HIV/AIDS Surveillance database, US Bureau of the Census and for each year from 1990-97 were taken from country specific epidemiological fact sheet, UNAIDS, 2000 update. We have cumulated the reported cases for each year. 1: Backcalculation approach with Mean=10, α=11.0786, β=3.7138, θ=0.5144; 2: Backcalculation approach with Mean=9, α=9.9928, β=1.5301, θ=0.5247 Incidence density: $h(s)=Exp(\theta s)$; $F(\alpha,\beta,\theta)=1-Exp[-\alpha t^{\beta}]$

In Table 2 we have shown the estimates up to year 2000 with Mean=10 and set1, the situation where the coverage rates are better. For this case back-calculated projections (after adjusting the under-estimation) indicate there may be 1.52 million to 2.3 million individuals will be living with AIDS (excluding the deaths) by the end of 2005. It is not understandable at present how much the interventions change these projections, but the ameliorated prevention strategies and IEC programs undertaken by government as well as non-government organisations in the country may alter largely any future projections. The under-estimation explained is likely to decline (ie. more case reporting) in future if the HIV/AIDS surveillance is strengthened further. The study is sensitive to the incubation parameters like mean etc., Admitting approximate uniform crude death rates at the National level; these AIDS related deaths are unfortunate for health sector reforms.

Summary and Conclusions

We estimated the cumulative number of AIDS cases and AIDS deaths in India by adjusting the under-estimation, with the available reported AIDS cases between 1986 and 2000 and current HIV infection estimates. Estimates indicate cumulative AIDS deaths up to 2000 varies between 0.058 million and 0.457 million. The estimated deaths are regrettable for the health services in India. The estimates are sensitive to the parameters of the incubation distribution considered. We considered pre-ART era deaths which were up to the year 2000 in this study. This method can be extended once ART related and non-ART related survival analysis data becomes available for the longer duration.

References

Rao ASRS, Thomas K, Sudhakar K, Maini PK (2009): HIV/AIDS Epidemic in India and Predicting the Impact of the National Response: Mathematical Modeling and Analysis. *Mathematical Biosciences Engineering (AIMS, USA)*; Oct; 6(4):779-813.

Brookmeyer R, Gail MH.(1986): Minimum Size of the Acquired Immunodeficiency Syndrome (AIDS) Epidemic in the United States. *Lancet*; ii: 1320-2

Hira SK, Rao Arni SRS, Thanekar J. (1999): Evidence of AIDS-related mortality in Mumbai, India. *Lancet*; 354:1175-6.

Lanjewar DN, Anand BS, Genta R, et al., (1996): Major Differences in the Spectrum of Gastrointestinal Infections associated with AIDS in India versus the West: An Autopsy Study. *Clin Infect Dis*; 23:482-85.

NACO. Surveillance of HIV Infection/AIDS Cases in India HIV/AIDS Indian Scenario. June 2009. (http://www.nacoonline.com)

PHLS. The Incidence and Prevalence of AIDS and Other Severe HIV Disease in England and Wales for 1992-1997: Projections using Data to the End of June 1992. *Communicable Disease Report* 1993; 3, Supplement 1.

Schwartlander, B., Stanecki, K.A., Brown T, et al., (1999): Country-specific Estimates and Models of HIV and AIDS: Methods and Limitations. *AIDS*; 13:2445-58.

12

Social Exclusion and Transgenders: A Study in Puducherry, India

P. B. Shankar Narayan, Sunitha Kuppuswamy

Introduction

Transgender

Transgender is an umbrella term that refers to people who's biological and gender identity or expression may not be the same. This can but does not necessarily include preoperative, postoperative or non-operative transsexuals, female and male cross-dressers, drag queens or kings, female or male impersonators, and intersex individuals (NLGJA, 2008). In its broadest sense, "transgender" encompasses anyone whose identity or behavior falls outside stereotypical gender expectations (Pluriels & Genre, 2008). Transgender is a term for any person whose internal gender identity differs from physiological gender (Wilson D, 2001). It is particularly important to realize that many individuals, despite the fact that they may appear transgender to some do not consider themselves to be transgender (Pluriels & Genre, 2008).

Social exclusion is a new and multidimensional concept, related to the relative position of an individual or a group in the society. Each type of societal "disadvantage" can contribute to social exclusion. Estivill J, (2001) defines "Social exclusion is an accumulation of confluent processes with successive ruptures arising from the heart of economy, politics and society; gradually distances and places persons, groups, communities and territories in positions of inferiority in relation to centre powers, resources and prevailing values". Further to Estivill, Jessicalive, (2009) identifies four aspects of social exclusion as exclusion from social society; exclusion from social goods; exclusions from social production; and economic exclusion. Beall and Piron (2005), suggest "a process and a state that prevents individuals or groups from full participation in social, economic and political life and from asserting their rights. It derives from exclusionary relationships based on power". Thus focusing on social inclusion means emphasizing things like access to services like education and health care, good social networks, decent housing, water facilities, adequate information and support, and the ability to exercise basic rights. In this study Social exclusion is viewed as denial of Transgender living in the society with equal to others.

Social Exclusion and Transgender in India

Transgender communities historically exist for centuries in most of the countries in the world and they are commonly called as *hijra* in India. The hijra—usually born physically male, but known throughout South Asia as a third gender because they identify as female—wear women's clothing and live in closed societies, banding together to brace against widespread discrimination (Elliott J, 2009). The transgender face discrimination and abuse ranging from rejection from their families to sexual abuse from classmates. They occupy an odd place in South Asian culture; though their societal roots are ancient, in most settings here they are pariahs (Elliott J, 2009).

Strong teasing, bullying and sexual abuse from classmates prompt many hijra to drop out of school, resulting in high illiteracy rates and increasing unemployment. But finding a job is also a difficult task for the hijra who do receive an education after a long struggle. It is estimated that more than

25000 transgender in Mumbai, one of the major cities in India are floating from one place to the other within the city and outside, to earn money by blessing and greeting individuals, couples or families for special occasion. Some are involved as professional dancer in bars or during ceremony and others go for begging at the signal, in the trains or on the street. The statistics about occupation of Transgender reveals that 60 percent of them are involved in commercial sex work; 20 percent of the transgender living or working in Mumbai are infected with the HIV virus (Vincenzi A, 2009). The main reason behind such an increased percentage is because of having unprotected sex. They avoid the usage of condom during sex works as the client is willing to pay more if not used.

The key contributing factors to social exclusion in India include poverty, non-dominant social identities, e.g. race, ethnicity, religion, and gender; social locations (migrants, refugees); demographic features (occupation, educational level); and health conditions, e.g. disability, stigmatized diseases, such as HIV and AIDS (UN, 2007). This clearly shows that understanding the socio-cultural and human rights aspects of discrimination against the *hijra* community and deprivation can help reduce HIV/AIDS transmission and safeguard this marginalized community.

Review of Literature

According to *D'Augelli* (1998), the summary of data from a number of surveys and research studies demonstrated that lesbian, gay, and bisexual youth were more likely to be victimized within their families and in the community. Violence against transgender youth, lesbians, gays and adults is still a present reality particularly at their workplace. The humiliation is in the form of verbal harassment by peers, threat of physical violence, physical attack, rape, incest and destruction of personal property.

In an empirical extension of the study on examining the ways in which transgender people challenge the assumption that gender is associated with sex; *Gagné* et al., (1998) explored the social context in which transgender individuals resist the normative expectations of sex and gender. Findings of the study indicated that the social pressures to conform to the gender binary were experienced as desires for relationship maintenance and self preservation.

According to *Bradford et.al.* (1994), fifty-two percent of the women that participated in the National Lesbian and Gay Health Foundation study reported that they had been physically assaulted. Also, Lesbian, gay, bisexual and transgender youth and adults are a stigmatized minority group. As such, they face the daily stress of being members of a stigmatized group (DiPlacido, 1998). Though sexuality minorities have always existed in India sometimes in forms, which are culturally sanctioned (such as the *hijra*) and at other times in invisibility and silence, their issues have never seriously been articulated. It is only recently that the rights of sexuality minorities as an issue have been taken seriously in India by various civil society organizations (PUCL-K, 2001)

The small amount of evidence available suggests that transphobic bullying exists and legislative protection for trans people in schools is inadequate. In one study, 75 per cent of trans respondents experienced problems in school (Keogh et al., 2006). Whittle et al., (2007) make some recommendations to reduce discrimination against trans employees. These include trans awareness training for managers and Human Resources staff, and the extension of the statutory definition of transsexuality to include non-transsexual trans groups, who at present are not fully protected under gender legislation.

According to Ramdas, R. *et.al.* (2003), along with subjection to physical violence such as beatings and threats of disfigurement with acid bulbs, the sexuality of the hijra also becomes a target of prurient curiosity, at the least, which leads to brutal violence, at the most. The 2006 Scottish Social Attitudes survey found that 50 per cent of respondents would be unhappy if a close relative entered a long-term relationship with a transsexual person, and 30 per cent felt that a transsexual person would be unsuitable as a primary school teacher (Bromley et al.,2007).

Objective

Keeping above concept of social exclusion of Transgender in view an attempt is made in this research paper

- To understand the treatment received by the transgender in their own family; and problems faced by them in health care settings
- To understand and analyze societal attitude towards the transgender;
- To study about the human rights violations of transgender at their workplace;

To achieve the above objectives contributing to social exclusion of transgender, a qualitative and quantitative study has been undertaken in Puducherry, which is a small coastal town formerly called as French colony in India. The study used 30 samples which were selected using non-probability convenient sampling method. The tools used for data collection were mainly structured interview schedules and case studies.

The universe of the study was considered as the transgender community that includes Kothis and Aravanis, of *Sahodaran* Community Oriented Health Development Society (SCHOD) in Puducherry. SCHOD was started in the year 1998, under the Trust Act. The organization works with the marginalized, stigmatized sections of the society, the MSM (Men who have Sex with Men), and the transgender. They work towards their welfare; the improvement of their health conditions, to protect them from STIs and HIV, and capacity building for their own empowerment.

Background Characters of TRANSGENDERS

The samples taken for the study (30 Transgenders) were born and brought up in the villages of Puducherry. They speak the local language, *tamil,* and were living with their parents like any other 'normal' child. Almost all the respondents preferred and put on female clothes to appear appealing and attractive during their childhood. They preferred playing with girls rather than with boys and enjoyed indulging themselves with the household activities that are usually taken over by females. They posed themselves to be 'soft' natured like girls and for some respondents, it turned into a problem when they entered into the stage of adolescence.

They were seen 'abnormal' in the eyes of their parents and neighbors. It is in this stage where they had to face laxity, mortification and are bound to go through a lot of scurrilous incidents due to increased dependency on others at home and at school both emotionally and economically. This fear factor was the main reason for the rest of the respondents for not sharing their physiological problems with their family members. Disclosure of their orientation and identity during adolescence and young adulthood is thus largely dependent on the social support they have from families and friends (D`Augelli - Hershberger - Pilkington, 1998).

Because of the uncongenial school environment, the respondents failed to find out a safe space at school. This increased the number of school drop outs which ultimately diminished future employment opportunities. Ostracized by their own family members, they were forced to stay with their friends and community members. Most of the transgender are involved in sex work; begging activities in trains/shops; or work on a daily wages basis to win their bread and butter. The analysis of sample transgenders are as follows.

Results

One third of the respondents (35.6%) have completed primary education; 31.1% of the respondents completed under graduation; 17.8% of the respondents passed SSLC and 11.1% of the respondents studied up to Plus two. About 2.2% of the respondents did Diploma course and 2.2% completed Post graduation.

75.6% of the respondents stay along with their family; 10.1% of respondents stay with friends; 12.1% stays with other transgender friends and 2.2% of the respondents stay with a partner. 51% of the respondents' family members do not know that they are transgender, and they fear about the fact that if they come to know about it, they might discriminate them. About 19% of the respondents' family members accepted them as a transgender. Around 14.3% of the respondents were not accepted by their family members. And 12.3% of respondents, though faced lots of discrimination when opened up the matter, were then accepted by their family members. They say that the main reason for their acceptance is that 'either they are the only son of the family or because they are an earning member at home'. Around 3.3% of respondents are accepted by their family members but are discriminated to a greater extent.

Treatment Received by their Family

Majority of the respondents (82.3%) had been subjected to societal abuse and discrimination from more than one source, of which gundas and police play the major role. About 15.7% of the respondents were subjected to discrimination to a greater extent from the society.

Among these respondents, 65.7% were subjected to police torture and 32.3% were not. This clearly indicates the violation of human rights of transgender by the law enforcing agency themselves.

Societal Attitude

All the respondents had undergone testing and among them, around 42.3% were treated by the health care practitioners indifferently. So they feel free to approach them when they are in need. But, majority of the respondents (55.7%) claim that they have been treated in an abusive manner, or with lack of concern and so they are not able to approach them during needy time. Even HIV and AIDS prevention, treatment, care and support programs do not reach this marginalized community.

Except a very little percent of respondents (4.2%), most of the respondents (95.8%) do not possess a ration card for their identity. About 34.3% of the respondents face discrimination from more than one source including colleagues, friends and other workers. Around 32.3% said that they don't face any discrimination as they work with the same community. About 29% of the respondents revealed that they face discrimination and torture from their customers. Around 2.3% of respondents are unemployed.

Case Studies

The society including their parents, neighbors, and friends were uncomfortable with their feminine behavior and attitude. Though most of the respondents are from moderately income yielding families, they were deprived of proper food, clothing, schooling and other opportunities because of their feminine behavior right from the adolescent stage. It is to be noted that the same were provided in abundance to their 'normal' siblings.

Case Study: 'Just because I am a transgender, my father threw me out from the house with a bag filled with my belongings; my mother said that I had born to deprive the societal-respect of my family; and my brother was much bothered about his friends and college mates as they might tease him if they come to know that his brother is a transgender' says *Mani,* who is living with his community members and working for daily wages in Puducherry. *'It has been almost three years now and still my parents could not accept me'*, he adds with a deepest emotional hurt in his heart. It was really pathetic to see him finding very difficult to control his tears rolling out of his eyes when he spoke out. On the other hand, *Muthu,* a 21 year old transgender says that *'It is because of this unacceptable truth that I never opened up the matter to my family members'. 'It's really hard and fearful to keep up the secret with me to win the love and affection of my family members'*, he adds with a shivering and sore throat.

'We could not even walk down the road peacefully. I am frequently abused by men on the roadside. They give a nasty look; touch my hip; and abuse me verbally' says Raghu, who travels daily to a garment factory, where she works. These poor people were not peaceful even at their workplace as they had

to face a lot of discrimination and humiliation. *'The manager used to pester me often; and insult me if I am not cooperating with him. At one point of intolerance, I had even thought of resigning my job'*, she adds. But they are forced to adapt with such kind of an environment due to their economical needs. They share their problems; awful experiences everyday with their community members and also discuss the ways and means to tackle such situations. *'But finally the talks/discussions about our problems end up with no solution'* says Tharani, one of the room-mates of Raghu, carrying a sorrowful smile on her face denoting their helplessness.

Conclusions

Change, however, appears to be on the horizon if the considerable gains won in various states are indicators of increasing success in the battle for inclusion of transgender. In an unprecedented move, various states have accorded official recognition for the community with the issue of ration cards with a separate 'third gender' category. This is, without doubt, a major step forward in the demand for citizenship rights, as only two sexes—male and female—are recognized in Indian civil law. Further, government orders have been issued announcing unfettered access to education and counseling services. More recently, the state's social welfare department announced the constitution of a separate welfare board for transgender (Sekhar A, 2008). Also, movement in favor of the transgender community must be initiated even by the policy planners of the government and non-government sectors.

The community-based organizations are involved in organizing a number of awareness programmes for the transgender and the common public for driving the change of inclusion of transgender. Interestingly, some campaigns to mainstream the community have also involved a conscious stepping away from making demands. Media communication tools could be used to achieve the desired behavioral change goals. Some efforts in terms of HIV interventions are being operated by CBOs. Since 2004, TAI's 'We Too for a Healthy Society' campaign has been actively encouraging TGs "to use their stamina for others". Dr. Lakshmibai explains the need for such developmental initiatives alongside disease prevention programmes in the context of STDs. "We realized that variables such as low self-esteem and guilt considerably affect the behaviour of TGs. So we included behavioral and life issues in our programmes, focusing on human values such as honesty, modesty, thrift and hard work rather than any moral preaching" (Sekhar A, 2008).

The Press Council of India and other watchdog institutions of various popular media (including film, video and TV) should issue guidelines to ensure sensitive and respectful treatment of transgender issues. The number of awareness programmes about the human rights of transgender need to be increased in the form of public service announcements.

The work has to be done collectively with representatives from the transgender community and the mainstream society who generally exclude them. Unless the mainstream society understands and co-operates in this issue, with an action-oriented realization, efforts of CBOs may be unsuccessful. Thus inclusion of transgender would be a successful attempt if the Indian government takes necessary steps to prevent the existing discriminations. Transgender will contribute to the community and to the society to a greater extent and hence the government should really think of the transgender in India, and they should get their rights, finally, after so many years of independence.

References

Beall J, Piron L-H.(2005): "DFID Social Exclusion Review" London: Overseas Development Institute, pp:32-7.

Bradford, J., Ryan, C., & Rothblum, E.D. (1994): National Lesbian Health Care Survey: Implications for Mental Health Care. *Journal of Consulting and Clinical Psychology, 62*, 228–242.

Bromley, C., Curtice, J. and Given, L. (2007), *Attitudes to Discrimination in Scotland: 2006 Scottish Social Attitudes Survey*. Edinburgh: Blackwell.

D'Augelli, Anthony R.–Scott L. Hershberger–Neil W. Pilkington. (1998): Lesbian, Gay, and Bisexual Youths and their Families:

Disclosure of Sexual Orientation and Its Consequences. *American Journal of Orthopsychiatry*, 68: 361-371.

D'Augelli, A.R. (1998): "Developmental Implications of Victimization of Lesbian, Gay, and Bisexual Youths" In G. M. Herek (Ed.), *Stigma and Sexual Orientation: Understanding Prejudice Against Lesbians, Gay Men, and Bisexuals* (pp. 187–210). Thousand Oaks, CA: Sage.

DiPlacido, J. (1998): "Minority Stress Among Lesbians, Gay Men, and Bisexuals: A Consequence of Heterosexism, Homophobia, and Stigmatization", InG.M.Herek (Ed.), *Stigma and sexual orientation:Understanding prejudice against lesbians, gay men, and bisexuals* (pp. 138–159). Thousand Oaks, CA: Sage.

Gagné, P.& Tewksbury, R. (1998): "Conformity Pressures and Gender Resistance Among Transgendered Individuals" *Social Problems*, 45(1), 81-101.

Elliott, Joel. (2009): "India's Transgender Strive for Rights".

Jessicalive (2009): "What is Social Exclusion?"

Keogh, P., Reid, D. and Weatherburn, P. (2006), *Lambeth LGBT Matters: The Needs and Experiences of Lesbians, Gay Men, Bisexual and Trans Men and Women in Lambeth*, Lambeth: Sigma Research

NLGJA.(2008): "National Lesbian and Gay Journalists Association's Stylebook Supplement"

Pluriels, Genre (2008): "Who are Transgender People? The Basics"

Sekhar, Anupama (2008): "Tamil Nadu Pioneers Transgender Inclusion". Info change agenda.

United Nations (2007): "Theoretical Concepts of Social Exclusion" Chapter 1. *In*: Literature Review on Social Exclusion in the ESCWA Region. New York, NY: United Nations, 2-7.

Vincenzi, Alessandro (2009): "India: The Transgender World" A Documentary Photo Story posted on Gaia Photos.

Wilson, Diane (2001): "Some Transgender Definitions"

"Human Rights Violations Against Sexual Minorities in India". A PUCL-K fact-finding Report about Bangalore. (2001).

Ramdas, Rao. et.al. (2003): "Human Rights Violations against the Transgender Community: A PUCL Report": A Study of Kothi and Hijra Sex Workers in Bangalore

Whittle, S. and Turner, L. (2007), '"Sex Changes"? Paradigm Shifts in 'Sex' and 'Gender' Following the Gender Recognition Act?', *Sociological Research Online*, 12 (1).

Whittle, S., Turner, L. and Al-Alami, M. (2007), *Engendered Penalties: Transgender and Transsexual People's Experiences of Inequality and Discrimination*, London: The Equalities Review.

13

Health and Poverty Among PLHIV and Its Impact on Women and Children in Household

Pradosh Debnath, Reeti Debnath

Introduction

Globally, the HIV/AIDS epidemic has become a major public health issue and is posing a serious challenge to the developed as well as the developing nations. Moses et al. concluded from their study that the epidemic is diverse, complex and heterogeneous, with considerable variation between the countries in the region, but share important characteristics. The epidemics are centered mainly on unprotected paid sex, the sharing of contaminated needles and syringes by injecting drug users, and unprotected sex among men who have sex with men. High consumption life-styles have raised aspirations of others and increased the consumption gap between the top and bottom sections. Along with the increasing value placed on material consumption, there has also been an increase in perception of sexuality as a commodity to be 'consumed' for pleasure. The gap between material aspirations and low socio-economic status of Indian women coupled with poverty has led to distortions such as the spread of promiscuity, corruption, growth of the Mafia, drug and women trafficking etc. Poverty greatly exacerbates both women and men's vulnerability by restricting access to information and services and making it more difficult to cope with the impact of the disease. All these factors have also contributed to the spread of HIV/AIDS.

A survey conducted by National AIDS Control Organization (NACO) to assess the modes of transmission among HIV positive cases during the period of January to October 2008 found that heterosexual mode is the largest mode of transmission which is nearly 85.6 percent, followed by parent to child transmission about 6.5 percent. A small fraction of HIV infections are caused by contaminated syringes and needles (1.3 percent), the transfusion of infected blood or blood products (1.2 percent). (Refer Figure 1 here).

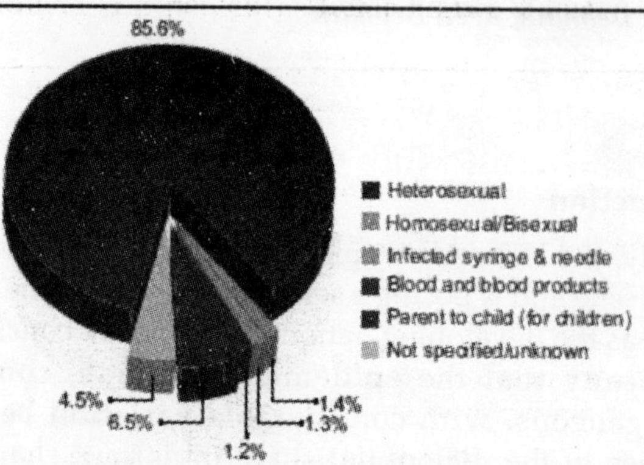

Source: NACO News, Volume IV, Issue 4, Oct- Dec 2008) available at http://www.nacoonline.org/upload/naco%20newsletters/July%202009/NACO%20-%20Newsletter%20-%20Voll-IV%20Issue-4%20-%20Oct.-Dec.%202008%20English.pdf

Figure 1: Modes of Transmission Among HIV Positive Cases (Jan-Oct, 2008)

Poverty, women trafficking, sex work, migration, lack of education, gender discrimination and violence against women are some of the factors responsible for the spread of HIV among women and girls in the Asia and the Pacific region (UNAIDS, UNFPA and UNIFEM 2004). Women's systematic lack of access to resources increases their vulnerability to the stresses of care in the context of HIV/AIDS - whether in the form of property rights that confer the assets of a deceased husband to his natal family, lack of skills and education owing to prior discrimination against female children, a lack of income-generating activities, or lack of political power to demand health and care support services. Often women have to search for new or additional livelihood after the illness of the earning member to meet with the new demands within the household. Women need to know their rights, that they can act in their own self interest and that they will be supported by families, communities and nations.

Objectives

This study is an attempt to assess the impact HIV/AIDS is likely to have over the health and the livelihood of the PLHIV's, particularly in the poor and its consequences on the women and children in India in terms of:

- The burden of domestic work and economic responsibilities on the women and their role as caregivers in the HIV affected households.
- Violence, abuse and discrimination experienced by the women and children in the HIV affected households and the status of HIV-positive widows.
- Gender disparities in the treatment seeking behaviour and out of pocket expenditure of the HIV affected households in the treatment of opportunistic infections (OIs).
- Enrolment pattern of the girl child in school, gender differences in the reasons for discontinuation of school and the type of school attended by the children from HIV and non-HIV households. (Data Source: Gender Impact of HIV and AIDS in India, NACO, NCAER and UNDP Report 2006).

The HIV/AIDS Prevalence in India

According to the Joint United Nations Programme on HIV/ AIDS (UNAIDS) 2006 report, out of an estimated 46 million people living with HIV worldwide, 5.7 million people were reported to be living with the virus in India, more than any other country in the world. However, the estimates released by NACO, supported by UNAIDS and WHO, in July 2007 led to a major revision of the prevalence estimate and indicated that the total number of people living with HIV/AIDS (PLHIV) in India in 2007 is approximately 0.36 - 0.4 percent, which corresponds to an estimated 2 million to 3.1 million. Most men who buy sex either are married or will get married. This puts a significant number of women, often perceived as 'low-risk' because they mainly have sex with their husbands, at risk of acquiring HIV. Many women are being infected by their husbands or partners who engage in paid sex or inject drugs. Females constitute around 39 percent of the burden (0.9 million). Biological, socio-cultural and economic factors make women and young girls vulnerable to HIV and AIDS. The HIV virus is more easily transmitted from men to women than from women to men; male-to-female transmission during sex is about twice as likely as female to male transmission. Children below 15 years constitute 3.5 percent of the estimated number of PLHA. Adults aged 15-49 years constitute 88.7 percent of the estimated number of PLHA. The HIV Sentinel Surveillance 2007 shows the trends of estimated adult HIV prevalence in India from 2002 to 2007 and the estimated number of PLHA in India. (Refer Figure 2 here)

Though different research groups have different opinion about the exact number of HIV/AIDS cases in the country the bitter truth is that ever since the detection of the first case of HIV amongst sex workers in Chennai, India in 1986, the national HIV prevalence has steadily grown, not only affecting most high-risk groups such as men having sex with men (MSM), female sex workers (FSW) and people who inject drugs (PWID) but also spreading into the general population in some States of India. At the national level, the overall HIV prevalence continues to portray the concentrated epidemic in India, with a high prevalence among High Risk Groups – IDU (7.2 percent), MSM (7.4 percent), FSW (5.1 percent) & STD clinic attendees (3.6 percent) and low prevalence among ANC clinic attendees (Refer Figure 3 here).

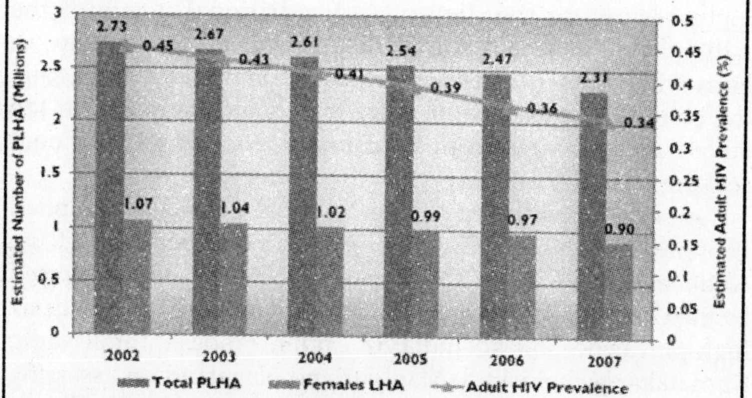

Source: HIV Sentinel Surveillance Report 2007

Figure 2: Trends of Adult HIV Prevalence and Number of PLHA (Total & Female), India, 2002-07

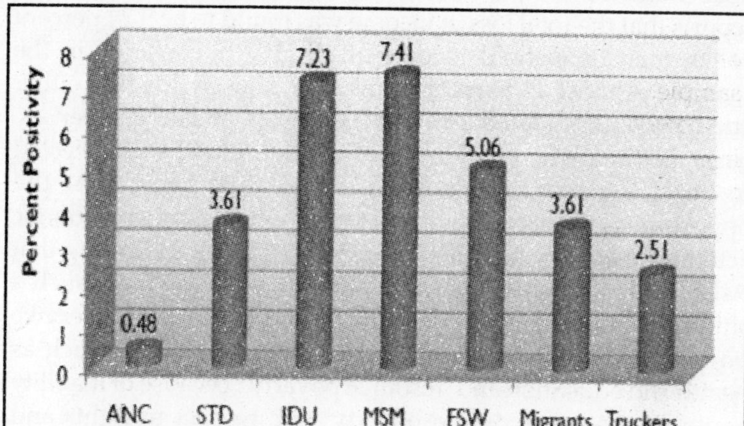

Source: www.nacoonline.org

Figure 3: HIV Prevalence Among Different Population Groups, India, 2007

The Impact of HIV/AIDS

At the micro level, though the impact of HIV/AIDS is difficult to quantify and depends on the individual's health, income does decline if the individual is unable to work and the caregiver curtails work outside the home to attend to the needs of sick family members. Expenditure on medical care increases, as do the dietary and nutritional needs of the patient. A few recent studies have revealed an increase in borrowing from friends and relatives, debt and mortgaging, the continued presence of older household members in the labour market, significant hardships especially in treatment seeking, and also widespread discrimination.

A survey conducted by the National Council of Applied Economic Research (NCAER), with the collaboration of the National AIDS Control Organization (NACO) and supported by the United Nations Development Programme (UNDP) in six high-prevalence states of India viz. Andhra Pradesh, Tamil Nadu, Karnataka, Maharashtra, Manipur and Nagaland on assessing the socio economic impact of HIV reports that the burden of non-hospitalized as well as hospitalized illnesses, the prevalence of which is substantial in HIV households, is very heavy on HIV households as compared to non-HIV households. The survey reports that the total loss in income was found to be 9.24 percent of the total household income of all HIV households in the sample. Almost 43 percent of the HIV households had either borrowed or liquidated assets to meet hospitalization expenses, from the time when a member of the household was detected to be HIV-positive. Studies in Thailand reveal that the opportunity cost of care giving in terms of curtailing of economic activities was very high for low-income groups, indicating that AIDS leads to impoverishment. Poverty resulting from such a situation can be categorised into two types namely 'service poverty', where people are unable to access services such as health and education and 'resource poverty', because of inability to access resources due to poverty with respect to rights and representation or governance.

Macroeconomic effects observed are reduction in aggregate savings and investments in the households. National economies are affected through illness and death of producers, diversion of resources from savings (and eventually investment) to care and a possible reduction in the rate of economic growth. Poorer countries are likely to have worse epidemics than rich nations as their health status is generally worse and income distribution is uneven, rendering the poorest particularly vulnerable to the disease. Indeed, since the poor are characterised by weak endowments of human and financial resources, few marketable skills and generally poor health, this leads to decreased productivity and increased risk of infection, such as from untreated STDs, which facilitate the transmission of HIV.

Poverty in HIV/AIDS Affected Households and Its Impact on the Women and the Children

The World Health Organisation considers poverty to be the world's most ruthless killer and the greatest cause of suffering. The World Health Report 1995 states that "indeed poverty is the main reason why babies are not vaccinated, why clean water and sanitation are not provided, why curative drugs and other treatments are unavailable and why mothers die in childbirth. It is the underlying cause of reduced life expectancy, handicaps, disability and starvation. Poverty is a major contributor to mental illness, stress, suicide, family disintegration and substance abuse. Every year in the developing world 12.2 million children under 5 years die, most of them from causes which could be prevented for just a few US cents per child. They die largely because of world indifference, but most of all they die because they are poor".

Strong links between HIV/AIDS and poverty have been demonstrated, with AIDS deepening poverty and increasing inequalities at every level- household, community, regional and sectoral. Recent studies in Botswana, Swaziland, Malawi, Zambia and Tanzania have shown associations between acute food insecurity resulting from poverty and unprotected transactional sex among poor women. Delegates at a major AIDS conference in Mexico cited the cases of fisherwomen in the Pacific and women in Kenya desperate for food being forced to sell their bodies, adding to concerns of a new twist in the spread of the deadly pandemic. "Fish for sex" deals are quite common in Kenya, on the shores of Lake Victoria, where women fish traders meet incoming boats and sleep with fishermen for a favorable price.

Poverty is also depriving people of access to health facilities, schools and media and thus limits their access to information and education on HIV/AIDS. Studies conducted in different states of India reveal that the poor have greater financial problems in accessing treatment, leading to adoption of various coping mechanisms like selling of assets and taking out loans, migration in search of new jobs, withdrawing the children particularly the girl child from school to take care for the sick or sending them to stay with relatives etc. Poverty pushes families, often unaware of the risks, to send children into the work force or to hand them over to recruiters promising jobs in a distant place where, unprotected, they might be forced into a childhood of harsh labor or sexual abuse. Many HIV affected families would resort to home based activities such as vending, to earn extra money to support medical expenditures. However, mounting medical fees, additional care related expenses, the reduced ability of care givers to work and later on the funeral expenses collectively push HIV affected households deeper into poverty. As HIV/AIDS affects the household, a vicious cycle of ill health and low productivity, increasing poverty and malnutrition develops in the society. (Refer Figure 4 here)

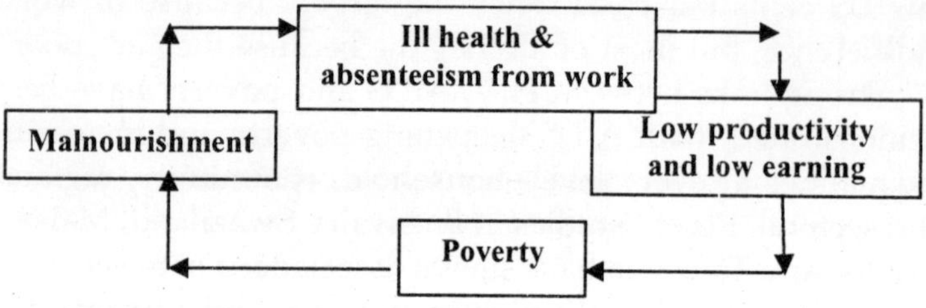

Figure 4: The Cycle of Poverty, Ill Health and Productivity

It is well researched in the developed as well as the developing countries that women are primarily responsible for domestic work, bringing up children and providing care for the sick and the elderly and India is no exception to this. Women in India tend to bear the burden of most of the household chores like cooking, cleaning the house, washing, bringing up children and taking care of the elderly and the sick and in rural India in addition to these activities, they have to travel a long distance to fetch water and fuel. In households, where an earning male member is infected by HIV, women may be forced to complement earning along with other household activities. They may have to take up paid work, and in addition to the routine household activities, they may have to take care of the patients suffering from AIDS related illnesses as well (UNDP, 2003). As the primary care giver, women invest enormous cost of time and resources to provide this care as well as have to face the impact of the loss of loved ones. They face emotional exhaustion, fatigue and burn out, in addition to the depletion of financial resources to meet the mounting medical expenses. Their role as a caregiver could be extremely taxing in terms of time as well as physical exertion. This would result in what is now termed as "time poverty" for women.

HIV/AIDS and Its Impact on Health and Health Seeking Behavior

As mentioned earlier in this study, patients infected with HIV are at an increased risk for a variety of physical ailments. Compared to many other diseases which can be cured, AIDS is costly because many of the opportunistic infections associated with AIDS (TB, pneumonia, and others) are expensive to treat. Medical expenses of the HIV households are almost four times higher than the per capita per month medical expenses of the non-HIV households. Reduced incomes and savings, increased expenditures and poverty in HIV/AIDS affected households have a direct impact on the women and children in the household. The study conducted by NCAER, NACO and UNDP reports that there are gender differences in the health-seeking behaviour and out-of pocket expenditure on healthcare in AIDS affected households. As compared to men, in the case of women, a higher percentage of illnesses are left untreated, clearly indicating a gender gap in the treatment-seeking behaviour. While in the case of men, only 4.4 percent of the illness episodes were left untreated, in the case of women this percentage was more than double at 9.7 percent. There is a substantial gender gap in the average cost of hospitalisation; while the average household expenditure per hospitalisation is Rs. 2,994 for men, this average is much lower at Rs. 1,953 for women. Women are more likely to wait longer periods of time before seeking services and treatments during the course of an illness, they are more likely to be at an advanced stage of HIV infection and present related opportunistic infections before they actually seek out treatment and services.

Recent studies of HIV affected people show that the PLHIV's also suffer from mental disorders and suicidal tendencies. The knowledge of a positive diagnosis will leave patients with intrusive, brooding thoughts, panic attacks, depression, social isolation, feelings of desperation and altered behavior. Dr Prabhat Sitholey, former head of the department of Psychiatry at Chattrapati Shahuji Maharaj Medical University (CSMMU) in Lucknow explains: "The world over, psychiatric disorders stemming from infectious diseases are widespread. All such individuals are doubly disadvantaged as they do not display expected health seeking behaviour and are prone to a diminished state of responsiveness." One such study of "Suicidal Ideation in HIV positive patients", conducted by CSSMU in September 2008 tracked 250 patients in the 18-60 age group to conclude that almost half of them displayed suicidal tendencies. The pre-disposition became more pronounced in those who also had depression, adjustment disorders, indulged in substance abuse or displayed other mental illnesses. Such tendencies are also more marked in females, those who are unemployed, unmarried and those who come from low socio economic status families (family income less than Rs.5000 a month).

Impact on Savings and Consumption Pattern

The NCAER, NACO and UNDP survey reveals how HIV and AIDS influence the level and pattern of consumption and savings of the households. Even though the proportion of food expenditure is much lower for the HIV households, the per capita per month expenditure on food of these households is slightly higher than that of the non-HIV households. The difference in per capita expenditure on food between the two types of households is mainly due to the expenditure on "other food" items, especially the need to have nutritious and balanced food resulting in higher expenses. A notable feature about savings is the lower average household saving of HIV households as compared to non-HIV households in both rural and urban areas. This is largely indicated by the large and negative savings in jewellery and agricultural land by the HIV households, even as savings in these forms are positive in the case of non-HIV households. The study empirically validates the assumption that HIV and AIDS result in a decline in savings and assets of the households and ultimately have a deleterious physical and mental impact on the members in the household.

HIV widows are fairly young, mostly in the age group of 20 to 30 years and their households are economically and socially worse off than the other HIV households. A comparison of the HIV widow households with the other HIV households reveals that their savings are lower; percentage of households which have either borrowed or liquidated assets after a family member became HIV-positive is higher. A higher percentage of widow households live in kutcha houses. The percentage of households owning agricultural land or having livestock is lesser among widow households than in the remaining HIV households, as the widow households would have disposed off their land and livestock in order to meet the medical expenses of their deceased husbands. Thus, a higher percentage of these widow households are below the poverty line as compared to the others. This can have serious financial consequences for them and their families that are likely to push them into activities that put them at higher risk of HIV infection, or compromise their ability to seek treatment and care.

Gender Discrimination and Violence

All women, whether married, single, divorced, widowed or adolescent girls are more vulnerable to the negative impact of HIV/AIDS than men. Some of the socio-economic and cultural reasons for this disparity are on account of inequalities within the family; violence against women; issues concerning women's inheritance and property rights; low priority for women's treatment; lack of education; and an inability to negotiate safe sex. Denial of information, discrimination, lack of security, being blamed for bringing in the "curse", and being evicted from their homes after the death of the husband are regular occurrences for HIV-positive women in India. The NCAER study highlights that women are more supportive of their HIV positive husbands (12.4 percent) than men of their HIV positive wives (8.4 percent). While nearly 5.5 percent of female PLWHA have been asked to leave home after being tested positive in comparison only 1.9 percent of the male PLWHA had been told to do so. Facts also reveal that an overwhelming majority (84 percent) of women in the sample informed their spouses immediately, the percentage of men who did the same is much lower (69 percent). A study conducted by Taraphdar et al; among 46 PLWHA's (consisting of 40 males and 6 females) regarding disclosure of the HIV status to one's sexual partner concludes that all the female patients had disclosed their serostatus to their sexual partners, as compared to 26 (65 percent) in the 40 males.

Negative outcomes including blame, abandonment, violence, anger, stigma and depression following disclosure was seen to be 16.6 percent in women as compared to 11.5 percent in men. A workshop titled 'Understanding Violence against Women and its Implications for Our Struggle against HIV/AIDS' undertaken by the School of Women's Studies, Jadavpur University, and Action Aid India in 2007 analyzed the interrelation between violence against women and the increasing incidence of HIV among women. The researchers interviewed 60 positive women from low income and lower middle class backgrounds in and around Kolkata and Siliguri in north Bengal. They concluded from their study that in a patriarchal society, the already inferior status of women becomes worse if she becomes HIV-positive. She may even be blamed for her husband's infection. "My in-laws blamed me for my husband's illness saying that because I couldn't satisfy him, he went to other women and developed the disease," said one woman quoted in the survey. When widowed or orphaned as a result of HIV/AIDS women and girls face more AIDS-related stigma, discrimination or even abandonment. The study by NCAER, NACO and UNDP reports that the economic and social situation of HIV-positive widows was particularly dire.

They "face a double burden (as a widow and an HIV-positive) of stigma and suffer discrimination from the family and society in which they live. The study shows that hardly 10 percent of widows were living with their husband's family and out of [the others] more than 90 percent had stopped living in their marital homes after the death of their husband. Only 9 percent of widows reported getting financial support from their in-laws and 79 percent of the widows complained that they were denied a share in their husband's property.

Impact on Schooling and Education of Children

House hold income is one of the important demand side factors that determine the schooling of children. As a result of reduced income and increased expenditure, many households have to compromise on their children's education. Many children in HIV/AIDS affected households leave school in order to take care of family members or provide income. This again magnifies the problem of child labour. The study by NCAER, NACO and UNDP measured the impact of HIV and AIDS on the schooling of children by comparing enrolment rates, school attendance rates across HIV and non-HIV households. The differences between HIV and non- HIV households are more marked in current enrolment percentages, indicating that the dropout rates are higher in HIV households. There is a gender difference in the current enrolment percentages especially in the case of rural children belonging to HIV households, which suggests that in the HIV households, girls are more likely to be withdrawn from school. The reason for discontinuation of schooling is largely unaffordability. The average number of days absent from school during the last academic year was higher for the children of HIV households.

Pradhan et al. reports that in the case of HIV households, the percentage of girls attending government schools is significantly higher than the percentage of boys attending government schools. The HIV-positive parents feel unhappy about shifting their wards from private to government schools however, given the limited resources they would rather spend more on the education of boys than girls. This is not surprising since girls are often forced to drop their education in favour of domestic and care related activities, which are obviously heightened in a situation of HIV. Previous research studies have already proved that more women than men are caretakers of people with HIV which may saddle them with the triple burden of caring for children, the elderly and people living with AIDS as well as financial responsibility for their family's survival.

Lost Childhood

Children and young people are at the forefront of the HIV/ AIDS epidemic today. The most vulnerable group to infections, millions of children face the socio economic and psycho social impact of the epidemic. Where AIDS deaths have forced many adolescents to take on adult roles, the transition from childhood to adulthood is disappearing. For children whose parents are living with HIV, life is likely to be a series of hardships. As the disease progresses, the parents fall ill repeatedly and this leads eventually to loss of jobs. AIDS consumes family budgets, fewer funds remain available for children's education, health care, and other needs. As mentioned earlier, children leave school to care for a dying parent or take care of younger siblings. Many children have to not only see their parents die, but they also have to live with the stigma of being associated with someone who had AIDS.

In India, the extended family system is still strong. Children are usually taken care of by their aunts, uncles or grandparents if their parents die suddenly. But if the death is due to AIDS, the extended family is much less helpful, either because of misplaced fears of becoming infected themselves, or because of the stigma of being associated with someone who is HIV-positive. Many children raised by grandparents face a second loss when their much older grandparents die. The children, who already have to deal with the loss of their parents, are left to fend for themselves in a hostile world where they are unwanted. For lakhs of AIDS orphans, the list of challenges is indeed daunting: social exclusion, economic uncertainty, denial of property and inheritance rights, illiteracy, malnutrition, illness and physical and sexual abuse. Shunned by their families and communities, they are often placed in situations that only increase their risk towards contracting the dreadful disease.

Conclusions

From the above discussion, it is well understood that the continuing high prevalence of HIV/AIDS in India is the 'S-factor' (silence, stigma, shame), which leads to discrimination, denial and speaking out for help. The only means to minimize the effect of AIDS is to enable people to *Know AIDS for No AIDS.* Community awareness is desirable to ease the stigma and discrimination attached with the disease and motivate people living with HIV to speak out to meet their reproductive health and treatment needs. More HIV/AIDS oriented programmes need to come up and such promotions need to be continued. Teachers, parents, counselors, doctors, social workers and professionals all can play a significant role in generating awareness about prevention and control of HIV/AIDS.

Discussion of sex matters between parents and their children has been a taboo, and this needs to be changed with time. There is lack of couple communication about sexual matters and in many instances the HIV status of one partner is not known to the other (Chattejee et. al; 2006, Schensul et al., 2009; NCAER study; 2006). The NFHS III data shows that only 57% of ever married women (15-49 years) have heard of AIDS. Lack of access and utilization of MCH services and weak outreach system continues to be a barrier to provide HIV prevention and treatment services to eligible HIV positive pregnant women. Of the six states where the NCAER survey was conducted, it was seen that in Manipur and Nagaland, a small but higher percentage of women than men took treatment from private health facilities. The expenditure per non hospitalised illness was also slightly more for women in Nagaland. An analysis of the profile of the sample households indicated that the sample households in these two states have higher annual income compared to others. Also, the level of education of the female PLWHA was better than that in the other states. Percentage of female PLWHA who are salary earners was also slightly higher in these two states. This leads to the conclusion that women who are better educated and have better income are likely to have better access to health facilities and seek treatment. Promotion and use of female condoms and microbicides will also give women more control over their bodies and lives.

Relatives who accept affected children find it difficult to manage them due their meager income, limited resources coupled with the discrimination they face. Hence, the caregivers of children affected by AIDS too need support, both financial and emotional. Subsidizing school expenses such as school uniforms and school fees, offering free meals and books can be of help to the children in HIV affected households. Interventions and activities should aim to provide social and financial support especially for poor infected persons and the care givers of orphaned children. Vocational training to those who have lost their jobs and to their family members can be given so that they can sustain themselves and earn a decent livelihood without being dependent on others.

AIDS has become a major challenge for human security. By eventually impairing economic growth, the epidemic has an impact on investment, trade and national security, leading to still more widespread and extreme poverty. Even if the country's epidemic does not match the severity of those in southern Africa, it is clear that HIV/AIDS will have a devastating effect on the lives of millions of Indians for many years to come. It is hence important to integrate and intensify HIV/AIDS programmes into an overall strategy to combat the root causes of the transmission of the disease, i.e. poverty, lack of education and awareness, inequality between classes, individuals, and between men and women–ignorance, discrimination and exploitation.

References

"More AIDS Risked as Poor Women Trade Sex for Food" The Financial Express, August 5th, 2008. http://www.financialexpress.com/news/more-aids-risked-as-poor-women-trade-sex-for-food/344966/0.

Chatterjee N, Hosain GM (2006): Perceptions of Risk and Behaviour Change for Prevention of HIV Among Married Women in Mumbai, India. Journal of Health Population Nutrition, 24(1):81–88.

Coursen-Neff; Zama (2004): "Future Forsaken: Abuses Against Children Affected by HIV/AIDS in India", Human Rights Watch, New York.

Debnath, R (2009): "The Socio- Economic Consequences of HIV/AIDS on Women, Children and the Vulnerable Population in India", Working Draft prepared for presentation at the National Consultation on HIV Social Research Priorities in India, December 17-19th, TISS, Mumbai.

Dilip, T. R. and Duggal, Ravi (2002): 'Incidence of Non-Fatal Health Outcomes and Debt in Urban India', Draft Paper prepared for Urban Research Symposium, December 9-11, The World Bank, Washington DC. (available online www.ucl.ac.uk/... / drivers_urb_change/urb_society/pdf_health_educ/CEHAT_Ravi_Non_Fatal_Health_india.pdf).

International Institute for Population Sciences, Macro International. National Family Health Survey (NFHS-3), 2005–06. India, Mumbai, International Institute for Population Sciences, 2007. JAMA, 2008, 300(6):703–710.

Knodel, John and Im-em, Wassana (2003): The Economic Consequences for Parents of Losing an Adult Child to AIDS: Evidence from Thailand, Population Studies Centre Research Report, University of Michigan.

Mehra, A.K. and Gupta, S. (2006): The Impact of HIV/AIDS on Women Caregivers in Situations of Poverty: Policy Issues, New Delhi: Indian Institute of Public Administration/UNIFEM

Moses S, Blanchard JF, Kang H, et al., (2006): AIDS in South Asia: Understanding and Responding to a Heterogenous Epidemic. Washington, DC: World Bank.

NACO (2007): 'HIV Sentinel Surveillance and HIV Estimation in India 2007: A Technical Brief'.

National AIDS Control Organisation, National Council of Applied Economic Research, et al. (2006): Socio-Economic Impact of HIV and AIDS in India. UNDP.

National Family Health Survey (NFHS-3) 2005-06, September 2007.

Pradhan, B, et al; (2006): Socio Economic Impacts of HIV/AIDS in India, NACO, NCAER and UNDP.

Schensul, S. L et al., (2009): Multilevel Perspectives on Community Intervention: An Example from an Indo-US HIV Prevention Project in Mumbai, India. American Journal of Community Psychology, 43(3–4):277–291.

Taraphdar P, Dasgupta A, Saha B. (2007): Disclosure Among People Living with HIV/AIDS. Indian Journal of Community Medicine, 32(4):280–282.

UNAIDS (2006): 'Report on the Global AIDS Epidemic'.

UNAIDS (2007): 'Press Release: 2.5 Million People in India Living with HIV, According to New Estimates', 6th July.

UNDP/UNFPA/UNIFEM (2004): "Women and HIV/AIDS: Confronting the Crisis".

World Health Organization (1995): The World Health Report 1995, Geneva.

World Health Organization (2005): 'India: Summary Country Profile for HIV/AIDS Treatment Scale-up', December.

URL's

http://www.avert.org/aidsindia.htm.

http://www.hivaidsonline.in/index.php/Vulnerable-Groups/violence-against-women-and-hivaids.html

http://www.indiatogether.org/2009/aug/hlt-hivmind.htm

http://www.jadavpur.edu/academics/sws/research.asp

http://www.nacoonline.org

*http://*www.ncaer.org

*http://*www.nfhsindia.org

http://www.reuterslink.org/news/HIVPuja.htm

http://www.saathii.org/ovc/context_and_response/children%20and%20AIDS%20_%20NACO%20program%20updates.pdf

http://www.savethechildren.in/india/key_sectors/hiv_aids.html

http://www.unicef.org/media/media_45451.html

14

Impact of Male Sexual Dysfunction on Sexually Transmitted Diseases

Anindita Chowdhury

Introduction

Sexual dysfunction is the persistent or recurrent inability to react emotionally or physically to sexual stimulation in a way expected of the average healthy person or according to one's own standards of acceptable sexual response. Sexual dysfunctions are disorders related to a particular phase of the sexual response cycle. It can occur during the desire, excitement, plateau, or orgasm stage of the sexual response cycle. For example, sexual dysfunctions include sexual desire disorders, sexual arousal disorders, orgasm disorders, and sexual pain disorders. If a person has difficulty with some phase of the sexual response cycle or a person experiences pain with sexual intercourse he /she may have a sexual dysfunction.

Any of the following factors can contribute to sexual dysfunction:

Psychological/Emotional Factors

Factors including stress, negative body image, performance anxiety, expectation of failure, fear of pregnancy, memory of negative sexual experiences, and fear of acquiring or transmitting a sexually transmitted disease

Biological/Physiological Factors

These include changes related to aging, certain medical conditions (arthritis, reproductive cancers, diabetes, cardiac disease, hypertension), physical injury (such as spinal cord injuries), the effects hormonal changes or of hormonal contraceptive methods, pregnancy, and substance abuse.

Interpersonal/Social Factors

These include peer pressure, poor communication with a partner, sexual abuse, attitudes toward sexual orientation, uncertainty of how to behave, and conflicts with one's partner.

Environmental Factors

These include cultural influences, gender dynamics, availability of partners (partner ratio), and physical setting (lack of privacy).

For example, one of the most common dysfunctions is inhibited arousal during the excitement stage. This presents as erectile dysfunction (*impotence*) in men or lack of lubrication in women. Occasional inhibited arousal is common and not dysfunctional; however, chronic inhibited arousal is a sexual dysfunction that can be caused by recreational drug use, certain medications, certain diseases, physical damage, or psychological factors.

Examples of Male Sexual Dysfunctions Include

Hypoactive Sexual Desire Disorder: This disorder may be present when a person has decreased sexual fantasies and a decreased or absent desire for sexual activity as a result. The person usually does not initiate sexual activity and may be slow to respond to his/her partner's sexual advances. This disorder can be present in adolescents and can persist throughout a person's life or be a response to a period of stress..

Sexual Aversion Disorder: A person who actively avoids and has a persistent or recurrent extreme aversion to genital sexual contact with a sexual partner may have sexual aversion disorder. In order to be considered a disorder, the aversion to sex must be a cause of difficulty in the person's sexual relationship. The individual with sexual aversion disorder usually reports anxiety, fear, or disgust when given the opportunity to be involved sexually. Touching and kissing may even be avoided. Extreme anxiety such as panic attacks may actually occur. It is not unusual for a person to feel nauseated, dizzy, or faint.

Male Erectile Disorder: If a male is unable to maintain an erection throughout sexual activity, he may have male erectile disorder. This problem must be either persistent or recurrent in nature. Erectile dysfunction is classified as either primary or secondary in nature. Males suffering from the former, have never been able to have intercourse while in the latter males have succeeded in having intercourse once twice or a thousand times before his dysfunction began. Secondary erectile dysfunction is about ten times more common than primary erectile dysfunction. Some males will be unable to obtain any erection. Others will have an adequate erection, but lose the erection during sexual activity. Erectile disorders may accompany a fear of failure. Sometimes this disorder is present throughout life. In many cases the erectile failure is intermittent and sometimes dependent upon the type of partner or the quality of the relationship.

Male Orgasmic Disorder: When a male experiences significant delay or total absence of orgasm following sexual activity, he may have male orgasmic disorder. In order to be qualified as a disorder, the symptoms must present a significant problem for the individual.

Premature Ejaculation: When minimal sexual stimulation causes orgasm and ejaculation on a persistent basis for the male, he is said to have premature ejaculation. In order to qualify as a problem the timing has to significantly affect the person or the relationship or both. Premature ejaculation is sometimes seen in young men who have experienced this since their first attempt at intercourse.

Performance Anxiety: Sexual performance anxiety can become a major issue within a relationship-and the more important the relationship is to you, the more anxious you are likely to become about sex and your own performance. Whether one suffers from premature ejaculation, impotence or some other sexual difficulty, anxiety around sex only makes things worse. Ultimately, a vicious circle is created, when worrying about your performance exacerbates the original problem, until the sexual performance anxiety becomes a problem in itself.

Sexually Transmitted Diseases

Infections that are transmitted by sexual contact are referred to as sexually transmitted diseases or STDs. STDs include infections that were formerly known as venereal diseases (VDs). Other than HIV, the most common STDs are chlamydia, gonorrhea, syphilis, genital herpes, human papillomavirus, hepatitis B, trichomoniasis and bacterial vaginosis. Adolescents and young adults are the age groups at the greatest risk for acquiring an STD.

Oral Sexual Transmission

Sexually Transmitted Diseases such as HIV and Hepatitis B are thought to not normally be transmitted through mouth-to-mouth contact, although it is possible to transmit some STDs between the genitals and the mouth, during oral sex. It is also responsible for the increased incidence of herpes simplex virus 1 (which is usually responsible for oral infections) in genital infections and the increased incidence of the type 2 virus (more common genitally) in oral infections. Infections like Cytomegalovirus infections, Herpes simplex virus (especially HSV-1) and Infectious mononucleosis are primarily transmitted through oral medium and may be caught through direct oral contact such as kissing, or by indirect contact such as by sharing a drinking glass or a cigarette.

Chlamydia:

It is one of the most common sexually transmitted diseases. The Center for Diseases Control and Prevention(2008) estimates that more than 3 million cases of chlamydia occur every year. The type of infection is bacterial in nature from Chlamydia trachomatis strain which lives in vaginal fluid and semen. The mode of transmission is mainly through vaginal and anal sex, although it is much less common it can also be passed on via oral sex and hand to eye contact.

Syphilis

It is a sexually transmitted disease caused by the bacteria Treponoma pallidum. It is often called the "Great Imitator" because syphilis symptoms resemble those of other common diseases. The majority of syphilis sufferers are male, accounting for about 60% of all cases. If .caught early on in syphilis test, syphilis can be easily treated. However, if left untreated, syphilis can cause heart problems, psychological disorders, blindness, and death Centers for Disease Control and Prevention,2006. Syphilis also increases the risk of contracting HIV, the virus that causes AIDS, by up to five fold. The type of Infection is bacterial. Syphilis is almost always transmitted through sexual contact with an infected person. The syphilis bacteria can easily spread from the ulcers on an infected person to the mucous linings of the mouth, genitals, and anus of an uninfected sexual partner. Though unlikely, it is possible to contract the infection by coming into contact with the broken skin of an infected person. Syphilis can also be passed from an infected mother to her unborn child. To prevent being infected with syphilis, contact with open sores needs to be avoided. Condoms will not completely safeguard from getting syphilis, as sores can occur on other parts of the body. Use a dental dam during oral sex is another preventive method.

Herpes Simplex Viruses (HSV)

There are eight types of human herpes virus. It is the herpes simplex viruses types I and II - known as HSV-1 and HSV-2 - that are responsible for genital herpes. HSV-2 is more frequently transmitted by sexual contact and is one of the most prevalent STDs worldwide. In general HSV-1 infects the mouth, lips or nose, causing cold sores. HSV-2 infects the genital and anal area. Although genital and anal infections used to almost always be caused by HSV-2 infection, HSV-1 is becoming more common in these parts of the body due to greater numbers of people having oral sex.

Gonorrhea

This is the oldest and most common form of STD. it is passed by any form of sexual contact ranging from sexual intercourse to fellatio, anal intercourse and infrequently cunnilingus or even kissing. A woman who has intercourse once with an infected man has a fifty percent chance of getting gonorrhea while a man who has intercourse with an infected person has a twenty to twenty five percent chance of getting infected.

Acquired Immune Deficiency Syndrome

The newest and most frightening STD to come to public awareness was first documented in 1981. Current evidence suggests that the number of new cases is doubling or tripling every year. It appears to be an unusually fatal disease, and in fact some researchers believe that no one survives a full blown case. These two facts–a high rate of increase and a high fatality rate combine to produce a public health threat almost without parallel in recent times. It is primarily spread through sexual contact with a virus HTLV-3. Non sexual transmission can also occur in cases of blood transfusion and needle sharing.

Objectives

The aim of the study is to find out the impact the sexual problem has on the health of the person, in terms of risk factors. Paucity of research from a cultural point of view regarding male sexual dysfunction in the Indian was another reason that the study was carried out using qualitative research method. The aim of the present study is to anchor the importance normal sexuality has in preventing sexually transmitted diseases and infection. This study also provides insight about the population at risk of incurring sexually transmitted diseases and infection.

Qualitative research method was used since the study is exploratory in nature and impact of sexual dysfunction on sexual health was conceptualized from analysis of narratives conversed during interview sessions.

Methodolgy

Coverage

This paper is based on a study conducted among 40 unmarried males of 18-35 years presenting with a history of multiple sexual exposures ranging over a period of month to over one year The study covered two groups of patients for comparative research purpose, with one group primarily taking treatment for sexual problem and another group taking treatment for sexually transmitted diseases and infections from a sexual health clinic in Kolkata. The selection was done purposively.

Research Technique

Interview is a part of daily life, it's an informal way of coming to know a person, entering his phenomenological world, gathering facts, or enhancing familiarity with an object or subject. However interview in qualitative method is much more critical than that, it goes beyond mere gathering of facts it is more of an attempt to construct meaning and interpretation in the context of conversation (Kvale 1996) Two types of interview schedules-semi-structured interview (schedule and unstructured interview schedule–were used. The semi-structured interview sometimes called guided interview was used to generate further questions to develop interesting areas of inquiry during the interviews. They provided the raw material for narratives generated in the unstructured interviews. So natural is the impulse to narrate wrote H white, (1989) that the form is almost inevitable for any report of how things happened, a solution to "the problem of how to translate the knowing into telling. Research interviews are no different respondents if not interrupted will organize replies into episodes of their ailment like a story with a beginning (precipitating factors), the suffering the mental and physical anguish and final reconciliation. A teller in a conversation takes a listener into a past time and recapitulates what happened then to make a point, often a moral one. Respondents narrativize particular experiences in their lives often where there has been a breach between ideal and real self and society. Embodying the self in stories can occur in settings where the self is being disembodied, such as medical examinations (Young, 1989).

The areas covered in the interview can be summarized in terms of the chief complaint , the identity crisis and coping with the problem . Any form of dysfunction has a debilitating effect it not just affects the soma but the psyche as well. Sexual identity is a component closely related to feeling of manliness and sexual confidence, therefore when a man faces sexual crisis there is a strong possibility that it might affect his interaction with his friends family and colleagues . the interview schedule was aimed at eliciting all these information.

Chief Complaint

1. Can you describe, what are chief problems that you are suffering from?
2. Could you tell me near about the time since which you have realized that you have the problem
3. What made you feel that you have the problem?
4. How does it affect your life or future?
5. What would you consider caused it?

Identity

1. How would you describe yourself as a person? Prompt what sort of a person are you , like happy moody nervy , anxious etc
2. How has the problem affected you as an individual?
3. How did you feel sexually before having had the problem?
4. Has it affected your interaction with your family, friends or colleagues?

Coping

1. What does the term sexual problem (as stated by patient) mean to you?
2. What did you do when you found out about the problem?
3. How have you dealt with the problem till now

Further probing was left to situational factors and information obtained within the larger frame.

Data Analysis

Logic of qualitative enquiry used in this study was that of 'Analytic induction'. This approach has been developed mostly by Strauss and Corbin (1998). In this, each case was taken to develop a working hypothesis to explain causality. After that the next case was examined against it to see the extent the existing hypothesis explains both. The hypothesis was refined with each progressive case to come up with a generalization that explains all the cases and would be useful to explain any new case. The trustworthiness of analytic induction depends upon the sampling procedure, which in this case was that purposive sampling

Analytical approach used in the study is called 'natural narrative', a term coined by Labov and Waletzky, 1967, since, narratives used were first person oral accounts of experience that took a particular form.

Using Labov's 1972, 1982 framework the simple narratives were organized for interpretative purpose. According to Labov narratives are made from a common set of elements and every clause has a function: to provide an abstract for what follows (A) orient the listener (O),carry the complicating action (CA) evaluate its meaning (E) and resolve the action (R). In the present research stories and other narrative segments were located from a stretch of talk and were inductively build into a framework for interpretative and analytical purpose using the above structure.

Procedure

The audio recording of interview was not possible in the clinical setup because of the sensitive nature of the topic under discussion. Therefore the entire conversation was handwritten. The narratives came about when the patient was asked to elaborate on some detail with an example. For instance while asking how he came to know of his problem, his history of sexual exposure was obtained and further probing provided a narrative of his experience and outcome of the exposure. Four to six sessions per patient were used for obtaining the data The paucity of elaborateness of discussion regarding cause and effect was one significant factor for large sample size. The transcripts were analyzed under the heads of (a) chief complaints, nature extent and duration of problem, (b)the extent of impact on the persons concept of self in the intrapersonal and interpersonal level (c) the behavioral manifestation of the problem and coping strategies (d) impact of the problem on health, physical and mental. Deeper level of analysis was carried out using Labov's(,1972, 1982)method. The rationale for using qualitative method lies in the fact that to understand the impact of sexual problem on the person and his life one has to understand the subjective world of the person with the person. The behavioral manifestation of the problem and subsequent actions of the client while in treatment cannot be gauged through scales. It has bearing upon the dysfunctional level of thinking which most patients having the dysfunction exhibit to a greater or lesser extent. Transcriptions were prepared simultaneously with the data collection. After each transcription the basic analysis of the data was carried out

Interpretation of Results

Background variables like age, educational qualification, occupation, area of origin, nature of sexual partner, chief reproductive health problems, duration of problem and condom usage behavior were obtained using the semi-structured interview schedule It was observed that 13 out of the 40 respondents belonged to the age group 31 years to 35 years, while 15, 7 and 5 were in the group 26 to 30 years, 21 to 25 years and below 20 years respectively.

All the respondents had some sort of formal education. About 14 out of 40 respondents were educated up to the secondary level. About 10 out of 40 respondents were graduate, while 8, 5 and 3 out of the remaining 40 respondents received higher secondary to below graduate, up to primary and post graduate education respectively.

Regarding occupation it was reported that 16 out of 40 respondents were employed in some organization either government or private while 17 were self employed and the rest 7 were un-employed.

About 20 out of 40 respondents came from semi urban area of origin while 11 were from rural background and the rest 9 were from urban origin.

Nature of sexual partner was categorized in terms of girl friend, commercial sex worker (CSW), multiple partner. During data collection another category developed under the head of 'boudi'. It was observed that about 10 out of 40 respondents had sex only with their girl friend. About 23 had sex with commercial sex workers as well as boudi's belonged to the category of multiple sex partners. About 7 had sex only with commercial sex workers.

Respondents were divided into two groups, one group taking treatment for sexual problem (n-25) while 15 respondents came with problem of sexually transmitted infection. Out of the 15, about 11 complained of underlying sexual problem as well. About 18 out of 36 respondents taking treatment for sexual problem complained of performance anxiety either due to history of failure in sex or premature ejaculation or quick loss in erection or small organ or due to naivety. About 9 out of 36 complained of size problem. 13 out of 36 respondents reported premature ejaculation as a chief sexual problem while 10 respondents reported erectile dysfunction.

Condom usage behavior revealed that 18 out of the 40 respondents never wore condom during their sexual intercourse, 10 respondents out of 40 always wore condom while 12 out of 40 respondents sometimes wore condom. Deeper probing revealed that none (0) of the 40 respondents took any form of protection during oral sex.

Among the respondents (15) who came with sexually transmitted disease to the clinic, 7 out of 15 wore condom always while 8 did not wear condom in the last episode or in previous ones. Condom burst, slippage, multiple partner unprotected sex, anal sex and oral sex were the causes attributed to their infection based on the type.

Table 1 displays excerpts for erectile problem as a chief complaint of sexual dysfunction for some of the respondents taking part in the study. Their nature of problem, behavioral manifestation of the problem, impact on attitude towards self as a result and its implication on health that is mental and physical has been tabularized. Due to paucity of space only few excerpts and one dysfunction are given.

a) chief complaints, nature extent and duration of problem, (b) the extent of impact on the persons concept of self in the intrapersonal and interpersonal level (c) the behavioral manifestation of the problem and coping strategies (d) impact of the problem on health, physical and mental.

Discussion

In any society of the world masculinity is often synonymous with sexual potency. Males consider their sexual prowess as a mark of manhood which imparts a sense of confidence in dealing with the opposite sex. Receding hairline and sexual competency are some of the most sensitive topics for most men. Sexual information lies in the list of tabooed topics in the Indian society, resulting in most people having the sexual dysfunction suffering in silence. The emphasis on sexual rights that are bestowed upon a man on marriage makes male sexual competency an yardstick for grooms to be. This results in sexual anxiety and depression leading to performance anxiety for virgin males. They seek advice of their married contemporaries who often advice them to use sildenafil citrate commonly branded as Viagra to overcome their fear of failure. Another common advice is to try out with a consenting adult to gauge the correctness of the fear. In the clinical setup, these consenting adults are often older women who are referred

Table 2
Relationship between Sexual Dysfunction and Sexually Transmitted Diseases

	Chief Complaints	*Impact on Self*	*Behavioral Manifestation and or Coping Strategies*	*Impact of the Sexual Problem on Overall Health*
Quotes from transcripts Some of the verbatim quotes of the respondents transcripts for problems of erection	I am unable to perform for a couple of years now I lose my erection the minute I am about to enter It takes very long to become hard It is not hard enough for penetration It becomes lose the minute I wear a condom Sometimes I lose the hardness when I trying to wear the condom I am losing my sexual desire slowly I don't enjoy intercourse as much as I used to I am unable to satisfy my partner I want to know whether I can perform	I feel so ashamed I know its because of my bad habits I have brought about my own problem My partner refuses to have sex anymore with me I am losing my self confidence I am afraid to go for marriage I fear relationships I just don't know what to tell my family they are pressurizing me for marriageI don't want to destroy someone else's life I know I won't be able to perform I think I am impotent	I thought it was something to do with my partner I tried with someone I know (Boudi), It becomes a little hard if she sucks it I try about everything to make it hard I don't get an erection even when I am watching porns with my friends. I tried to have sex many times but I could not My friend suggested a medicine I tried it She tried to make it hard over a long time but nothing happened. I am unable to perform even with medicines She 'boudi' told me to consult a doctor, she knew I had a problem I tried all sorts of medicine, I was fine as long as I took the drug.	I feel very depressed I am afraid I fear I will not be able to perform My body seems to grow weak I am not able to concentrate on work My partner is very irritated with me , we have frequent fights over this I keep having a burning sensation during urination Pus comes out when I urinateI keep getting small rashes on the inner side of penis every now and then

to as *"boudi"* by the client. They are used as testing ground to ascertain the sexual performance. Men suffering from any form of sexual dysfunction are helpless since there are no test to diagnose sexual failure or the extent of failure.

The fear of failure, embarrassment and legal battles over divorce are among some of the significant factors that bring about premarital anxiety.

" I am afraid , I fear that if I am unable to perform, my whole life would be at stake, moreover I can't destroy someone else's life for my mistake. My family members would be harassed."

Secondly the feelings of guilt over masturbation add to the repertoire of anxiety. For males in Kolkata, masturbation is evil, which they are assured by traditional system of thoughts like ayurveda and Unani is a harmful habit leading to various forms of mental and physical weakness. Most males have at least once in their adolescence indulged in the act of masturbation and therefore condemn themselves.

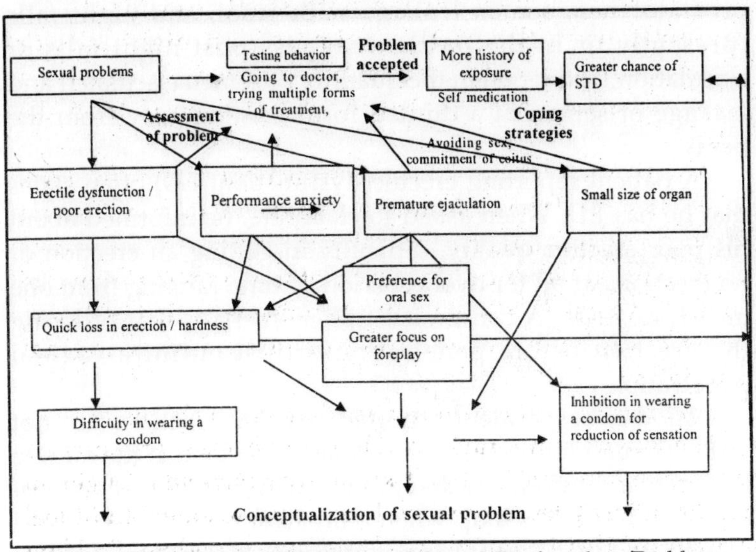

Chart I: Network Showing Impact of Sexual Dysfunctions/Problems with Sexually Transmitted Diseases

"I know I have caused my own problem , I had the bad habit of mausturbation (hostomaithun), it was because of the bad company I used to keep when I was a teenager, once I was caught and scolded. My parents told me the harm that I was causing to myself, I could not concentrate on my studies and mentally I was becoming weak, especially I was forgetting things very fast ,I started underperforming in school". In most cases the guilt becomes a part of their self concept and they feel they are being punished for their bad deed.

According to the Chart I, the most prevalent sexual problems or dysfunctions reported were

- Erectile dysfunction
- Premature ejaculation
- Performance anxiety
- Small organ

Some of the commonly reported sub problems associated with the already stated ones were general weakness, loss in appetite, severe gastric problems, weight loss, tiredness, difficulty in concentrating on work for long, dilute semen, prostatorrhea, semen leakage with stool, and night falls (presently or in the past), weakness post night falls or ejaculation., reduction in the quantity of semen ejaculated and leakage of semen in a diluted form continuously from the penis

A patient reporting erectile dysfunction(ED) often states that he has ED. When asked to elaborate, he informed about his poor erection quality, difficulty in getting an erection or no erections at all for over a period of time ranging from one month to years. A concomitant phenomena is that of losing the erection before penetration or just on intra-vaginal penetration.

Another respondent reported that his erections are not stable enough for wearing a condom, or he loses it the minute he wears a condom. " I don't know why but even if I get an erection it just goes limp when I am about to enter, and I feel so ashamed that I want to avoid wearing a condom. Problem is that wearing a condom, *"I feel committed for sex when I wear a condom but no matter how hard I try I can't sustain it beyond few seconds."*

In case of premature ejaculation , the person ejaculates or climaxes before penetration or on few strokes post penetration. Most of the patients coming for treatment came with complaint of ejaculation within 2 to 4 strokes. *"I am unable to perform, I come before I can push inside". "I can hold my ejaculation at the most for about 10 seconds". "I have tried many times but I can't push inside because of my early discharge". "I keep having nightfall regularly , I feel very weak when I wake up". "every time I talk to some female or think about women a wet slimy discharge comes out of my penis".*

In cases of performance anxiety, most times the profile of the patient is unmarried or settled to be married soon. They are virgin having very little knowledge about sexual performance. For them the necessity is to find whether they will be able to perform after marriage. They fear loss in potency or weak potency. *"my family is pressurizing me to get married but I think I am not totally fit". "I think my sexual desire is going down , and I wont be able to perform after marriage". " I have noticed that my erections are not hard enough", " I have noticed that I ejaculate very fast and the quantity of ejaculation is also very little , and watery".*

Patients with small organ size complain of fear of failure. They are more interested in increasing the size of their penis while taking treatment for any other sexual problem. They attribute their failure to organ size rather than underlying sexual problem. *" I am very embarrassed of my penis size" " I don't think I will be able to satisfy any woman". " I have gone to many women they told me I have a small penis , they don't feel anything during sex".*

Misinformation and myths about sexuality are the root cause of sexual problems of psychogenic nature. The guilt over masturbation has an undeletable mark in the psyche of Indian males from the very childhood which makes them enter adult life with anticipation of disaster. The taboo on sexual discussion chokes their concerns till about the time of late adolescence or marriage. The fear of failure after marriage poses a threat to the concept of self as perfect husband so they initiate a journey of finding out the truth. The available grounds of testing are sex-workers or local 'boudis' or 'familial boudis' who to them are the councils for certification of sexual potency.

But the psychology of fear is a vicious cycle of 'fears-spectator -failure -greater fears'. Thus failure at first attempt which is inevitable launches a history of exposure and chances of sexual contamination in the process.

The predilection for oral sex comes from overexposure to pornography where in oral genital contact is a definite prelude and or sequence to any sexual act. However in the given sample, oral genital contact was used more as a crutch for getting an erection or sustaining it. This mode of erection generation work on reflex path way and in a sense is the genital equivalent of a knee jerk. Overindulgence to oral sex again is a risk behavior for contacting a range of sexually transmitted diseases.

The male, who persistently ejaculates unintentionally during non coital sexual foreplay or while trying to enter his partner has a problem which is a cause of distress is explicit . He often tries to cover up for the lack of timing by participating in a variety of sexual activities considering the fact that he loses his ejaculatory control soon after initiation of intercourse.

The sexually dysfunctional male may change his behavior to avoid sexual situations (owing to fear of failure); he may cope by framing his partner for his failure or through other ego-defense mechanisms; or he may try to overcome his problem by industriously "working" at sex, which usually makes the situation worse and again increases the chance of contamination owing to multiple partners and multiple exposures.

Condom Usage Behavior

Another part of analysis was regarding their feelings about condom. This was based on responses tapped both for respondents taking treatment of sexual problem or sexually transmitted diseases. About 15 out of 40 respondents came with complaints of sexually transmitted infection of which 7 always used condom for sexual intercourse and the rest 8 did not wear it at the last attempt or were occasional users of condom. Overall 18 among the 40 respondents never wore condom , 12 marked it as occasional preference while the rest 10 out of 40 used it always. Out of 10 respondents who always used condom, 3 had post graduate qualification, 5 were graduates while rest 2 had HS to below graduate educational qualification.

On questioned about preference of contraceptives, all men informed condom framed as the preferred mode of choice. The data revealed that, the realization that condom needs to be worn to avoid sexually transmitted disease was accepted by almost all men, but their behavior pattern was guided by other reasons. Facts like the *'boudi'* was not contaminated with any sexual dysfunction, or that the partner was faithful to them were often the reasons given for non usage of condom during sexual intercourse. More often the men had selected partners or 'Boudis' whom they would frequent , as a result a sort of emotional understanding would develop along with a trust which would slacken their defenses and they would try performing without a condom. Another significant finding was that often they lost their erections after wearing a condom, so they avoided wearing it. On probing further it was found that on losing the erection they indulged in some form of foreplay to regain it, usually oral sex; and the condom as a second skin was not really conducive to getting back the erection since it reduced sensation. *"wearing the condom I don't feel anything" ,"I like the feeling of her mouth on my penis".* Another fact that came about is that women partners did not prefer oral sex when the male counterpart wore condoms, especially when the erection was flaccid with the condom and any form of oral contact would upset its hold on the penis.

Men with premature ejaculation reported that ejaculating early, was often delayed when they wore a condom but not beyond 5 to 6 strokes over their normal ability. But on the flip side it affected their enjoyment during oral sex so they used condom post oral foreplay.

Men with performance anxiety were settled to be married in the near future, acknowledged condom usage from health perspective but reported erections not hard enough for wearing a condom, or losing erection prior to or on penetration or inability to penetrate. Most men belonging to this category reported no erection or early loss in erection. *"going to her I just don't get the sufficient hardness, not even hard enough to wear a condom, after a lot of working at it the little hardness that came went away the minute I was about to penetrate inside, it became limp and soft instantly"* {"onar kache giye kichu tei amar shokto hochce na , condom je porbo temon shokto nei , onek chesta korte giye jaob aektu shokto holo, prbesh korar agei norom hoye gelo"} " *my partner tried to help me get an erection but I ejaculated in the semi flaccid state, and I could not get a second erection after that, she tried sucking but that did not elicit another erection, she went on massaging it for over half an hour , I don't know why but I just could not get an erection"* .

Men with small organ reported that their partner complained about their size and diameter of penis, and wearing a condom reduced the sensation further for their partner, so they preferred not wearing one. They also reported that their partners were faithful so not wearing a condom did not bear significant risk of sexually transmitted diseases. When further probed about their feelings whether they considered exclusive rights on the women partner they were convinced otherwise but considered them safe because of common recommendations from some source.

Another significant finding was that women preferred to have coitus with men without a condom to enhance sensation to which the men acceded. This was more common for *"boudis"* from familial origin who were already using other forms of contraceptives like birth control pills owing to their marital status.

The reasons enumerated for wearing a condom was mostly to avoid uncalled for pregnancies rather that sexually transmitted diseases. Other forms of contraceptives mostly used were that of withdrawal method of coitus, followed by emergency pill and finally birth control pill.

The anlaysis indicates that men with sexual problem, exhibit a particular behavior termed as testing behavior, and they become their own spectator. They try to test their potency through sexual encounters. More often than not it is the sex workers or local *'boudis'* who frame as the board of sexual certification. Failure to perform or the fear of losing sexual power makes the man revisit multiple such women over the course of his life. The actual reason for sexual encounter becomes more of a test rather than pleasure. Indulging in various forms of foreplay especially oral sex is more often a common pathway for transmission of sexually transmitted diseases. In certain cases condom is either avoided or ignored for reasons already stated. Physiological conditions like weak erection or quick loss in erections makes condom usage a frustrating process for men with sexual dysfunction. In cases where men were taking treatment primarily for STD it was found that they suffered from sexual problem and were unsatisfied with their sexual life. Most men suffering with sexual dysfunction were anxious and were dissatisfied with their quality of life. Thus the sexual dysfunction, condom non usage, indulgence in oral sex and multiple partners makes this section of population extremely vulnerable to contamination with sexually transmitted diseases. Ongoing patients often visit brothels and *'boudis'* or their fiancée to ascertain their success in treatment.

Limitations of the Present Study

- Narratives are just one side of the story the behavior pattern can be better understood when obtained from both partners.
- More information regarding quality of life especially psychological aspect can be better understood on administration of standardized scales like BAI and BDI.

Conclusions

Aim of this research was to find the impact of male sexual problem or dysfunction on sexually transmitted diseases and infection by exploring the causal relation between the two. The levels of analysis revealed certain behavioral manifestations of patients with sexual problem and coping strategies used by them. It was found that males suffering from sexual dysfunction more often than not exhibit a 'testing behavior' just like a litmus test, to ascertain their virility/ potency. The size of their organ as compared to ones seen in pornography, lack of proper sexual guidance and information and deep rooted guilt feelings over masturbation are among the important factors exacerbating the fear of failure and testing sexual ability. This poses a great risk of sexually transmitted diseases because of associated unsafe sexual behaviors like trying out with multiple partners, idiosyncratic arousal strategies, oral sex, oral anal contact, dismissal of condom etc. It was found that on the causal hierarchy male sexual dysfunction precedes sexually transmitted diseases. Thus combating sexual dysfunction through means which promote non sexual testing procedures reduces risk behavior and chances of contamination. The findings of this study helps in generating measures to combat sexually transmitted diseases by pinpointing the population at risk and psyche of risk taking behavior.

Directions for Future Research

Develop a study among the sex workers as they can be a rich source of data about the population at risk of contamination.

The effect of sex education on the sexual confidence and sexuality of individuals

Methods for screening of local 'boudis' who are potential carriers of STDs.

References

Akhtar S. (1988): Four Culture Bound Psychiatric Syndromes in India. Int J Soc Psychiatry; 34:70-4

Avasthi A, Biswas P. (2004): Pharmacotherapy of Sexual Dysfunctions: Current Status. *Indian J Psychiatry; 46:213-20.*

Chadda RK, Ahuja N. Dhat (1990): Syndrome: A Sex Neurosis of the Indian Subcontinent. Br J Psychiatry; 156:577-9.

Centers for Disease Control and Prevention. Sexually Transmitted Diseases Treatment Guidelines 2006. MMWR 2006;55(No. RR-11).

Centers for Disease Control and Prevention. Sexually Transmitted Disease Surveillance, 2008. Atlanta, GA: U.S. Department of Health and Human Services, November 2009.

Centers for Disease Control and Prevention. Sexually transmitted diseases treatment guidelines 2006. MMWR 2006;55(no. RR-11).

Centers for Disease Control and Prevention. Sexually Transmitted Disease Surveillance, 2006. Atlanta, GA: U.S. Department of Health and Human Service, November 2007.

Denzin, N. K., & Lincoln, Y. S. (1994): '*Introduction: Entering the Field of Qualitative Research*'. In N. K. Denzin & Y. S. Lincoln (Eds.), Handbook of Qualitative Research (pp. 1-17). Thousand Oaks, CA: Sage.

Epigee Health and Fitness: *M.T. Williams, Ph.D. Dr. Williams: http://www.epigee.org.*

Kvale, Steiner (1996): *Interviews: An Introduction to Qualitative Research Interviewing.* Thousand Oaks, CA: Sage.

Labov, W & Waletzky, J. (1967): *Narrative Analysis: Oral Versions of Personal Experience.* In J Helm (Ed.), 'Essays on the Verbal and Visual Arts'(pp 12-44). Seattle: University Of Washington Press.

Labov, W (1982): *Speech Action and Reaction in Personal Narratives.* In D Tannen (Ed.) '*Analyzing Discourse : text and talk*' (pp.219-247) Washington, DC: Georgetown University Press.

Labov, W.(Ed.) (1972): '*The Transformation of experience in narrative syntax'. In W. Labov (Ed.), 'Language in the inner city: Studies in Black English Vernacular'* (pp.354-396) Philadelphia: University of Pennsylvania Press.

Masters, W.H. and Johnson, V.E. (1966): '*Human Sexual Response*'. Boston: Little Brown, *In* William H Masters, Virginia E Johnson, Robert C Kolodny (Ed.) '*Sex and Human Loving*', 1988. Jaico Publishing House.

Patton, M.Q. (1990): '*Qualitative Evaluation and Research Methods*' (2nd ed.). Newbury Park, CA: Sage.

Reissman, Catherine Kohler (1939): *Narrative Analysis–Qualitative Research Method's*; V.30.

Strauss, A., Corbin, J. (1998): '*Basics of Qualitative Research*', 2nd ed., Sage, London, .(1998), in Symon, G., Cassell, C. (Eds),'*Qualitative Methods and Analysis in Organizational Research: A Practical Guide*', Sage, London.

White , H. (1989): '*The Rhetoric of Interpretation. In P Hernadi (Ed), The Rhetoric of interpretation and interpretation of rhetoric*' (pp 1-22). Durham, NC: Duke University Press.

Young, K. (1989): '*Narrative Embodiments: Enclaves of the Self in the Realms of Medicine*'. In J Shotter& K J Gergen (Ed.), Texts of Identity (pp.152-165). London; Sage.

15

Poverty Issues Among Women in Sex Work: A Comparative Study of Andhra Pradesh and Karnataka

S. Radhakrishnan, C.P. Prakasam, ULIMIRI. V. Somayajulu

Introduction

As HIV/AIDS is the major public health challenge and India being a developing country with second largest population in the world is facing continual developmental problem. The main route of HIV transmission is through unprotected heterosexual activity and mainly Women in Sex Work (WSWs) are more vulnerable facing high risk (UNAIDS, 2002). Poverty is one factor that influences the sex work which in turn leads to HIV transmission. As precisely quoted (below) by Dr. Nelson Mandela, poverty is purely made by man and frantically affects different dimensions of human activities.

"Like slavery and apartheid, poverty is not natural. It is man-made and it can be overcome and eradicated by the actions of human beings"

– Nelson Mandela

One of the dimensions that poverty affects the human is HIV/ADIS which shakes the whole world attention. Unlike developed countries, third world countries are affected both directions i.e. poverty and HIV infection rate. There is a close link between the poverty and the HIV/AIDS, i.e. there are two sets of issues: (a) AIDS as a cause of poverty or AIDS deepening poverty and (b) the combined effect of poverty and income inequalities on social transactions–including sex, patterns of vulnerability and patterns of risky behaviour in relation to HIV infection and AIDS (UNAIDS, 2000).

Many research studies show that there is direct association between poverty and HIV infection. John Lekan Oyefara (2007), explains in his paper that more than one third (35%) of the respondents joined the sex industry because of poverty and lack of other means of getting daily food. There was a significant relationship between poverty, food insecurity and consistent use of condoms by female sex workers at $P<0.01$

The countries in the South Asia region support about one-quarter of the planet's population, with a large number of people unemployed and living below the poverty line (Ahmed, 2005).

The vulnerable groups namely unwed mothers, young widows, orphans, economically weaker women and the people who are outside the normal family setup are more susceptible to falling victim to prostitution. Traffickers living abroad have been reported to arrive in a village and marry a woman and sell her upon arrival in the destination country (Ahmed, 2005).

Nick Waterman narrates, although CSWs' poverty is contingent upon a variety of entrenched structural factors and also need to be addressed through macro socio-economic policies, interventions at the micro and macro levels are able to positively impact upon poverty reduction. He further adds that adult education interventions should aim to alleviate multi-faceted aspects of poverty, by enhancing human capital, developing social capital and utilizing financial capital for alternative income-generating activities.

Poverty drives them to lack of skills, education, information, lower access to services, migrate to work and which in turn lead to commercial sex work, both establishment-based and other types (Bhushan WHO/WPRO, Manila).

On the other hand, poverty may be one of the "causes" of the "sugar daddy" phenomenon in Africa, Jamaica, and elsewhere. This refers to older men offering gifts of cash or kind to young unmarried women in exchange for sexual favors. This has become sufficiently widespread that it often provokes little or no negative social sanction (Gupta and Mahy 2001).

Thus, the evidence suggests that any relationship between poverty and AIDS is complex and multi-directional. Ogbogu describes that poverty has also been fingered as a twin problem militating against the effective prevention and impact mitigation of HIV/AIDS in Nigeria among this group. Poverty was a key theme in the findings of Bloem, (2002), where almost a third of CSWs were employed and undertook commercial sex work to supplement their income. Poverty drives sex trafficking and that leads the delivery system for young, poor women and girls to prostitution as a means to provide for themselves, and their dependents in the family with no option.

As many studies reveal that the causal effect of poverty on HIV transmission has a significant role. Poverty and demand are two equally stronger forces linked with the issue of Commercial Sexual Exploitation of women and children. These contribute to the human degradation in the form of Commercial Sexual Exploitation of Children, such as: demand by the adults (usually the economically well off men) to satisfy their sexual desires and the economic deprivation of the victims or poverty.

This socio-economic situation has resulted in increasing social crimes, especially human trafficking of women and children. Prostitution, which is also included in human trafficking, is an intolerant social reality and a major issue in South Asia (Naqvi, 2005).

Hence, this study focuses on the poverty issues among the WSWs with comparison of two states viz., Andhra Pradesh-AP and Karnataka-KA.

Objectives

The major objectives of the paper are

1. To understand and compare the knowledge, attitude and behaviour among WSWs

2. To understand the poverty situation and linkages among WSWs in these two states

Data and Methods

Data for the present study were collected from the large survey conducted in Andhra Pradesh and Karnataka with a total sample size of 494 women in sex work (276 in Andhra Pradesh and 218 in Karnataka). Simple statistics, Univariate and bivariate analysis are applied

Profile of Respondents

Current Age by Income

Among BPL (with monthly income of less than Rs 1500), more than one third of the WSW from Andhra Pradesh and one fifth from Karnataka are of 20-25 years. On the other hand, in the APL (monthly income more than Rs 1500) group, three fifth in AP and about two fifth in Karnataka are below 25 years of age. Thus the WSWs from the BPL group are older to their counterparts from the APL group.(Table 1)

Knowledge on HIV/AIDS Prevention Ways by Income

Knowledge about reducing HIV risk behavior through use of condom is more among the WSW from BPL group, while knowledge of HIV prevention through single sex partner is more among the WSW from APL group, in AP. The BPL WSW from AP recorded higher level of HIV prevention knowledge and this could be due to the reach of intervention programmes implemented. (Table 1)

Awareness of HIV/AIDS Transmission Ways by Income

As Fig 1 indicates, WSW from the APL group in AP have two times higher awareness about HIV/AIDS transmission ways - 55% vs 26%. This is true for Karnataka as well though the difference is marginal - 31% vs 24%. As in the case of HIV prevention ways, awareness of HIV transmission ways is more in AP, than Karnataka.

Table 1
Profile of WSW by Monthly Income

	Andhra Pradesh			*Karnataka*		
	Income (Rs)			*Income (Rs)*		
	<=1500	*>1500*	*Chi Sqr (p val)*	*<=1500*	*>1500*	*Chi Sqr (p val)*
Current Age(years)						
< 20	9.1	13.6	2.16	11.9	12.7	6.29
20-24	36.4	47.5	(.705)	21.4	26.1	(.178)
25-29	27.3	19.2		27.4	36.6	
30-39	27.3	15.5		28.6	20.1	
>= 40	0.0	4.2		10.7	4.5	
Reducing Risk Behaviour						
Using condoms	54.5	29.8	13.58	46.4	32.8	13.28
One partner	9.1	28.3	(.009)**	2.4	0	(.021)***
Frequency of Sex Per Day (*)						
1-2 times	36.4	20.6	129	40.5	21.6	8.95
3-5 times	63.6	40.0	(.005)**	42.9	56.7	(.030)***
6-8 times	0.0	20.9		13.1	16.4	
More than 8 times	0.0	21.5		3.6	5.2	
Duration of Sex Work						
< 5 Years	63.6	62.6	.835	54.8	64.9	15.1
5 +	36.4	37.4	(.934)	45.2	35.1	(.004)**

(*) The total may exceed 100 because of multiple responses.
** Significant at 0.001 level
*** Significant at 0.010 level

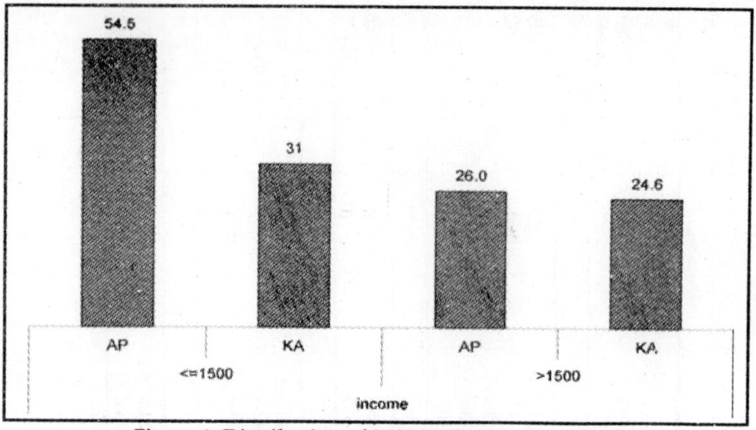

Figure 1: Distribution of WSW Who Aware of HIV Transmission by Income

Sexual Behaviour by Income

Table 1 gives the sexual behaviour of the WSW in terms of frequency of sex. Frequency of sex per day is more among the WSW from BPL groups in both the states with the difference being more striking in AP.

Age at First Sex by Income

The analysis of the data on age at first sex presented in Fig. 2 indicates that the poverty situation among WSW of Karnataka drives them to enter the sex industry at early age. Of the WSW from BPL group in Karnataka, four fifth (80%) had the first sex before attaining the age of 18 years, while one fifth had it after attaining the age of 18. In case of the APL WSW, 70 % had the sex debut below 18 years, while 29% had it after 18 years. IN AP, 55 % and 61% of WSW from BPL and APL groups had sexual debut below 18 years, while 46% and 39% had sexual debut after 18 years.

Duration of Sex Work by Income

As Table 1 indicates, more than three fifth of the WSW in AP irrespective of income are in the sex industry for less than 5 years, while in Karnataka, this proportion is less in case of APL WSW.

STD Symptoms and Treatment

Table 2 gives the reported incidence of STI symptoms and the treatment seeking practices adopted. Reported incidence of any of the STI symptoms is more in AP, than in Karnataka. The WSW from BPL group reported higher incidence of STI symptoms in AP, while the reverse holds good in Karnataka. STI treatment was sought from Doctor and STI clinic in both the states. The income differentials in treatment seeking behaviour are more visible in AP, than in Karnataka.

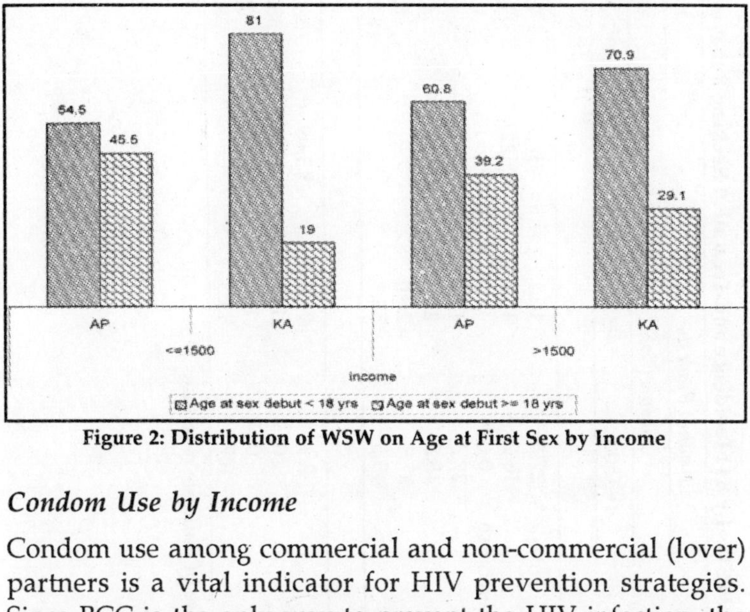

Figure 2: Distribution of WSW on Age at First Sex by Income

Condom Use by Income

Condom use among commercial and non-commercial (lover) partners is a vital indicator for HIV prevention strategies. Since BCC is the only way to prevent the HIV infection, the Targeted Interventions (TI) are mainly focusing on changing the behaviour of the WSW to adopt condom use with various partners. These critical indicators are analyzed by income level to understand the behaviour of the WSW.

Commercial Partner: The consistent use of condom with commercial partner by level of income (Fig 3) is an important indicator to understand the risk of WSWs. IN AP, consistent use of condom with commercial partner is more among the WSW from APL group, compared to BPL group- 72% vs 55%.

Table 2
Distribution of WSWs by STI Incidence and Treatment Seeking Behaviour by Income

	Andhra Pradesh			*Karnataka*		
	Income (Rs)			*Income (Rs)*		
	<=1500	*>1500*	*Chi (p val)*	*<=1500*	*>1500*	*Chi (p val)*
STI Incidence (*)						
Thin water discharge from Vagina	27.3	12.1	56.7	7.1	9.7	22.3
Thick candy discharge	18.2	13.6	(.522)	1.2	6.7	(.617)
Excessive bleeding during/after intercourse	0.0	7.5		0.0	3.0	
Discharge with foul smell	27.3	15.1		4.1	5.2	
Genital swelling	45.5	21.5		4.8	7.5	
Burning sensation during urination	27.3	26.0		6.0	8.2	
None	45.5	55.1		84.5	79.9	
Treatment Seeking Behaviour (*)						
Doctor	3.1	96.9	15.99	33.3	66.7	3.31
STD Clinic	0	100	(.100)	33.3	66.7	(.768)
Self Medication	0	100		20	80	
Other	6.7	93.3		28.6	71.4	

(*) The total may exceed 100 because of multiple responses.

In Karnataka, the reverse holds good. But proportion of WSW who never used condom with commercial partner is higher in case of BPL WSW, compared to APL WSW- 4% vs 2%.(Fig3)

Non-commercial Partner (lover): Table 3 indicates considerable differentials in use of condom with lover by income in AP as 19% WSW from APL used condom, against none from the BPL group. The difference in case of Karnataka seems marginal - 38% vs 36%.

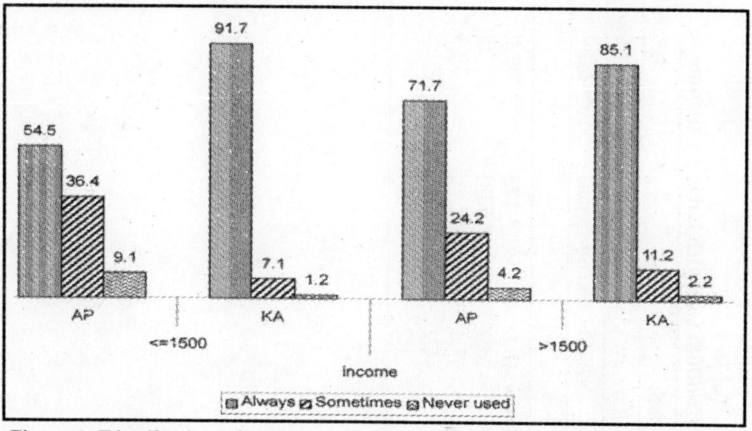

Figure 3: Distribution of WSW on Condom Use with Commercial Partner by Income

Condom Negotiation Power by Income

As the negotiation power is a key component for protecting oneself against this epidemic, Table 4 gives the condom negotiation power of the WSW. The analysis clearly indicates higher condom negotiation power/skill of the WSW from APL groups, compared to theur counterparts from BPL group. Though similar trend is observed in Karnataka also, the income differentials narrowed down significantly. As such, insisting for condom use seems to be low in Karnataka irrespective of income status.

The condom use negotiation is done after collecting money or going to the room, customer removed his clothes, and just before sex with income as well as state differentials.

Table 3
Distribution of WSW by Condom Use with Lover by Income

	Andhra Pradesh			*Karnataka*		
	Income (Rs)			*Income (Rs)*		
	<=1500	*>1500*	*Chi Sqr(p val)*	*<=1500*	*>1500*	*Chi Sqr(p val)*
Condom use with lover						
Yes	0	18.5	3.123	35.7	38.1	2.59
	27.3	20.4	(.538)	25	29.1	(.459)
No	72.7	57.4		39.3	32.8	
NA	0	4.2				
DK	0	4.2				

Table 4
Distribution of WSW by Negotiation of Condom and Time of Negotiation by Income

	Andhra Pradesh			*Karnataka*		
	Income (Rs)			*Income (Rs)*		
	<=1500	*>1500*	*Chi Sqr(p val)*	*<=1500*	*>1500*	*Chi Sqr(p val)*
Condom use with lover						
Action taken during negotiating on condom use (*)						
Accept the client	27.3	5.7	8.09(.004)**	92.9	88.8	3.86(.276)
Complain the brothel keeper	45.5	60.4	.978(.323)	27.4	20.1	6.25(.100)
Explain about safety	63.6	92.1	10.37(.001)**	63.1	70.9	5.73(.125)
Tell the customer to try	81.8	92.8	1.82(.177)	51.2	57.5	4.63(.201)
Use of nirodh is compulsory	72.7	89.1	2.74(.097)	22.6	29.9	4.99(.172)
Time of negotiation on condom use (*)						
Brothel keeper tells	0	0.4	6.35(.385)	3.6	1.5	13.19(.022)
After collecting money	18.2	13.6		19	23.9	
After going to the room	27.3	18.9		34.5	47	
After customer has removed his cloths	18.2	34.7		23.8	13.4	
Just before he is ready to begin sex	27.3	28.7		15.5	6	
Others	9.1	1.1		3.6	8.2	

* The total may exceed 100 because of multiple responses.n** Significant at 0.001 level

Self Risk Perception

A set of questions was asked to the WSW regarding their self risk perception of getting HIV infection, and the analysis is presented in Fig 4. More than half of the WSW in Karnataka from both the income groups (51%, 57%) reported that they are risk of getting HIV infection. In AP, 27% WSW from BPL group and 16% from APL group reported to be at risk. The income differential in HIV risk perception seems broader in AP.

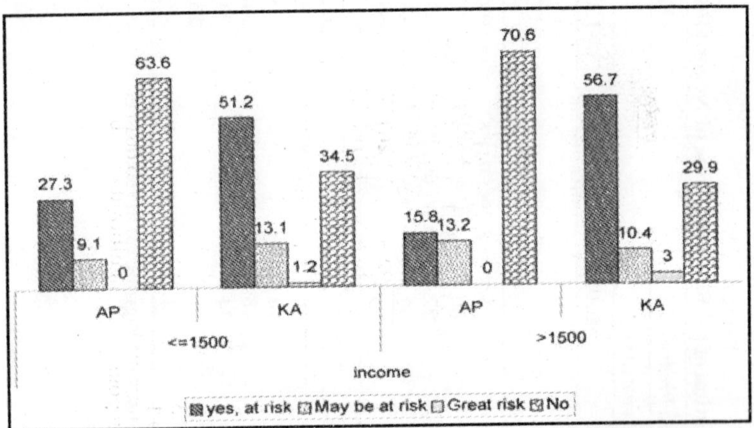

Figure 4: Distribution of WSW by Self Risk of Getting HIV/AIDS

Conclusions

The analysis highlights several gaps in the knowledge, attitudes and practice and indicate the need to strengthen the targeted interventions by focusing on improving the economic condition of the WSW by strategically developing the SHGs and to enhance their livelihood. This stems from the fact that poverty emerges as a main factor associated with the sex work. STI Treatment seeking behaviour among the WSW from low income group needs to be addressed since the risk of getting HIV is higher among this group.

There is also need to strengthen the intervention to increase the consistent condom use with all partners. Along with this it should focus on the negotiating power and skills of the WSW regarding condom use with clients even in the crucial situation. It is observed that in Andhra Pradesh, WSWs are negotiating clients on condom use just before the sexual act which is risky and sometimes it may lead to failure of condom.

The mobilization of sex workers all over the world has led to successes in prevention programmes. As it is evident in sonagachi, it is essential to strengthen the community mobilization in targeted intervention and management of HIV prevention. The Community Led Structural Intervention (CLSI) is being evolved to fight against the HIV beyond the traditional targeted intervention. Thus, the female autonomy needs to be addressed along with structural components namely social, economical and political perspectives.

Policy and Programme Implications

In both the states, there is a need to address the capacity building of CBO where these WSW are affiliated to develop the SHG and strengthen the same so as to improve the economic situation of the WSW. The ongoing intervention should focus on increasing the consistent condom use among commercial as well as non commercial partners. There is need to evolve the intervention for the clients of those WSW through Community Led Structural Intervention so as empower the women to demand for their rights.

References

Anjana Bhushan WHO/WPRO, Manila: 100% CUP: Poverty, Gender and Human Rights Issues.

Bloem J. (2002): Reported Behavioural Surveillance Surveys for HIV/ STD Risk-related Behaviour, (BSS) round 1, Unpublished Report, Maseru, Sechaba Consultants.

Gupta, N. and Mahy, M. (2001): Sexual Initiation Among Adolescent Women and Men: Trends and Differentials in Sub-Saharan Africa. Calverton, Md.: Demographic and Health Research Division, Macro International.

John Lekan Oyefara: Food Insecurity, HIV/AIDS Pandemic and Sexual Behaviour of Female Commercial Sex Workers in Lagos

Metropolis, Nigeria. Journal of Social Aspects of HIV/AIDS VOL. 4 No. 2 August 2007.

Naqvi, L., Jerar (2005): Prostitution, Human Trafficking Thrive as a Lucrative Immorality, The Japan Times Online. Available at: http://202.221.217.59/print/features/life2005/f1200502 09 a1.htm

Nick Waterman, South Africa: Commercial Sex Workers: Adult Education and Pathways out of Poverty.

Ogbogu IO, Odutolu O, Ogbogu OI; HIV Positive Sex Workers and Poverty: *Int Conf AIDS.* 2004 Jul 11-16; 15: Abstract No. WePeC6224, WHED, Abuja, Nigeria.

UNAIDS (2000a), pp. 26-36: AIDS, Poverty Reduction and Debt Relief.

Zahid Shahab Ahmed (2005): Poverty, Globalization, Social Customs & South Asian Children in Prostitution.

SECTION - 4

Strategies and Programmes

16

Strategy Towards Achieving Safe Motherhood in India: A Case Study of GVK EMRI

Biranchi Jena, Debasis Bhardwaj, G.V. Ramana Rao

Introduction

Higher levels of maternal mortality remains one of the most daunting public health problems in India, as it accounts for 23 per cent of the global burden of maternal deaths (WHO, 2007). India witnessed very low institutional births (40.7%) and only 50% women had at least three antenatal care visits for their last birth (NFHS-3, 2005-06). Births attended by the trained health personnel still remained at very low level of 48.3%. With such low proportion of institutional deliveries and births assisted by trained personnel, it is not surprising at all to have a disturbing Maternal Mortality Ratio (MMR) of 301 per 1,00,000 live births (SRS, 1997-2003, Registrar General, India).

The Millennium Development Goals (MDG) have been set as to achieve 200 maternal deaths per lakh of live births by 2007 and 109 per lakh of live births by 2015 (Sample Registration System, 2009). India has the highest number of maternal deaths in the world with 117,000 women dying due to complications of pregnancy and childbirth (WHO, 2007).

Maternal mortality in resource-poor nations has been attributed to the "3 delays"; delay in deciding to seek care, delay in reaching care in time, and delay in receiving adequate treatment (NIHFW, 2000). The first delay is on the part of the mother, family, or community not recognizing a life-threatening condition. The second delay is in reaching an appropriate health-care facility due to lack of affordable and accessible quality emergency transport or may be due to road conditions. The third delay occurs when appropriate or adequate care or is not available at health care centre (NIHFW, 2000).

India has relatively poor health outcomes, despite having a well-developed administrative system, good technical skills in many fields, and an extensive network of public health institutions for research, training, and diagnosis. This suggests that the health *system* may be mis-directing its efforts, or alternatively be poorly designed (India's Public Health System, 2004). Despite several interventions in the health care sector, the health system continues to be inadequate and insufficient to cover the population efficiently. It continues to be disconnected with public health goals, inadequately equipped to address people's expectations and fails to provide financial risk protection to those unable to access care for want of ability to pay. Accessibility and availability of a proper health care facility is still an issue.. Estimated 25 percent of people in Madhya Pradesh and Orissa could not access medical care due to reasons related to location, while it was 11 percent for Uttar Pradesh (National Commission on Macroeconomics and Health 2005).

Private health care sector has grown up at a larger scale in the last few years. However private health care system is unregulated and is withinreach to urban people only. It is highly affected by several factors such as technology, education and training, public expectations and perceptions, regulatory frameworks, societal values, etc; thus provides a high value addition to only a smaller segment. With an intention to reap profit, experience shows that the private sector is hardly concerned with public health goals, making state intervention essential. Thus when overall health sector develops, vulnerable groups like infants, women, elderly and especially the rural segment get proportionately lesser benefit. Evidence suggests that not-for-profit sector, particularly community-based organizations, seem to have had a beneficial impact on access, equity and quality of services in rural and backward areas (National Commission on Macroeconomics and Health, 2005). In such context an unique proposition in health care in the form of Public Private Partnership (PPP) was thought to be a novel strategy to bring desired result with synchronization of public goals with private sector commitments. GVK Emergency Management and Research Institute (GVK EMRI) is India's first integrated Emergency service provider operating under the PPP framework.

Objectives

It is not that strategies were not taken in India to reduce the maternal deaths. A good number of programmes like Reproductive and child health have been initiated and unfortunately the outcome is far from satisfactory. The current study tries to examine the new strategy in terms of processes and operations of GVK EMRI in bringing down the Maternal Mortality by reducing the delays at different level and achieving the safe motherhood. The specific objectives of the current study are as follows:

- To assess the socio-demographic and operational profile of pregnancy cases reported as medical emergencies
- To evaluate the processes of the EMS system adopted by GVK EMRI in effectively managing the medical emergencies during pregnancy.
- To assess the type of medical complications reported to EMS during pregnancies
- To estimate the impact of the free EMS service on the Maternal Mortality Ratio (MMR)

Methods

The current study emphasizes and evaluates the process being followed to manage pregnancy related emergencies. Each process was studied to measure its impact on factors affecting maternal complications.

The study also is a retrospective study of all the pregnancy related medical emergencies reported to GVK Emergency Management and Research Institute (GVK EMRI) during 2009 (January-December 2009) in Andhra Pradesh. GVK Emergency Management and Research Institute (GVK EMRI) started running the first professional and comprehensive free emergency services in Andhra Pradesh from August 2005 under the Public Private Partnership (PPP) by establishing a single toll free number 108. GVK EMRI has set up an Emergency Response Centre (ERC), where the calls from emergency victim are received from all over the state and the emergency service is provided within 18 minutes in urban area and 24 minutes in rural areas with the support of technologies like GPS/GPRS/AVLT etc. As part of a routine protocol being followed, details of the emergency victim including demographics, chief complaints and other details are captured by the GVK EMRI emergency services after the call is recorded on dialing 108. A total of 3,23,495 cases of pregnancy related emergencies were reported to GVK EMRI during 2009, of which 1,05,951 cases were analyzed for the purpose of the study.

The low level of institutional deliveries has been a matter of concern in India and many studies have cited it as one of the major cause of higher ratio of maternal mortality. Since the free EMS services provided by GVK EMRI facilitates to convert the non-institutional deliveries into institutional deliveries, there would be a definite impact on MMR. GVK EMRI's contribution is indirectly estimated through preventable maternal deaths attributed to deliveries done at institution. To obtain preventable maternal deaths due to institutional deliveries, a regression model is developed by taking the MMR as the dependant variable and level of institutional deliveries as the predictor variable. The regression model is developed by obtaining the state level MMR data from NSS and institutional delivery data from NFHS 3. The degree of variation (R^2) was taken as the factor for preventable deaths in the following regression model;

$$\text{Log MMR}_i = a + b \log \text{ID}i$$

Where

MMR_i = Maternal Mortality Ratio for i^{th} State

ID_i = Level of Institutional Deliveries for i^{th} State

For the purpose of the study, the survival status of victim is defined as whether the emergency victim is alive or not after 48 hours of providing the emergency transport with pre hospital care to the patients. GVK EMRI has a robust process in collecting the survival status of the victims after 48 hours of the incident. GVK EMRI collects the information on survival status in four major categories viz. "alright and discharged from hospital", "Stable, out of danger but still in the hospital", "critical and still in the hospital" and "expired". For statistical analysis simple cross tabulations and frequency tables were used. Statistical analysis was performed using SPSS 16.0 version.

Results

During the calendar year 2009, a total of around 14,00,000 medical emergencies reported to GVK EMRI in Andhra Pradesh, of which 3,23,495 emergencies were pertaining to Pregnancy related complications. Around one fourth of the total emergencies are pregnancy related and this shows the requirement and usefulness of an EMS in managing the unmet needs in provision of safe motherhood in India. GVK EMRI invented the process of SENSE- REACH- CARE to provide the emergency medical services. Sense process explains the access to a EMS system which would ensure a emergency medical services, where as Reach and Care process deals with the quick response and appropriate care.

The total proportion of pregnancy cases reported to GVK EMRI has increased to around 21% in 2009 as compared to only 2% in 2006 (Table 1). Majority (67%) of the pregnancy complicated victims were in the age group of 20-30, with mean age of 23 years (SD=3.5 years). Almost a quarter were in the age group of less than 20 years, who used the GVK EMRI services for maternal complications.

Table 1
Total Number of Pregnancy Cases Reported to GVK EMRI and Its Share in Total Medical Emergencies

Year	*Total Number of Pregnancy Cases Reported to GVK EMRI*	*% Share of Total Emergencies Handled*
2006	2528	2%
2007	65009	17%
2008	293095	20%
2009	323495	21%

Source: GVK EMRI, AP Operations.

It has been noticed that GVK EMRI provided more support to the rural health system by handling more pregnancy related emergency cases in rural areas than urban. Seventy four percent of the pregnancy related emergencies were reported from rural areas and 7% were reported from tribal areas. From 2nd quarter of 2007 there was a spurt in the total pregnancy cases handled by GVK EMRI and from this period GVK EMRI started its operation in rural Andhra Pradesh. Although the service covered the entire state, services were sought from only 66% of the villages for the pregnancy related medical emergencies. However, the service usage has gone up significantly from less than 20% in 2007 to 66% in 2009.

Around 51% of the calls were reported at night (from 6 PM to 6 AM) and marginally higher proportion of calls (54%) were reported to be from tribal areas than rural areas (51%) and urban areas (52%) ($p<0.001$). More than 40% of the service users were either scheduled caste or scheduled tribe and 45% belong to backward caste. Again more than 95% of the service users were belong to lower economic status (white card holders).

Almost 90% of the pregnant women have called GVK EMRI and used the services while they were in labor pain (Table 2). GVK EMRI witnessed delivery occurring in emergency ambulance in around 2% of the total cases reported. This translates to almost 17 deliveries happening everyday inside the ambulance.

Table 2
Percentage Distribution of Type of Medical Emergencies in Pregnancy

Type of Emergency in Pregnancy	*% Share*
In Labor pain	89.57%
Abortions/Foetal Loss	1.19%
Excessive Bleeding in Pregnancy	1.41%
Delivery in Ambulance	1.90%
Eclampsia (Convulsionsin Pregnancy)	0.45%
Others (Not specified)	5.48%
Total (N)	109553

The strategy to increase the seeking of the EMS services for pregnancy related complications included Ambulance demonstration at village level, introduction of Volunteers in case of Emergency (VoICE). The VoICE process is an indigenous process developed at GVK-EMRI to create awareness of 108 services across the GVK-EMRI operating states. To carry forward the mission of GVK-EMRI- *"your right to safety- saving lives"*. Each field supervisor is involved in developing a panel of responsible citizens from the villages, who not only improve the lives of vulnerable people but also themselves. Volunteers would be assisting the emergency victims in case of emergency by stabilizing them and connecting to 108 centers. Once recruited, they are inducted with first aid training. Necessary social recognition is a part of the process to involve more volunteers towards realizing the millennium goal of safe motherhood.

Considering concept of *"Seeing is believing"*, GVK- EMRI has pioneered in the strategy of Ambulance demonstration for creating awareness at community level to use appropriate transport and out of hospital care during medical emergencies pertaining to pregnancy. This has not only created awareness, moreover it has a gone a long way in promoting institutionalization of pregnancy related emergencies. Such strategies has reduced the delay drastically at first instance i.e. delay in sensing the medical attention during third trimester pregnancy and seeking the medical services.

Reaching to the victim at the earliest ensures the reduction and avoidance of delay in accessing the appropriate health care. On an average the response time (receiving the call to reaching of ambulance at victim) in handling the pregnancy related emergencies was 23.15 minutes (SD=15.49). Around 34% of the total cases were handled in less than 15 minutes, whereas 70% cases were handled within 30 minutes. However, a significant variation was observed in the mean response time in rural area (24.17 minutes), tribal area (25.28 minutes) and urban areas (18.37 minutes) ($p<0.001$). As far as the total time is concerned the emergency service (from call to hospital) was provided on an average in 52.76 minutes (SD= 26.7 minutes). A significant difference was also noted in total time for provision of service in rural area (55.08 minutes), tribal area (56.73 minutes) and urban area (42.24 minutes) ($P<0.001$). GVK EMRI ambulance run on an average of 13.33 kilometers (SD= 9.9 Kilometers) for each pregnancy related case for provision of medical emergency services. The mean distance travelled from base to scene was 14 kilometers for rural and tribal area and 10 kilometers for urban area. This indicated that the accessibility of ambulance in terms of distance and time ensured the efficient management of delay in accessing to the appropriate health care system. Strategies like introduction of GPRS, Automated Vehicle Location Tracking (AVLT), GIS, segmentation of ambulances, and prior dispatch system helped to reduce the response time to a greater extent, so also the delay.

GVK EMRI ambulances are manned by Emergency Medical Technician (EMTs) who were trained in Basic Life Support (BLS), Advance Cardiac Life Support (ACLS) and other medical training. Thus accessibility to the emergency ambulances ensures the accessibility to at least to a BLS system before being transported to a health care facility. Of the total cases handled, 2.5% cases (2746), the EMT performed the delivery at the woman's residence, as it was too late to carry the pregnant woman in ambulance. In 94% cases the EMT successfully transported the pregnant woman with labor pain to the appropriate health care unit with effective pre hospital care. A process of Hospital Information System (HIS) in GVK EMRI provides strategy to transfer cases to appropriate hospital. In 2% cases, the deliveries occurred in the ambulance itself. More critical cases required the intervention of a medical doctor and GVK EMRI also introduced a process of intervention of a medical doctor to provide guidance to EMT during pre-hospital care and transport. The data showed that 12.2% of the total reported cases were provided with Emergency Response Centre Physician (ERCP) intervention. About 70% of the cases were shifted to Government hospitals, whereas 28% cases were shifted to private hospitals. It has also got a process to follow up the victim's condition after 48 hours of hospital admission. The data showed that 76% victims were alright and discharged from hospital, where as 23% were found to be stable but still continue staying at hospital. Around 0.07% victims (80) were found expired and 0.03% (22) were found critical after 48 hours of follow up.

GVK EMRI's contribution is also indirectly estimated through preventable maternal deaths attributed due to deliveries done at institution. It is hypothesized that proportion of institutional deliveries explains the maternal mortality outcome. Thus a model is developed by taking the information on MMR and institutional deliveries in 16 states.

$$\text{Log } MMR_i = a + b \log ID_i \quad \text{.....................................(1)}$$

Where

MMR_i = Maternal Mortality Ratio for i^{th} State

ID_i = Level of Institutional Deliveries for i^{th} State

The model was noted to be statistically significant ($p<0.001$) with a R^2 of 75% (Table 3). The degree of variation (R^2) was taken as the factor for preventable deaths in the model. Or in other words it was assumed that MMR could be prevented up to 75% if all deliveries are assured for institutional deliveries. If it is assumed that GVK EMRI contributed to the reduction of MMR by ensuring institutional deliveries, its contribution can be estimated by taking into account the proportion of total live births taking place in Andhra Pradesh.

$$LB_{ap(t)} = Pop_{ap(t)} * CBR_{ap(t)} \quad \text{...(2)}$$

Where

$LB_{ap(t)}$ = Live Births in AP at time t

$Pop_{ap(t)}$ = Projected AP population at time t (RGI)

$CBR_{ap(t)}$ = Crude Birth Rate in AP at time t (SRS, Oct. 2007)

GVK EMRI share in handling the live births was estimated as

$$LB_{ap(GVK\ EMRI)\ (t)} = Case_t / LB_{ap(t)} \quad \text{...(3)}$$

Where

$LB_{ap(GVK\ EMRI)\ (t)}$ = Proportion of Live births (deliveries) handled by GVK EMRI at time t

$Cases_{t}$ = Total number of cases handled by GVK EMRI at time t

The preventable maternal deaths contributed by GVK EMRI can be estimated as;

$$C_{GVK\ EMRI\ (t)} = PMD_t * LB_{ap(GVK\ EMRI)\ (t)} \quad \text{...(4)}$$

Where

$C_{GVK\ EMRI\ (t)}$ = GVK EMRI's contribution in preventable maternal deaths

PMD_t = total preventable deaths at time t [R^2 of the regression model (1)* total maternal deaths]

Once the GVK EMRI's contribution to the preventable maternal deaths is estimated, it is easier to estimate the revised MMR by controlling GVK EMRI's contribution in the following way;

$$MMR_r = \{(MMR_t - C_{GVK\ EMRI\ (t)}) / LB_{ap(t)}\} * 1,00,000 \quad \text{...(5)}$$

Where

MMR_r = Revised MMR

MMR_t = Original MMR

The results of the estimation indicated that the strategy adopted by GVK EMRI was able to reduce the MMR by 15% (Table 4).With appropriate data the model can be used for rural, tribal and urban areas. However there is a challenge in obtaining the MMR for rural, tribal and urban areas though NFHS has the data for institutional deliveries.

Table 3
Model Results

Variable	*Coefficients*	*Standard Error*	*t Stat*	*P-value*	*Lower 95%*	*Upper 95%*
Intercept	8.511	0.4621	18.41	0.000	7.519	9.502
Institutional Deliveries (x)	-0.803	0.1226	-6.55	0.000	-1.066	-0.540
R Square	0.754144137					

Table 4
Estimation Results of GVK EMRI's Contribution in Reduction of MMR

Variables	*Value*
$Pop_{ap(t)}$	83178000
$CBR_{ap(t)}$	18.9
$LB_{ap(t)}$	1572064
$Case_t$	323495
$LB_{ap(GVK\ EMRI)\ (t)}$	21%
MMR(srs)	197
Total Maternal Deaths	3097
PMD_t	2323
$C_{GVK\ EMRI\ (t)}$	478
MMR_r	167
Reduction in MMR	15%

Applying such estimation for India under various assumptions of utilization of such services would bring down the MMR by 23% to 35%, as the impact is expected to more at the bigger MMR base (India MMR stands at 301 per one lakh live births) than a smaller base.

Discussion

Early age pregnancy and late age pregnancy are less likely get the delivery done at a health care institution (NHFS-3, AP, 2005-06). GVK EMRI services were utilized more by the younger pregnant mothers with mean age of 23, with more than a quarter from the age group less than 20 years. With teen age pregnancy posing more risk of maternal complications, strategies to cover a higher proportion of such pregnancies by this EMS would further bring down the maternal deaths. GVK EMRI started a new strategy to cover more risky pregnancy cases by coordinating with other organization, ASHAs and forming a data base on Expected Date of Deliveries (EDD). The urban and rural variation in the deliveries occurring at an institution remained significantly wide with 55.9% in rural area and 81.5% in urban area (NHFS-3, AP, 2005-06). Thus a strategy mitigating such urban rural difference in institutional deliveries would definitely bring down the maternal deaths. GVK EMRI ensured a higher proportion (81%) of maternal complications being handled from rural and tribal area. Social and cultural factors also affect the maternal outcomes. Many studies indicated low rate of institutional deliveries among the lower caste in the society. The institutional deliveries were as low as 27% among scheduled tribe and around 60% among the scheduled caste and backward caste in Andhra Pradesh (NHFS-3, AP, 2005-06). The EMS provided by GVK EMRI has strategized to provide more services among such group and in 2009, 85% of the total users were from scheduled tribe, scheduled caste and backward caste. This would no doubt improve the maternal outcome among the lower social group.

Timely transport affects women's ability to receive preventative and emergency obstetric care that is essential for their survival. As per World Health Organization (WHO) estimates, 75 per cent of maternal deaths can be prevented through timely access to child-birth related care (WHO, 2005). The model in this paper found that 75.4% of the maternal deaths could be avoided by ensuring cent percent institutional deliveries. For managing pregnancy related emergencies effectively, it is essential to ensure that comprehensive emergency obstetric care is reached within 12 hours, with the exception of obstetric hemorrhage which requires attention within 2 hours (Maternal Health and Transport Key Issues Guide). The "reach" process in GVK EMRI ensured all the pregnancy related medical emergency cases were managed with 23.15 minutes of response time and 52.76 minutes for accessing the appropriate health care facility. Timely access to care also helps reduce other long term maternal health problems including obstetric fistula caused by obstructed labor (Porter, 2007). Travelling long distance without proper transport deteriorated the condition of the pregnant women and adds risk to negative hospital outcome. A significant proportion of the women died after reaching a hospital, who had travelled 10 kilometers or more for treatment without a proper medical support (Biego, G). Although GVK EMRI travels on an average 13 kilometer to provide services, it was supported by faster transport and effective pre hospital care. Half of the maternal deaths reported occurred before the women reached a treatment facility; most of them had travelled by bus, rickshaw or bullock cart and only 9 percent by ambulance (Pendse, 1999). The strategy by GVK EMRI is poised to cater 100% transport of all trimester pregnancy cases through state of art ambulances with trained EMTs.

Focusing on high risk pregnancies may not be the right strategy for reducing maternal mortality, as low risk population also experience complications during child birth. Thus substantial reduction in maternal mortality requires that all pregnancies should be treated as 'at risk (Ranjan, 2004). GVK EMRI in its process included all pregnancy related medical emergencies as high priority ambulance dispatch.

Basic emergency obstetric care services can be delivered by professionally trained service providers in out of hospital settings. This is important in a country like India where most of the deliveries take place in out of hospital settings and majority of the maternal deaths are the result of the delay either in identifying a complication that requires emergency care or in transporting the woman in distress to a place where emergency obstetric care services are available (Ranjan, 2004). The strategy of pre hospital care by trained EMTs and supported by ERCP would add a huge value to the present state of affairs in the maternal mortality. The presence of a 'skilled' attendant at the time of the delivery in such situations can help in reducing both the delay in identifying an obstetric emergency and the delay in referring the woman to a health facility where emergency obstetric care services are available (Ranjan, 2004). Daily averages of 17 deliveries happening in emergency ambulances and a sizable number of deliveries assisted by EMTs at the victim's residence have substantially reduced the risk of maternal mortality.

Conclusions

Maternal mortality in India is at a substantially higher level. It is urgent and important to bring down the maternal deaths for an overall socio-economic development. Although many programmes and strategies have been launched for this objective, expected changes were not observed. Handling the issue through Public Private Partnership (PPP) framework was initiated by GVK EMRI and a set of strategies were launched to improve the maternal outcome. The GVK EMRI invented process of Sense-Reach-Care (S-R-C) brought a new dimension in reducing the MMR in India. Other strategies like VoICE, ICE, HIS, training and Research, use of technology would strengthen the flagship S-R-C process to speed up in bringing the desired result. In a nutshell, the strategy of introduction of emergency health transport along with pre hospital care plays an important role in achieving the millennium development goal-to reduce maternal mortality by 75 per cent by 2015-as well as improving maternal health in general.

References

Biego, G. (eds): Survey on Adult and Childhood Mortality, Tanzania. Calverton, MD: Macro International.

India's Public Health System (2004): How Well Does It Function at the National Level? World Bank Policy Research Working Paper 3447, November 2004.

International Institute for Population Sciences (IIPS) and Macro International (2008).

National Family Health Survey (NFHS-3), India, 2005-06: Andhra Pradesh. Mumbai: IIPS.

Maternal Health and Transport Key Issues Guide: http://www.eldis.org/go/health/maternal-health-and-transport (accessed on 12th February 2010).

Ministry of Health and Family Welfare(2005): Report of the National Commission on Macroeconomics and Health, Government of India, New Delhi.

National Institute of Health and Family Welfare (2000): Module for Health Worker Female (ANM). Reproductive and Child Health, Integrated Skills Development Training. New Delhi, India: NIHFW; June 2000:175–253.

Pendse V (1999): Maternal Deaths in an Indian Hospital: A Decade of (No) Change? Reproductive Health Matters - Special Issue on Safe Motherhood Initiatives , 1999: 119-127.

Porter G (2007): Transport, Immobility and Spatial Poverty Traps: Issues for Rural Women and Girl Children in Sub-Saharan Africa. A paper prepared for "Understanding and addressing spatial poverty traps: an international workshop". London: CPRC/ODI.2007.

Ranjan Aloaak; Maternal Health in India; Studies in Population and Development, No.04-06, Shyam Institute.

Sample Registration System (2003): Maternal Mortality in India 1997-2003, Trends, Causes and Risk Factors, Registrar General of India, New Delhi.

World Health Organisation (2005): Reducing Maternal Deaths: A Challenge for the New Millennium in the African Region. Brazzaville: WHO Regional Office for Africa, Brazzaville, Congo; 2005.

World Health Organization (2007): Maternal Mortality in 2005: Estimates developed by WHO, UNICEF and UNFPA and the World Bank, WHO, Geneva.

17

Involvement of Men in Reproductive Health: An Intervention Strategy of Addressing Couples in Slums of Mumbai

Balaiah Donta, D.D. Naik, Umesh Iddya, Anil Bandivedekar

Introduction

Men have their own sexual and reproductive health needs, which are not adequately met. Due to culturally promoted gender role, men tend to have little or incorrect information about their own sexual and reproductive health. By addressing these issues through interventions directed to men and provision of correct knowledge about sexual and reproductive health of men and women and identifying the areas needing co-operation and support of both men and women in dealing with their health issues improvement could be brought about in men concerning their own acceptance of reproductive health and also their participation in activities which support their wives and other persons. On the other hand it may also be considered that as most sexual. Family planning (FP), child bearing and reproductive health (RH) decisions require mutual support of men and women, there is a need to carryout programmes aimed at both partners and enable them to have greater interaction which will facilitate decision making based on informed choice. These husband

and wife interactions also enable man to seek solutions to his own sexual and reproductive health (SRH) problems and also to get reoriented to playing his role in family making and also contributing to gender equity.

In India, men play a dominant and many times decisive role in allowing, as also regulating women's access to RH services. They follow masculine role models and hold leadership position in the community. Traditionally they are not being involved in parenting responsibility. Due to lack of correct knowledge they also shy away from seeking RH services in public. Under these circumstances, male participation is vital in enabling them to seek RH knowledge and services for themselves and to come forward to extend support to women as also to undergo change in their negative attitudes toward sex, gender and power. Male involvement includes the number of men who encourage and support their partner and their peers to use family planning and who influence the policy environment to be more conductive to developing male related programmes. In this context, "male involvement" should be understood in a much broader sense than male contraception, and should refer to all organizational activities aimed at men as a discrete group, which has the objective of increasing the acceptability and prevalence of family planning practice of either sex (Green and Chens, 2003).

In patrichial society where men largely make household decisions, the need to include men in all matters that required joint spousal decision is critical in achieving key reproductive health goals. Despite this fact until recent year's men role in couple's fertility decision making was ignored, however since the past few years demographic studies examined this role of men in family planning and many of them showed the importance of involving husbands for couple"s family planning adoptin (Medicam, 2004).

The significance of enhancing male participation in reproductive health programme is well recognized because of the sexual and reproductive behaviour of men which puts them at risk, and also has an impact on the health status of their sex partners. Both The Cairo 1994 and the Beijing 1995 conferences have recognized the need for behavioural research to study factors inhibiting male participation so as to find ways of enhancing male involvement and responsibility in FP and reproductive health. While traditionally FP research and programmes have focused on women, a few studies which have begun to study attitudes and behaviours of men with regard to reproductive health issues have found that men play a key role in their partners' adoption of contraception (Davies J., et. al; 1987).

Despite the recognition that male involvement is important and urgently needed, not many programmes have been exclusively directed at men or at couples. Hence, there is a need to address the safe motherhood and family planning concerns of men, as also of the couple for improving the reproductive health in relation to safe motherhood and family planning.

Objectives

The overall objective of the study is to identify programme strategies contributing to effective participation for men in programmes aimed at improving safe motherhood and family planning. Specific objectives of the study are To study the awareness, perception and practices among married men regarding safe motherhood and family planning; determine decision making process on issues related to safe motherhood, family planning; investigate the reproductive health seeking behavior and the support they had received from their spouses.

Methodology and Study Design

The data for this study derived from the study entitled "Interventions in urban slums for enhancing participation of men in reproductive health" which was conducted in collaboration with Municipal Corporation of Greater Mumbai (MCGM) and funded by Ministry of Health and Family Welfare, Government of India. Three comparable slum areas were selected (on the basis of similar population, infant mortality rate and infrastructure) with the help of Municipal Corporation of Greater Mumbai after surveying 12 health post areas for the purpose of this research study. These areas were named as; Intervention area-1 (Mohili Village) where interventions addressed to husbands only, Intervention area-2 (Bail Bazar) where interventions addressed to couples and control area (Asalfa Village) where no intervention were proposed. The ongoing government reproductive health and family welfare programmes continued in all three-study areas.

The data from intervention area-2 and control area utilized for this study and the information collected for the awareness and practice of Safe Motherhood, Family Planning methods is listed in Table 1. In intervention area, baseline data obtained from a random sample of married men from experimental (561) and control (588) areas through a semi-structured interview schedule during 2005. Based on the baseline information, the interventional strategy designed and implemented both at community as well as clinic level, through providing information, education, counselling and clinic services for couples. Interventions were carried out for couples for 21 months, followed by post-intervention survey carried out in both the experimental (555) and control (575) areas in 2007. Analysis was carried out for Safe Motherhood and Family Planning and Contraceptive methods and the information collected from the questions listed in Table 1.

In the sample population, large number of male (husband) were in the age group 30-39 and women (wife) belong to less than 30 years of age.Average age at marriage of male found to be around 24 years and women were below 20 years (18.38). Male were educated up to 10th standard and most of the female were up to primary level. Majority of study population (88 percent) belongs to Hindu religion. Baseline and end line information was collected for control and Intervention (Expermental) areas and results have discussed understand the male involment in Safemotherhood and family planning activities and their perception, awareness in experimental and intervetion areas.

Table 1

List of in Information Collected about Safe Motherhood and Family Planning and Contraceptive Use from the Respondent in Slum Area of Mumbai

Safe Motherhood	*Abortion Issues*
	Past history of abortion
	Prevalence of induced abortions (MTP)
	Decision-making about induced abortion (MTP)
	Who accompanied wife to abortion (MTP) services
	Current pregnancy status:
	Decision-making regarding number of children
	Antenatal Care
	Awareness
	Awareness of ANC registration
	Number of antenatal check-ups a pregnant woman should have
	In which month of pregnancy a pregnant woman should register?
	Husbands' perception
	Discussion between husband and wife regarding antenatal check-ups wife need to have
	In which month of pregnancy did wife first go for antenatal check-up?
	Decission
	Who decided about wife going for antenatal check up?
	Who accompanied wife to the antenatal check-up
	Did husband accompany wife during her last delivery
	Reasons for husband not accompanied wife during last delivery reported by wife
	Kind of antenatal services did wife receive during pregnancy
	Reasons for wife not attending antenatal check-up

Contd.

Safe Motherhood	*Abortion Issues*
Family Planning and Contraception	Knowledge of contraceptive methods among husbands *Source* of Contraceptive information reported by husbands Had spouse ever discussed using spacing method? If yes, when? Had spouse ever *discussed* about using Permanent method? If yes, when? *Current contraceptive use* Current contraceptive use by method Reason for not using F.P. method currently by couple Opinion of husband and wife regarding vasectomy and tubectomy

Results

Safe Motherhood

Abortion Issues: Past History of Abortion: During the baseline survey, 19 per cent women from intervention and about 20 per cent from control area reported history of abortion in past. Whereas post-intervention survey indicates that; 22 per cent of husbands from intervention and 11 per cent from control area reported the same. There was about 9 percentage point decrease observed in control area whereas 3 percentage point increase was observed in intervention area with no significant difference in intervention area with respect to past history of abortion.

Distribution of Induced Abortions (MTP) by Study Areas: During the baseline survey 10 per cent of wives from intervention and about 11 per cent from control area reported that they had one abortion, whereas 2 per cent from intervention as well as control area had multiple abortions. Post-intervention survey indicates that; 11 per cent from intervention and 6 per cent from control area reported that they had one abortion whereas 3 per cent from intervention and less than one per cent from control area had multiple abortions. Significant difference was observed with marginal decrease in control area and marginal increase in intervention area with respect to distribution of induced abortions (Fig.1).

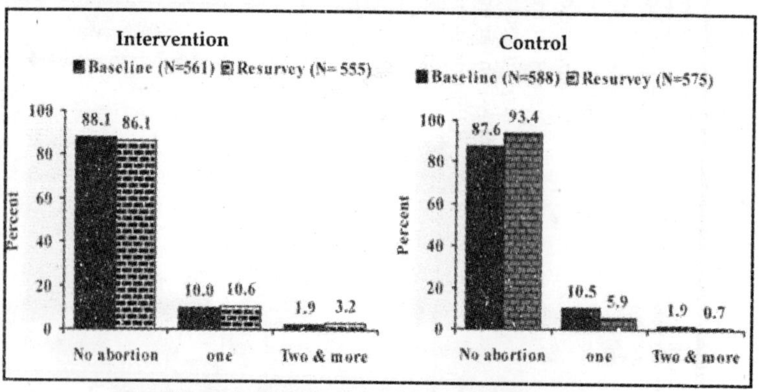

Figure 1: Distribution of Induced Abortions

Decision-making regarding going for Induced Abortion (MTP): A question was asked to wives who decided that wife to go for abortion (last abortion). Baseline information indicates that 55 per cent wives from intervention and 73 per cent from control area reported that the decision to go for abortion was taken jointly by husband and wife. Whereas post-intervention survey indicates that 66 per cent wives from intervention and 58 per cent from control area reported the same. Significant difference was observed intervention area regarding decision-making regarding MTP. Eleven percentage point increase was observed in intervention area regarding joint decision making for wife to go for induced abortion (Fig.2).

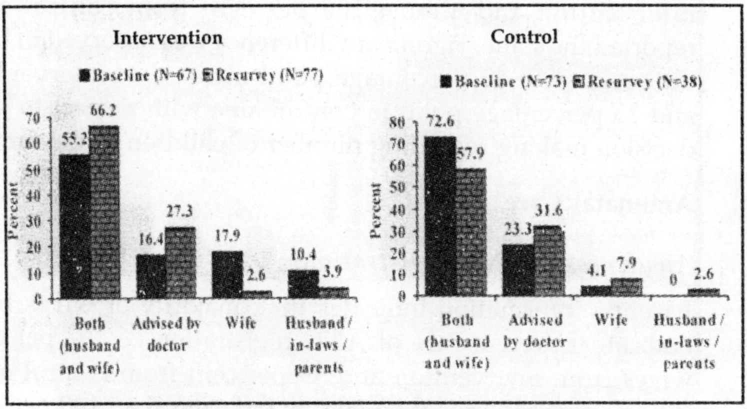

Figure 2: Decision Making regarding Induced Abortions

Who Accompanied Wife to Abortion (MTP) Services?: Baseline information indicates that majority of wives from both the areas i.e. 73 per cent wives from intervention and 93 per cent from control area reported that their husbands accompanied them to abortion services. Post-intervention survey also indicates that majority of wives from both the areas i.e. 78 per cent from intervention and 79 per cent from control area reported the same. About 5 per cent increase observed in intervention area in husband accompanying wife to abortion (MTP) services with no significant difference in both the areas.

Current Pregnancy Status: Baseline information indicates that; 8 per cent wives from intervention and 7 per cent from control area reported currently pregnant. Whereas post-intervention survey indicates that 8 per cent wives intervention and 3 per cent from control area reported the same. No significant difference was observed in both the areas with respect to current pregnancy.

Decision-making Regarding Number of Children: A question was asked to wives who decide how many children should be there in your family? Baseline information indicates that 78 per cent wives from intervention and 87 per cent from control area reported that both husband and wife jointly take the decision regarding the number of children in their families. Whereas during post-intervention, 93 per cent wives from intervention and almost 100 per cent from control area reported the same. Significant difference was observed in both the areas with 15 percentage point increase in intervention and 13 percentage point in control area with respect to joint decision making regarding number of children in the family.

Antenatal Care

Awareness of ANC Registration

Baseline information indicates that; majority of wives from both areas were aware of ANC registration i.e., 97 per cent wives from intervention and 99 per cent from control area. Whereas post-intervention survey indicates that; 100 per cent wives from both the areas were aware of ANC registration. Marginal increase with significant difference was observed intervention area.

Number of Antenatal Check-ups a Pregnant Woman should have?

Baseline information indicates that; 13 per cent husbands from intervention and 20 per cent from control area said that a pregnant woman should have at least two to three check-ups during pregnancy. About 21 per cent husbands from intervention and 8 per cent from control area felt that a pregnant woman should have at least seven check-ups during pregnancy. Whereas post-intervention survey indicates that 11 per cent husbands from intervention and 36 per cent from control area said that a pregnant woman should have at least two to three check-ups during pregnancy. Fifty-two per cent husbands from intervention and 47 per cent from control area felt that a pregnant woman should have at least seven check-ups during pregnancy. Significant difference was observed among husbands in both the areas with respect to awareness regarding number of ANC check-ups pregnant woman expected to have.

In Which Month of Pregnancy a Pregnant Woman should Register? Husbands' Perception

Baseline information indicates that 28 per cent husbands from intervention and 23 per cent from control area reported that pregnant woman should register for ANC check-up during 2nd or 3rd month (early registration). Whereas post-intervention survey indicates that 65 per cent husbands from intervention and 35 per cent from control area reported that pregnant woman should register for ANC check-up during 2nd or 3rd month (early registration), whereas Significant different observed in both the areas, with 37 per cent increase in awareness about early registration of pregnancy among

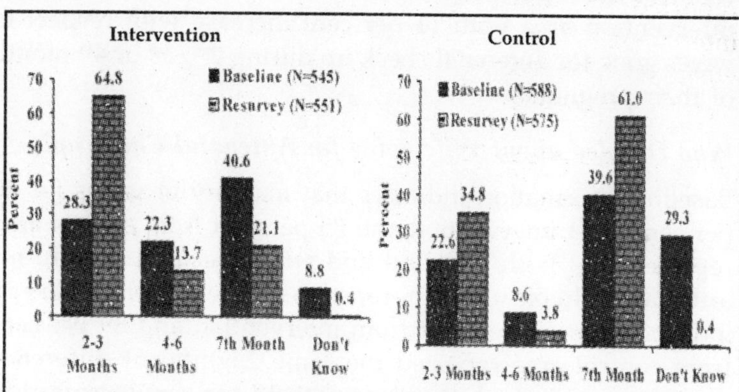

Figure 3: In Which Month of Pregnancy a Pregnant Woman should Register?

husbands in intervention and 12 per cent in control area with respect to awareness regarding ANC registration among husbands (Fig.3).

Discussion between Husband and Wife regarding Antenatal Check-ups Wife need to have

Baseline information indicates that 96 per cent husbands from intervention and 99 per cent from control area said that they discussed with their wives about antenatal check-ups they need to have. Whereas post-intervention survey indicates that 99 per cent from intervention and 100 per cent from control area said the same. No significant difference was observed in intervention and control area with 3 percentage point increase in intervention and 0.7 percentage point in control area with respect to husbands reporting discussion with wives regarding antenatal check-ups they need to have.

In Which Month of Pregnancy did Wife first go for Antenatal Check-up?

Baseline information indicates that; 55 per cent wives from intervention and 71 per cent from control area under went antenatal check-up during 2nd, 3rd or 4th month of pregnancy. Whereas post-intervention survey indicates that 66 per cent wives from intervention and 73 per cent from control area reported the same. Significant difference was observed in intervention area with 11 per cent increase with respect to wives gone for antenatal check up during 2nd, 3rd or 4th month of their pregnancy.

Who Decided about Wife going for Antenatal Check up?

Baseline information indicates that majority of wives i.e. 59 per cent from intervention and 85 per cent from control area reported that both husband and wives decided wife to for antenatal check-up. Whereas post-intervention survey indicates that 77 per cent from intervention and 89 per cent from control area reported the same. Significant difference was observed in both the areas with 18 per cent increased in intervention and 4 per cent in control area with respect to joint decision making regarding wife to go for antenatal check-up.

Who Accompanied Wife to the Antenatal Check-up

Baseline information indicates that 52 per cent wives from intervention and 49 per cent from control area reported that their husbands accompanied them to the antenatal check-up. Whereas post-intervention survey indicates that 58 per cent wives from intervention and 56 per cent from control area reported the same. Significant difference was observed with 6 per cent increase in intervention area, whereas 7 per cent increase observed in control area with no significant difference with respect person accompanying wife to antenatal check-up.

Kind of Antenatal Services did Wife receive during Pregnancy

Those who had antenatal check-ups during pregnancy were asked what type of services they had received. Baseline information indicates that majority of wives from both the areas reported that they had abdominal examination, BP check-up, blood test, urine test, TT injection and IFA tablets. Post-intervention survey indicates that nearly 100 per cent of wives from both the areas reported that they have received the same services. Significant difference was observed in all ANC services in control area with respect to all antenatal check-ups mentioned above, whereas, significant difference was observed only in TT injection in intervention area.

Reasons for Wife not Attending Antenatal Check-up

Baseline information indicates that 6 (3%) out of 196 wives from intervention and 4 (2.7%) out of 150 from control area did not go for antenatal check up. From intervention; area one wife said services were far, three felt it is not necessary and two decided to go for abortion. From control area; one wife said could not afford to go and three felt it is not necessary. Whereas during post-intervention all pregnant wives during last three years from both the areas reported that they had ANC check up during last pregnancy.

Did Husband Accompany Wife during her Last Delivery

Baseline information indicates that 66 per cent wives from intervention and 59 per cent from control area reported that their husbands accompanied them during their last delivery. Whereas post-intervention survey indicates that 72 per cent wives from intervention and 75 per cent from control area reported the same. About 6 per cent increase with no significant difference was observed in intervention area, whereas significant difference was observed in control area with 16 per cent increase with respect to husband accompanied wife during her last delivery.

Reasons for husband not accompanied wife during last delivery reported by wife

The most common reasons for husband not accompanied during last delivery were husband was out of station or he could not get the leave from his job. Baseline information indicates that 57 per cent wives from intervention and 61 per cent from control area reported that their husbands were out of station so they could not accompany them during last delivery, whereas 25 per cent wives from intervention and 24 per cent from control area reported that their husbands could not get the leave from the job.

Post-intervention survey indicates that 64 per cent wives from intervention and 77 per cent from control area reported that their husbands were out of station so they could not accompany them during last delivery, whereas 29 per cent wives intervention and 23 per cent from control area reported that their husbands could not get the leave from the job. No significant difference was observed in intervention area whereas significant difference was observed in control area with respect to reasons for husband not accompanied wife during last delivery.

Family Planning and Contraception-Correct Knowledge of Contraceptive Methods Among Husbands

Baseline information indicates that 99 per cent husbands from intervention and 99 per cent from control area were aware about condom whereas post-intervention survey indicates that 100 per cent husbands from intervention and 100 per cent from control area had reported the same. Baseline information indicates that 93 per cent husbands from intervention and 98 per cent from control area were aware about oral pills whereas post-intervention survey indicates that 100 per cent husbands from intervention and 99 per cent from control area had reported the same. Baseline information indicates that 89 per cent husbands from intervention and 63 per cent from control area were aware about IUD whereas post-intervention survey indicates that 99 per cent husbands from intervention and 98 per cent from control area had reported the same.

Baseline information indicates that 100 per cent husbands from intervention and 99 per cent from control area were aware about tubectomy whereas post-intervention survey indicates that 100 per cent husbands from intervention and 99 per cent from control area had reported the same. Baseline information indicates that 98 per cent husbands from intervention and 80 per cent from control area were aware about traditional vasectomy whereas post-intervention survey indicates that 100 per cent husbands from intervention and 96 per cent from control area had reported the same. Baseline information indicates that two per cent husbands from intervention and 0.7 per cent from control area were aware about non-scalpel vasectomy whereas post-intervention survey indicates that 96 per cent husbands from intervention and 61 per cent from control area had reported the same.

Baseline information indicates that 29 per cent husbands from intervention and 13 per cent from control area were aware about injectables whereas post-intervention survey indicates that 97 per cent husbands from intervention and 61per cent from control area had reported the same. Baseline information indicates that 1 per cent husbands from intervention and 0.5 per cent from control area were aware about emergency contraception whereas post-intervention survey indicates that 72 per cent husbands from intervention and 56 per cent from control area had reported the same. Baseline information indicates that 5 per cent husbands from intervention and 3 per cent from control area were aware about female condom whereas post-intervention survey indicates that 70 per cent husbands from intervention and 14 per cent from control area had reported the same.

Baseline information indicates that 57 per cent husbands from intervention and 41 per cent from control area were aware about withdrawal whereas post-intervention survey indicates that; 99 per cent husbands from intervention and 94 per cent from control area had reported the same. Baseline information indicates that 17 per cent husbands from intervention and 17 per cent from control area were aware about rhythm whereas post-intervention survey indicates that 99 per cent husbands from intervention and 88 per cent from control area had reported the same. Baseline information indicates that 55 per cent husbands from intervention and 9 per cent from control area were aware about abstinence whereas post-intervention survey indicates that 99 per cent husbands from intervention and 91 per cent from control area had reported the same. Significant differences was observed in intervention area with respect to awareness about all contraceptive methods except tubectomy whereas in control area significant differences was observed with respect to awareness about all contraceptive methods except condom, oral pills and tubectomy (Table 2).

Source of Contraceptive Information Reported by Husbands

Husbands who were aware of contraceptive methods were asked about the source of contraceptive information. Television, Hospital, Radio, News Paper, Displayed IEC material, Printed IEC material, Private clinic and awareness programmes were mentioned as their sources of information during baseline survey as well as post-intervention survey.

As a source of contraceptive information, during baseline survey; 64 per cent husbands from intervention and 54 per cent from control area mentioned displayed IEC material; 19 per cent husbands from intervention and 18 per cent from control area mentioned printed IEC material; 28 per cent

Table 2
Awareness about Contraceptive Methods Among Husbands

Contraceptive Method	*Intervention* Baseline (N=561)	*Intervention* Post-intervention (N=555)	*Control* Baseline (N=588)	*Control* Post-intervention (N=575)
Condom	98.6	100.0	99.5	99.7
Oral Pills	93.2	99.8	98.3	99.0
IUD	88.6	99.5	63.3	74.2
Tubectomy	99.8	100.0	99.1	99.0
Vasectomy (Traditional)	98.0	100.0	80.3	95.7
Vasectomy (Non Scalpel Vasectomy)	2.0	96.4	0.7	60.5
Injectables	29.2	97.3	12.7	60.7
Emergency Contraception	1.4	71.9	0.5	56.2
Female Condom	5.2	69.9	2.7	13.7
Withdrawal	57.0	98.9	40.8	94.4
Rhythm	16.6	98.9	17.0	87.7
Abstinence	55.1	99.3	9.2	91.3

husbands from intervention and 3 per cent from control area mentioned private clinic; 9 per cent husbands from intervention and 1 per cent from control area mentioned awareness programmes as their source of contraceptive information which contributed less.

During post-intervention survey drastic increase was observed in these sources as 93 per cent husbands from intervention and 33 per cent from control area mentioned displayed IEC material; 93 per cent husbands from intervention and 24 per cent from control area mentioned printed IEC material; 87 per cent husbands from intervention and 68 per cent from control area mentioned private clinic; 74 per cent husbands from intervention and 17 per cent from control area mentioned awareness programmes as their source of contraceptive information. Significant difference was observed in both the areas with respect to all sources of contraceptive information except television.

Had Spouse Ever Discussed Using Spacing Method? If Yes, When?

Baseline information indicates that 78 per cent husbands from intervention and 60 per cent from control area reported that they discussed with their spouses about using spacing method. Whereas post-intervention survey indicates that; 75 per cent husbands from intervention and 89 per cent from control area reported the same. Significant difference was observed with 19 per cent increase in control area whereas 3 per cent decrease with no significant difference was observed in intervention area with respect to discussion with spouse regarding use of spacing method. Majority of husbands discussed regarding use of spacing method after the birth of first child.

Had Spouse Ever Discussed about Using Permanent Method? If Yes, When?

Baseline information indicates that 70 per cent husbands from intervention and 59 per cent from control area reported that they discussed with their spouses about using permanent method. Whereas post-intervention survey indicates that 51 per cent wives from intervention and 60 per cent from control area reported the same. Significant decrease observed in control area with respect to discussion with spouse regarding use of permanent method. Majority of husbands discussed regarding use of permanent method after the birth of second child. About 14 per cent husbands from intervention and 22 per cent from control area were discussing with their wives regarding use of permanent method soon after marriage or first child.

Current Contraceptive Use

Current Contraceptive Use by Method

Baseline information indicates that 27 per cent couples from intervention and 39 per cent from control area reported that they were using spacing contraceptive method, 44 per cent from intervention and 41 per cent from control area were using permanent method and 29 per cent from intervention and 20 per cent from control area were not using any contraceptive method. Whereas during post intervention survey 36 per cent couples from intervention and 33 per cent from control area, reported that they were using spacing contraceptive method, 34 per cent from intervention and 39 per cent from control area were using permanent method and 31 per cent from intervention and 28 per cent from control area were not using any contraceptive method. Highly significant ($p<0.001$) difference was observed in intervention area whereas significant ($p<0.05$) difference was observed in control area with respect to type of contraceptive method couples using currently (Table 3).

Table 3
Current Contraceptive Use by Type of Methods

	Intervention	*Control*		
Type of Method	*Baseline*	*Post Intervention*	*Baseline*	*Post Intervention*
Spacing	26.7	35.5	39.1	32.9
Permanent	44.1	33.7	40.5	39.3
No Method	29.2	30.8	20.4	27.8
	$\chi^2 = 14.78$ d.f.=2 P<0.001		$\chi^2 = 9.89$ d.f.=2 p <0.05	

Current Contraceptive Use by Male/Female Method

Baseline information indicates that 14 per cent couples from intervention and 20 per cent from control area, reported that they were using male methods (condom, withdrawal, traditional vasectomy, non-scalpel vasectomy), 57 per cent from intervention and 60 per cent from control area were using female methods (oral pills, IUD, abstinence, rhythm, injectables, tubectomy) and 29 per cent from intervention and 20 per cent from control area were not using any contraceptive method.

Whereas during post intervention survey 22 per cent couples from intervention and 16 per cent from control area, reported that they were using male methods (condom, withdrawal, traditional vasectomy, non-scalpel vasectomy), 47 per cent from intervention and 56 per cent from control area were using female methods (oral pills, IUD, abstinence, rhythm, injectables, tubectomy) and 31 per cent from intervention and 28 per cent from control area were not using any contraceptive method. Highly significant ($p<0.001$) difference was observed intervention area with 8 per cent increase in use of male contraceptive methods whereas significant ($p<0.01$) difference was observed in control area with marginal (4%) decrease in use of male method (Table 4).

Table 4
Current Contraceptive Use by Male/Female Methods

	Intervention		*Control*	
Type of Method	*Baseline*	*Post Intervention*	*Baseline*	*Post Intervention*
Male Method	13.6	22.0	19.7	16.2
Female Method	57.2	47.2	59.9	56.0
No Method	29.2	30.8	20.4	27.8
	$\chi^2 = 16.77$ d.f.=2 P<0.001		$\chi^2 = 9.44$ d.f.=2 p <0.01	

Reason for Not Using F.P. Method Currently by Couple

Among those who were not using any contraceptive during the baseline survey; 49 per cent husbands from intervention and 64 per cent from control area reported the major reason as wanted a child whereas during post-intervention 78 per cent husbands intervention and 55 per cent from control area reported the same. Other reasons mentioned by husbands were; wanted a/another son, wanted additional child, wanted a daughter, no proper knowledge, against contraceptive use or use of contraception is against religion, medical problem etc. Significant difference was observed in both the areas with respect to reasons for not using family planning methods currently by couple.

Opinion of Husband and Wife Regarding Vasectomy and Tubectomy

Baseline information indicates that 4 per cent husbands from intervention and 4 per cent from control area felt that vasectomy is better than tubectomy whereas during post-intervention 41 per cent husbands from intervention and 4 per cent from control area reported the same. Significant difference was observed in husbands' opinion regarding vasectomy and tubectomy in both the areas, with increase in husbands opinion as vasectomy is better than tubectomy in intervention and control areas.

Discussion

The intervention strategy adopted in this study promoted joint decision making regarding abortion and number of children wanted, increased awareness about antenatal check-up, antenatal registration, health seeking behaviour, awareness and knowledge of non-scalpel vasectomy, emergency contraception, injectables and female condom significantly. Condom use increased significantly.

It is critical that men's involvement be seen as frame work that can be applied to all areas of RH including safe motherhood, post abortion care, cervical cancer prevention, adolescent health and gender-based violence[6]. Current study indicates 11 per cent increase in joint decision making for wife to go for induced abortion and 5 per cent increase in husband accompanying wife to abortion (MTP) services.

The effect of son preference and hence non-use of contraception on fertility was high in Maharashtra, along with other states. Son preference can also affect family planning behaviour. In every state woman with two sons are more likely to use contraception than women with two daughters[7]. Efforts should be made to educate and motivate the men towards small family norms and hence to use contraception. A study conducted in Mumbai by our group reported that men have strong desire for sons, nine out of ten men had preference for one son and one in every twelve had preference for at least two or more sons, mainly to continue family name and old age support[8]. Current study indicates significant increase (15.5%) in joint decision making regarding number of children in the family which has reflected in 6.6 per cent decrease in discussion between husband and wife about desire for more sons than daughters.

Dev in his study conducted in 1998 observed a positive impact of interventions in improving the health seeking behaviour of pregnant women when husbands were contacted compare to when they were not[9]. In current study, spousal communication regarding need for antenatal check-up increased marginally as well as there were significant increase (17.8%) in joint decision making regarding wife to go for antenatal check-up. ME Khan et al in their study emphasized need for joint counselling of husband and wife during ANC care during "on-the-job training" of doctors as well as other health providers at the grassroots level[10]. Awareness regarding early registration of pregnancy among husbands increased by 37 per cent with 11.3 per cent increase in women going for antenatal check-up during 2nd, 3rd or 4th month of their pregnancy. All the pregnant women from intervention area prior to three years of post-intervention survey underwent antenatal check-ups.

Mishra VK el al., reported that misconceptions about contraceptive use and negative image of family planning programme are also sometimes mentioned as reason for discontinuation and non-use of contraception. In their study 8.2 per cent men did not use any contraceptives because they had poor or no correct knowledge about the methods[11].

Awareness about Condom, Oral Pills, IUD, Tubectomy and Vasectomy reached to 100 per cent whereas drastic increase was observed in awareness of NSV, Injectables and Female Condom whereas about 38 per cent increase observed in husbands' opinion as vasectomy is better than tubectomy in this study after interventions.

Conclusion and Recommendations

The intervention strategy adopted in this study decreased son preference, promoted joint decision making regarding abortion and number of children wanted, increased awareness about antenatal check-up, antenatal registration, health seeking behaviour, awareness and knowledge of non-scalpel vasectomy, emergency contraception, injectables and female condom significantly. Condom use increased significantly.

Sustainability of prograamme can be ensured by continuing IEC programmes along with routine MCH programmes. ANMs and MPWs with the help of Community Health Volunteers (CHVs) can cover the topics on safe motherhood, immunization and contraception when women visit health post for ante-natal and post-natal check-up or during their field visits. Information can be provided in small group meeting or during educational programmes in the community. Medical Officer, ANMs, MPWs and CHVs trained in counselling on safe motherhood and contraception can provide counselliong as and when required. The programme can be implemented in other health posts in similar situation to reach the large population. This will bring down the cost of the programme. Hence the programme can be sustainable, replicable and cost effective.

References

United Nations International Conference on Population and Development "Programme of Action of a Conference" Cairo, September 1994.

National Population Policy for India 2000, Department of Family Welfare, Ministry of Health and family Welfare, Government of India. Website: www.mohfw.nic.in.

Green,P.C. and J. Chens (2003): HBC Male Involvement in Reproductive Health. CPD UNFPA. Paper 27. Report available at http://www.epd.org.bd/pub_attach/unfpa27.pdf

Medicam (2004): Male Involvement is Key to Reproductive Health Promotion Working Group (RHPWG). USAID policy project. October, Retrived from :htpp://www.policyproject.com/pubs/brochures/CAM_MaleInvolveEng.pdf

Davies J., Mitra S.N. and William P Schellstede (1987): "Oral Contraception in Bangladesh: Social Marketing and the Importance of Husbands". *Studies in Family Planning* 18, 3: 157-168.

Manisha Mehata (2001), "Communicating with Men to Promote Family Planning: Lessons Learned and Suggestions for Programming", paper presented at the World Health Organization (WHO) meeting of Regional Advisers on Programming for male involvement in Reproductive Health" Washington, DC Sept. 5-7.

Mutharayappa R, Choe MK, Arnold F, Roy TK. (1997): "Son Preference and Its Effect on Fertility in India". In: *National Family Health Survey Subject Reports*, International Institute for Population Sciences, Mumbai, India and East-West Centre Program on Population, Honolulu, Hawai, U.S.A. March 1997: No 3.

Balaiah D, Ghule M, Naik DD, Tapase P, Iddya U, Parida RC, Hazari KT, Kanbur A. (2001): "Son Preference and Family Planning Practices among Married Men in Mumbai, India", *Reproduction and Contraception*, 12(4): 226-239.

Dev A. (1998): "Involvement of Husbands' in the Antenatal Care Evaluation of Deepak Charitable Trust; Outreach Programme", Paper presented at the Workshop on Men as Supportive Partner in Reproductive and Sexual Health, Kathmandu, Nepal, June 1998 Population Council, New Delhi, India.

ME Khan, Irfan Khan and Nupur Mukherjee (1997): "Involving Men in Safe Motherhood" *The Journal of Family Welfare* 43(2): 18-30.

Mishra VK, Retherford, Nair PS and Feeney G. (1999): "Reasons for Discontinuing and Not Intending to Use Contraception in India", *National Family Health Survey Subject Reports*, International Institute for Population Sciences, Mumbai, India and East-West Centre, Population and Health Studies, Honolulu, Hawai, U.S.A. June 1999: No 13.

18

Socio-Economic Inequalities in Self-Rated Poor Health Among Indian Elderly: Evidence from NSSO 60th Round Data

Pallavi Banjare, J. Pradhan

Introduction

Ageing is a universal phenomenon in both developing as well as developed countries (UN, 2007; WHO, 2008). While the population of more developed countries have being aging for over a century but this process has began recently in most less developed countries, and this will take far less time than that of the developed nations (Kinsella & David, 2005).

Population ageing may be seen as a human success story of medical advancements, economic development over diseases and injuries that has raised the human life expectancy to the millennium. By 2050, nearly 1.2 billion of the expected 1.5 billion people age 65 or older will reside in today's less developed region (Kinsella & David, 2005). More over global population ageing is a by-product of demographic transition, in which both mortality and fertility decline from higher to lower levels (UN, 2007). Currently, the total fertility rate is below replacement level in almost all develop nations and this is speedily heading towards the less developed ones.

India is in a phase of demographic transition. As per the 2001 census, the population of the elderly in India was 76 million as compared with 20 million in 1951. It is estimated that this will cross 125 million by the year 2025 (UN, 2001).

In developing countries, gaps in health related outcomes between the rich and the poor are large (Baker & Garg, 1993; Gwatkin, 2000; Leon and Walt, 2001; Wagstaff, 2002a, 2002b). These gaps limit poor peoples' potential to contribute to the economy by reducing their capacity to function and live life to the fullest. Moreover, health plays vital role in the well-being of the elderly, in any country including India. There is a well documented but poorly understood '*gradient*' linking socioeconomic status to wide range of health outcomes (Adler et al., 1994). Studies from both the developing and developed countries have noted an inverse association between socio-economic status and mortality, morbidity and disability among the elderly (Kabir et al, 2003; Liang and Liu, 2001). Studies from India have noted a negative association between socio-economic status and parameters of social mobility such as widowhood and economic dependence among the elderly (Soneja et al., 1996).

Many studies have assisted the level of socio-economic inequalities in health using concentration index and concentration curve. Though the values of concentration indices (CIs) show the degree of socio-economic inequality, it does not highlight the pathway through which inequality occurs. Decomposition of inequalities is critical to explore pathways of socio-economic inequalities in elderly health.

To our knowledge, there has been virtually no study that attempted decomposition of socio-economic inequalities in health among elderly population in India. Given the recent methodological developments and the policy relevance, an effort has been made in this paper for the first time to decompose health inequalities in terms of self reported poor health in India.

Data and Methodology

Data from the 60th round of National Sample Survey (NSS-2004) has been used in this study. NSSO survey data provides generous information on elderly's health, health care, disability, deaths and cause of deaths in last 365 days, use of medical facilities and socio-economic and demographic background characteristics. For core analysis, we considered self rated poor health status as dependent variable. NSSO provides information on perceived current health status (grouping responses to *'what is your own perception about current state of health'* using a three point scale –'Excellent/ Very good'; 'Good/Fair'; and 'Poor'). Subsequently, responses are recoded into binary variable (good health[1] =0; and poor health=1).

Use of self-reported health status may be questioned, particularly as it is subjective (Gupta and Sankar, 2003). Self-reporting may also be shaped by the social context in which the person is situated (Sen, 1993). However, there is a large volume of literature suggesting that self-reported health is an acceptable indicator of general health with good construct validity (Manton et al., 1997; Smith, 1994; Soldo and Hill, 1995; Wallace, 1995), and a powerful predictor of mortality risks (Idler and Benyamini, 1997), disability (Idler and Kasl, 1995), and morbidity (Beckett et al., 2000; Schechter et al., 1998). A medical study in Bangladesh also finds strong correspondence between self-reported health and actual physical measures of health (Rahman and Barsky, 2003).

Independent variables for decomposition analysis included: age (70+/others), economic status (poor/non-poor), sector (rural/urban), social group (SC-ST/others), sex (female/male), and education (illiterate/literate) economic dependence (dependent/not dependent). In this paper we consider per capita monthly consumption expenditure (PCMCE) as a measure of household economic status (poverty). This measure is used in many studies and gives an idea about the economic environment of the individuals (Deaton and Paxson, 1995; Deaton, 1997; Pal and Palacious, 2008; Dreze and Srinivasan, 1997; Alam, 2008). Though some studies have criticized PCMCE as a true indicator of poverty, in particular in the context of its inability to capture age-specific poverty level (Alam, 2008), it is still the best available measure of standard of living. In fact, Deaton (1997) and Blundell (1995) have shown that household monthly consumption expenditure could be used as a proxy variable for income. Then entire population is divided into five wealth quintiles (Q1 to Q5). The wealth quintile distribution was used to determine poor-rich household for subsequent modeling and estimation of concentration index. For the decomposition analysis, quintiles 1 & 2 and quintiles 3, 4 & 5 were grouped together.

Table 1 provides description of variables considered for decomposition analysis. The decomposition analysis is confined to seven possible socio-economic determinants that could explain the maximum dimensions of socioeconomic inequality particularly in developing countries like India. The predictors variables of interest are: i) Age above 70+; ii) Poor economic status (sum of Q1 and Q2); iii) residence in rural areas; iv) belong to SC/ST; v) female elderly; vi) illiterate; and vii) economically dependent.

Table 1

Definition of Variables Considered for Decomposition Analysis

Health Variable	*Predictive Variables*	*(Yes=1, Otherwise=0)*
Current health status (self rated) (Poor=1, Good=0)	Age	*70+ =1, ≤69=0*
	Poor economic status	*Poor=1, Non-Poor=0*
	Residence	*Rural=1, Urban=0*
	Social groups	*SC/ST=1, OBC/General=0*
	Sex	*Female=1, Male=0*
	Education	*Illiterate=1, Literate=0*
	Economic status	*Economically Dependent=1, Economically Independent=0*

Measuring Socio-economic Inequalities in Elderly Health

The literature on the measurement of socioeconomic inequalities in health has mainly drawn on the development of rank-dependent measures in the income inequality literature. A long-standing issue in the literature on healthy inequality is whether all inequalities ought to be measured or only those which show some systematic association with indicators of socioeconomic status (Gakidou et al., 2000; Wagstaff, 2001). Some of the earlier contributions used Lorenz curves and the Gini index to measure inequality in mortality rates (LeGrand, 1989). Lorenz curve describes the cumulative distribution of health in a population ranked by health and the Gini index, hence forth denoted as G, measures the deviation from an equal distribution as (twice) the area between Lorenz curve and the diagonal.

Wagstaff et al., (1991) have proposed the use of related concepts of concentration curve and index to measure the extent to which inequalities in health are related to indicators of socioeconomic status like income or education. They argued that the concentration index meets three minimal requirements of an inequality index: (i) it reflects that the experience of the entire population studies, (ii) it reflects the socioeconomic dimension of health inequalities and (iii) it is sensitive to changes in the composition of the underlying socioeconomic ranking variable. A concentration curve describes the cumulative distribution of health in a population ranked by socioeconomic status and the concentration index, henceforth denoted as C, measures the deviation from an equal distribution as (twice) the area between the concentration curve and the diagonal.

The concentration index is defined with reference to the concentration curve. The concentration index is defined as twice the area between the concentration curve and the line of equality (the 45-degree line). So, in the case in which there is no socioeconomic-related inequality, the concentration index is zero. The convention is that the index takes a negative value when the curve lies above the line of equality, indicating disproportionate concentration of the health variable among the poor, and a positive value when it lies below the line of equality.

If the health variable is a "bad" such as ill health, a negative value of the concentration index means ill health is higher among the poor.

Formally, the concentration index is defined as

$$C = 1 - 2\int_0^1 L_h(p)dp$$

The index is bounded between – 1 and 1. For a discrete living standards variable, it can be written as

$$C = \frac{2}{N\mu}\sum_{i=1}^{n} h_i r_i - 1 - \frac{1}{N}$$

Where h_i is the health sector variable, μ is its mean, and r_i = i/N is the fractional rank of individual i in the living standards distribution, with i = 1 for the poorest and i = N for the richest. For computation, a more convenient formula for the concentration index defines it in terms of the covariance between the health variable and the fractional rank in the living standards distribution (Jenkins 1988; Kakwani 1980; Lerman and Yitzhaki 1989).

$$c = 2\frac{1}{\mu} \text{ cov (h,r)} \quad \text{.................................(1)}$$

It may be noted that the concentration index depends only on the relationship between the health variable and the rank of the living standards variable and not on the variation in the living standards variable itself. A change in the degree of income inequality need not affect the concentration index measure of income-related health inequality.

The sign of the concentration index indicates the direction of relationship between the health variable and position in the living standards distribution, and its magnitude reflects both the strength of the relationship and the degree of variability in the health variable. Although this is valuable information, one may also wish to place an intuitive interpretation on the value of the index.

Decomposing Determinants of Inequalities in Elderly Health Indicators

Health economists have widely adopted the Gini coefficient and concentration indices to provide summary measures of inequalities of health within population (Wagstaff 2002a, 2002b; van Doorslaer et al., 1997). Like the Gini coefficient of income inequality, the Gini and concentration indicies for health have the attraction that they can be decomposed by factors (Kakwani, 1980, Hosseinpoor et al., 2006, Yiengprugsawan et al., 2007, Lauridsen et al., 2007). A recent contribution by Wagstaff et al., (2003) has used this property to show how a linear regression approach can be used to decompose the concentration indices into the contributions of different explanatory variables. In this regression-based decomposition approach, the contribution of each factor to overall inequality depends on the elasticity of health with respect to that variable, capturing the health gradient, and on the concentration index for that factor, capturing how much inequality in the distribution is attributable to the factor.

In this paper, the method proposed by Wagstaff et al., (2003), has been used to decompose socioeconomic inequality in elderly health in India. The decomposition analysis allows us to estimate how the determinants proportionally contribute to inequality (the gap between the poor and rich) in a health variable.

Wagstaff et al., (2003), showed that for any linear regression model linking the health variable of interest, y to a set of k health determinants, x_k:

$$y = \alpha + \sum_k \beta_k x_k + \epsilon \quad \text{.................................(2)}$$

Where, ϵ is an error term. Given the relationship between y_i and x_{ki} the concentration index for y 'C' can be written as

$$C = \sum_k \left(\frac{\beta_k \bar{x}_k}{\mu}\right) C_k + \frac{GC_\varepsilon}{\mu} \quad \text{..........................(3)}$$

Where, μ is the mean of y, $\bar{x}_k$ is the mean of x_k, C_k is the concentration index for x_k, and β_k is the regression coefficient. In the last term (which can be computed as a residual), GC_ε is the generalized concentration index for ε.

The above equation therefore shows that C comprises of two components. The first is the deterministic or explained components. This is equal to weighted sum of the concentration indices of the regressors, where the weights are simply the elasticities. The second is a residual or 'unexplained' component. This reflects the inequality in health that cannot be explained by systematic variation in the x_k across socioeconomic groups.

Methodological Steps of Decomposition of Socioeconomic Inequalities in Child Health

The steps of decomposition analysis are as follows:

(i) Regress the health variable against its determinants, which provides coefficients of explanatory variables (β_k)

(ii) Generate the means of the health variable and each of its determinants (μ and $\bar{x}_k$)

(iii) Calculate the concentration indices for the health variable and for the determinants (C and C_k) using equation (1). At this stage, the values of all the variables included in equation (3) are known. Finally, the contribution of each of the determinants included in the model to the inequality in the health variables can be quantified through the following steps:

(iv) Compute the absolute contribution of each determinant by multiplying the health variable elasticity with respect to that determinant and its concentration index $(\beta_k/\mu)C_k$ and

(v) Calculate percentage contribution of each determinant simply by dividing its absolute contribution by the concentration index of the health variables $(\beta_k\bar{x}_k/\mu)$ C_k/C.

Results

Table 2 Presents the mean value of the selected covariates considered in this analysis. Results show that about 24% of the elderly perceived that their health status is poor during time of survey. Forty two per cent of the elderly belong to poor economic status, and majority of them come from rural areas (63%).

Table 2
Descriptive Statistics of Individual Covariates (N=34831)

Variables	*Mean*	*Std.Dev*	*Min*	*Max*
Self reported poor health	0.247612	0.431631	0	1
Age 70 (above)	0.352703	0.477818	0	1
Poor economic status	0.421665	0.493833	0	1
Living in rural areas	0.639229	0.480231	0	1
SC/ST	0.244925	0.430049	0	1
Female	0.490396	0.499915	0	1
Illiterate	0.611834	0.48734	0	1
Economically dependent	0.655263	0.475289	0	1

Table 3 presents the decomposition analysis of socio-economic inequality in self rated poor health among Indian elderly. Concentration indices provide insights on the poor-rich distribution of the socio-economic determinants. A positive CI value implies that the extent of inequality is greater in favor of rich and a negative CI value implies that the inequality is in favor of the poor. The CI value of self reported poor health among elderly is -0.0854 at national level.

Table 3
Contribution of Various Socio-economic Covariates to Total Health Inequality in Elderly Health for India, 2004

Variables	*Mean*	*Marg Effect*	*CI*	*Contribution to CI*	*% Contribution*
Age 70 (above)	0.3527	0.1506	0.0316	0.0068	-8.9
Poor economic status	0.4216	0.0448	-0.571	-0.0436	57.0
Living in rural areas	0.6392	0.0259	-0.1968	-0.0132	17.2
SC/ST	0.2449	-0.0048	-0.1956	0.0009	-1.2
Female	0.4939	-0.0204	-0.0047	-0.0002	-0.3
Illiterate	0.6118	0.0255	-0.0108	-0.0108	14.1
Economically dependent	0.6553	0.1397	-0.0169	-0.0169	22.1
Self reported poor health	0.2476		-0.0854	-0.0765	100.0
Residuals =				-0.0089	

Decomposition approach reveals that variables, poor economic status (57%) economically dependent (22%) and living in rural areas (17%) contribute to about 96% of predictable socioeconomic inequalities in self rated poor health status. This analysis has also demonstrated that measuring socio-economic inequalities in elderly health provides critical insights for understanding the determinants of health inequalities in term of their contributions which are immensely valuable for specific health interventions strategies and achieving health equity.

Discussion and Conclusions

This paper presented first hand evidence on the decomposed contributions of socio-economic determinants of inequalities in the elderly. Such precise decomposition outcomes demonstrate evidence that most socioeconomic inequalities primarily arise from these three socio-economic predictors namely: poverty, economic dependence and rural residence.

So, elderly belong to poor economic status and all those elderly who are economically dependent on others are facing most of the problem. Therefore, special attention to these people who live in poverty especially in rural areas and are dependent on others is essential. The new health policy by the government should look into this through various methods like: i) it must have a financing system for all those elderly who belong to BPL (below poverty line) with a public and private partnership; ii) many of the elderly in rural areas don't know about any of the schemes launched by the government like the National pension scheme and many other beneficiaries by the government due to lack of awareness, so certain awareness programs should be promoted with the help of NGOs and other private voluntary organizations in health to keep them updated. Various educational programs have been started to educate the elderly but the success rate is quite low this should be monitored properly as education too plays an important role in their poor health status.

References

Alam, M. (2008): Ageing, Socio-economic Disparities and Health Outcomes: Some Evidence from Rural India, Working Paper Series No. E/290/2008, Institute of Economic Growth, University of Delhi Enclave, North Campus, Delhi-110007, India.

Alder, Nancy E., Thomas Boyce, *et al.*, (1994): Socioeconomic Status and Health: The Challenge of the Gradient, *American Psychologist*, 49, 15-24.

Baker, J.L., J. van der Gaag (1993): Equity in Health Care and Health Care Financing: Evidence from Five Developing Countries. In Equity in the Finance and Delivery of Health Care: An International Perspective Edited by: van Doorslaer E, Wagstaff A, Rutten F. New York, Oxford University Press.

Beckett, M., Weinstein, M. Goldman, N. & Yu-Hsuan, L. (2000): Do Health Interview Surveys Yield Reliable Data on Chronic Illness Among Older Respondents? *American Journal of Epidemiology*, 151-23.

Blundell, R. (1995): Income, Expenditure and Living Standards of UK Households, *Fiscal Studies*, 16(3): 40-54.

Deaton, A. (1997): The Analysis of Household Surveys: A Micro Econometric Approach to Development Policy, World Bank, Washington DC.

Deaton, A. and C. Paxson (1995): Measuring Poverty Among the Elderly, NBER Working Paper, National Bureau of Economic Research, Inc.

Dreze, J. and P.V. Srinivasan (1997): Widowhood and Poverty in Rural India: Some Inferences from Household Survey Data, *Journal of Development Economics*, 54, 217-234.

Gakidou, E.,C.J.L. Murray, J. Frenk (2000): Defining and Measuring Health Inequality: An Approach based on the Distribution of Health Expectancy. *Bulletin of World Health Organization* 78: 42-54.

Gupta, I. & Sankar, D. (2003): Health of the Elderly in India: A Multivariate Analysis. *Journal of Health & Population in Developing Countries*, June 24, 2003.

Gwatkin, D.R. (2000): Health Inequalities and the Health of the Poor: What Do We Know? What Can We Do? *Bulletin of the World Health Organization* 78 (1): 3 -17.

Hosseinpoor, A.R., E.v. Doorslaer, N. Speybroeck et al., (2006): Decomposing Socioeconomic Inequality in Infant Mortality in Iran. *International Journal of Epidemiology* 35: 1211-1219

Idler, E.L. & Benyamini, Y. (1997): Self-rated Health and Mortality: A Review of Twenty-seven Community Studies. *Journal of Health and Social Behaviour* 38, 21-37.

Idler, E.L. and S.V. Kasl (1995): Self-Rating of Health: Do They Also Predict Change in Functional Ability?, Journal of Gerontology, 50(6): S344-53.

Jenkins, S. (1988): Calculating Income Distribution Indices from Micro Data. National Tax Journal 61: 139-42.

Kabir ZN, Tishelman C, Torres-Aguero H, Chowdhury AMR, Windblad B, Hojer B. (2003): Gender and Rural-urban Differences in Reported Health Status by Older People in Bangladesh. *Arch Gerontol Geriat* 37: 77-91.

Kakwani, N,C. (1980): Income Inequality and Poverty: Methods of Estimation and Policy Application. Oxford University Press, New York, NY.

Kinsella, K & David R.Philips (2005): Global Ageing: The Challenge of Success. *Population Bulletin.*

Lauridsen J, Christiansen T, Gundgaard J, Häkkinen U, Sintonen H. (2007): Decomposition of Health Inequality by Determinants and Dimensions. *Health Economics* 16: 97-102.

LeGrand, J. (1989): An International Comparison on Distributions of Ages-at-death. In: Fox J., ed. Health inequalities in European countries. Adelshot, Hants, England, Gower Pub. Co.

Leon, D.A., G. Walt (2001): Poverty, Inequality and Health: An International Perspective. In Oxford Medical Publications Oxford ; New York , Oxford University Press.

Lerman, Robert I. & Yitzhaki, Shlomo (1989): Improving the Accuracy of Estimates of Gini Coefficients. *Journal of Econometrics.* 42(1): 43-47.

Liang J, Liu X, Gu S. (2001): Transitions in Functional Status Among Older People in Wuhan, China: Socio-economic Differentials. *J Clin Epidemiol* 54: 1126-38.

Manton, K.G, Stallard, E. and Cordel, R. (1997): Changes in Age Dependence of Mortality and Disability: Cohort and Other Determinants. *Demography* 34, 135-157.

NSSO (2006): Morbidity, Health Care and the Condition of the Aged, ational Sample Survey Organization, 60th round, Report No. 507(60/25.0/1), Ministry of Statistics and Programme Implementation, Government of India.

Pal, S. and R. Palacios (2008): Understanding Poverty Among the Elderly in India: Implications for Social Pension Policy, IZA Discussion Paper No. 3431, April, 2008.

Rahman, M.O. & Barsky, A.J. (2003): Self-reported Health Among Older Bangladeshis: How Good a Health Indicator is it? *The Gerontologist* 43, 856-863.

Schechter, S., Beatty, P. & Willis, G.B. (1998): Asking Survey Respondents Aboul Health Status: Judgment and Response Issues. In Schwarz., N., Park, D., Knauper, B. & Sudman, S. (eds.) Cognition, Aging, and Self-reports. Taylor & Francis, Ann Arbor, MI: pp. 229-247.

Sen, A.K. (1993): Positional Objectivity. *Philosophy and Public Affairs* 22(2), 126-145

Smith, J. (1994): Measuring Health and Economic Status of Older Adults in Developing Countries. *Gerontologist* 34, 491-496.

Soldo B.J. & Hill, M. (1995): Family Structure and Transfer Measures in the Health and Retirement Study: Background and Overview. *Journal of Human Resources*, Supplement 30(5), S108- S37.

Soneja S, Nagarkar KM, Dey AB, Khetrapal K, Kumar V. (1996): Socio-economic Status and Its Relationship to Parameters of Social Morbidity Among Elderly Patients Seeking Outpatient Medical Care. In: Kumar V, editor. Aging: Indian perspective and global scenario. New Delhi: All India Institute of Medical Sciences; p. 137-9.

United Nations (2001): World Population Ageing 1950-2050. Population Division, DESA, United Nations.

United Nations (2007): World Economic and Social Survey 2007. Development in an Ageing World. New York: United Nations

Van Doorslaer, E.,A. Wagstaff, Bleichrodt, S. calonge, U.G. Gerdtham, M. Gerfin, J. Geruts. L. gross, u. Hakkinen, R.E. leu O.O' Donnell, C. Propper, F. Puffer, M. Rodriguez, G. sundberg, and O. Winkelhake (1997). "Income-related Inequalities in Health: Some International Comparisons. *Journal of Health Economics* 16(1): 93-112.

Wagstaff, A,P. Paci, E.van doorslaer (1991): On the Measurement of Inequalities in Health, *Social Sciences and Medicines* 33:545-557

Wagstaff, A (1991): QALYs and the Equity-efficiency Trade-off .*Journal of Health Economics* 10(1):21-41

Wagstaff, A. (2001): Poverty and Health. WHO Commission on Macroeconomics and Health. Geneva.

Wagstaff, A. (2002a): Inequalities in Health in Developing Countries: Swimming Against the Tide? Policy Research Working Paper 2795. Washington, DC , World Bank.

Wagstaff, A. (2002b): Poverty and Health Sector Inequalities. *Bulletin of the World Health Organization* 80(2): 97-105

Wagstaff, A.,E. Van Doorslaer, and N. Watanabe (2003): On Decomposing the Causes of Health Sector Inequalities, with an application to malnutrition inequalities in Vietnam. *Journal of Econometrics* 112(1): 219–27

Wallace R.B. & Herzog A.R. (1995): Overview of the Health Measures in Health and Retirement Study. *Journal of Human Resources,* Supplement 30(5), S84-S107.

WHO Commission on Social Determinants of Health (2008): Closing the Gap in a Generation. Health equity through action on the social determinants of health. WHO, Geneva.

Yiengprugsawan ,V.,L.L.Lim, G.A Carmichael, A.Sidorenko et al., (2007): Measuring and Decomposing Inequity in Self-reported Morbidity and Self-assessed Health in Thailand. *International Journal For Equity in Health* 6: 23.

19

Real-Time Bio-Surveillance Program: Field Experiences from Tamil Nadu

M. Ganesan, Suma Prashant, N. Janakiraman, Nuwan Waidyanatha

Introduction

In India, there were outbreaks of major diseases in the past. One of the major outbreaks, which occurred in 1996, was dengue hemorrhagic fever/dengue shock syndrome (Dar et al., 1999). Also in the month of November 2009, there was a fever like disease outbreak: chikungunya, recorded in the southern part of rural Tamil Nadu, India (The Hindu, 2010). This went unnoticed, due to the lag in reporting by paper-based system. Some times, number of diseases is being undetected due to lack of rapid communication system for spatial and temporal analysis to detect their occurrence well in advance. The Directorate of National Vector Borne Disease Control Programme in India has regularly been publishing the status on State-wise disease outbreak such as dengue fever and chikungunya on their website. But, it was not on real time basis, as the data are being collected through paper-based system (DNVBDCP, 2009).

Similarly, health workers in India working in Primary Health Centre (PHC) and Health Sub Centres (HSC) carry to the field 20 registers weighing almost ten kg to aid in documentation of health information. The village health nurses (VHN) along with sector health nurses (SHN) meet on a weekly basis to assess their work and report the consolidated weekly health record statistics gathered from the field at the PHC level and send it to the Deputy Director of Health Services (DDHS) at the district level. They in turn will prepare a location and week wise disease monthly count details and share it to the Directorate of Public Health and Preventive Medicine at State level (DPHPM) (NIC, 2010). It takes one month for DDHS to communicate the disease count details to the directorate located at state level. Hence, it is very clear that the present health information reporting system is entirely paper-based and does not permit to get real time information. This is really a time consuming process and is not effective in detecting the disease outbreak well in advance. Real Time Bio-surveillance Program (RTBP) provides the ability to detect and monitor a wide variety of health events, involving multiple kinds of disease, including communicable and non-communicable, as well as reportable and non-reportable ones, following the general recommendation for disease surveillance systems (WHO, 2004). Implementation of RTBP essentially means to make available right information in the correct form to right place, at right time.

According to Telecom Regulatory Authority of India, the number of mobile phone users increased to 525.15 million, which is an alarming growth rate in India as compared to previous years (TRAI, 2009). It is because of available inexpensive technology and instruments. Therefore the project was designed in appropriate manner with the goal of collecting patient information real-time through mobile phone that would help the health officials to identify the cases affected with particular serious disease before it spreads to other people or regions.

This pilot project was jointly formulated by LIRNEasia, Sri Lanka and Indian Institute of Technology Madras's Rural

Technology and Business Incubator (IITM's RTBI), India with the financial support from International Development Research Centre (IDRC), Canada. Thiruppathur block of Sivaganga district located in southern rural area of Tamil Nadu has been chosen and pilot testing is done since July 2008. Based on the experiences gained so far from this pilot project, this paper has been designed to emphasize lessons learnt in terms of benefits and drawbacks, so as to take the improved technology to other regions and efficient scaling-up.

Methodology

This paper specifically highlights the experiences of 25 health workers from selected PHCs in a district of Tamil Nadu. DDHS selected Thiruppathur block of Sivaganga district in Tamil Nadu, India for pilot testing of the project. Sivaganga district is one of the most economically backward districts located in southern part of rural Tamil Nadu, which has 47 PHCs and 275 HSCs. Rural health care systems in this district is decentralized and the smallest component is HSC and this covers the population of 3000-5000. The HSC is staffed by one VHN covering from 10 to 15 km^2 and the PHC covers a population level of 20,000 and staffed by mainly paramedical health staff as well as medical doctors. The project area comprised of four PHCs (Nerkuppai, Thirukostiyur, Keelasevalpatty and Sevanipatty) and 25 HSCs covering a range of distance from 10 to 25 km with a rural population of about 68092. Twenty-four health workers spreading over 24 HSCs were selected and the remaining one VHN was not included, as she did not attend the technology-training workshop. One SHN was also inducted, as she was very much interested in mobile phone data entry.

In the initial stage of the pilot project, after getting the consent letter from the Health Secretary, Department of Health and Family Welfare, Tamil Nadu, a project orientation programme for 25 health workers working in the jurisdiction of Thiruppathur block was conducted to create awareness about pilot project's goals and objectives. One mini survey was carried out among these 25 health workers, who are willing to participate in this pilot project, to understand their background and characteristics followed by a two-day technology-training workshop organized in May 2009. In this workshop they were trained in mobile phone data entry by adopting standard operating procedures of m-HealthSurvey application which is developed by IITM's RTBI for RTBP involves three basic steps: (1) install and configure the application; (2) submission of data; (3) transmitting the patient data using General Packet Radio Service (GPRS), which is a wireless data service deployed as a standard feature in a many mobile phones. The GPRS transmits patient data over the mobile operator's network to an Internet gateway, further to which it goes to a central database for storage and analysis

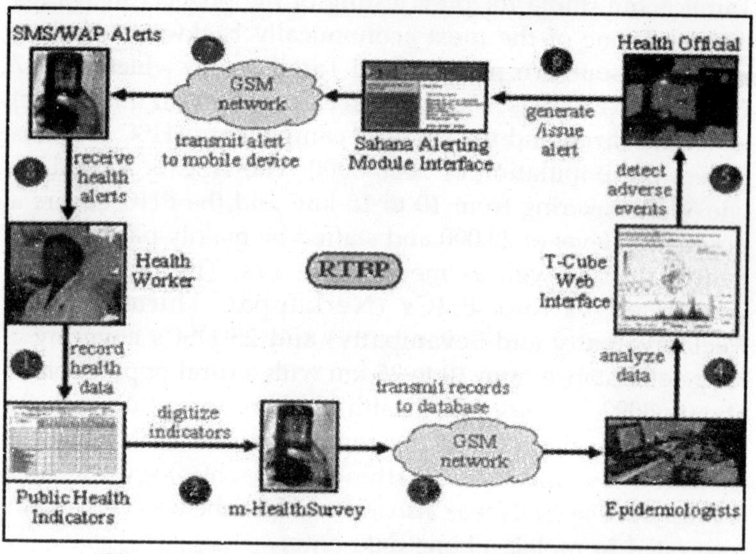

Figure 1: Data Collection Method and Information Flow

(Nuwan *et al.*, 2009). Submission of data is done on the mobile phone using an installed java-based application (Kannan and Sheebha, 2009).

The Fig. 1 depicts the data collection method and information flow. The health workers participating in RTBP project were given free mobile phones with GPRS connectivity from the project. From June 2009, they started entering health data (patients' location, age, gender and disease/syndrome) and entered data were stored on back end database. A RTBP staff was stationed in the field to monitor them and to give timely trouble-shooting support. At regular intervals, their feedbacks were collected, deliberated and most appropriate ones incorporated in m-HealthSurvey application.

Findings

Demographic Characteristics of Health Workers

Table 1 summarizes the health workers' demographic characteristics. All the health workers were female with higher number of health workers belong to the age group between 41 and 50. Most of the health workers (68 %) had studied up to the 10th standard and only 28 per cent had studied up to the 12th standard. They all had attended various short terms training courses on reproductive child health, HIV/AIDS etc from the reputed organization called Gandhigram Rural Institute of Health and Family Welfare, Tamil Nadu. A

Table 1
Distribution of Demographic Characteristics of Healthcare Workers

Demographic Characteristics	*n = 25n (%)*
Age Group (years)	
30 to 40	7(28)
41 to 50	14(56)
51 to 60	4(16)
Educational Qualifications	
10th Std	17(68)
12th Std	7(28)
Graduation	1(4)
Years of Service	
0 to 5	4(16)
6 to 10	3(12)
11 to 15	3(12)
16 to 25	15(60)
Total	25 (100)

majority (60%) had been working as health workers for the last 16 to 25 years in their respective centers and was well integrated to their village community.

Experiences with the Health Workers during the Technology-training Workshop

During this workshop, it was observed that most of the health workers had ever used Short Messaging Services (SMS) and some of them were totally illiterate in handling mobile phone even for voice interaction. In the workshop, most of the health workers shared with us that they would seek help from their children or young relative or neighbours when they use mobile phone for voice. This technology-training workshop was their first experiences using mobile keypad for entering text. At the end of two-day workshop, all the health workers had become aquatinted and showed interest in learning to enter data for project purpose and eventually were able to collect the health data independently. During the workshop, it was noted that some of the health workers learnt very quickly and started helping others. They also gave a lot of suggestions to improve the m-HealthSurvey application and report generation page on the backend database. There was initially some resistance to getting involved and complying with the proposed technology intervention. However, we also observed in this workshop that all the health workers who attended the training were familiar with the project objectives and other details, as we had already conducted an initial awareness meeting with them.

Experiences with Health Workers during Submission of Health Data

As soon as the technology-training workshop was over, the health workers were requested to submit health data up to 30th May 2009 through their mobile phone, this was to acclimatize them to the usage of application. The official launch of data collection began from June 1, 2009. The health workers were continuously monitored and given trouble-shooting support by the staff stationed in the field. The data started coming in from day one to our backend database and it was found that there were erroneous spelling mistakes mainly on disease/syndromatic information. The project team initiated analysis on the data by week-wise and disease-wise to understand the patient inflow status with respect to their health sub centers. To know the mobile phone expertise level of health workers after four months from the technology-training workshop, one small mock exercise was done. The study revealed that the time taken to submit health data per patient by a health worker through mobile phone was two minutes for all the health workers affiliated to four PHCs' except Nerkuppai PHC. However, the health workers working under the jurisdiction of Nerkuppai PHC were unable to enter data on their mobile phone and the training session was not taken seriously. It was also found that they had not been actively involved in mobile phone data entry since the launch when compared to other health-workers from the remaining PHCs. The possible reason could be that those health-workers presumably had a perceived fear in entering data which will further be seen and reported to their higher officials and might result in unnecessary administrative problems to them in future. This claim was later checked with DDHS office and the DDHS denied and stated this excuse framed by the concerned health-workers.

After observing this fact, each health workers of this group was met individually and explained the purpose and objective of the project and assurance was given to them that this was only for testing purpose and this pilot testing would never affect their official activity. Healthworkers were convinced and assured of regular data entry. The field staff was advised to make regular periodical field visits to the respective HSCs attached to Nerkuppai PHC and build good rapport and continuous motivation.

Experiences with Paramedical Staff and Medical Officers (MO) at PHC Level

During one of the visits to PHCs, it was observed that there were more patients' inflow in the PHC when compared to

HSC and maintenance of registry information was an arduous task. Hence it was thought upon to collect those data also through a web based data entry (Internet method) as they had computer with Internet connectivity. But considering the constraints faced at PHC in respect of human resource availability for doing this activity and also frequent failure of internet connectivity, the web based data entry task was dropped and switched over to mobile phone data entry at PHC level. The DDHS requested to appoint field assistants to enter data through mobile phone at the respective PHC level. The field assistants recruited by the project reported to PHC on daily basis from October 2009 and the patients' information was taken from the following registers and the same was entered over RTBP mobile phone application. This was one of the important steps that we had adopted during the pilot phase.

- Out Patient Diagnosis (OPD) register contains OPD Number, Date & Time of visit, Village name, Name of the Patient, Age and Sex. The person who is assistant for staff health nurse before the patient meets with MO for check-up usually enters this information.
- Nominal Register contains Diagnosis (Disease/ Syndrome), Symptoms, Sign and prescription details. This information is actually collected in this register while the patients are meeting with MO.

Experiences with Staff at DDHS

In the beginning stage of the project, it was found that there was lack of rapport building among RTBP Project staff with DDHS officials. In view of this, it was suggested that the staff who are working in the field on behalf of IITM's RTBI to meet DDHS officials at Sivaganga fortnightly in order to have constant rapport building, as for desired results to be achieved we need utmost cooperation from the DDHS office. It was mentioned in one of the meetings with DDHS, the Health Inspector from the respective PHC while submitting the cumulative records on a weekly basis to DDHS uses a standard format and DDHS will further consolidate all the information collected from each PHC/HSC and submit it to Directorate of Public Health and Preventive Medicine (DPHPM) on a monthly basis. The DDHS suggested that in order to show the advantage of RTBP, a cost benefit analysis can be worked out (present paper based reporting cost vs. RTBP cost) and the cost could be associated with reporting, analysis and notification system to health workers and health officials.

m-HealthSurvey Certification Exercise

In the month of October 2009, an m-HealthSurvey certification exercise was conducted with the active participation of 23 health workers (two health workers did not take part due to prior commitments) to assess and certify them in operating the m-HealthSurvey mobile phone software used for digitizing and submitting patient records. Prior to the start of this exercise, a four-page document titled "Standard Operating Procedures" in Tamil version through our field staff circulated to the same to all the health workers. A well-structured questionnaire consisting of the following, i) installation and configuration of m-HealthSurvey; ii) data entry submission and iii) standard operating procedures were introduced.

The install and configure m-HealthSurvey exercise was to judge their ability to install and configure the m-HealthSurvey application on their own. In the data entry submission exercise, they were asked to enter only the mandatory fields: case date/time, location (village name), symptoms, gender and age group. In some cases they were requested to submit the disease and their signs as well as determine using "unknown" or "other" options for the disease. The exercise was timed and evaluation of their performance was based on how much they could accomplish within the stipulated time frame. Total time in minutes from starting time to end time for Part I and II exercises was computed. The number of records entered by them in the part II exercise was stored in the back end database. In the part III, three general questions related to standard operating procedures were asked to choose the correct answers for each question. After completing the three exercises, each part was given points/marks as per marking scheme and finally the health workers were evaluated towards the certification. It was decided that if a health worker scored above 70 points, she is a certified as m-HealthSurvey user and if a health worker scores above 95 points, then she is awarded with potential m-HealthSurvey certificate.

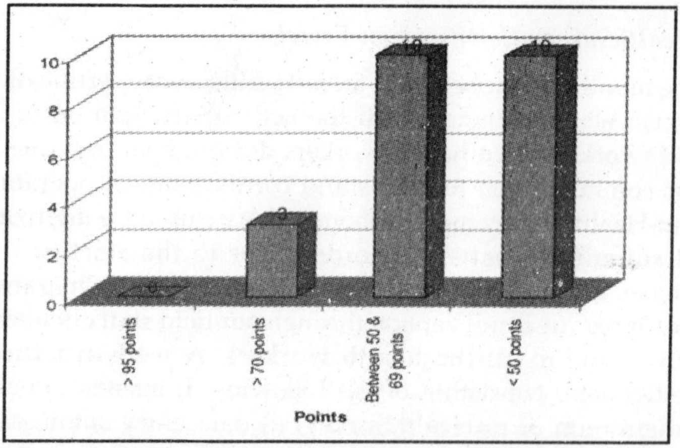

Figure 2: Points Scored by Health Workers in the Certification Exercise

The certification exercise (Fig. 2) revealed that only three of the 23 health workers who participated in this exercise scored above 70 points, while the remaining 20 were below the expected level. It was also observed that standard operating procedures for data entry were not fully understood by some of the health workers. The results of this excerise was very much helpful to design refresher training schedule for the health workers. It was decided collectively that individual performance of the low scoring candidates should be provided targeted attention in order to improve their skill and knowledge of using mobile phone for data submission. The reason for poor performance might be due to their middle age factor and also majority of them did not use the mobile phone for any other purpose prior to this RTBP pilot project's technology training workshop. The results from this exercise stimulated the project staff to further motivate and train the health workers to become a familiar and certified m-HealthSurvey user in future.

RTBP Mobile Phone Health Data Analysis

Number of Records: The patients' health data collected through m-HealthSurvey application using mobile phone starting from June 2009 to December 2009 its weekly analysis is graphically presented. The analysis of data on number of patients' (Fig. 3) shows that the total number of records was gradually increasing at an average of 14 per cent over weeks and the total number of records recorded was 36428 as on the last day of December 2009. In the initial weeks (1 to 11), the number of records entered by them was fewer and in the 12th and 13th week since launch it was observed a drastical reduction when compared to previous weeks and this was attributed due to lack of inflow of patients. The reason for poor number of records could also be due to lack of monitoring of the health workers during this period. On observing this trend at our back end database, each health worker was given close monitoring and trouble shooting support. The data collection was also initiated at the PHCs where number of patients'

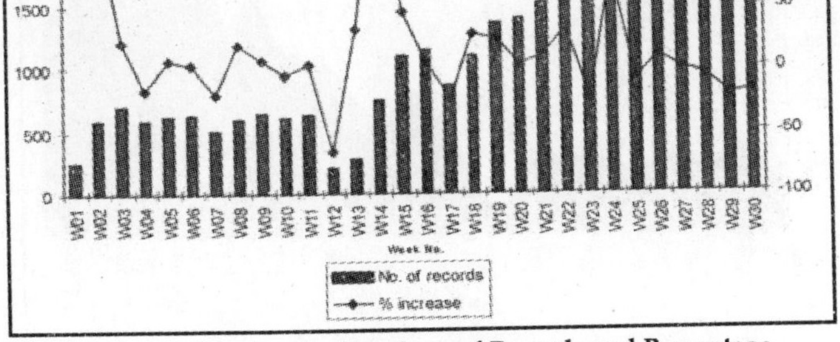

Figure 3: Week wise Numbers of Records and Percentage Increase During Jun '09 to Dec '09

inflow was higher when compared to HSC. In view of this, the number of records did increase tremendously from 14th week onwards. The higher number of records over the weeks might also be due to acquiring knowledge and skill of using mobile phone. The data was analyzed to understand the gender bias among the patient records. It was observed that the highest numbers of patient were female which might be due to the gender factor of the VHN who influenced female patients to visit health care centers.

Real Time (RT) vs Off Time (OT) Data Submission: When a patient is seen on a given day and if his/her data is submitted before the following morning, then that data is treated as Real-Time (RT) whereas if the data is submitted further to that then it is treated as Off Time (OT) data. Based on this classification, the week wise data was analyzed and it is presented in terms of real time vs off time records in the Fig. 4. There was an undulate increase of real time data submission as compared to off time data at the rate of 300 plus per week. Though the off time data submission was less as compared to real time data, there was a pattern of unsteady increase and decrease. The reason for this is that many of them enter data after working hours and even in the weekend when they have time. As a result highest records was found to be entered in the real time,

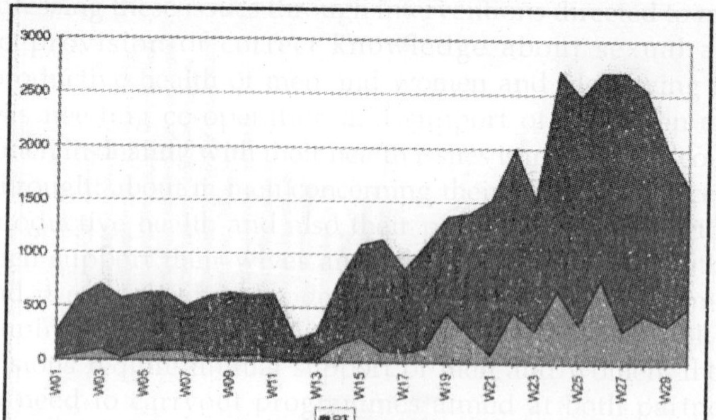

Figure 4: Week wise Real Time (RT) vs Off Time (OT) Records

in the data analysis. This has to be taken into consideration while reviving the m-HealthSurvey in the further study.

Recommendations

Based on the experiences gained from the pilot project, the following recommendations are made.

- The health workers need to be continually trained and monitored in order to enable them to achieve the desired results.
- To further study of ways to simplify data entry on m-HealthSurvey
- DDHS already has a system of health data management and a culture of storing health information in its management systems. It is felt that this system should be compared with RTBP tool in terms of workload and time availability.
- Since the PHC has a dearth of human resource for mobile phone data entry, project needs to evaluate the feasibility of appointing a separate project staff to enter data when the project further expands to other regions.

Conclusions

RTBP researchers conclude the health workers have acquired the ability to enter data through m-HealthSurvey application using mobile phone. However, there are some hurdles that need to be overcome like error rates, which have to be reduced, and simplification of the process of the data entry submission is required to improve real time records counts.

References

Dar, L., S. Broor, S. Sengupta, I. Xess, and P. Seth (1999): "The First Major Outbreak of Dengue Hemorrhagic Fever in Delhi, India", *Emerging Infectious Disease*, 5, 4: 589–580.

Directorate of National Vector Borne Disease Control Programme (DNVBDCP), (2009): http://nvbdcp.gov.in.

Kannan, T. and R. Sheebha (2009): *Software Requirements Specifications for the Real-Time Biosurveillance Program (RTBP) Information Communication Technology System*. Chennai: IITM's Rural Technology and Business Incubator. http://lirneasia.net/wp-content/uploads/2009/06/srs_mobile_ application_rtbp_v20.pdf.

National Informatics Centre (NIC), Directorate of Public Health and Preventive Medicine (2010): http://intra.tn.nic.in/dph/pcm/

Nuwan Waidyanatha, M. Ganesan, Pubudini Weerakoon, Gordon Gow, Maheshkumar Sabhnani and Artur Dubrawski. (2009): Real Time Biosurveillance Pilot in India and Sri Lanka: http://lirneasia.net/wp-content/uploads/2009/11/Waidyanatha_eAsia2009_web_paper.pdf

Telecom Regulatory Authority of India (TRAI) (2009): http://www.trai.gov.in

The Hindu (2010): http://www.hindu.com/2009/11/29/stories/2009112959790400.htm

World Health Organization (WHO) (2004): *Comprehensive Assessment of National Surveillance System in Sri Lanka, Joint Assessment Report*. New Delhi: World Health Organization.http://www.searo.who.int/LinkFiles/Publication_Comprehensive_assessment__NSS_Srl.pdf

20

Human Development Index: Does Alternative Weights and Scaling Would Be More Apt?

Ranjeeta

Introduction

The Human Development Index (HDI) is a measure of average achievement in basic human capabilities. Based on three components, viz. indicators of longevity, educational attainment and a decent standard of living, it is not exclusively focused on economic opulence (as the GNP is), and it certainly has served to broaden the empirical attention in assessing the process of development. Since the first publication of the yearly Human Development Reports in 1990 by the United Nations Development Programme (UNDP, 1990–2001), the human development index (HDI) provided by the UNDP has been widely used in measuring the relative human development in all nations. Countries are ranked according to the HDI frequently in the literature and general public. It is also widely used as a decision-making instrument for public policy decisions.

The human development index is a composite number that values between 0 and 1. The greater value of the HDI indicates a relatively better human development. The HDI is computed as the average of the measurement in three dimensions: i) longevity index based on life expectancy, ii) educational attainment index based on the percentage of the literacy of the adult population and the children's school enrolment and iii) resource index based on the per capita GDP in the dollars of purchasing power parity ($PPP) (UNDP, 1990–2001).

From the outset of its introduction in 1990, the HDI caught the attention of academics, researchers, policy makers, and development activists. It was praised for its broader perspective of human well-being, yet it was seriously scrutinized in terms of its analytical framework, methodology, data etc. There have been several academic critiques of the index, reviewing its internal consistency, robustness, predictive power. Therefore since the inception of HDI, its merits and weaknesses have been a continuous debating topic in the Development literature (Srinavasan 1994). As a result of this there are many modifications and extensions proposed for the human development index.

Objective

The first objective of this paper is to look at the issue of weightage in HDI and how the ranking of the states changes when the method of assigning weights changes. Since the weightage issue has be one of the most frequent and important criticism of the Human Development Index by UNDP method, therefore in this paper attempts have been made to calculate the HDI using the same indicator but different methods of assigning weights. After that the ranking of all the states by different methods has been compared. The second objective of this paper is to look at the issue of scaling in HDI and how the ranking of the states changes when the method of scaling the indicators is changed. There is a prolonged debate on the method of scaling in constructing the composite index. Therefore in this paper it has been looked into that how the ranks of the states changes when two different method of scaling is applied and if is there any comparability between these two methods.

Data Source

For this study the data for the years 2006-2007 from various sources have been used. The data on per capita net state domestic product has been taken from Central Statistical Organisation (CSO). Life expectancy at birth has been taken from the Office of the Registrar General, India. Gross enrolment ratio has been taken from the selected educational statistic. Literacy rate has been taken from the NFHS 3.

Literature Review

According to the UNDP, the Human Development Index (HDI) is a summary measure of human development based on three dimensions: life expectancy at birth; knowledge; and standard of living. Life expectancy at birth measures the relative achievement of each country in prolonging life. The knowledge component is a combination of two indices: adult literacy rate and combined (primary, secondary and tertiary education) gross enrolment ratio. The index for literacy and the index for enrolment are combined with adult literacy receiving a two-thirds weight and enrolment a one-third weight. The standard of living is calculated using the logarithm of adjusted GDP per capita (PPP US$).

Performance in each dimension is expressed as a value between 0 and 1 by applying the following formula:

$$\text{Dimension Index} = \frac{\text{actual value} - \text{min imum value}}{\text{max imum value} - \text{min imum value}}$$

The HDI is then calculated as a simple average of the dimension indices. The maximum and minimum values for each of the dimensions have been established by the UNDP as follows: 85 years and 25 years for life expectancy at birth, 100% and 0% for the adult literacy rate and the combined gross enrolment ratio, and US$40,000 and US$100 for per capita income (UNDP. 2002).

The HDI applies a very simple weighting scheme: equal weights for each component. This is obviously convenient but not justified. The variables are given equal weights not because of simplicity, but because of the philosophical reasoning, that all the dimensions included in the HDI are equally important and desirable in their own right for building human capabilities. The ideal approach would presumably involve using as weights the impact of each component on the ultimate objective. For the HDI, this means that each of the components should receive weights according to its contribution to human development (Chowdhury 2005). Some people argue that the method of assigning weights on the basis of a correlation matrix, such as Principal Component Analysis, has not been considered appropriate here since the pattern of interdependencies is likely to change as the technology takes firm root in the region. As one has no other empirical basis to work out the relative importance of indicators, it has been decided to assign the equal weights to all the indicators (Kundu 2004).

The other important problem to be sorted out is the elimination of the bias of scale that characterises each indicator. Scaling and the normalized value are required for two reasons. First, the variables included in the HDI have different units. Thus, life expectancy is in years, adult literacy rate is in percentages and the GDP per capita is in PPP$. By normalization, one gets rid of units and derives pure numbers. Such transformation is needed for additive purposes while constructing a composite index. Second, scaling enables one to carry on comparisons as to how in each dimension countries have fared relatively and what are the unfinished paths. In computing HDI, UNDP adopts the Range Equalisation (RE) method wherein each indicator is divided by the range (after subtraction of the lowest value) so that scale-free values vary between 0 and 1. In recent years UNDP has changed its methodology slightly as it uses a fixed range computed on the basis of predetermined 'goalposts' reflecting the feasible upper and lower limits to the values. This enables one to make temporal comparisons, not only of the rank scores of countries but also of their HDIs. The disadvantage in this method is that the three constituent indices pertaining to life expectancy, education and GDP have lost the feature of having a fixed range of unity. The highest value in each index falls short of unity as the value for the top ranking country is below the goalpost. The same explanation holds for the minimum value being higher than zero. In view of the familiarity and popularity of this method among practitioners and policy makers, it has been the first choice for constructing composite indices in the present analysis.

HDI and Weights

The HDI assigns equal weights to all its three indicators. The simple addition of the components of HDI has little justification. Since the three components of HDI are spread around different means with different variances, the simple averaging of these components for the purpose of building a composite index is questionable. In addition the means and variances of different components would vary with respect to the selected extreme values (maximum and minimum) for each indicator. Also a priori determination of weights for various components implies the existence of a universally acceptable human welfare/development function, which is not the case. As there is no firm agreement on the definition of human development and therefore not directly observable, we are essentially dealing with a hypothetical construct (Noorbaksh, 1998).

In concomitant with the methodology of HDI in the latest Human Development Report, the indices of life expectancy at birth (LEB), adult literacy rate (ALR) and combined gross enrolment (CGE) in education index (EDU) and income (GDPPC) can be expressed as follows:

$$\text{LEB index} = (\text{LEB} - 25)/(85-25) = (\text{LEB}/60) - 0.416666$$
$$= 0.01667 * \text{LEB} - 0.41666 \quad (1)$$
$$\text{ALR index} = (\text{ALR} - 0)/(100 - 0) = \text{ALR}/100$$
$$\text{CGE index} = (\text{CGE} - 0)/(100 - 0) = \text{CGE}/100$$
$$\text{EDU index} = 2/3 * (\text{ALR}/100) + 1/3 * (\text{CGE}/100)$$
$$= 2/300 * \text{ALR} + 1/300 * \text{CGE}$$
$$= 0.00667 * \text{ALR} + 0.00333 * \text{CGE} \quad (2)$$
$$\text{GDPPC index} = (\ln \text{GDPPC} - \ln 100)/(\ln 40000 - \ln 100)$$

$$= (\ln GDPPC - 4.60517)/\ (10.59663 - 4.60517)$$
$$= 0.16690 \ln GDPPC - 0.76802 \qquad (3)$$

Now HDI = 1/3*(LEB index + EDU index + GDPPC index) (4)

Substituting equation (1), (2) and (3) in (4), the HDI can be expressed as a linear combination of its constituent indicators in the following manner:

$$HDI = 0.00556\ LEB + 0.00222\ ALR + 0.00111\ CGE + 0.05563 \ln GDPPC - 0.39489$$

This algebraic expansion of the UNDP method of HDI construction produces results quite contradictory to their claims of all dimensions included in the HDI being "equally important and desirable in their own right for building human capabilities."

However, the equation above implies that the UNDP method of scaling variables results in implicit weights due to which their "effort" towards equal treatment of variables during aggregation does not quite materialize in practice. Also, UNDP does not provide any justification for the resultant higher weight to the income variable or lower weights to the education variables.

In this paper Principal Component Analysis (PCA) and Modified Principal Component Analysis (MPCA) have been used to objectively determine the weights to the components in HDI. Since the standardization of the variables in the PCA, in order to eliminate the bias of scale, involves a considerable loss of information as it equalizes mean and variance of all the indicators. The Modified Principal Component Analysis (MPCA) aims to minimize this loss of information. The PCA method enables one to determine a vector known as the first principal component/factor, linearly dependent on the constituent variables, having the maximum sum of squared correlations with the variables. The eigen vector corresponds to the maximum eigen value of the correlation matrix gives the required factor loadings (weights). The composite index for a particular geographical unit may be obtained by linearly combining the standardized variable values, the weights being the corresponding elements of the eigen vector.

The first principal component has the property of having the largest sum of squared correlations with the original data matrix. The successive components are generally ignored. This method therefore gives higher weights to indicators having higher correlations with other selected indicators. However development variables exhibit substantial disparity in space. The PCA approach does not consider this disparity while aggregating the variables. In PCA the standardization of the variables in order to eliminate the bias of scale, involves a considerable loss of information as it equalizes mean and variance of all the indicators.

The Modified Principal Component Analysis (MPCA) aims to minimize this loss of information. Instead of standardization, scaling is done by dividing each indicator value (observation) by the respective means. By this method, the ratios of the observations before and after scaling are the same. The MPCA approach therefore rejects the correlation matrix as the basis for working out factor loading or weights. The MPCA has got certain advantages over the traditional PCA.

- Scaling of variables by division by mean ensures the protection of the disparity factor in each indicator.
- MPCA ensures non-negativity of weights and hence the final index values are always positive.

So, using Principal Component Analysis and Modified Principal Component Analysis composite indices of Human Development has been computed for major 19 Indian states. The indicators used in this analysis are exactly the same which are used by UNDP for computing HDI. Since in this analysis the number of states or we can say the number of observation are very less therefore it is useless to construct the frequency distribution of the rank change. From Table: 1 it can be seen that the maximum shift in rank is by two position by either method as compared with the UNDP's method.

HDI and Scaling

Range Equalisation Method

Another most debatable problem of HDI is the scaling technique of scaling the indicator. UNDP uses range

Table 1
Composite Indices of Human Development (2006-07)

	HDI	*Rank*	*HDIPCA*	*Rank*	*HDIMPCA*	*Rank*	*HDIDM*	*rank*
Andhra Pradesh	0.753396	11	-0.20684	11	1.947108	11	0.995203	11
Assam	0.73799	12	-0.68266	12	1.857061	12	0.900896	12
Bihar	0.631907	19	-2.47723	19	1.386744	19	0.685846	19
Chhattisgarh	0.714574	16	-1.58365	15	1.808489	16	0.869332	15
Gujarat	0.798247	6	0.708825	7	2.192465	6	1.108068	7
Haryana	0.794911	7	1.468877	5	2.268683	5	1.212413	2
Himachal Pradesh	0.845794	2	1.884224	2	2.362807	3	1.192353	4
Jharkhand	0.695356	17	-1.6143	16	1.656812	17	0.821351	17
Karnataka	0.785375	8	0.380474	8	2.067599	9	1.040961	8
Kerala	0.889351	1	3.345447	1	2.40671	1	1.238334	1
Madhya Pradesh	0.724086	15	-1.85335	18	1.846778	13	0.85057	16
Maharashtra	0.839953	3	1.760531	3	2.365903	2	1.201002	3
Orissa	0.726056	14	-1.12261	13	1.812887	15	0.875819	14
Punjab	0.80616	5	1.701176	4	2.176328	7	1.158614	5
Rajasthan	0.727859	13	-1.35774	14	1.824945	14	0.886438	13
Tamil Nadu	0.828735	4	1.184706	6	2.290475	4	1.141569	6
Uttar Pradesh	0.689317	18	-1.80101	17	1.639798	18	0.792866	18
Uttarakhand	0.777694	9	-0.02551	10	2.0861	8	1.019752	9
West Bengal	0.774746	10	0.290629	9	1.997454	10	1.008611	10

Source: Central Statistical Organisation (CSO). Office of the Registrar General, India. selected educational statistics. And National Family Health Survey 3.

equalisation (RE) method to calculate HDI. Following the RE method, the component index for a category has been obtained by first making each indicator scale free by subtracting its minimum value from each observation and then dividing it by its range. The average of these values across the indicators (within the category) for each state then becomes the value of its component index. If a state has maximum values for all the indicators in a category, it will score an index value of 1. Similarly, a state will obtain a component score of zero only when it has the minimum value for all the indicators.

Division by Mean Method

In applying the DM method, the indicators in each category have been divided by their respective means. The values thus obtained have been added for each state to obtain the component index for the category. In the Table: 1, HDI by UNDP rank equalisation method and division by mean method both have been calculated and the states have been ranked accordingly. Attempts have been made to analyse the difference in ranking due to change in scaling method. The maximum shift in rank due to change in method of scaling as compared to the range equalisation method of UNDP is by 5 positions. Haryana accounts for this shift, its position by UNDP (RE) is 7th where as in HDIDM its position is 2nd.

Comparison of Results

Although the three methods discussed above use different procedures for scaling of indicators, it would be interesting to look into the explicit weights that each method assigns to the indicators. Table: 2 compares the explicit weights assigned to the indicators by different methods. It shows clearly that while the UNDP method and Principal Component Analysis method gives least importance to the education variables, the MPCA gives the second highest importance to the same during composition. The highest weight in MPCA goes to life expectancy.

Table 2
Comparing Weights Using Alternative Methodology

	HDI	*HDIPCA*	*HDIMPCA*
Adult Literacy Rate	0.222	0.56628642	0.49805408
Gross Enrolment Ratio	0.111	0.05182501	0.49417111
Life expectancy at Birth	0.333	0.5934145	0.51349125
Per Capita NSDP	0.333	0.56964295	0.49402812

In this part of the paper the rank correlation coefficients (Kendall's) between HDI values obtained by the different methods have also been calculated. From Table 3 it can be seen that the correlation is minimum (0.848) in HDIPCA and HDIMPCA followed by HDIMPCA and HDIDM (0.89) followed by HDIPCA and HDI (RE) (0.9). The correlation of HDIMPCA is high with HDI (RE). All the composite indices show high correlation but the HDI (RE) and HDIMPCA shows the highest correlation among all the other indices.

Table 3
Kendall's Correlation between HDI(RE), HDIDM, HDIPCA, and HDIMPCA

	HDI(RE)	*HDIDM*	*HDIPCA*	*HDIMPCA*
HDI(RE)	1			
HDIDM	0.9064	1		
HDIPCA	0.9064	0.9064	1	
HDIMPCA	0.9181	0.8947	0.848	1

Table 4
Percent Variation of Principal Component

Methods	*Highest Eigen Value*	*% of Variation Explained*
Principal Components Analysis	2.451097	61.2
Modified Principal Component Analysis	4.074782	97.7

Changes in States Ranks

Table: 5 in appendix show the changes in rank on account of the application of the MPCA, division by mean and PCA vis-à-vis the UNDP method of 19 states for the year 2006-07. By the method of PCA about 37% states showed an improvement in ranks against only 21% in case of MPCA. In both the methods the percentage of states showing fall in ranks is about 26%. There is very nominal variation in the rank of states by the method of division by mean. One thing is notable from this analysis that the states which show higher rank changes are common in all the method, mainly in MPCA and DM. This implies that the direction of change in relative position arises from the methodology of scaling the indicators which is the same in case of HDIDM as well as HDIMPCA. The difference in the magnitude of change however can be attributed to the different weights assigned to each indicator by the two methods.

Table 5
Changes in States Ranks

	HDIMPCA	*HDIPCA*	*HDIDM*
Fall in Rank	5	5	4
Unchanged	10	7	13
Rise in rank	4	7	2

Axiomatic Approach to Different Methods of HDI

The demands for good social indicators are well-known: indicators should be reliable, consistent, sensitive to responses, measurable, user friendly, cost-effective, policy-relevant and valid, among other requirements. The difficulty in building indicators with these properties and in aggregating and using them should not be underestimated. But all these desirable qualities cannot be simultaneously satisfied.

The composite indices of Human Development are not just numbers but they are the indicator of the achievement in three basic dimension of well being of regions. Therefore an ideal composite index of measuring Human Development should follow some axioms. It is also suggested that they should be more subjective. There are basically three axioms which are suggested to be followed by a composite index.

Non Dictatorship Axiom: According to this axiom no single indicator in a composite index should be dominant enough to solely determine the overall rank of the composite index.

Monotonocity Axiom: According to this axiom other things remaining same if any country has any improvement in any indicator then the country should get a higher rank and the value of composite index should go up.

Independent from Irrelevant Alternatives Axiom: According to this axiom the value of a composite index for a country should not depend on the change in the value of an indicator for another country.

The calculation of HDI using UNDP method without goalpost violates the third axiom. Whereas the calculation of HDI using UNDP method with goalpost violates the non dictatorship axiom, and the rank is solely influenced by the income component. The testing of all the methods for all the axioms is beyond the scope of this paper, but it can be said that any of the alternative methods of calculating Human Development Index does not satisfy all the axioms. So it is very difficult to say that which is the perfect and ideal for calculating Human development Index. It is also said that HDI by UNDP is not very theoretically sound as far as the weights are concern but it gives a very indicative picture which shows the relative achievement of a country in what Amartya Sen calls the 'freedom' and 'choice'. So, it can be said that over all the methods, the one which UNDP is using is not the best but since according to Arrows impossibility theorem, it is impossible to have a best method, given different alternative methods.

Conclusions

To conclude it can be said that the lower weight it assigns to the education variable in UNDP method is unjustified. The high weight assigned to the income component does not conform to the concept of human development, which intends to put people at the centre-stage of development. The MPCA method on the other hand values the longevity dimension most highly followed by the education dimension. Income gets the lowest weightage by this method. Intuitively, this is appealing because per capita income merely provides the 'means' to attain the 'ends' and having command over resources does not always ensure proper access to it. So, the UNDP methodology of constructing the HDI is not at all robust to different weights as is evident from this exercise.

The another thing which can be concluded is in spite of the fact that there are high correlation between MPCA, DM and HDI(RE), the above discussion makes it clear that change in the methodology of composition can and does bring about significant changes in the values of component indices and alters even the ranking of the states. Issues of value judgment, implicit in the methodology cannot, therefore, be dismissed.

HDI by UNDP method is not theoretically very sound as far as the issues of weights and scaling are concern, but since it has been shown that there is no method that can satisfy all the three required axioms therefore can be said axiomatically perfect, so the choice of method should depend the requirement of the research.

References

Allen C. Kelley (1991): The Human Development Index: "Handle with Care" Population and Development Review, 17, No . 2 (June 1991).

Chowdhury Shyamal and Squire Lyn (2005): 'Setting Weights for Aggregate Indices: An Application to the Commitment to Development Index and Human Development Index, Global Development Network.

Kundu Amitabh (2004): ICT and Human Development: Towards Building a Composite Index for Asia, UNDP.

Noorbakhsh Farhad (1998): Human Development Index: Some Technical Issues and Alternative Indices, Journal of International Development.

Sen Amartya and Anand Sudhir (1994): 'Human Development Index: Methodology and Measurement', UNDP Occasional Paper.

Srinavasan, T.N. (1994): 'Human Development: A New Paradigm or Reinvention of the Wheel?,' American Economic Review, Papers and Proceedings 84: 238–243.

UNDP (2002): Human Development Report 2002. New York, Oxford University Press.

21

Communicating Nutrition Through School Science Curricula—A Content Analysis of Textbooks

G.M. Subba Rao, T. Vijayapushapm, Vinod Pavarala

Introduction

Nutrition education at a young age is a key element in promoting sustainable healthy eating behaviours. Schools provide the most effective and efficient way to reach children and their families (Perez-Rodrigo and Javier, 2001). Although school children prefer to learn in the classroom setting through the teacher, choosing to teach nutrition education is not a clear-cut choice for teachers or schools, as nutrition has to compete with other subjects (Lytle, 1994). Nutrition education curriculum programmes are unlikely to work well if they are not part of the 'core' school curriculum (Stuart and Achterberg, 1995). Integrating nutrition education into curricular areas helps to resolve the problem of not having time to teach nutrition (Lytle, 1994). Development of innovative nutrition education component that can be effectively blended along with other health related issues in the science curricula is a continuous and demanding process. Before developing such content, there is a need to evaluate the nutrition component in the existing school science textbooks. Content analysis of curricula and textbooks can thus be the basis for improving school-based nutrition education (Kondracki et.al., 2002).

In the Indian context, there are three different streams of school education – (1) through the schools affiliated to Central Board of Secondary Education (CBSE) (2) schools affiliated to the Council for the Indian School Certificate Examination that gives Indian Certificate of Secondary Education (ICSE) certification on completion of Class X; and (3) schools that follow the syllabi of the respective State School Education Boards. Across the country, 9689 schools are affiliated to CBSE (CBSE, 2008). For the CBSE schools, the syllabus is prescribed by the Board and the schools usually follow the textbooks published by the National Council for Educational Research and Training (NCERT) or by private publishers. There are several thousands of schools affiliated to the respective State Education Boards. These schools follow the syllabi prescribed by the respective Boards. In case of Andhra Pradesh, the textbooks are published by the AP State Council for Education Research and Training (APSCERT).

Krippendorf (1980:21) defines Content Analysis as "a systematic, replicable technique for compressing many words of text into fewer content categories based on explicit rules of coding". He also suggests that it is a technique for making replicable and valid inferences from the text/data to their context (Krippendroff, 1986). It is a technique that is used to develop objective inferences about a subject of interest in any type of communication (Berg, 1998). For the present study, the CBSE and AP State Board textbooks were selected with the following objectives:

Objectives

1. To analyse the biological science content in relation to the over all general science component of the textbooks of all classes from primary to high school (I - X classes).
2. To do quantitative content analysis for finding out the proportion of space allocated for the nutrition component in relation to the other topics in the biology textbooks.

3. To conduct qualitative analysis of the nutrition component for finding out the topics dealt with, importance assigned to them, continuity of the topics from one class to the other.

Materials and Methods

Sample

All science text books from Classes I-X of two streams - NCERT and AP State Board were selected for the study. ICSE textbooks were not considered for the study as they are not printed by the Council (which only prescribes the syllabus) and the schools rely on books from private publishers, but the books used by each school differ greatly from the others.

As regards the NCERT and AP State Board textbooks, most schools in Hyderabad use books published by private publishers for classes I-V, for class above VI, the schools use either NCERT or APSCERT books based on their school affiliations. For primary classes (I to V), books published by Navneet publishers were selected for CBSE syllabus and textbooks by Holy Faith Publishers were selected for AP State Board as they are commonly used many schools.

Content Analyses

The process of content analysis involves coding raw messages according to a classification scheme that allowed for easy identification, indexing and retrieval of content relevant to research questions (Berg, 1998). For the purpose of the study all the content related to physics, chemistry and environment (excluding sanitation, cleanliness and safety of water) were categorized under 'Physical and Environmental Sciences' and content related to life sciences were categorized as 'Biology'. Under biology, the terms 'nutrition', 'food safety', 'health' and 'others' were operationally defined before carrying out the study. The operational definitions in terms of inclusion and exclusion criteria have been listed in Table-1.

In the present study quantitative and qualitative content analysis methods were used. Physical measurement of space

Table 1
Operational Definitions of Categories for Content Analysis

Theme	*Inclusion*	*Exclusion*
Nutrition	All topics that pertain to food, food intake, its functions, nutrients, their role in human health Nutrient deficiencies and diseases or disorders arising there of Food consumption, Unhealthy foods, over nutrition/ obesity and lifestyle diseases	Food borne diseases. All human, plant and animal processes like respiration, digestion, reproduction, excretion etc fall under this category. Topics related to food / water handling, storage, preservation and cooking. Food borne illnesses. Food additives and impact on healthDisease prevention and cure Nutrition, nutrition deficiency disorders and related topics mentioned above
Food Safety Health	Topics related to food / water handling, storage, preservation and cooking. Food borne illnesses. Food additives and impact on health Wellbeing of individual. Disease prevention and cure.	Disease prevention and cure Nutrition, nutrition deficiency disorders and NCDs due to overweight and obesity food borne diseases Food Safety (as mentioned above)
Others	All human, plant and animal processes like respiration, digestion, reproduction, excretion etc fall under this category	Health, Nutrition and food safety

(in terms of pages) allocated, number of illustrations and exercise questions were measured as part of the quantitative analysis (Shepherd and Achterberg, 1992).

Degree and Emphasis for Quantitative Analysis

Chapters: While counting the total number of chapters, only those lessons which were completely dedicated to the subjects of interest (nutrition, food safety or health) were considered. Those chapters with one or two units or sub-units dedicated to the topics were not considered.

Space Allocated (No. of Pages): While counting the number of pages allocated for each subject, irrespective of the theme of the chapter, if the topic dealt with fell into the categories of interest (as per the operational definitions/inclusion and exclusion criteria) and was covered in more than a quarter page, then it was counted under the respective subject area.

Illustrations: All illustrations in the science textbooks were categorized into physical and environmental science according to the chapters in which they were placed. Of the illustrations in the biology segment, those occurring in the lessons categorized as Nutrition, food safety and health and hygiene were counted under the respective themes. Of these, all those pictures which showed fruits, vegetables, grains, pulses, eatables or activity of eating were considered under nutrition whereas the visuals related to hand washing, cleanliness, hygiene, street foods, food vending, food in covered containers etc were considered under food safety.

Qualitative Analysis

This was carried out to understand the latent meanings of the content by analyzing quality of narration, illustrations and other general elements like font, print, etc. The latent meanings were first interpreted by the investigator and were later independently reviewed by a sociologist and an expert committee comprising of nutritionists and communication professionals. Only those interpretations that were commonly agreed by all have been included in the results.

Results

Quantitative content analysis showed that the biology component occupied relatively less space in relation to physical and environmental science in the NCERT textbooks in the higher classes, while at least one chapter in them was dedicated to nutrition from I to VII classes, there is no special chapter on nutrition in the high school science textbooks (from VIII to X classes) (Table-2). Similarly, the number of chapters allocated for biology is relatively less when compared to

Table 2
Distribution of Number of Chapters in NCERT Textbooks

Class	*Total*	*Physical & Environmental Science*	*Biology*	*Nutrition*	*Food Safety*
I	18	7	11	1	0
II	19	9	10	1	0
III	18	5	13	1	0
IV	14	7	7	1	0
V	17	7	10	1	0
VI	16	11	5	2	0
VII	15	9	6	1	0
VIII	14	11	3	0	0
IX	15	11	4	0	0
X	17	12	5	0	0

physical and environmental science in classes VI to X even in the AP State Board textbooks. Special chapters on nutrition appear only in classes IV and V. Although nutrition topics are dealt with in the IX and X classes they appear as sub-units in other chapters related to health (Table-3). As regards food safety, there are hardly any dedicated chapters for the subject in the science textbooks of both NCERT and AP Board.

As regards the space allocation for each of the topics of interest, within the biology component in the school textbooks, nutrition has been provided over 10% of the space in all classes up to VII in the NCERT curriculum. However, it is not the same in the AP State Board syllabus. Food safety got about 1% of all space allocated for biology in primary classes in NCERT (Figure-1). In AP State Board Science syllabus, it was

Table 3
Distribution of Number of Chapters in AP State Board Textbooks

Class	*Total*	*Physical & Environmental Science*	*Biology*	*Nutrition*	*Food Safety*
I	7	3	4	1	0
II	9	4	5	1 unit	0
III	10	6	4	0	0
IV	11	7	4	1	2
V	11	7	4	1	0
VI	11	8	3	0	0
VII	11	9	2	0	0
VIII	14	9	5	0	1 unit
IX	19	13	6	1 unit	1 unit
X	15	11	4	2 units	0

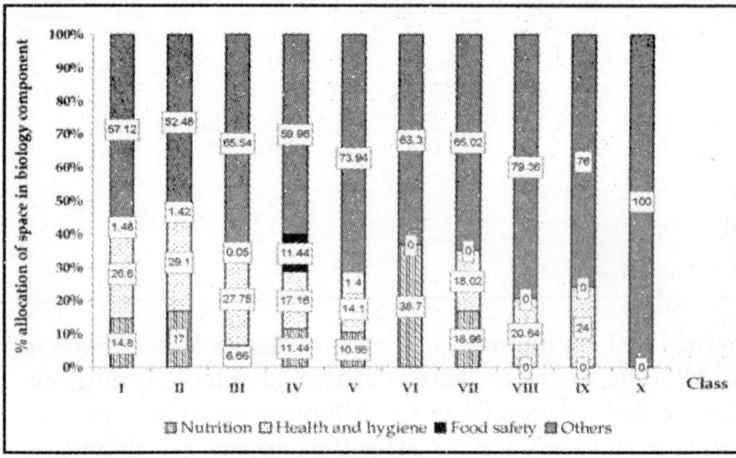

Figure 1: Subject wise Allocation of Space (%) in Biology Component of NCERT Textbooks

observed that although there were no dedicated chapters for nutrition, 10-23% of the space was allocated for nutrition component in the biology content in the primary classes. About 10% of the biology content was allocated for nutrition in Class–X. However, there was almost no allocation of specific space for food safety in AP Textbooks at all, except in V and VII classes where 15% and 5% of space in biology component was allocated respectively (Figure-2).

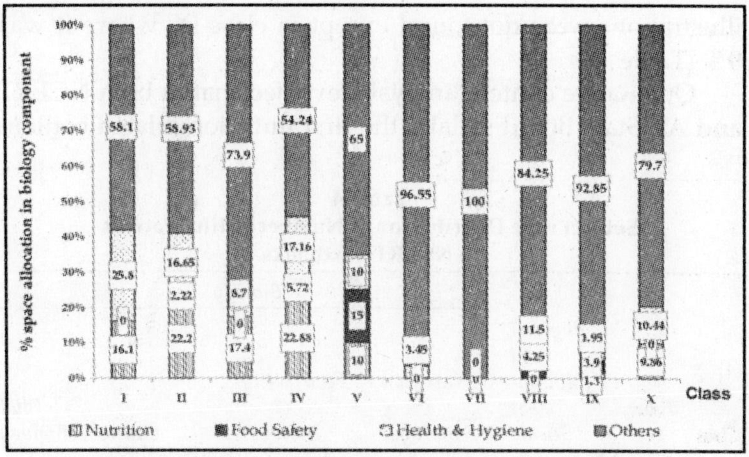

Figure 2: Subject wise Allocation of Space (%) in Biology Component of AP State Board Textbooks

Physical counting of the illustrations revealed that in the primary classes (I-V), the number of illustrations allocated for biology were more than half of all the illustrations in both NCERT as well as AP State Board science textbooks. However, the number of illustrations related to nutrition was more than 25% of all biology illustrations only in the first two classes.

However, the number of illustrations pertaining to biology vis-à-vis nutrition and food safety, decrease in the textbooks of classes of subsequent classes. In the high school text books (VIII-X) there were no illustrations pertaining to nutrition at all, quite obviously because there is no reference to this topic anywhere. Similarly in the AP state textbooks, more than a quarter of all biology illustrations in classes I-IV relate to nutrition while it is almost nil in classes V-X. Food safety related illustrations are almost nil in NCERT textbooks of I through X classes, with the highest of 6% of all biology illustrations only in class IV (Table-4). In the AP State Board textbooks, illustrations related to food safety occupied relatively higher proportion of the biology illustrations. At least one percent of all biology illustrations from classes I–V depicted food safety, with least (1%) in Class-I and highest (15%) in class-V. Thereafter, in higher classes the food safety illustrations were not found except in class-IX, where it was 9% (Table -5).

Qualitative content analysis revealed that in both NCERT and AP State Board syllabi, the first nutrition related content

Table 4
Subject wise Distribution of Number of Illustrations in NCERT Textbooks

Class	Total No.	Physical and Environment Science	Biology: Nutrition (% of Biology)	Food Safety (% of Biology)	Others	Total Biology
I	226	36	52 (27.6)	0 (0)	111 (58.1)	190
II	264	85	46 (25.8)	1 (0.6)	111 (62)	179
III	169	45	6 (4.9)	0 (0)	83 (66.9)	179
IV	155	80	11 (16.2)	4 (5.9)	47 (69.1)	68
V	150	78	3 (4.2)	1 (1.4)	61 (84.7)	72
VI	237	146	25 (27.5)	0 (0)	66 (72.5)	91
VII	191	116	3 (4)	0 (0)	70 (93.3)	75
VIII	160	113	0 (0)	0 (0)	41 (87.2)	47
IX	170	113	0 (0)	0 (0)	49 (86)	57
X	196	138	0 (0)	0 (0)	58 (100)	58

Table 5
Subject wise Distribution of Number of Illustrations in AP State Board Textbooks

Class	Total No.	Physical and Environment Science	Biology: Nutrition (% of Biology)	Food Safety (% of Biology)	Others	Total Biology
I	316	55	67 (26.1)	2 (0.8)	184 (70)	261
II	222	58	71 (43.3)	5 (3.1)	68 (41.4)	164
III	176	56	29 (24)	2 (1.7)	78 (64.8)	120
IV	105	46	25 (42.5)	5 (8.5)	22 (37.2)	59
V	127	58	0 (0)	10 (14.5)	52 (75.4)	69
VI	184	42	0 (0)	0 (0)	138 (97.2)	142
VII	143	88	0 (0)	0 (0)	55 (100)	55
VIII	187	123	0 (0)	0 (0)	61 (95.3)	64
IX	181	113	0 (0)	6 (8.8)	62 (91.2)	68
X	285	156	7 (5.5)	0 (0)	109 (84.4)	129

in the first three classes was devoted to recognizing various foods, creating awareness about the foods that are derived from plant and animal sources. Thereafter in higher classes wherever nutrition topics are covered, topics like food groups, functions of foods and nutrition deficiency disorders are dealt with in greater or lesser detail (Table-6).

The data also indicated that the colour visuals and tables have been interspersed in the NCERT textbooks both for visual relief and easy understanding. However, in AP State textbooks, text dominates and visuals are simple black and white line drawings which sometimes are not easily comprehensible. In both the syllabi in all classes except in Classes I and II, the nutrition lessons appear in the back pages of the books. The text uses vague terms like "all nutrients in required quantities" while defining concept of balanced diet, but no where in the textbook it is mentioned what required quantities are. Moreover, some factual errors were also observed in the content in the X class textbook of AP State Board where in obesity was listed as a nutrition deficiency disorder.

The illustrations depicting good food habits, eating habits, cooking etc., in the NCERT science textbooks of the primary classes seem to have an urban bias with pictures of children consuming foods on a 'dining table' using modern cutlery and crockery.

Discussion

In various national plans and policies, the government has time and again reiterated its unequivocal commitment to incorporate nutrition into the school curriculum. For instance, the National Nutrition Policy 1993 and the National Plan of Action on Nutrition (NPAN), 1995 in its indirect policy measure through the Ministry of Education, clearly emphasizes the need for incorporating 'nutrition' in school text books (FNB, 1995a). The National Policy of Education (1986–modified in 1992) and National Curricular Frame Work (2005) also highlight the need and importance of nutrition and physical activity as part of health education in schools (WHO-

Table 6
Nutrition Topics Covered in NCERT and AP State Board Textbooks

Class	*NCERT*	*AP State Board*
I	'Plants around us' illustrations of fruits and veg. are given'Food from Plants' – cereals, pulses, nuts, fruits (illustrations)'Good Habits' – Eat at regular intervals, take just enough, Don't waste /over eat, chew	Plants give us food - Grains, vegetables, fruits, oils pulses and spices(illustrations for easy identification)
II	"Uses of Plants" - 'Plants give us food' – cereals, pulses, oilseeds, tubers, roots leaves, veg (colour illustrations)Lesson 'Our food' – functions of foodsEnergy yielding, body building and protective.***Eat food four times a day***	Small unit in Chapter on 'Plant Life" deals with plants as sources of foods A Unit on 'Animal Life' - Milk, poultry and meat shown as foods from animalsUnder the chapter on Human body, a unit on "food for health' deals with kinds of food
III	One complete chapter on nutrition 'Food for body' Food groups Milk highlighted as 'complete Food' Foods – raw and cooked Advantages of cooking – kills germs, easy to digest, made soft & tasty	One complete chapter on 'Food' What is food? Functions of food, why do we eat foodo Food sources Food groups Carbohydrates -rich foods Fats–rich foods Protein –rich foods Vitamins and minerals–foods rich in these In a brief running text towards the end of the page "The food which contains all the nutrients in required quantities needed by the body is called balanced diet" (not even highlighted) "Population and food shortage"
IV	In a lesson on 'Uses of plants and animals', Under uses of plants, "Plants give us food is discussed with illustrations – roots, tubers, cereals, fruits, nuts etc. Similarly in half a page, foods from animals also discussed – egg, chicken, meat	One Complete chapter on Nutrition under the title "Food we eat" - Raw foods - Why fruits and vegetables salads/sproutso Care in selecting raw foods Why should we cook food and methods of cooking

Contd.

		protecting foods from flies and insectso"population and shortage of food" discussed with illustration
V	Under "Our body, diseases and sanitation" , a unit on 'Deficiency diseases', which discusses 'Balanced diet'Recommended intakes of cereals, pulses GLVs etc. given in a tableDiscussion on Deficiency disorders – protein def., energy def. Vit A, B, C, D Def, Mineral Def. (iron and iodine)Causes for deficiencies – diarrhoea and hookworm infestation Culminates in importance of washing vegetablesDo not over wash and do not overcook	No Chapter on Nutrition
VI	"Components of food" – Elaborate discussion on meal. Some common meals of different states. Small experiments to measure carbohydrate, protein or fat in foods What's the function of various nutrients – Carbohydrates, proteins, vitamins minerals (vit A, B, C, D and iron, calcium, iodine, phosphorous)Balanced dietDeficiency disordersElaborate with colour illustrations	No Chapter on Nutrition
VII	Chapter 'Our food" What is food Why do we need food, Foods we consumeNutrition, Need for variety of foods What are nutrients –Chart on balanced diet Components of foods Box item on Saturated fatty acids (SFAs), Hydrogenated oils and ill-effects on heart Vegetable oils – Unsaturated fats food for health Combination of Saturated fatty acids (SFAs) and Unsaturated fats Food substitution with low cost nutritious food… Examples given in a table A table on cutting energy consumption by food replacement a list of 21 items given	No Chapter on Nutrition

Contd.

VIII	No chapter	No Chapter on Nutrition
IX	No chapter	None on human nutrition Nutrition in Animals as a unit in 'Life processes" - Nutrition in various animals, Need for digestion and digestive enzymes,
X	No chapter	One complete chapter titled 'Nutrition'Nutritional requirements - Macro and Micro nutrients and their importance for bodyCarbohydrate, protein and fat, vitamins and minerals and Balanced dietDeficiency diseases - Calorie Malnutrition, Protein Malnutrition, PEM, Kwashiorkar, Marasmus, <u>Obesity</u>. Vit Deficiency Diseases - Vit A, Vit D, Vit E, Vit K (Vit B with pellagra illustration Vit D Deficiency with line drawings) Table showing vitamins - deficiency disorders - rich foods

India, 2008). The analysis of nutrition component in school curricula reveals that despite all the above policy measures, nutrition seems to have not got its due in the school curricula. This observation is in concurrence with an earlier review of school health programmes in 10 Indian states, which observed that there is no priority for health promotion in actual practice due to lack of commitment from education departments (WHO-India, 2008). The present analysis of curricula also indicated that there are too many inconsistencies in presentation of topics related to nutrition. This observation is in concurrence with an earlier study carried out in Delhi in 1996 to assess the micronutrient nutrition related content in the school curricula, which also observed inconsistencies in presentation of topics related to micronutrients (ICCIDD, 1996).

In their analysis of the nature of science and technology presentation in NCERT science textbooks for classes IV through X, the development of conceptions on some physical science topics (like force, work, and energy); Koul and Dana (1997) found that there was 'excessive' physical science content with prime emphasis on established concepts, laws, and theories. Similar observation was also made earlier by Ramanathan and Siddiqi (1994). In the current study too we found that the emphasis on physical sciences was increasing in classes VI through X allocating lesser proportion of space for the biology component, thereby, limiting the scope for coverage of nutrition and food safety. Some researchers have suggested integration of nutrition into diverse curricular areas (Lytle, 1994), but in the present study, we found that integrating nutrition and food safety related topics in subjects other than science, say in physical and environmental sciences actually dilutes the importance of nutrition and food safety education because it gets masked under other related topics. For instance, although nutrition (more precisely, importance of regular but small meals) was covered in some primary classes in the lessons pertaining to 'good habits' along with aspects like 'sitting in good posture', 'wearing washed clothes', 'combing hair' etc., understandably this does not give adequate scope for the child to comprehend the scientific rationale or importance of inculcating the above nutritional or food safety habits.

Considering that India's adolescents are confronted with the problems of undernutrition (NNMB, 2006) on the one hand and overweight and obesity on the other (Laxmaiah *et.al.*, 2007; Krishnaswamy, 1999), the school system can be effectively used to educate the school-going children. The science textbooks of all classes after class III in both NCERT and AP syllabi, however, only deal with food groups or nutrient deficiency disorders. There is hardly any mention of important deficiency disorders like anaemia and iodine deficiency disorders and steps to be taken to control them. Similarly, there is hardly any information on contributing factors to overweight and obesity like consumption of unhealthy/junk foods, lifestyle factors etc. Similarly there is no mention of obesity and resultant chronic diseases like diabetes, hypertension and cardiovascular diseases.

Conclusions

The present study revealed that the space allocation for biology in relation to physical sciences is lesser in higher classes. Nutrition component is dealt at primary school level but very little at high school level. Nutrition when covered after class III in both NCERT and AP syllabi, only deals with food groups or nutrient deficiency disorders. Similarly, food safety deals only with cleanliness of surroundings, not consuming fly swarming or insect infested foods.

The analysis clearly brings out the lacunae in the nutrition component covered in the school curricula. It could be recommended that many important topics such as nutrition and growth, link between childhood malnutrition and non-communicable diseases in adulthood, adolescent nutrition, nutrition for girl child, hidden hunger, lifestyle factors and obesity, nutrition during pregnancy and lactation, importance of breast feeding, unhealthy foods, fortification etc. be covered in the curricula. Considering that many of our earlier studies indicated that school based nutrition education is preferred mode of learning and effective way of education, the results of this study will be useful during future revisions of the textbooks for strengthening the nutrition and food safety components.

References

Berg, B. (1998): "Content Analysis", In: Berg B. *Qualitative Research Methods for the Social Science,* Boston: Allyn & Bacon. 233-252.

CBSE (Central Board of Secondary Education) (2008): *Directory of Schools Affiliated to CBSE.* Available at: http://www.cbse.nic.in/welcome.htm (accessed: 31st May 2008).

FNB (Food and Nutrition Board) (1995): *National Plan of Action on Nutrition,* New Delhi: Food and Nutrition Board (FNB), Department of Women and Child Development Ministry of Human Resources, Government of India.

ICCIDD (International Council for Control of Iodine Deficiency Disorders) (1996): "Curriculum Development in Micronutrient Malnutrition", *Proceedings of the Workshop on Micronutrient Malnutrition: Curriculum Development for Schools, 30th March 1996,* New Delhi: All India Institute of Medical Sciences.

Kondracki, N.L., Wellman, N.S. and Amundson, D.R. (2002): "Content Analysis: Review of Methods and their Applications in Nutrition Education", *Journal of Nutrition Education and Behavior,* Vol. 34(4): 224-230.

Koul, R. and Dana, T. (1997): "Contextualized Science for Teaching Science and Technology", *Interchange, Vol.28* (2&3): 121-144.

Krippendorff, K. (1980): *Content Analysis: An Introduction to Its Methodology,* Newbury Park, CA: Sage. 21.

Krippendorff, K. (1986). *Content Analysis: An Introduction to Its Methodology,* Beverley Hills, London: Sage Publications.

Krishnaswami, K. (1998): "Country Profile: India. Nutritional Disorders–Old and Changing", *The Lancet,* Vol. 351(9111): 1268–9.

Laxmiah, A., Balakrishna, N., Sharad Kumar, Ravindrnath, M., Brahmam, G.N.V. and Sesikeran, B. (2007): *Prevalence and Determinants of Overweight and Obesity Among 12-17 year Old Urban Adolescents in Andhra Pradesh–A Report,* Hyderabad: National Institute of Nutrition, ICMR in Collaboration with India Representative Office, WHO, New Delhi.

Lytle, L. (1994): *Nutrition Education for School-aged Children: A Review of Research*, Alexandria, Virginia: Food and Consumer Service, US Department of Agriculture.

Perez-Rodrigo, C. and Javier, A. (2001): "School-based Nutrition Education: Lessons learned and New Perspectives", *Public Health Nutrition*, Vol.4(1A): 131–139.

Ramanathan, S. and Siddiqi, N. (1994): "Representation of Science in Upper Primary Science Textbooks: An Assessment", *Indian Educational Review*, Vol. 29 (1-2): 1-12.

Shepherd, S.K. and Achterberg, C.L. (1992): "Quantitative Research Methodology: Data Collection, Analysis and Interpretation, and Verification", In: Monsen, E.R. (Ed.), *Research: Successful Approaches*, Chicago: American Dietetic Association, 82-88.

Stuart, T. and Achterberg, C. (1995): "Nutrition Education and Communication Strategies for Different Groups and Settings", In: *Nutrition Education for the Public–Report of an FAO Expert Consultation*, (*Rome, 18-22 September 1995)-FAO Food and Nutrition Paper No.59*, Rome: FAO. 19-23.

WHO- India (2008): *Towards Health Promoting Schools*, New Delhi: WHO- Country Office, India. 2-3.

Index

I

T

U